VISUAL QUICKSTART GUIDE

MACROMEDIA DREAMWEAVER 8

FOR WINDOWS AND MACINTOSH

Tom Negrino
Dori Smith

Peachpit Press

Visual QuickStart Guide
Macromedia Dreamweaver 8 for Windows and Macintosh
Tom Negrino and Dori Smith

Peachpit Press
1249 Eighth Street
Berkeley, CA 94710
510/524-2178
800/283-9444
510/524-2221 (fax)

Find us on the Web at www.peachpit.com
To report errors, please send a note to errata@peachpit.com
Published by Peachpit Press, in association with Macromedia Press
Peachpit Press is a division of Pearson Education

Copyright © 2006 by Tom Negrino and Dori Smith

Editor: Nancy Davis
Production editor: Lisa Brazieal
Proofreader: Liz Welch
Compositor: Kelli Kamel
Indexer: Julie Bess
Cover design: Peachpit Press

ISBN 0-321-35027-8

9 8 7 6 5 4

Printed and bound in the United States of America

Dedication

To our son, Sean Smith,
with love from Mom and Dad.

Special Thanks to:

Virginia DeBolt, who stepped in and contributed several chapters when we needed it most. Her work was terrific, and we are grateful for her help. Thanks also to Virginia for the use of her photographs in Chapters 5 and 6.

Our wonderful editor, Nancy Davis, who pulled this book together, made it better, and encouraged us when we were flagging.

Thanks to Lisa Brazieal, as always, for her excellent production work.

Thanks to the book's compositor, Kelli Kamel, and thanks to Julie Bess for the index.

Thanks to Peachpit's Angela Kozlowski for being our liaison with Macromedia.

Thanks to Peachpit's Nancy Ruenzel and Marjorie Baer for their support.

Our appreciation to Al Sparber, of Project Seven (www.projectseven.com) for providing and allowing us to use his company's Dreamweaver extensions.

Dori would like to thank the Wise-Women's Web community (www.wise-women.org) for their help and support, for contributing their years of Dreamweaver expertise, and for being the best darn Web-related mailing list around.

We would like to thank the Dreamweaver Task Force of the Web Standards Project (www.webstandards.org) for their work with Macromedia to improve Dreamweaver.

Of course, our gratitude to the members of the Dreamweaver team for creating a terrific product.

In Tom's office, the soundtrack for this book included music by Lene Marlin, Joydrop, Maria Mena, Bowling for Soup, Natalie Imbruglia, and lots more bouncy pop music.

TABLE OF CONTENTS

Chapter 10: **Using Forms and Fields** **291**

Chapter 11: **Adding Frames** **309**

Chapter 12: **Using Behaviors and Navigation Objects** **333**

Chapter 13: **Making Life Easier: Using Templates, Libraries, and Snippets** **363**

TABLE OF CONTENTS

TABLE OF CONTENTS

INTRODUCTION

Welcome to *Macromedia Dreamweaver 8 for Windows and Macintosh: Visual QuickStart Guide*! Macromedia Dreamweaver has long been the premier visual tool for Web site developers, allowing you to build great-looking Web pages and smoothly running Web sites. Dreamweaver's ease-of-use takes much of the pain out of creating Web sites, without sacrificing flexibility. It's possible to use Dreamweaver to create terrific Web sites without knowing much about HTML and JavaScript (though you will create better Web sites if you familiarize yourself with at least the basics of these languages).

Dreamweaver is a rich, powerful, and deep program, and at first glance, it can be a bit intimidating. We've written this book as a painless introduction to Dreamweaver and its features, and with our help, you will use Dreamweaver to build an excellent Web site.

Using this book

We've organized the different elements of building Web sites with Dreamweaver 8 into chapters, and within each chapter are numbered, step-by-step directions that tell you exactly how to accomplish various tasks. You don't have to work through the entire book in order, but it is structured so the more complex material builds on the earlier tasks.

We start with an overview of Dreamweaver, move on to setting up your Web site and creating your first Web page, then discuss how to add content and interactivity to your pages. Finally, we show you how to work with HTML code and manage your Web site.

When we decided to write this book, we wanted to take a fresh look at Dreamweaver—at how people use it, and how people *should* use it. Throughout the book, we've tried to show you how to use Dreamweaver using its most modern features, rather than using some of the features that are still in the program, but are "old school." Specifically, we'll show you how to apply styles and position your page elements using Cascading Style Sheets, rather than older, obsolete methods. If you don't know what that means, don't worry; it's all explained in Chapters 5 and 6.

✔ Tips

- Throughout the book we've included many tips that will help you get things done faster, better, or both.

- Be sure to read the figure captions, too; sometimes you'll find extra nuggets of information there.

- When we're showing HTML or JavaScript code, we've used this `code font`. We also use the code font for Web addresses.

- You'll also find sidebars (with gray backgrounds) that delve deeper into subjects.

For keyboard commands, we've included Mac keyboard shortcuts in parentheses immediately after the Windows shortcut, like this:

To open the Find & Replace dialog, press Ctrl-F (Cmd-F).

While writing this book, we've made the assumption that you're familiar with the basics of using Windows or Mac OS X. You don't need to be a computer expert by any means, but you shouldn't be stumped by concepts like selecting text, using menus, clicking and dragging, and using files and folders. Naturally, you should be familiar with Web surfing and how to use a Web browser to view a Web site.

A note for our Mac-using friends

If you've flipped through this book already, you probably noticed that the vast majority of the screenshots were taken on machines running Windows. That doesn't mean that the book (or its authors) don't welcome Dreamweaver users on the Mac. Far from it; in fact, both of us are primarily Mac users, and we are frequent contributors to *Macworld* magazine and other Mac-oriented publications.

INTRODUCTION

However, our crack research department tells us that most Dreamweaver users are running the program on Windows machines, so we have included screenshots that will reflect the experience of the majority of our readers. Happily, Dreamweaver (and especially Dreamweaver 8) works almost identically on both platforms. In the few cases where there are differences, we've included separate procedures for Windows and for Mac users.

There is one other thing that we *haven't* done in this book that we have done in all of our previous Mac books. We are no longer telling Mac users to Control-click to bring up a contextual menu (which we sometimes call shortcut menus in this book). Instead, we've adopted right-click, because Apple is now shipping its multiple-button mouse (which it calls Mighty Mouse) with all of its computers that come with a mouse. If you still have one of the old Apple mice with a single button, just substitute Control-click wherever you see right-click in the book. Better yet, we suggest that you get any USB or wireless mouse with multiple buttons and a scroll wheel. It will really increase your productivity.

There's more online

We've prepared a companion Web site for this book, which you'll find at:

`http://www.dreamweaverbook.com`

On this site, you'll find news about the book and links to other online resources that will help you use Dreamweaver 8 more productively. If we discover any mistakes in the book that somehow got through the editing process, we'll list the updates on the site, too.

If you have any questions, please first check the FAQ (Frequently Asked Questions) page on the companion Web site. It's clearly marked. If you've read the FAQ, and your question isn't answered there, you can contact us via email at `dw8@dreamweaverbook.com`. We regret that because of the large volume of email that we get, we cannot, and will not, answer email about the book sent to our personal email addresses. We can only guarantee that messages sent to the `dw8@dreamweaverbook.com` email address will be answered. Unfortunately, due to the danger of computer viruses being spread with e-mail attachments, we cannot accept any messages with attachments.

Let's get started

Every journey begins with a first step, and if you've read this far, your journey with Dreamweaver has already begun. Thanks for joining us, and let's get started building your great Web site.

Tom Negrino and Dori Smith

November 2005

INTRODUCING DREAMWEAVER

1

Welcome to the world of Dreamweaver! The premiere Web design and development tool from Macromedia may appear a little daunting at first, so this chapter will show you what's what and what's where. Once you understand what all the parts of its interface do, you'll soon find that Dreamweaver is an invaluable application for creating and maintaining Web sites.

In this chapter, you'll learn about the Dreamweaver Start Page and document window. Then you'll see the plethora of toolbars included with the software: the menu bar, the Insert Bar, the Document toolbar, the Style Rendering bar, and the Standard bar. The Status bar, Property Inspector, and panels are next, and then you'll learn about the included workspace layouts, and how to set up your own custom workspace. Finally, there's a summary of the new features in Dreamweaver 8.

A Quick Tour of Dreamweaver

In this section, you'll learn about the different windows, panels, pages, views, toolbars, and inspectors that make up the Dreamweaver experience. Whether you're a novice to Web design, an experienced pro who's new to Dreamweaver, or someone who primarily wants to know what's new in Dreamweaver 8, this will bring you up to speed.

The Start Page

The first time you launch Dreamweaver, you'll see the Start Page, as shown in **Figure 1.1**. This page (which changes based on what you've recently done in Dreamweaver) is your starting point for both creating and modifying pages and sites. If you close all your open Dreamweaver windows, the Start Page reappears.

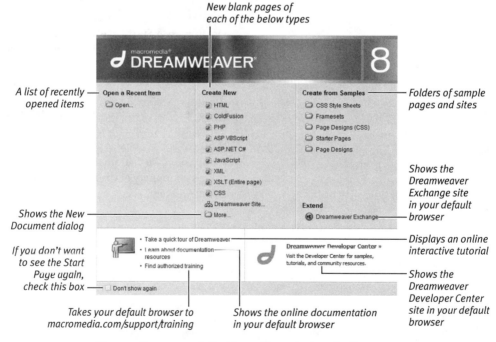

Figure 1.1 Dreamweaver's Start Page will soon become familiar—but if you don't want to see it, you can make it go away.

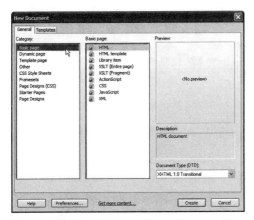

Figure 1.2 The New Document dialog offers a multitude of choices.

The Start Page consists of several sections:

◆ **Open a Recent Item:** This section contains a list of the ten most recently opened items in Dreamweaver. If you've opened fewer than ten, it will show just that number; if you've never used Dreamweaver, it will appear as in Figure 1.1 with just an "Open..." folder.

◆ **Create New:** If you want to create a new page or site, this is the column for you. Choosing one of these options creates a new HTML, ColdFusion, PHP, ASP, JavaScript, XML, XSLT, or CSS file. Next to last, you can create a new Dreamweaver site. And lastly, you can choose "More...", which will display the New Document dialog (**Figure 1.2**) about which we'll learn more later.

◆ **Create from Samples:** If you're just learning about building Web sites, these are the choices for you. This section contains folders, each of which contains many beautifully laid-out pages ready for your content. Clicking on any one of these opens up the New Document dialog again, but with a different category chosen: Choosing CSS Style Sheets selects the CSS Style Sheets category, choosing Framesets selects the Framesets category, and so on, through Page Designs (CSS), Starter Pages, and Page Designs. Even if you're an experienced designer, it can be worth your time to look at the previews to get your creative juices flowing.

◆ **Extend:** Dreamweaver is built with an extensible architecture—that is, it's easy to add functionality to Dreamweaver that wasn't included when it shipped. That's done through a technology called extensions, which are bits of software that extend Dreamweaver's capabilities. You can get additional extensions through the

Continues on next page

Macromedia Dreamweaver Exchange at `www.macromedia.com/exchange/dreamweaver/`. Some of them have an additional charge, and some are free, but it's worth checking out what's available when Dreamweaver alone doesn't scratch your itch. See Appendix B for more information about extending Dreamweaver.

◆ **Quick Tour:** Choosing this option gives you, as it says, a quick tour of Dreamweaver's functionality. You'll see a short online tutorial from Macromedia.com using their Breeze Web presentation product.

◆ **Documentation Resources:** This displays the online Dreamweaver documentation using your default browser.

◆ **Authorized Training:** If, despite having this book, you still want further training, you can follow this link to `www.macromedia.com/support/training/`. There, you'll find resources that can get you any kind of training you're looking for.

◆ **Dreamweaver Developer Center:** If you want to learn more about Dreamweaver from a developer's perspective, this will take you to `www.macromedia.com/devnet/dreamweaver/`.

◆ **Don't show again:** Macromedia knows that while some people love the Start Page, other people aren't so fond of it. Throughout this book, you'll see many examples of how you can personalize your copy of Dreamweaver so that it works just the way you want it to. Here, you can choose to never see the Start Page again.

If you reconsider, though, it's easy to bring back the Start Page: in Dreamweaver, choose Edit (Windows)/Dreamweaver (Mac) > Preferences > General > Document Options, and check the "Show Start Page" box.

Workspace Setup (Windows only)

If you've just launched Dreamweaver for the first time, and you're on Windows, you'll see a dialog before the Start Page (**Figure 1.3**). The Workspace Setup dialog lets you choose which of the two layouts you prefer: the Designer or the Coder. If you've spent years working with HomeSite and that's what you're comfortable with, choose Coder. If you're more of a visual type, or you don't even know what HomeSite is, choose Designer. Click OK, and you'll see the Start Page.

This dialog only appears the first time you run Dreamweaver. If you change your mind later, you can change your layout by choosing Window > Workspace Layout and selecting the alternate in the menu that appears (**Figure 1.4**).

This book assumes that all you Windows users (the Mac users don't have a choice) will pick the Designer Layout, so that's what you'll see from here on out. The Dual Screen layout option, available for both Windows and Mac users (even those with only a single monitor), isn't an actual layout choice. What it's used for is discussed below.

Pick a choice from the Start Page, and you're off and running.

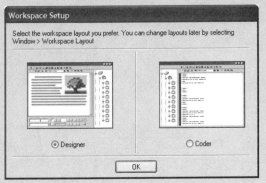

Figure 1.3 Windows users will see the Workspace Setup dialog the first time they launch Dreamweaver.

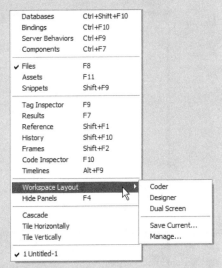

Figure 1.4 If you decide later that you picked the wrong option, you can always switch using this menu.

The Document Window

Now that you've opened a file, you see the document window and all its surrounding panels, inspectors, etc. (**Figure 1.5**). It may look busy and cluttered at first, but you'll soon learn your way around.

The document window shown here is a blank white Web page, ready for you to add your design and content. If you want, you can just click inside the window and start typing away! The details of creating a Web page will be covered in Chapter 3.

Panel groups

Menu bar

Insert bar

Toolbar

Tag Selector

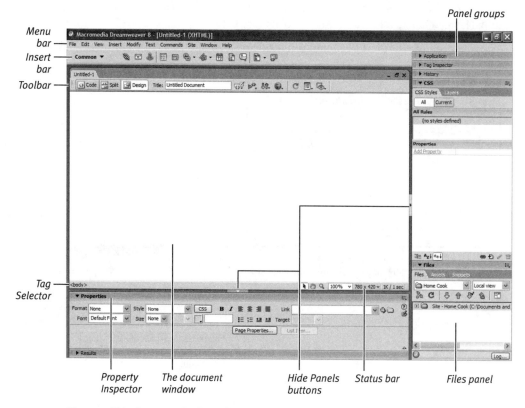

Property Inspector

The document window

Hide Panels buttons

Status bar

Files panel

Figure 1.5 This shows your basic vanilla Dreamweaver document window, but you can modify it to fit your work habits.

Figure 1.6 Switch from document to document by clicking on the tab with the document name.

Figure 1.7 The Restore Down button changes Dreamweaver from a tabbed view to a multiple document view.

If you have multiple files open at once (a fairly common occurrence), you'll see a row of tabs across the top of the document window (**Figure 1.6**). To go from one file to another, just click on the name of the file you want to edit.

Don't like tabs? Dreamweaver lets you get rid of them:

◆ **Windows:** When you open a document in Dreamweaver, click the Restore Down button (**Figure 1.7**) in the top-right corner of the document window (*not* the one in the Dreamweaver window). Once one document has been moved into its own window, all the others will automatically move, too. To go back to the original, click the Maximize button (which has replaced the Restore Down button) in the top-right corner.

◆ **Mac:** Tabs are the normal interface in Windows, so Windows users have to manually lose the tabs any time they want to do without them. Mac users, though, are only getting tabs with Dreamweaver 8. Because of that, Dreamweaver allows Mac users to choose whether to get rid of tabs permanently (older Dreamweaver/Mac behavior), to force windows to always show tabs (Windows behavior), or to open documents in tabs, but only when two or more documents are open (new Dreamweaver/Mac behavior). These can be set by going to Dreamweaver > Preferences > General > Document Options and choosing your preferred combination of "Open documents in tabs" and "Always show tabs."

A QUICK TOUR OF DREAMWEAVER

The Menu Bar

The Dreamweaver menu bar is about what you'd expect to see on your platform. There is one big difference between the Windows menu bar (**Figure 1.8**) and the Mac menu bar (**Figure 1.9**): the latter also contains a "Dreamweaver" menu. On it are the "About Dreamweaver," "Keyboard Shortcuts," and "Preferences" menu options. On Windows, the first can be found under Help, and the latter two under Edit. And of course, the Windows menu bar is part of the Dreamweaver window, while on the Mac the menu bar is always at the top of the screen.

The Insert Bar

Directly under the menu bar is what's called the Insert Bar. The Windows version is shown in **Figure 1.10** and the Mac version in **Figure 1.11**. As you might have guessed, the Insert Bar is used to insert content and objects into your page. The Insert Bar comes in eight different flavors (as seen in **Figure 1.12**):

◆ **Common:** This set of objects contains those that are the most commonly used such as links and images.

Figure 1.8 The Dreamweaver menu bar on Windows.

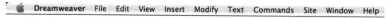

Figure 1.9 The Dreamweaver menu bar on a Mac, which includes an additional "Dreamweaver" menu.

Figure 1.10 The Insert bar on Windows.

Figure 1.11 The Insert bar on a Mac.

Figure 1.12 The Insert bar contains eight different layouts.

◆ **Layout:** This set includes tables, divs, layers, and frames: all objects that let you describe how you want to lay out your page.

◆ **Forms:** The forms set includes form elements such as text fields, buttons, and check boxes.

◆ **Text:** The text set doesn't actually contain objects to insert on the page; instead, it lets you style text that's already on the page. It's better, though, to just use the Property Inspector (see below) to do this instead.

◆ **HTML:** The HTML set is another less-than-useful group: it allows you to insert objects such as tables, frames, and scripts that are better done elsewhere.

◆ **Application:** If you're someday going to work with external data such as databases, that's when you'll use the Application set.

◆ **Flash elements:** Oddly enough, this set only holds one object, the Flash image viewer. If you want to add other Flash elements (such as Flash buttons, text, or video), go back to the Common set, where they can be found under Media Plugins.

◆ **Favorites:** This starts off empty, but you can modify it to contain just what you'd like it to have. To do this, choose the Favorites set, and then right-click (or Control-click, for Mac users with only a single-button mouse or trackpad). You'll be presented with a dialog that will allow you to add your most commonly used objects.

If you're ever wondering what an icon on the Insert Bar does, just move your cursor over it—a tool tip will appear with the icon's name. If there's a small black triangle to the right of an icon that means this object contains related tools and objects. Click on the object to view the pop-up menu of choices.

A QUICK TOUR OF DREAMWEAVER

The Document Toolbar

Underneath the Insert Bar, and below any tabs you have open, you'll find the Document toolbar (Windows: **Figure 1.13**, Mac: **Figure 1.14**). The Document toolbar itself consists of three parts:

◆ **View mode buttons:** These let you choose between Design, Code, and Split views of your document. See "Using Document Views" for more on what each of these does and when you'd want to choose each.

◆ **The page title:** Every page needs a descriptive title, and here's where you'll change yours. The page title, and how it differs from the name of a page itself, will be covered in Chapter 3, "Building Your First Page."

◆ **Miscellaneous buttons:** These contain everything from a "preview in browser" button, to a button to validate content, to a button to show additional visual aids inside Dreamweaver itself.

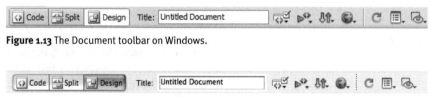

Figure 1.13 The Document toolbar on Windows.

Figure 1.14 The Document toolbar on a Mac.

Using document views

The three document views allow you to choose which version of the document you want to see:

◆ **Design: Figure 1.15** shows a typical Web page in the design view. This mode, known as WYSIWYG (What You See Is What You Get) allows you to get an idea of how your page will appear when viewed in a browser. For the most part, almost everything you want to do in Dreamweaver can be done in the design view, and this book will be entirely about what you can do here (except for Chapter 15, "Editing Code").

Continues on next page

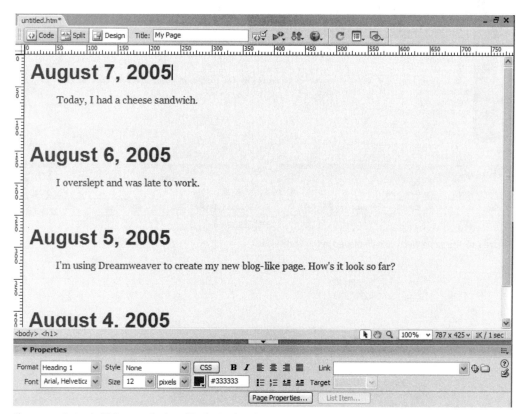

Figure 1.15 A simple Web page displayed in the Design view.

◆ **Code: Figure 1.16** shows the exact same page in the code view. Here's what the underlying markup and tags look like. While Chapter 15 will cover the ins-and-outs of tags, many people work quite well with Dreamweaver without ever using the code view.

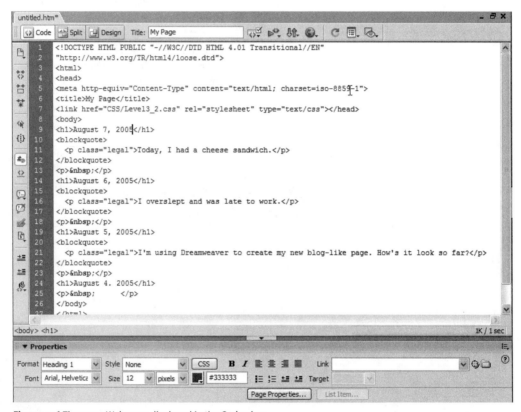

Figure 1.16 The same Web page displayed in the Code view.

◆ **Split: Figure 1.17** shows the same page, again, in the split view. If you can't decide whether you want to look at code or design, split lets you have the best of both, with code on the top, and the WYSIWYG view below. It's a great way to start to learn about markup, and it's also handy for control freaks who want to tweak their tags to be just so, and simultaneously see how their design looks. You can resize the amount of space taken up by each of the two views by dragging the split bar between the two panes up or down.

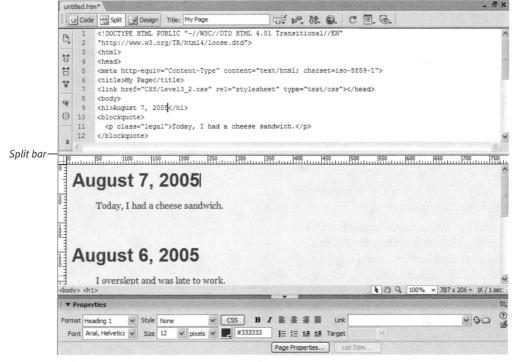

Split bar

Figure 1.17 And the same Web page, displayed in the Split view.

Other toolbars

If you right-click in the Insert Bar or Document toolbar, you'll see that there are two other bars that aren't enabled by default:

◆ **Style Rendering bar:** If you've set up your CSS stylesheets so that your pages appear differently in, for example, a screen view versus a page designed for printing, this is what you'll use to switch between the two style renderings. Most of the time, you'll just want the default screen view. The button at the far-right end of the bar works a little differently: it toggles the page between a view that includes the rendered CSS styles and a view with CSS styles turned off.

◆ **Standard bar:** While Macromedia refers to this bar as "standard," it's actually used to make Dreamweaver feel more like a word processing application. Some examples of what it contains—New, Open, Save, Print, Cut, Copy, Paste—will give you an idea of what's here. As with the Style Rendering bar, the chances are that Macromedia's default for these toolbars (off) is what you'll want to use.

You can also turn off the Insert Bar and Document toolbar in the same fashion if you want the cleanest possible layout (for instance, if you're working on a very small screen). To turn them back on, choose View > Toolbars, and select the ones you want to see again.

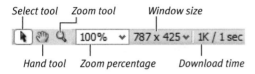

Figure 1.18 The tag selector makes it easy to select all the contents of a tag.

Select tool   Zoom tool   Window size

Hand tool   Zoom percentage   Download time

Figure 1.19 The controls on the right-hand side of the status bar.

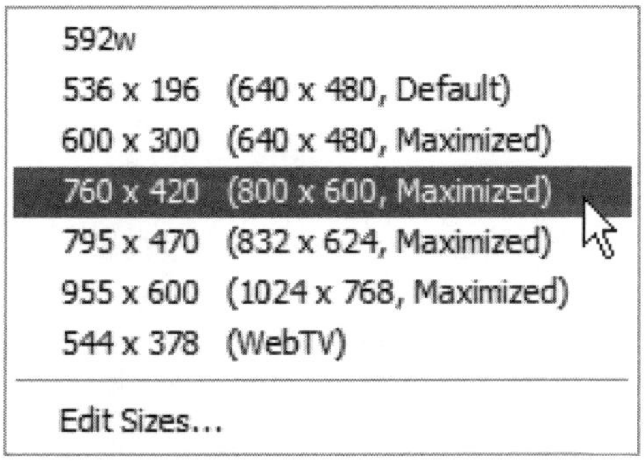

```
592w
536 x 196   (640 x 480, Default)
600 x 300   (640 x 480, Maximized)
760 x 420   (800 x 600, Maximized)
795 x 470   (832 x 624, Maximized)
955 x 600   (1024 x 768, Maximized)
544 x 378   (WebTV)

Edit Sizes...
```

Figure 1.20 Use this popup menu to choose the dimensions of your document window.

The Status Bar

The status bar is the bottom-most part of the document window. It's often also referred to as the *tag selector*, although that's really the correct name for just the left-most part. Click anywhere in a document, and the tag selector will show you the current tags based on the current location of the cursor. You can then click on any of the tags in the tag selector (**Figure 1.18**) to select everything contained within that tag. Clicking on the <body> tag always selects the entire contents of the page.

The right-most side of the status bar contains more controls (**Figure 1.19**). The Select, Hand, and Zoom tools let you (respectively) select objects on the page, scroll around the page, and zoom into the page. The next control shows the current zoom percentage of the page. After that is the window size currently being displayed; you can click on this to get a popup menu of available window sizes (**Figure 1.20**). And finally, there's an estimate of how long it would take a browser to download this page. If you don't like the default values for the last two controls, you can change either or both by selecting "Edit Sizes" from the popup menu. These will be covered more extensively in Chapter 6.

A QUICK TOUR OF DREAMWEAVER

The Property Inspector

At the bottom of the screen is the Property Inspector (**Figure 1.21**, Windows; **Figure 1.22**, Mac). Based on what is selected in the document window, different options appear in this inspector; that is, if you've selected some text, you'll see text options, while if you've selected an image, image options appear. The Property Inspector can be used to both view and modify the displayed options. The many uses of the Property Inspector will be covered throughout the rest of the book.

In the lower-right corner of the inspector is an expand/collapse triangle. Depending on its current state, this will either expand or collapse the inspector. This lets you choose whether you want to display the extra information shown in the bottom half.

Figure 1.21 The Property Inspector on Windows.

Figure 1.22 The Property Inspector on the Mac.

Panel grip   Panel title bar   Panel options button

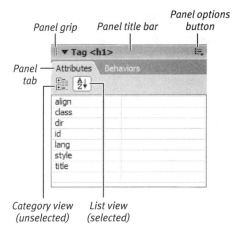

Panel tab   Attributes   Behaviors

Category view (unselected)   List view (selected)

Figure 1.23 A panel and its parts.

Panel group bar

Figure 1.24 And undocked panel has a panel group bar.

The Panels

Along the right side of the Dreamweaver window are *panels*. In the default installation of Dreamweaver, the CSS, Application, Tag Inspector, and Files panels are visible and docked. Also available, although not visible until you turn them on, are Frames, History, Results, Code Inspector, and Timelines. These can all be found under the Window menu.

Each panel has its own unique features designed to make it easy to inspect and modify their respective objects. They do have a few things in common, shown in **Figure 1.23**:

◆ **Panel grip:** At the top left of each panel are two vertical rows of dots. This is the *panel grip*. Click and drag the grip to move the panel to a new location. If you drag the panel out of the dock area, you will *undock* the panel (**Figure 1.24**), and the panel group bar will appear. To dock the panel again, use the panel grip to drag the panel back into the dock area.

◆ **Panel group bar:** The bar across the top of an undocked panel is the *panel group bar*. Click and drag the panel group bar to move the panel to a new location. Clicking the close box (Windows) or close button (Mac) closes the panel group; It does not re-dock it. On the Mac, a group of docked panels share a single panel group bar.

◆ **Panel tab:** Almost every panel contains two or more tabs; this one contains two: "Attributes" and "Behaviors." What displays in the remainder of the panel depends on which tab within that panel is active.

Continues on next page

◆ **Category view:** This example (the Attributes tab in the Tag panel) has two possible views: category and list. The category view is currently not selected. If it was, the attributes would be shown grouped by category.

◆ **List view:** Here, the list view of the Attributes tab in the Tag panel is selected, so the attributes are listed below in alphabetical order.

◆ **Panel options button:** If you click the panel options button, a menu appears that gives you a variety of options (**Figure 1.25**) based on which panel and tab you're currently on. This example shows the options for the Layers tab of the CSS menu. From here, you can group Layers with one of the other panels, close the Layers tab, rename the CSS panel group, maximize the CSS panel group, or close the CSS panel group. If you choose to group the Layers tab with another panel, you can choose the Application, Frames, Code Inspector, Timelines, Results, History, or Files panels, or you can create a new panel group. The ability to close tabs and move tabs from one panel to another allows you to set Dreamweaver up to work just the way you want it.

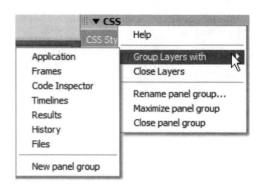

Figure 1.25 Different panels have different options, but these are the most common.

✔ Tip

■ Panels have an occasional tendency to go missing. If you've got a situation where the Window menu says a panel is open but you can't find it anywhere, choose Window > Arrange Panels to make all currently open panels visible again.

Setting Up Your Workspace

It's not just a matter of deciding what you do want to see—setting up your workspace also means figuring out what you *don't* want to see. Given all the toolbars *and* all the possible panels *and* the Property Inspector, you can run out of room for the actual Web page you're trying to work on (**Figure 1.26**). Here's how to set up a workspace that works for you.

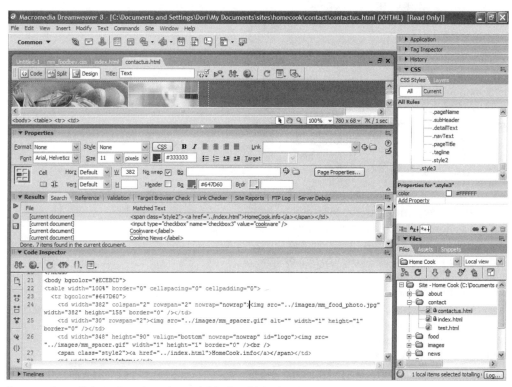

Figure 1.26 Not all the tools and panels are visible, but this is already an unusable workspace.

The Included Workspace Layouts

As mentioned earlier, if you're on Windows, you have two default layouts to choose from: Coder and Designer (Figure 1.4). If you're a Mac user, you have one default layout named, originally, *Default* (**Figure 1.27**). The Mac Default layout is similar but not identical to the Windows Designer layout. If at any point you've added, deleted, and moved around panels and documents to the point where everything's all over the place, you can always go back to your original layout by choosing Window > Workspace Layout > Default.

There's one other option that comes on both platforms: the Dual Screen layout. If you're lucky enough to have two (or more) monitors, the Dual Screen layout attempts to make the most of all of them. For example, the Files panel is expanded to show both local and remote sites, and so it splits off from the (new) Assets and Snippets panel.

Although its appearance in the menu implies otherwise, the Dual Screen layout isn't an option that you can check, and then uncheck to reverse its results. It's available whether you're on a multi-screen system or not, so if you choose it on a computer with only one monitor, you might get some odd results that aren't quite what you might expect. If you do that, and then want to go back, choose one of the other options from Window > Workspace Layout.

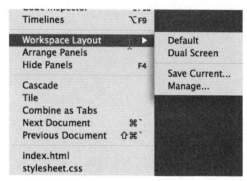

Figure 1.27 On a Mac, the default layout is what Windows users call the Design layout.

Modifying your layout

If you're on a computer with a smaller monitor, you may wish that you could hide and show panels with a quick click of a button. Thankfully, you can.

If you're on Windows, there are two buttons in between the document window and the panels/Property Inspector—one on the side, and one at the bottom (**Figure 1.28**). These are the Hide Panels buttons. Click one, and the adjacent panels go away. Click it again, and they return.

On both platforms, you can also press F4 to toggle the visibility of all your panels and the Property Inspector.

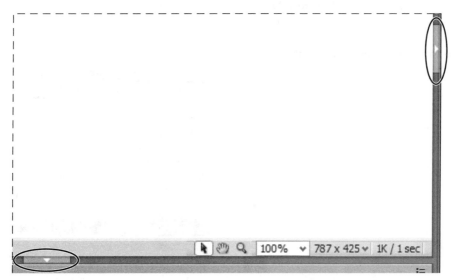

Figure 1.28 The bottom and right sides of the document window have Hide Panels buttons on Windows.

Saving custom layouts

No matter which platform you're on, what comes with Dreamweaver isn't likely to be exactly what you want. No problem! Set up your layout just the way you want it, and then choose Window > Workspace Layout > Save Current. A dialog appears asking you to name this new layout (**Figure 1.29**). The next time you look at Window > Workspace Layout (**Figure 1.30**), you'll see your own custom layout (here, named "Standard") listed above the others.

If you later decide that you don't want that layout any more, or want to give it another name, choose Window > Workspace Layout > Manage… to bring up the Manage Workspace Layouts dialog (**Figure 1.31**). From there, you can choose to delete or rename your custom layout (but you can't do this to any of the included layouts).

Figure 1.29 To create a custom Workspace Layout, just enter its name.

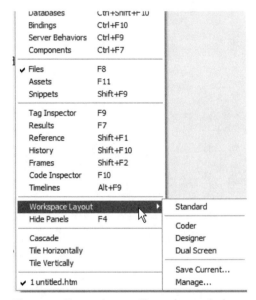

Figure 1.30 The new layout will now show up in the Workspace Layout menu.

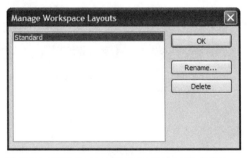

Figure 1.31 The Manage Workspace Layouts dialog lets you rename or delete your custom layouts.

Managing windows

You may want your documents to open in tabs sometimes and in their own windows sometimes. It's easy to go back and forth between these two options and to set your documents to appear just the way you want them. It's a little different on each platform:

To manage windows (Windows):

◆ Starting with the default tabbed layout (**Figure 1.32**), choose Window > Cascade. Your document windows will appear in a cascade: each slightly lower and to the right than the one behind it (**Figure 1.33**).

or

Continues on next page

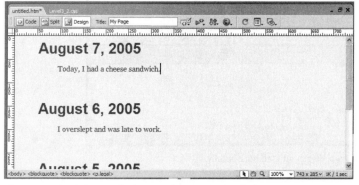

Figure 1.32 The default tabbed layout that you've seen before.

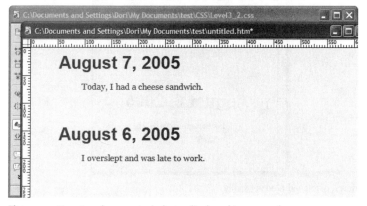

Figure 1.33 Your two document windows, displayed in a cascade.

◆ Starting with the default tabbed layout (Figure 1.32), choose Window > Tile Horizontally. Your document windows will appear tiled horizontally, with the available space split evenly between them (**Figure 1.34**).

or

◆ Starting with the default tabbed layout (Figure 1.32), choose Window > Tile Vertically. Your document windows will appear tiled vertically, with the available space split evenly between them (**Figure 1.35**).

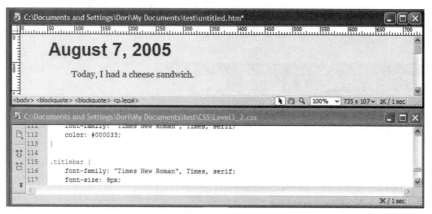

Figure 1.34 Your two document windows, displayed tiled horizontally.

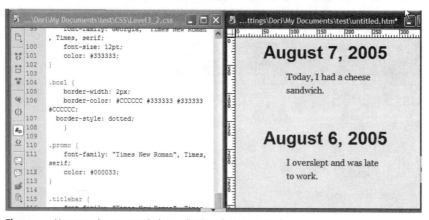

Figure 1.35 Your two document windows, displayed tiled vertically.

Figure 1.36 The default tabbed layout, on the Mac.

✔ Tips

■ To return to the tabbed window view, click the Maximize button in the right-top corner of any document. This will put all open windows back in their place.

■ There's one good reason to have your documents opened in separate windows: it's the only way a Windows user can use the popup menu of available window sizes (Figure 1.20).

■ Having trouble getting from document to document because one is behind another? All open documents are available for the choosing at the bottom of the Window menu.

To manage windows (Mac):

◆ Starting with the default tabbed layout (**Figure 1.36**), choose Window > Cascade. Your document windows will appear in a cascade, each slightly lower and to the right than the one behind it (**Figure 1.37**).

or

Continues on next page

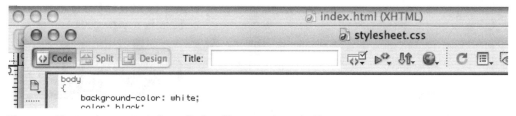

Figure 1.37 The two document windows, displayed in a cascade on the Mac.

SETTING UP YOUR WORKSPACE

◆ Starting with the default tabbed layout (Figure 1.36), choose Window > Tile. Your document windows will appear tiled vertically, with the available space split evenly between them (**Figure 1.38**).

✔ Tips

■ To return to the tabbed window view, choose Window > Combine as Tabs. This will put all open windows back in their places.

■ Having trouble getting from document to document because one is behind another? The Window menu has a list of all open documents, as well as Next Document and Previous Document commands, so you can use it to choose the file you want.

■ Note that on Windows, you have a choice of horizontal or vertical window tiling, but on the Mac, the only tiling option is vertical.

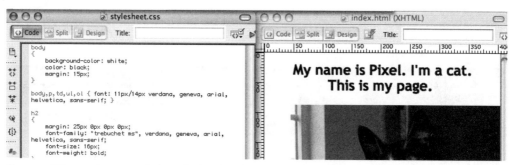

Figure 1.38 The two document windows, displayed tiled vertically on the Mac.

What's New in Dreamweaver 8

If you've used Dreamweaver before, you'll notice that while some things look very similar, some things also look very different. A comprehensive description of all the new features in Dreamweaver 8 would take up an entire chapter or possibly an entire book, so here are just a few of the highlights:

◆ **Background file transfer:** Tired of twiddling your thumbs while Dreamweaver is uploading files? Now you can keep working while files transfer in the background. See Chapter 2 for more details.

◆ **Zoom:** You can now zoom in on a page to inspect images or work with a complex table layout, or zoom out to preview how a page looks. There's more about the Zoom tool in Chapter 6.

◆ **Guides:** If you're used to guides in other graphical applications, you'll be thrilled that they're now in Dreamweaver. They're great for making sure that images and divs are placed exactly where you want them to be. Chapter 6 gives the details about laying out your pages.

◆ **Workspace layouts:** As mentioned earlier in this chapter, you can use one of the included default layouts, or customize and save your own.

◆ **Tabbed documents for Mac:** Mac users are no longer second-class citizens having to do without tabs. With Dreamweaver 8, tabbed document windows make it simple to move between open documents.

◆ **Compare files:** You can now use your own preferred file comparison tool when you want to compare files to find out what's changed. You can compare two local files, a local file to a remote file, or two remote files.

- **Paste Special:** Dreamweaver has new pasting options: you can retain any Microsoft Word or Microsoft Excel source formatting or just paste the text. Chapters 4 and 14 cover making Dreamweaver work with other applications.

- **A new approach to CSS:** There are a multitude of new CSS-related enhancements in Dreamweaver 8, from the new CSS panel to CSS rendering improvements. These will all be covered in detail in Chapter 5.

- **The Style Rendering toolbar:** Mentioned briefly above, you can use the Style Rendering toolbar to view content based on CSS media types.

- **And many, many more**...

STARTING YOUR FIRST SITE

Dreamweaver is all about building sites. Sure, it has all of the tools you need to create great Web pages. But the basic building block is the site, not the page. You need to define a site in Dreamweaver, which will then be the container for all of the files and folders that will make up your Web site.

When you build sites, you will start by creating and testing the site on your local machine. Then, when the site is ready, you will send it over the Internet to your Web server, where it will go live for all the world to see. Dreamweaver has all the tools you'll need to create the site, work with its files and folders, and then transfer it to the Web server. That's what we'll be covering in this chapter. So let's get started!

Understanding Local and Remote Sites

Dreamweaver 8 can do a great job of helping you manage all the files and folders that make up your Web site, but for the best results, you'll need to use the program's site management tools to set up and maintain the site. First, you need to understand some of the terminology Dreamweaver uses for sites. You'll want to build and test your Web site within a single folder on your hard disk, which Dreamweaver calls the *local root folder*. This folder contains all of the files and folders that make up the site. For example, let's say that you're building a company site that has two sections in it, one for product information (called products), and the other for information about the company (called companyinfo). Each of the two sections gets its own folder. These folders are located inside the local root folder (which in this example I'm calling MyCompany). Because each section shares some of the same graphic images, there is also an images folder in the local root folder. The site structure would look something like **Figure 2.1**. With one exception, each of the Web pages that you build for the site will go into either the products or companyinfo folder. The exception is the main site page (the one that people see when they load your site in their browsers). That's called the *index page*, and it usually goes in the local root folder (which is also called the *local site*).

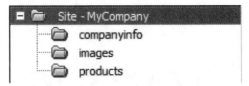

Figure 2.1 The top folder here is the local root folder, which contains all of the files and folders that make up the Web site.

After you build the pages for your site, you will use Dreamweaver to copy all of the files and folders (usually over the Internet) to the Web server. Dreamweaver replicates the folder structure from your hard disk on the Web server, so the site's structure and all of the links between the pages are preserved. Dreamweaver refers to the copy of the site on the Web server as the *remote site*. The remote site should always be a mirror image of your local site, and Dreamweaver has tools that can synchronize the two sites (you'll learn more about that later in this chapter and in Chapter 16).

✔ Tips

■ Strictly speaking, you don't have to create all of your site's files within the local root folder. But if you do not, Dreamweaver will often put up dialogs complaining that files aren't in a local site, and you'll lose access to very useful Dreamweaver features, such as the ability to automatically update all links to a file that has been moved to another location in the site. We strongly recommend that you always build your pages in a local site, and keep all of the elements that make up those pages in the local root folder.

■ If you were using Dreamweaver's ability to work with sites built using a database, you could have a third copy of your site on a *testing* or *staging server*.

Static versus Dynamic Sites

There are two main kinds of Web sites that you can create in Dreamweaver: *static* sites, where you build all of the pages of the site on your local machine, then upload them to the Web server; and *dynamic* sites, in which all the pages are created from information drawn from a database. The content from a dynamic page is created when the user loads the page. Many e-commerce sites are dynamic sites; for example, when you go to Amazon.com and see pages that greet you by name and offer personalized recommendations, those pages are created and served just for you, based on the programming of Amazon's database.

We're covering how to build static sites with Dreamweaver in this book. When we run into options that Dreamweaver offers to work with dynamic sites, we'll mention that, but we generally will not cover those options in detail in this book. If you're interested in using Dreamweaver to create dynamic pages, check out *Macromedia Dreamweaver 8 Advanced for Windows and Macintosh: Visual QuickPro Guide*, by Lucinda Dykes.

UNDERSTANDING LOCAL AND REMOTE SITES

Using the Site Definition Dialog

Because the process of setting up your local and remote sites has many steps, Dreamweaver provides a handy Site Definition dialog that walks you through the process. Once you're familiar with setting up local and remote sites, the Site Definition dialog provides Basic and Advanced modes. The Basic mode (**Figure 2.2**) uses many screens, like a Wizard, which is a friendlier way of entering all the needed information. The Advanced mode (**Figure 2.3**) allows you to enter information on one screen with several categories, and provides more detailed options in each category.

You'll use the Site Definition dialog to create both the local and remote sites. In this section, however, we'll just create the local site. See "Defining the Remote Site," later in this chapter, for instructions to tell Dreamweaver about the remote site.

To create the local site:

1. In the Dreamweaver Start Page, click the Dreamweaver Site link (**Figure 2.4**).

   The Site Definition dialog appears, set to the Editing Files screen of the Basic tab.

   or

   Choose Site > New Site.

   The Site Definition dialog appears, set to the Advanced tab.

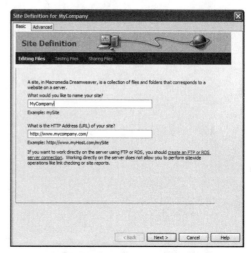

Figure 2.2 The Basic mode of the Site Definition dialog walks you through the information that you need to enter to define a site in a friendly fashion.

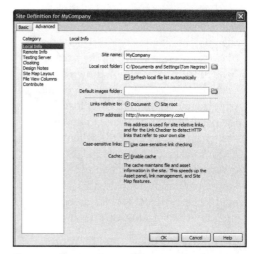

Figure 2.3 Once you've used Dreamweaver for a while, you'll be ready to define sites or make changes using the Site Definition dialog's Advanced mode.

Create New

- HTML
- ColdFusion
- PHP
- ASP VBScript
- ASP.NET C#
- JavaScript
- XML
- XSLT (Fragment)
- CSS
- Dreamweaver Site...
- More...

Figure 2.4 Click the Dreamweaver Site link in the Start Page to begin creating your site.

Figure 2.5 In the first screen of the Site Definition dialog, enter the name and Web address of your site.

2. If the dialog is set to the Advanced tab, click the Basic tab, which switches the dialog to show the Editing Files screen. Then, in the field under "What would you like to name your site?", enter the name.

The site name is only for your reference; it won't be visible to users of the site.

3. In the field under "What is the HTTP Address (URL) of your site?", enter the Web address of your site including the leading http:// (**Figure 2.5**).

4. Click Next.

The Editing Files, Part 2 screen appears.

5. Dreamweaver asks, "Do you want to work with a server technology such as ColdFusion, ASP.NET, ASP, JSP, or PHP?" Click the button next to "No, I do not want to use a server technology."

Server technologies such as the ones listed are used for sites that have pages that are generated *dynamically*, that is, the contents of the page are drawn from a database when the page is requested by the user. Using server technologies is beyond the scope of this book; instead, we'll be creating *static* pages.

Continues on next page

USING THE SITE DEFINITION DIALOG

6. Click Next.

The Editing Files, Part 3 screen appears (**Figure 2.6**).

7. Dreamweaver asks, "How do you want to work with your files during development?" Click the button next to "Edit local copies on my machine, then upload to server when ready (recommended)."

The other choice, "Edit directly on server using local network," is for specialized situations where your Web server is on the local network, rather than accessible over the Internet.

8. On the same screen, Dreamweaver asks, "Where on your computer do you want to store your files?" Click the folder icon to the right of the text field, which will bring up a dialog titled "Choose local root folder for site `sitename`," and browse to the folder on your hard disk that will contain all of the files for your site.

On Windows, select the folder in the dialog and click Open, then click the Select button.

or

On Macintosh, select the folder in the dialog and click the Choose button.

The dialog will close and you will return to the Site Definition dialog.

9. Click Next.

The Sharing Files screen appears (**Figure 2.7**).

Figure 2.6 Next, you'll need to tell Dreamweaver where to put your local site folder.

Figure 2.7 For now, we won't connect to a remote server, so None is the correct choice.

Figure 2.8 The Summary screen recaps the information you entered.

10. From the pop-up menu labeled "How do you connect to your remote server?", choose None.

    In this case, we are only creating the local site. If you want to continue on and define the remote site, go to step 4 in "Defining the Remote Site," later in this chapter.

11. Click Next.

    The Summary screen appears (**Figure 2.8**).

12. Click Done.

Getting Yourself Organized

Before you dive deeper into Dreamweaver, it's useful to spend some time deciding the structure and design of your site. In fact, this is a great time to push away from the computer and pick up a much older design tool: a pencil and pad of paper. While a primer on site design would take up much more space than we have in this sidebar (indeed, entire books are devoted to the subject), before you begin building your site with Dreamweaver, consider the following, then sketch out your designs.

◆ **What do your customers need from your site?** Your site's visitors are your customers. Create your sites for *them*, not for you. Customers can visit your site for a variety of reasons: to purchase something, to get information or entertainment, or to be part of a community. Sites centered on your customer's needs are sites that visitors will return to. Sites driven by company structure, or by the designer's ego—not so popular.

◆ **What is the best structure and navigation for your site?** Site structure is generally like an upside-down tree, or an organization chart. The index page is the main trunk, and branches off to folders with other pages inside (and often other folders with their own pages). On your pad, add the main folders that you'll create from the index page (the home page of your site). Your structure will also determine the site navigation you choose. Again, put yourself in the place of the customer, and imagine what they'll need to get around your site. Remember that they may not enter your site at your home page, so make sure the navigation is clear and consistent throughout the site.

Take the time to work out your customer's needs, and then the site's structure and navigation, on paper before you start creating things in Dreamweaver. You'll end up saving much more time by avoiding dead ends and wasted effort.

USING THE SITE DEFINITION DIALOG

Defining the Remote Site

The remote site lives on your Web server, and it is the destination for the files and folders from the local site on your computer's hard disk. Dreamweaver can connect to your Web server in several ways. The most common connection, called *FTP* (see the sidebar "What's FTP, SFTP, and WebDAV?"), is used when your server resides on the Internet or on your company's intranet. Another way to connect is called *SFTP*, for Secure FTP. A third way to connect is via a protocol called *WebDAV*.

Before you begin creating a connection to the remote site, you need to ask your network administrator for some information about the Web server you're using. You will need:

◆ The connection type, which will be FTP, SFTP, or WebDAV

◆ The FTP, SFTP, or WebDAV address for your server

◆ The login (sometimes called the user-name) for the server

◆ The password associated with the login

◆ The folder's path on the server that contains your Web site

Once you gather this information, you're ready to define the remote site in Dreamweaver. You'll begin by editing the site definition.

✔ Tip

■ Dreamweaver offers two other ways to connect to remote sites, RDS and Microsoft Visual SourceSafe (Windows only), which are used for database-backed sites, and will not be discussed in this book.

Figure 2.9 Begin adding the remote site to your site definition in the Manage Sites dialog.

Figure 2.10 You'll need to enter the FTP information in the Sharing Files screen. I've blurred some private information here.

To define the remote site with FTP or SFTP:

1. Choose Site > Manage Sites.

   The Manage Sites dialog appears (**Figure 2.9**).

2. Select the site you want, then click Edit.

   The Site Definition dialog appears. If you last used this dialog in Basic mode, it will appear still set to that mode. If you last used it in Advanced mode, it will appear that way.

3. If necessary, click the Basic tab, then click the Next button until the Sharing Files screen appears.

4. From the pop-up menu labeled "How do you connect to your remote server?", choose FTP.

   The dialog changes to show fields you need to fill in for the FTP connection type (**Figure 2.10**). If you will be making an SFTP connection, choose FTP from the pop-up menu, then check the "Use Secure FTP (SFTP)" check box when the dialog changes to show that option.

5. In the field labeled "What is the hostname or FTP address of your Web server?" enter the hostname or FTP address of your Web server.

   The hostname could be a name like www. peachpit.com or ftp.dori.com. It will usually be the name you would enter into a Web browser, without the http://. It must begin with www or ftp, and cannot be just the domain name, such as dori.com. The name should not contain directories or slashes, such as www. negrino.com/books/. You can also enter a numeric IP address in this field, such as 66.39.104.128.

   Continues on next page

Continues on next page

DEFINING THE REMOTE SITE

6. In the next field, enter the name of the folder on the Web site that contains your site's files and will serve as the root folder for your site.

This folder is also called the *host directory*, and is usually a path from the FTP folder to the root folder. Depending on your Web hosting company, this path could be named many different things. Typical host directory names are `htdocs`, `public_html`, or `www/public/docs/`. If you're unsure of the exact name of the host directory, check with your Web hosting company. Sometimes, the FTP host connects to the correct directory automatically, and you can leave the field blank.

7. Enter the FTP login name.

8. Enter the FTP password.

Don't forget that FTP logins and passwords are case-sensitive on many servers.

9. If you want Dreamweaver to remember the FTP login and password (recommended), make sure the Save check box is selected.

10. Click the Test Connection button to make sure that Dreamweaver can connect successfully to your Web server. If Dreamweaver reports an error, check the information you entered.

11. Click Next.

The Sharing Files, Part 2 screen appears.

12. Dreamweaver asks, "Do you want to enable checking in and checking out files, to ensure that you and your co-workers cannot edit the same file at the same time?" Click the radio button next to "No, do not enable check-in and check out."

    Check in and check out is a useful feature when you are working on the site with others, because it helps keep different people from accidentally editing a page at the same time. We will explore this feature further in Chapter 16.

13. Click Next.

    The Summary screen appears, with the information that you have entered for the local and remote sites.

14. Click Done.

What's FTP, SFTP, and WebDAV?

If you've never done any Web site maintenance before, you might be baffled by the term *FTP*. It stands for "File Transfer Protocol," and is a common method for transferring files (such as Web pages and images) between two computers connected to the Internet. Web servers often use FTP to send files between the server and the computer of whomever is maintaining the Web site. In order to do this, the server machine runs an *FTP server* program in addition to the Web server software. Normally you need a program called an *FTP client* on your computer in order to transfer files to and from an FTP server. Dreamweaver has the FTP client functions built in.

One of the drawbacks to FTP is that it is a protocol with no built-in security; all information is sent "in the clear," including your username, password, and the files themselves. The Secure FTP (SFTP) protocol solves this problem by encrypting all information sent between the SFTP client (in this case, Dreamweaver) and the SFTP server.

The WebDAV protocol provides both security and deals with another problem faced by Dreamweaver users: that of ensuring that only one person at a time is modifying a particular Web page. WebDAV locks a file while it is being edited, and releases the lock when the page is completed. Dreamweaver has its own system of locking and unlocking files when you use protocols other than WebDAV; in practice, you won't see a difference in the way Dreamweaver works no matter which connection protocol you select.

To define the remote site with WebDAV:

1. Choose Site > Manage Sites.

   The Manage Sites dialog appears.

2. Select the site you want, then click Edit.

   The Site Definition dialog appears.

3. If necessary, click the Basic tab, then click the Next button until the Sharing Files screen appears.

4. From the pop-up menu labeled "How do you connect to your remote server?" choose WebDAV.

   The dialog changes to show fields you need to fill in for the WebDAV connection type (**Figure 2.11**).

5. Enter the URL of your WebDAV server.

6. Enter the WebDAV login name.

7. Enter the WebDAV password.

   If you want Dreamweaver to remember the WebDAV login and password (recommended), make sure the Save check box is selected.

Figure 2.11 If you connect to your Web server via WebDAV, you'll need to enter the connection information.

8. Click the Test Connection button to make sure that Dreamweaver can connect successfully to your Web server.

If Dreamweaver reports an error, check the information you entered.

9. Click Next.

The Sharing Files, Part 2 screen appears.

10. Dreamweaver asks, "Do you want to enable checking in and checking out files, to ensure that you and your co-workers cannot edit the same file at the same time?" Click the radio button next to "No, do not enable check-in and check out."

11. Click Next.

The Summary screen appears, with the information that you have entered for the local and remote sites.

12. Click Done.

Editing Site Definitions

Once you have created your site definitions, you might need to change them. For example, you might want to change the location of the local root folder, or you may change the path on the remote server. You'll use the Site Definition dialog, but this time we'll use the Advanced tab to get things done a bit faster.

To change a site definition:

1. Choose Site > Manage Sites.

   The Manage Sites dialog appears.

2. Select the site you want, then click Edit.

   The Site Definition dialog appears.

3. If necessary, click the Advanced tab.

   The dialog changes to the Advanced mode (**Figure 2.12**).

4. Choose the category on the left side of the dialog for the kind of change you want to make.

   The right side of the dialog changes to show the options for the category you chose.

5. Make the changes you need to make.

6. Click OK.

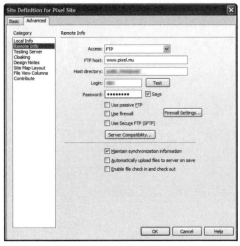

Figure 2.12 It's faster to edit site definitions in the Advanced tab of the Site Definition dialog.

Working with the Files Panel

To work with the files and folders that make up your Web sites, you'll use Dreamweaver's Files panel. This panel allows you to add and delete files and folders; view and change the local or remote sites; and do other maintenance tasks for your sites.

The Files panel appears at the right side of the Dreamweaver window, docked with other panels. By default, the Files panel is at the bottom of the group of panels. The panel consists of a couple of pop-up menus, a toolbar, and the files area below (**Figure 2.13**).

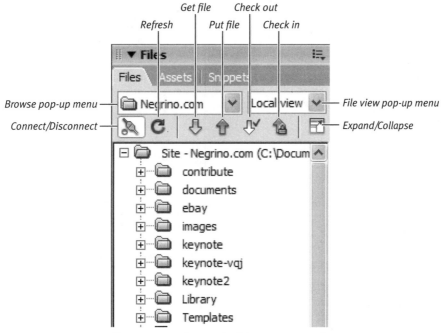

Figure 2.13 The Files panel will be your command center for working with files in Dreamweaver.

Navigating Disks and Sites

The Browse pop-up menu at the top of the Files panel allows you to browse through your hard disk, and easily switch between sites that you have defined. The menu looks a bit different on Windows and Mac, reflecting the differences between the operating systems (**Figure 2.14**). On both platforms, sites you have defined appear in the menu as folders.

To browse your hard disk:

1. In the Files panel, choose the disk you want from the Browse pop-up menu.

The disk's contents appear in the files area (**Figure 2.15**).

2. Navigate to the folder and file that you want.

To switch between defined sites:

◆ In the Files panel, choose the site from the Browse pop-up menu.

Figure 2.14 The Browse menu in the Files panel reflects the differences in the Windows (left) and Mac (right) operating systems.

Figure 2.15 If you choose your hard disk from the Browse pop-up menu, you can then navigate to any file or folder on the disk.

Figure 2.16 To see the files on the remote site, choose Remote view from the File view pop-up menu.

Switching Between Local and Remote Views

The File view pop-up menu, next to the Browse pop-up menu, allows you to switch the view in the Files panel between the local and remote sites.

To switch between local and remote views:

1. Choose a site you have defined from the Browse pop-up menu.

The site's local files appear in the files area, and the File view pop-up menu switches to Local view.

2. From the File view pop-up menu, choose Remote view (**Figure 2.16**).

Dreamweaver will connect to the site (you can tell because the Connect/Disconnect button in the Files panel toolbar will highlight), and the remote files will appear in the files area.

✔ Tip

■ The File view pop-up menu has two other choices: *Testing server* and *Map view*. We won't be discussing Testing server in this book, but you'll find an explanation of Map view in Chapter 16.

Refreshing Views

When you switch to the local or remote views of a site, Dreamweaver scans the contents of your local or remote site folders, and displays the current contents. On occasion, the view you're looking at in the Files panel may become out of date. For example, if you happen to upload or delete items on the remote site with a program other than Dreamweaver, those changes won't be shown in the Files panel. Similarly, if you move files into the local root folder by working in the Windows or Mac desktop, you may need to tell Dreamweaver to rescan and refresh its display of the local site.

To refresh the local or remote view:

1. Choose the site you want to refresh from the Browse pop-up menu.

2. Choose the view (local or remote) you want from the File view pop-up menu.

3. Click the Refresh button in the Files panel toolbar.

   Dreamweaver rescans the site you selected, and updates the files area.

Working with Files and Folders

The Files panel is great for organizing all of the files on your site, and creating new files and folders. You should do most of your file creation and management in the Files panel, because it can often save you quite a bit of time compared to using another method in Dreamweaver.

For example, you can create a new page by choosing File > New, then choosing the kind of page you want from the New Document dialog, then editing the page. When you save the dialog, you must navigate to the correct folder in the local site folder, name the page, then save it. In contrast, to create a new page in a particular folder using the Files panel, you select the folder that you want to contain the page, then choose the New File command.

✔ Tip

■ Just because the Dreamweaver files area is reminiscent of the Windows Explorer or Macintosh Finder, don't be fooled into thinking that it is the same, and that you could do your local file management on your computer's desktop. Dreamweaver is designed for working with Web pages, and it can do incredibly useful things like updating the links on a page to work correctly, even if you move the page that contains the links to a different folder on the site.

To create a new file or folder:

1. Use the File view pop-up menu to select the local or remote site. You will usually create files or folders in the local site.

2. Right-click a file or folder in the files area.

   A shortcut menu appears that gives you many options (**Figure 2.17**).

3. From the shortcut menu, choose New File or New Folder.

   The new file or folder appears in the files area. If you had selected a folder in step 2, the new file or folder will be created inside of the selected folder.

4. The name of the newly created file or folder will be selected in the Files panel. Type the name you want.

✔ Tip

- You can instead use the panel options button at the upper-right corner of the Files panel, which gives you a different shortcut menu, but it's easier to use the right-click shortcut menu.

To move files or folders:

1. Select a file or folder in the files area. To move multiple items, Ctrl-click (Cmd-click) to select each of the items you want to move.

2. Drag the selected item(s) to the new location.

   The Update Files dialog appears (**Figure 2.18**).

3. Click Update.

   Dreamweaver updates all of the links in the site that are affected by the move.

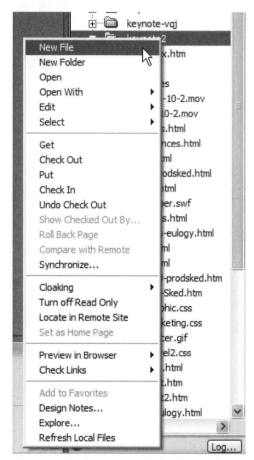

Figure 2.17 The shortcut menu in the Files panel is the fastest way to create a new file or new folder.

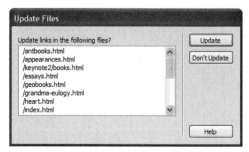

Figure 2.18 If you move files that are the target of links, Dreamweaver will ask to update the pages that link to the file you moved.

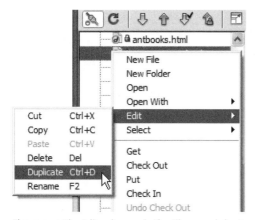

Figure 2.19 The Edit submenu in the Files panel shortcut menu gives you several options for working with files or folders.

To rename files or folders:

1. Select a file or folder in the files area.

2. Click the name of the file or folder.
   The name will become highlighted.

3. Type the new name. Don't forget to add the correct file extension for the file that you're renaming. For example, most Web pages will have the file extension .htm or (preferably) .html.

4. Press Enter (Return).
   The Update Files dialog appears.

5. Click Update.
   Dreamweaver updates all of the files in the site that are affected by the renamed file.

To edit files or folders:

1. Right-click a file or folder in the files area.

2. From the resulting shortcut menu, choose the Edit submenu (**Figure 2.19**).

3. Choose one of the items in the Edit menu.
   You can Cut, Copy, Paste, Delete, Duplicate, or Rename the file or folder. If a file operation will affect other files, Dreamweaver may display an "Are you sure?" dialog or the Update Files dialog.

✔ Tip

■ Note the shortcut keys listed next to each of the items in the Edit menu. As you become more comfortable working with files in Dreamweaver, using the shortcut keys can save you time.

Putting and Getting Files

You can copy selected files or folders (or the entire site) between the local and remote sites with the Files panel. The Dreamweaver term for moving an item from the local to the remote site is called *putting* the item; moving the item from the remote to local site is *getting* the item. If a put or get operation will overwrite a file, Dreamweaver will warn you. If you select a folder, Dreamweaver will move the folder and all of the items that it contains. So if you select the local root folder, you can put the entire site up on the remote server in just a couple of clicks. Sometimes, however, you'll want to use Dreamweaver's site synchronization feature, rather than put or get individual items. See "Synchronizing the Local and Remote Sites," later in this chapter.

To put or get a file or folder:

1. In the Files panel, choose Local view or Remote view from the File view pop-up menu.

   The local or remote view is displayed in the files area.

2. Select the file or folder you want to move.

3. Click the Get file or Put file button in the Files panel toolbar.

4. If any of the files that you're transferring are open and have unsaved changes, Dreamweaver will ask if you want to save the files before they are sent. Click Yes, or if there are multiple files, click Yes to All.

5. Dreamweaver may also display a dialog asking if you want to transfer any *dependent files*. An example of dependent files would be the graphics on the pages that you are uploading. If the dependent files have already been uploaded to the server, click No; there's no reason to reupload files that haven't changed. If you want to transfer dependent files that have changed, click Yes.

Checking files in and out

Operations with the Check in and Check out buttons in the Files panel toolbar will be discussed in Chapter 16.

Expanding the Files Panel

Normally, the Files panel will only show either the local site or the remote site. But if you would like to compare the list of files and folders on both sites, you can do that by expanding the Files panel. This feature works slightly differently on Windows and on Macintosh. On Windows, expanding the Files panel causes it to grow to take over the entire screen, replacing the rest of the Dreamweaver interface. On Mac, expanding the Files panel opens the panel in a new window that allows you to see the remote site on the left and the local site on the right (**Figure 2.20**).

To expand the Files panel:

◆ Click the Expand/Collapse button in the Files panel toolbar.

✔ Tip

■ To collapse the Files panel, click the Expand/Collapse button again.

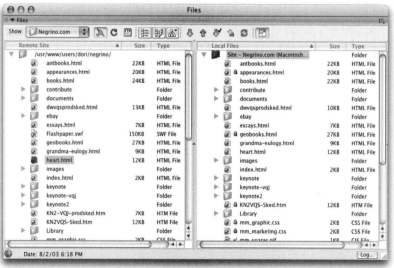

Figure 2.20 On the Mac, when you expand the Files panel, it opens in a new window, with the remote site on the left and the local site on the right.

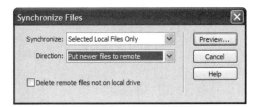

Figure 2.21 In the Synchronize Files dialog, you'll need to select the synchronization method you want to use.

Synchronizing the Local and Remote Sites

Having two copies of a Web site—one on your local machine and the other on a Web server—can potentially lead to trouble. It's possible, for example, for you to update several pages on your local site, and lose track of just which files you changed. In that case, it might be difficult for you to determine which copy of the site (local or remote) has the latest version of the files. Dreamweaver's Synchronize command compares the local and remote sites and transfers the newer files in either direction.

To synchronize local and remote sites:

1. Right-click in the Files panel. From the shortcut menu that appears, choose Synchronize.

or

Choose Site > Synchronize Sitewide.

The Synchronize Files dialog appears (**Figure 2.21**).

2. From the Synchronize pop-up menu, choose the files you want to update.

Your choices are to synchronize all the files in the site, or just files or folders that you selected in the Local view.

3. From the Direction pop-up menu, choose how you would like to copy newer files:

▲ **Put newer files to remote** sends newer files from your local site folder to the Web server.

Continues on next page

▲ **Get newer files from remote** finds newer files on the Web server, and copies them to your local site folder. This option will also copy *completely new* files that are on the Web server (ones, for example, that may have been placed there by a coworker) to your local site folder.

▲ **Get and Put newer files** synchronizes files both ways. New files on the local site will be transferred to the remote site and vice versa.

4. (Optional) If you want, turn on the "Delete remote files not on local drive" check box.

This is a good option to choose when you've made substantial deletions in the local site (perhaps because you did a big site cleanup). The wording of this option changes depending on what you chose in step 3. If you chose to transfer newer files from the remote site, the wording changes to "Delete local files not on remote server." If you chose to get and put files, this option becomes inactive.

5. Click Preview.

Dreamweaver connects to the remote site, and compares the files you chose to synchronize, then displays the Synchronize dialog (**Figure 2.22**). This allows you to preview the changes that will be made on the site. The Action column in the dialog tells you what Dreamweaver proposes to do to each file.

6. If desired, select one or more files in the Synchronize dialog and choose one of the action buttons at the bottom of the dialog. You have the following choices:

▲ **Get** marks the selected files to be retrieved from the remote site.

▲ **Put** marks the selected files to be sent to the remote site.

▲ **Delete** marks the selected files for deletion.

▲ **Ignore** tells Dreamweaver to ignore the selected files for this synchronization.

▲ **Mark as synchronized** tells Dreamweaver to consider the selected files as already synchronized, so no action will be taken.

▲ **Compare** opens the local and remote versions of the file so you can compare their differences.

7. Click OK.

Dreamweaver performs the synchronization.

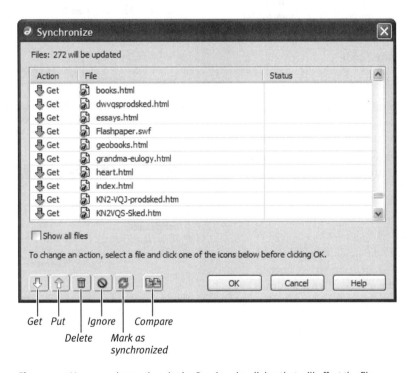

Figure 2.22 You can select actions in the Synchronize dialog that will affect the files as they are synchronized.

Cloaking Files

Not every folder in your local site needs to be uploaded to the remote site on the Web server. Dreamweaver allows folders to be *cloaked*, which means that they will be exempt from synchronization. This can save you a lot of time. Imagine that you're working on a site that contains large movie files. Cloaking the folder that contains the movie files means that while you're working on other parts of the site, Dreamweaver won't take the time to scan through the folders when synchronizing, and won't upload any of the files. When you're ready to upload the files, uncloak the movies folder and synchronize the local and remote sites.

To cloak a site folder:

1. Right-click a folder in the files area.

2. From the resulting shortcut menu, choose the Cloaking submenu, then from the submenu, choose Cloak (**Figure 2.23**).

   Dreamweaver displays the folder with a slash through it, indicating that it is cloaked.

✔ Tip

■ You can only cloak folders; you can't cloak individual files. But you *can* cloak all files of a particular type. Choose Site > Manage Sites, then select the site you're working on. In the Advanced tab of the Site Definition dialog, choose the Cloaking category. Enable the "Cloak files ending with" check box, then enter the file extensions of the kinds of files you want to cloak (**Figure 2.24**).

To uncloak a site folder:

1. Right-click a cloaked folder in the files area.

2. From the resulting shortcut menu, choose Cloaking > Uncloak or Cloaking > Uncloak All.

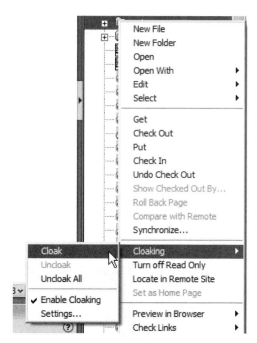

Figure 2.23 Choosing Cloak from the Files panel shortcut menu keeps a folder and its contents from being affected during synchronization operations.

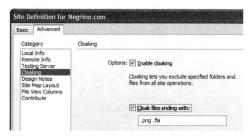

Figure 2.24 The Cloaking category in the Site Definition dialog allows you to set particular kinds of files to always be cloaked.

BUILDING
YOUR FIRST PAGE

3

After you've set up your local site, you can begin filling the site with pages. To do that, you'll need to create a page, give it a title, add some content to the page, and save it. To check your work, you should view the page in one or more Web browsers before you upload it to your Web server. Luckily, Dreamweaver makes it easy to view your work in different browsers.

If you need a little inspiration, Dreamweaver offers a variety of sample pages that you can use as a jumping-off point for your own creative efforts. You can also choose from a variety of page designs created entirely with CSS.

In this chapter, we'll also briefly discuss how you add text, links, and images to your pages, although we go into those subjects in much greater detail in Chapters 4, 7, and 8, respectively.

Creating a New Page

The first HTML page that you create in a new site should be the *index page*, which is the page that a Web browser loads automatically when a visitor goes to the site. Depending on how you are naming pages on your site, the index page could have a variety of names, but it is most often named index. html. After you create the index page, you will want to create other pages for the site.

As you'll see is often the case with Dreamweaver, there is more than one way to do the task at hand. You can create a new page using the Start Page, or you can use the New Document dialog.

Using the Start Page

The Start Page is the fastest way to create a new HTML page. It appears when you have closed all other document windows.

To create a new page from the Start Page:

1. Close any open document windows.

   The Start Page appears (**Figure 3.1**). Each of the items in the Start Page is a link.

2. In the Create New section, click HTML.

   Dreamweaver creates the new blank HTML page (**Figure 3.2**).

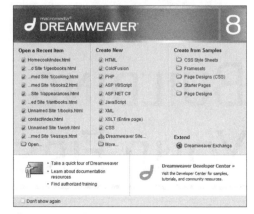

Figure 3.1 Click the links in the Start Page to open a recent item, create a new item, or create a new item from Dreamweaver's sample pages.

✔ Tips

- You can also use the Start Page to open pages that you recently worked on. Just click the item's name in the Open a Recent Item section of the Start Page.

- Clicking ColdFusion or PHP in the Start Page also creates an HTML page. Clicking CSS creates a new CSS style sheet. Clicking any of the other choices creates documents designed for different Web programming languages that you would normally work with in Code view.

- If you click any of the items listed in the Create from Samples section of the Start Page, Dreamweaver opens up the New Document dialog so you can choose the sample page you want. See "Using Sample Pages," later in this chapter.

- If you don't want to use the Start Page at all, you can turn it off in Dreamweaver's Preferences. Choose Edit > Preferences (Dreamweaver > Preferences), and click the General category. Then clear the check box next to "Show start page."

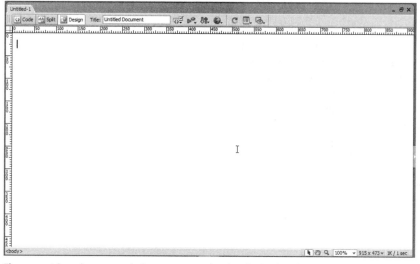

Figure 3.2 A brand-new page in Dreamweaver, showing the Design view.

Using the New Document dialog

The New Document dialog gives you a bit more flexibility than the Start Page when creating new documents. Like the Start Page, you can create several different types of new documents, plus it allows you to choose the doctype of the new document.

To create a new page from the New Document dialog:

1. Choose File > New, or press Ctrl-N (Cmd-N).

   The New Document dialog appears (**Figure 3.3**), set to the General tab.

2. Click to choose one of the items in the Category column.

   The second column changes to show the available items for the category you selected. The name of this column also changes to match the name of the category.

3. Click the item you want in the second column.

   If Dreamweaver has a preview image of the item you selected available, it will appear in the Preview pane (previews are mostly available for sample pages and templates), with its description below the preview area.

4. (Optional) Some of the kinds of documents you can create in this dialog allow you to declare their doctype, and for those the Document Type (DTD) pop-up menu will be available. Most of the time the default choice will be fine, but if you want to you can change the doctype from the pop-up menu (**Figure 3.4**).

5. Click Create.

   Dreamweaver creates the new document and displays it in a new window.

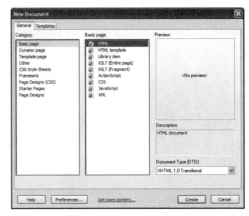

Figure 3.3 You'll probably create most of your new pages from the New Document dialog.

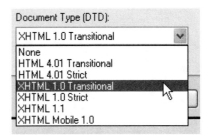

Figure 3.4 You can choose from the available DTDs in the New Document dialog.

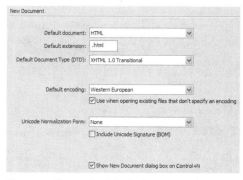

Figure 3.5 Change the defaults for new pages in the New Document category of Dreamweaver's Preferences dialog.

✔ Tips

- If you want to change any of the defaults for a new document, click the Preferences button in the New Document dialog. In the resulting dialog (**Figure 3.5**), you can change the default document type for the New Document dialog; the extension used for that document; the default DTD; and the default character encoding. You can also choose whether or not you want the New Document dialog to appear when you press Ctrl-N (Cmd-N), or if you just want Dreamweaver to create a new default document.

- We'll cover the Templates tab of the New Document dialog in Chapter 13.

Behind the Doctype

If you're not familiar with doctype, it's a declaration at the start of an HTML page that specifies the DTD (Document Type Definition) that is in use for the file. Web browsers use the doctype declaration in order to determine how the page should be rendered.

By default, Dreamweaver 8 inserts the "XHTML 1.0 Transitional" doctype, and the code it creates is consistent with that standard.

Using Sample Pages

Dreamweaver has many sample pages available, which do some of the work of creating new pages for you. The sample pages are often good jumping-off points for your own pages. After you create a document from one of the sample pages, you can customize and modify it as you wish.

The sample pages come in five categories:

◆ **CSS Style Sheets** are external CSS style sheet documents that contain style definitions for a wide variety of looks for your pages. You can click on any of the sample style sheets to see a preview and description (**Figure 3.6**).

◆ **Framesets** have 15 premade frameset pages with different frame layouts (**Figure 3.7**). This makes creating framesets considerably easier than doing it by hand.

◆ **Page Designs (CSS)** provides six page layouts that use only CSS (rather than tables) for layout and positioning (**Figure 3.8**).

◆ **Starter Pages** gives you dozens of pages you can use to create whole sites. There are several categories of sites, such as Entertainment, Travel, Spa, and more. Each site type has a home page, a product page, a text page, a catalog page, and a calendar page, all sharing the same basic design (**Figure 3.9**). These are useful, but are built around tables for layout, which may not be what you want to do (see Chapter 5 for more about page layout with Dreamweaver).

◆ **Page Designs** give you basic layouts for various tasks, such as a login window, a catalog page, or a comments form (**Figure 3.10**). These are also built using tables for layout.

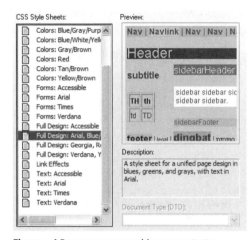

Figure 3.6 Dreamweaver provides many starter CSS Style Sheets, which you can preview in the New Document dialog.

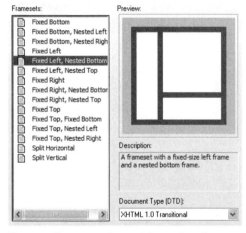

Figure 3.7 You can preview and choose from the predefined framesets.

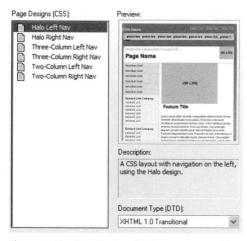

Figure 3.8 The Page Designs (CSS) category provides six good sample pages based entirely on CSS for their layout.

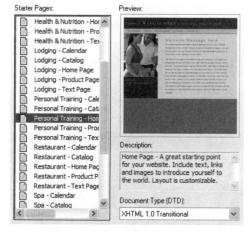

Figure 3.9 The Starter Pages give you many attractive pages that you can easily customize for your own sites.

To create a page from a sample page:

1. Choose File > New, or press Ctrl-N (Cmd-N). The New Document dialog appears.

2. Click to choose one of the sample pages categories in the Category column.

   The second column changes to show the available items for the category you selected. The name of this column also changes to match the name of the category.

3. Click the item you want in the second column.

   The preview image of the item you selected will appear in the Preview pane (previews are mostly available for sample pages and templates), with its description below the preview.

4. Click Create.

   Dreamweaver creates the page in a new window.

5. Modify the sample page as you like.

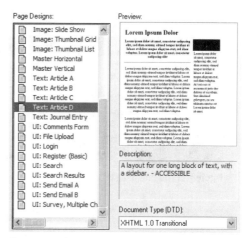

Figure 3.10 The Page Designs sample pages provide many pages that you can adapt for your own sites.

Titling Your Page

The first thing you should do with your new page is to add a *title*. The title is the text that appears in the title bar of Web browser windows, at the top of the window (**Figure 3.11**). You'll enter this text in the Dreamweaver document window.

To add a title to your page:

1. If necessary, open the page you want to title.

2. Click in the Title field at the top of the page's document window.

3. Type in the title (**Figure 3.12**).

✔ Tip

■ Don't forget to add the title; it's easy to forget, and when you do forget, it makes it harder for people to find your pages using a search engine. As we wrote this, a quick Google search for "Untitled Document" in the title of pages brought up more than 21 million hits. Don't be one of them!

Figure 3.11 The title of an HTML document appears at the top of a Web browser's window.

Figure 3.12 Enter the title in, well, the Title field.

Adding Text to Your Page

In this section, we'll cover adding a bit of text to your page, just enough to get you started. You'll find a much more detailed discussion of working with text in Dreamweaver in Chapter 4. In short, adding text is a lot like typing text in any word processor.

To add text to a page:

1. On the new page, click to set a blinking insertion point. You can press Enter (Return) to move the insertion point down on the page.

2. Type your text.

   The text appears on the page, aligned to the left.

To format the text:

1. On the Insert Bar, choose Text from the pop-up menu.

   The Text category of the Insert Bar appears (**Figure 3.13**).

2. Using the Insert Bar and the Property Inspector, apply any formatting you want, as you would with a word processor.

   See Chapter 4 for much more detail about using the Text category of the Insert Bar.

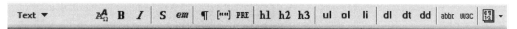

Figure 3.13 Use the Text category of the Insert Bar to format your text.

Creating Links

To add a hyperlink to a page, you need to select the text you want to turn into a link, then provide the URL for the link. A URL (Uniform Resource Locator) is the Web address that you would type into the Address bar of a Web browser.

You will find much more information about adding links to your pages in Chapter 7. You'll see how to add links to either text or graphics, and lots of other linky goodness.

To add a link to a page:

1. Select the text you want to turn into a link (**Figure 3.14**).

   In this example, I want to turn the "HomeCook.info" text at the top of the page into a link to the home page of the site, so I've selected that text.

2. Do one of the following:

   If you are linking to a page in your site, click the Point to File button in the Property Inspector (**Figure 3.15**), then drag to a file in the Files panel (**Figure 3.16**). When you release the mouse button, the file name appears in the Link field.

   or

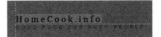

Figure 3.14 Begin creating a link by selecting the text that you want to turn into the link.

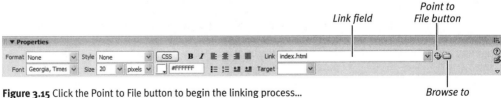

Link field

Point to File button

Browse to File button

Figure 3.15 Click the Point to File button to begin the linking process...

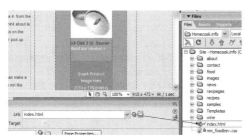

Figure 3.16 ... then drag to point at the file you want to link to in the Files panel. As you drag, Dreamweaver follows your mouse pointer with an arrow to make it clear which file you're pointing at.

Figure 3.17 You can also create a link by clicking the Browse to File button in the Property Inspector, which brings up this Select File dialog.

Figure 3.18 If the file you are selecting is outside your local root folder, Dreamweaver offers to copy the file to that folder as part of the linking process.

If you are linking to a file on your hard drive (inside or outside of your local site folder), click the Browse to File button in the Property Inspector. The Select File dialog appears (**Figure 3.17**). Navigate to the file you want to link to, select it, then click OK (Choose). The file name appears in the Link field. If the file is outside of the local root folder, Dreamweaver lets you know and offers to copy the file into the local root folder (**Figure 3.18**).

or

If you are linking to a Web address, click in the Link field in the Property Inspector and type the full URL of the link destination. You must include the `http://` portion of the address.

✔ Tips

■ You can also copy a URL from the Address bar of a Web browser (or anywhere else) and paste the URL into the Link field.

■ You aren't limited to Web links, which begin with `http://`, of course; you can put any valid URL in the Link field, including links for FTP, email addresses, and more. Again, see Chapter 7 for more information.

Adding Images

Much of the visual interest in Web pages is provided by images, and Dreamweaver makes it easy to add images to your pages. For much more information about adding images, sound, or movie files to your pages, see Chapter 8.

To add an image to your page:

1. In your document, click where you want the image to appear.

2. In the Common category of the Insert Bar, click the Image button (**Figure 3.19**).

   The Select Image Source dialog appears (**Figure 3.20**).

3. Navigate to the image file you want, and select it.

   Dreamweaver shows you a preview of the image in the Select Image Source dialog.

Image button

Figure 3.19 To add an image to your page, click the Image button in the Common category of the Insert Bar.

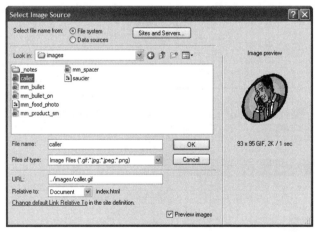

Figure 3.20 The Select Image Source dialog lets you pick an image, and shows you a preview of it as well.

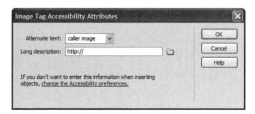

Figure 3.21 Use this dialog to enter the alternate text for an image.

Figure 3.22. The image appears on the page at the insertion point.

4. Click OK (Choose).

   If the image is not inside the /images directory of your local root folder, Dreamweaver copies the image to that location. Dreamweaver next displays the Image Tag Accessibility Attributes dialog (**Figure 3.21**).

5. (Optional, but strongly recommended) Enter the Alternate text for the image.

   Alternate text is text attached to the image for use by screen readers for the visually impaired, or for people who are browsing with images turned off.

6. Click OK.

   The image appears in your document (**Figure 3.22**).

✔ Tips

■ The Long description field in the Image Tag Accessibility Attributes dialog links to a file that can contain a full description of the image. This option is not often used.

■ If you don't want to add alternate text, you can turn the prompt dialog off in the Accessibility category of Dreamweaver's Preferences.

ADDING IMAGES

Naming and Saving Your Page

After you've built your page, you'll want to name it and save it in your local site folder. After you work on the page, you'll need to save your changes. You should get in the habit of saving often; there's nothing more annoying than lost work due to a power failure or because your computer decides to lock up.

It's important to understand the difference between a page's *title* and its *name*. The *title* appears at the top of the page in a Web browser; the *name* is the file's name, and will be part of the Web address, or URL, of the page. For example, "Welcome to HomeCook. info!" is the page's title, but index.html is the page's name.

To save your page for the first time:

1. Choose File > Save, or press Ctrl-S (Cmd-S). The Save As dialog appears (**Figure 3.23**).

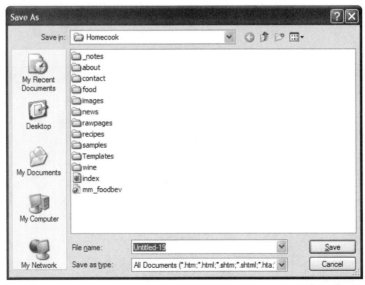

Figure 3.23 Use the Save As dialog to place your new document where you want it inside your local root folder, and also to give it a file name.

Figure 3.24 The Mac version of the Save As dialog shows you the document's extension, and selects the Untitled name for you.

2. Enter the name for the page.

Dreamweaver gives the page a default name of Untitled-*x*, where *x* is the number of pages you've created since you launched Dreamweaver. On Windows, the dialog shows the name in the "File name" field without showing the extension; on the Mac, the name appears with the extension, but only the name is selected, ready for replacement with whatever you type (**Figure 3.24**).

Not all characters are acceptable in a file name; be sure to read the "What's in a Name?" sidebar.

3. You should save the file inside your local site folder. If you want the file to be in a particular folder inside your site, navigate to that folder.

4. Click Save.

To save changes you make in your pages:

◆ Choose File > Save, or press Ctrl-S (Cmd-S).

What's in a Name?

Your computer may allow you to enter characters in a file name that aren't acceptable in a URL. For example, on the Mac, it's perfectly okay to use the slash (/) in a file name. But you can't use a slash in a URL (Web servers can't handle a slash in a file name), so you *shouldn't* include slashes. Similarly, you can use spaces in file names on both Windows and Mac, but you cannot have spaces in a URL, so don't use spaces in your file names. Other characters to avoid include #, $, &, and %. We recommend that for safety's sake, you use only letters, numbers, and the underscore character (to substitute for a space). Remember that some people may want to manually type a URL from your site into a browser, so make things easy for them by using relatively short file names. Using all lowercase makes it easier for visitors, too.

Opening a Page

Opening a page is straightforward; you'll usually want to use Dreamweaver's Files panel. You can also use the File menu or the Start Page if you like.

To open a page:

1. In the Files panel, find the page you want to open, and double-click it.

   The page opens.

   or

   Choose File > Open, or press Ctrl-O (Cmd-O).

   The Open dialog appears (**Figure 3.25**).

2. Navigate to the file, select it, and click Open.

   The file opens in a new window (or in a new tab, if you already have open windows).

✔ Tip

■ If you want to open up a page that you worked on recently, find the page in the Open a Recent Item category in the Start Page, and click it.

Figure 3.25 Use the Open dialog to find a page and open it.

Figure 3.26 You can see the difference in rendering the same page among different browsers here. Note that Internet Explorer 6 for Windows (top) fails to display the clouds next to the large page title, while Mozilla Firefox (middle) and Safari on the Mac (bottom) have no problem displaying everything on the page.

Previewing in a Browser

The page preview you see in Dreamweaver's Design view is useful, but it's no substitute for previewing your pages in real Web browsers. The reason is simple: the Design view shows one rendering of the HTML page, but Web browsers, which may be based on different rendering software (often called "rendering engines"), may show the same page differently. For example, you'll often see pages that look different in Internet Explorer 6 for Windows, Mozilla Firefox, and Safari on the Mac. That's because each of those browsers uses a different rendering engine, and they each lay out and draw pages differently (**Figure 3.26**).

By default, Dreamweaver makes your computer's default Web browser the default browser for previewing pages, but you can change that if you prefer.

Continues on next page

To preview a page in a Web browser:

1. Save your page.

Dreamweaver requires that the page be saved before it can create a preview. If you forget, you'll be asked with a dialog if you want to save. If you click No in this dialog, the preview will be of the last saved version of the page, not necessarily the latest version, so get used to saving before previewing.

2. Press F12 (Opt-F12).

The page opens in the default preview browser.

or

Choose File > Preview in Browser, then choose a browser from the submenu (**Figure 3.27**).

The page opens in the browser you selected.

or

Click the Preview/Debug in Browser button on the Document toolbar (**Figure 3.28**). This brings up a pop-up menu with the browser choices available on your system.

✔ Tips

■ If you're using a Mac laptop, you must press Fn-Opt-F12.

■ Depending on which version of Mac OS X you're running, F12 may be assigned by the system to either Exposé (Panther) or Dashboard (Tiger). On the Mac, Dreamweaver 8 requires that you use Opt-F12 for the primary browser, and Cmd-F12 for the secondary browser. If you have any Exposé or Dashboard features that use these keys, you can change them to different keys in the Dashboard and Exposé panel of System Preferences.

Figure 3.27 Choose the browser you want to use for the preview from the Preview in Browser menu.

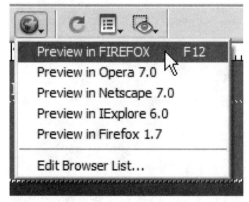

Figure 3.28 You can also choose your preview browser from the Preview/Debug in Browser button on the Document toolbar.

To set the browsers that appear in the Browser list:

1. Choose File > Preview in Browser, then choose Edit Browser List from the submenu.

   The Preview in Browser category of Preferences appears (**Figure 3.29**).

2. Do one or more of the following:

   ▲ To add a browser to the list, click the + button, then fill out the information in the resulting Add Browser dialog.

   ▲ To remove a browser from the list, select the browser and click the – button.

   ▲ To set a browser as the primary preview browser (this will cause it to open when you press F12 (Opt-F12)), select it and click the Primary browser button.

   ▲ To set a browser as the secondary preview browser (this will cause it to open when you press Ctrl-F12 (Cmd-F12)), select it and click the Secondary browser button.

3. Click OK to close the Preferences dialog.

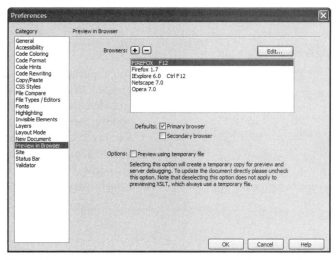

Figure 3.29 You can choose which browsers on your system appear in the Preview in Browser list, and also set browsers as your primary and secondary preview browsers.

Setting Page Properties

Information that is contained in the <head> tag concerns the entire page. These *page properties* include information about the appearance of the page, how links should be displayed, the font settings for headings, and the *encoding* to be used, which is the character set a browser should use to render the page.

For example, pages in English usually use the Western European encoding on Windows, and the Western (ISO Latin 1) encoding on Mac (these encodings are technically different, but you won't see much, if any, difference in your work). Dreamweaver and Web browsers both use the encoding to load the appropriate character set for the page. If you set the encoding to, say, one of the Chinese encodings, Dreamweaver and the Web browser will load the appropriate Chinese character set.

To set page properties:

1. Choose Modify > Page Properties, or choose Ctrl-J (Cmd-J).

   The Page Properties dialog opens (**Figure 3.30**).

2. Click the category you want.

   See the following sections for details on each of the categories and their options.

3. Set the options as you like.

4. Click Apply to see the changes on the open document without closing the Page Properties dialog.

   or

   Click OK to save your changes.

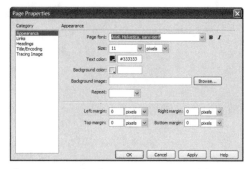

Figure 3.30 Use the Appearance category of the Page Properties dialog to set the page font and size, text and background colors, background images, and margins.

✔ Tip

■ Note that the available encodings are different on Windows and Mac. This is not a problem for English, but if you will be working in languages other than English, you should make sure that you use an encoding for that language that will work well across platforms, and test your site using browsers on Windows and Mac.

Appearance

The Appearance category of the Page Properties dialog (Figure 3.30) has the following options:

- **Page font** specifies the default font family your Web pages will use. Dreamweaver will use the font family you specify unless the font is overridden by a CSS style sheet. You can also set the font to be bold or italic.

- **Size** sets the default font size. Dreamweaver will use this font size unless the size is overridden by a CSS style sheet. You can choose an absolute size (such as 9, 10, 12, and so forth) or relative sizes, (such as small, medium, large, x-large, and so on). Choosing an absolute size allows you to pick any of the measurement units (pixels, points, in, cm, mm, picas, ems, exs, and %).

- **Text color** lets you set the default color for text. Click the color well to bring up a color picker to help you set the color.

- **Background color** lets you set the default color for the page background. Click the color well to bring up a color picker to help you set the color.

- **Background image** allows you to set an image that will appear behind all the text and images on the page. Click the Browse button to bring up the Select Image Source dialog, navigate to the image, then click OK (Choose). If you set a background image, it overrides the background color.

◆ **Repeat** sets how the background image will be displayed if it doesn't fill the whole page. You can choose **repeat** to tile the image horizontally and vertically; **repeat-x** to tile the image horizontally; **repeat-y** to tile the image vertically; or **no-repeat** to display the image only once.

◆ **Margins** allows you to set the Left, Right, Top, and Bottom margins of the page. You can use any of the measurement systems as units, as you can with text size.

Links

You find the following options in the Links category—unsurprisingly all affecting how links are displayed (**Figure 3.31**):

◆ **Link font** specifies the default font family your Web pages will use to display links. Dreamweaver will use the font family you specify unless the font is overridden by a CSS style sheet. You can also set the font to be bold or italic.

◆ **Size** sets the default font size for link text. Dreamweaver will use this font size unless the size is overridden by a CSS style sheet. You can choose an absolute size or a relative size. Choosing an absolute size allows you to pick any of the measurement units (pixels, points, in, cm, mm, picas, ems, exs, and %).

◆ **Link color** sets the color to apply to link text. Click the color well to bring up a color picker to help you set the color.

◆ **Visited links** sets the color to apply to visited link text. Click the color well to bring up a color picker to help you set the color.

◆ **Rollover links** sets the color to apply to link text when you place the mouse cursor over the text. Click the color well to bring up a color picker to help you set the color.

Figure 3.31 You can control many aspects of how links display with the Page Properties dialog, but you get even more control by setting link properties through CSS.

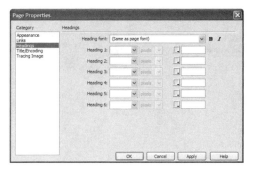

Figure 3.32 You can set the default font, size, and color for headings in the Headings category.

◆ **Active links** sets the color to apply to link text when you click the text. Click the color well to bring up a color picker to help you set the color.

◆ **Underline style** sets the way links will be underlined. Your choices are **Always underline**, **Never underline**, **Show underline only on rollover**, and **Hide underline on rollover**.

✔ Tip

■ If your page already has an underline style defined through an external CSS style sheet, the Underline style pop-up menu will display **Don't change**. You can actually change it; the option is there to tell you that there is already a style defined. If you change the underline style in Page Properties, it overrides the previous underline style definition.

Headings

The Headings category (**Figure 3.32**) has the following options for headings:

◆ **Heading font** specifies the default font family used for headings. Dreamweaver will use the font family you specify unless the font is overridden by a CSS style sheet. You can also set the font to be bold or italic.

◆ **Heading 1** through **Heading 6** allows you to set size and color options for each heading size. The size pop-up menus allow you to set absolute sizes or relative sizes, and you can choose from any of the available measurement units. Click the color well to bring up a color picker to help you set the heading color.

✔ Tip

■ You'll get more control over the text if you use a CSS style sheet to redefine a Heading style. See Chapter 5 for more information about redefining HTML styles.

Title/Encoding

The Title/Encoding category allows you to change the title and some of the more arcane items in a Web page (**Figure 3.33**):

◆ **Title** allows you to change the page title. It's equivalent to the Title field at the top of a document window.

◆ **Document Type (DTD)** allows you to change the <doctype> of the page. When you make a change here, Dreamweaver changes the page's code (if necessary) to make it compliant with the selected DTD.

◆ **Encoding** sets the encoding used for the page.

◆ **Unicode Normalization Form** and **Include Unicode Signature (BOM)** are only enabled when you use Unicode UTF-8 as the encoding. Choose Help > Dreamweaver to learn more.

Tracing Image

Some people prefer to design their pages in a graphics tool such as Adobe Photoshop or Macromedia Fireworks. They can then export that image and bring it into Dreamweaver as a background image. It isn't a background image for the page; rather, it is a guide that you can use as a reference to re-create the same look in Dreamweaver. This guide is called a *tracing image*. The tracing image only appears in Dreamweaver; it doesn't show up when you preview the page in a browser.

The tracing image category only has two options (**Figure 3.34**):

◆ **Tracing image** has a Browse button that, when clicked, brings up the Select Image Source dialog. Navigate to the image, then click OK (Choose).

◆ **Transparency** is a slider that controls the opacity of the tracing image. You can set the image from zero to 100% opacity.

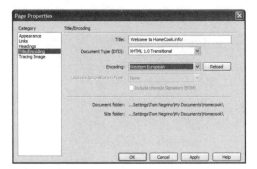

Figure 3.33 Set the title, document type, and encoding for the page in this dialog.

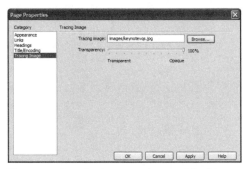

Figure 3.34 A tracing image can be a useful guide for re-creating page designs created in a graphics program.

Defining Meta Tags

Information about the page is contained in a kind of HTML tag called a *meta tag*. Meta tags can include a variety of the page's summary information, including keywords to help search engines index the page, a text description of the page, and links to external documents, such as a style sheet.

When you insert meta information, it appears within the document's `<head>` tag, inside a `<meta>` tag:

```
<meta name="keywords" content="HomeCook.
→info, food, wine, cooking, home
→cooking, homecook, dining">
```

You can set six categories of meta tags:

◆ **Meta** is a general category that allows you to add any information you want. You must give it a name and specify the content.

◆ **Keywords** adds one or more words to the document for use by search engines, to aid them in indexing the page.

◆ **Description** adds a text description of the site, again for use by search engines.

◆ **Refresh** reloads the current document after a specified interval of seconds, or redirects the document to another URL.

◆ **Base** sets the base URL for the page. All of the document-relative paths in the page are considered relative to the base URL. For more information about document-relative links, see Chapter 7.

◆ **Link** adds a link to an external document. It's used most often to define the location for an external CSS style sheet.

To add a meta tag:

1. Choose Insert > HTML > Head Tags, then choose the tag you want from the submenu (**Figure 3.35**).

   Depending on the kind of tag you chose, the appropriate dialog appears. For example, if you choose Keywords, the Keywords dialog appears (**Figure 3.36**). In this dialog, you need to enter the page's keywords, separated by commas.

2. Fill out the dialog, then click OK.

✔ Tip

■ Don't go overboard with your Keywords or Description. Search engines have long since figured out that lots of keywords or a very long description are attempts to artificially improve search engine rankings, and sites with excessive keywords or descriptions will be screened *out* of search results.

Figure 3.35 Dreamweaver allows you to set many meta tags for your document.

Figure 3.36 Separate Keywords with commas; Dreamweaver will turn these keywords into a meta tag for you.

Adding Text
To Your Pages

4

The main message of most Web sites is conveyed by the site's text, and a major part of your job in working with any site will be adding, modifying, and styling that text. Dreamweaver gives you the tools you need to effectively put text on your pages and get your message across.

When you add text, you need to deal with two different aspects of the text: its *structure* and its *presentation*. Structural elements are things like paragraphs, headings, lists, and the like; presentation is how the text looks, including things like the font, font size, text color, and so on. Most sites these days separate the structure and the presentation. Structure is about organizing the content on the page, and presentation is concerned with making the content look good.

In this chapter, we'll concentrate on getting text onto your page, and how to apply structure using headings and lists. We'll also cover using basic HTML text styles to change the look of your text. You'll learn how to more precisely style text and present it using Cascading Style Sheets in Chapter 5.

Adding Text

Most of the text on a Web page is formatted in *blocks*, which are enclosed by beginning and ending HTML tags. For example, the HTML for a line of text with paragraph tags wrapped around it looks like this:

```
<p>This text is wrapped in beginning
→ and ending paragraph tags.</p>
```

In order for a browser to understand that this is a paragraph, you (or in this case, Dreamweaver) have to make it one by adding the surrounding <p> tags.

Of course, in Dreamweaver's Design view, you won't see the HTML tags. All of the text contained between the opening <p> tag and the closing </p> tag is considered by a Web browser to be within the same paragraph, no matter how much text is between the tags. The <p>…</p> combination is an example of a *container tag*. Virtually all of the structural formatting that you can apply with Dreamweaver is done with container tags.

When you add text to a page with Dreamweaver, the program automatically wraps the text with paragraph tags when you press the Enter (Return) key on your keyboard. You can see this if you switch to the Code view, by clicking the Code button at the top of the Dreamweaver editing window, as shown in **Figure 4.1**.

Dreamweaver also has special commands that help you import entire Microsoft Word or Excel documents as Web pages. (See "Using Paste Special," later in this chapter, and Chapter 14 for more information.)

To insert text:

1. In Dreamweaver's Design view, click on the page where you want to add text.

2. Type the text you want.

Figure 4.1 Dreamweaver adds paragraph tags around text when you press the Enter (Return) key.

Cutting, Copying, and Pasting Text

Just like a word processor, you can cut, copy, and paste text on a page in Dreamweaver, which shares the same menu commands with virtually all standard Windows and Mac word processors and text editors. When pasting text in Design view from one part of a Dreamweaver page to another, or between Dreamweaver pages, text formatting is automatically maintained.

Dreamweaver also allows you to paste text and maintain some or all of the text's formatting. This is especially useful when moving text from applications such as Microsoft Word or Excel to a Web page. See "Using Paste Special," later in this chapter.

To cut or copy text:

1. Select the text you want to cut or copy.

2. To cut the text to the Clipboard, choose Edit > Cut, or press Ctrl-X (Cmd-X) on the keyboard.

   or

   To copy the text to the Clipboard, choose Edit > Copy, or press Ctrl-C (Cmd-C) on the keyboard.

   The text is placed on the Clipboard.

✔ Tip

■ When you have text selected, most of the time you can right-click to cut or copy the text using a shortcut menu. You can also right-click to paste text from the shortcut menu. If you have a single button mouse on the Mac, you can Ctrl-click to bring up the shortcut menu.

Selecting Text

Besides selecting text by dragging over it with the mouse cursor, Dreamweaver also gives you some text selection shortcuts:

◆ Double-click on a word to select it.

◆ Move your cursor to the left of a line of text until the cursor changes from an I-beam to an arrow pointing at the text. Then click once to highlight a single line, or drag up or down to select multiple lines.

◆ Triple-click anywhere in a paragraph to select the entire paragraph.

◆ For finer control over selecting individual letters, hold down the Shift key and press the left or right arrow keys to extend the selection one letter at a time.

◆ Ctrl-Shift (Cmd-Shift) plus the left or right arrow key extends the selection one word at a time. Ctrl (Cmd) plus the left or right arrow key moves the cursor one word to the left or right.

◆ Press Ctrl-A (Cmd-A) to Select All (the entire contents of the current document).

To paste plain text:

1. Click to place the insertion point on the page where you want the text to appear.

2. Choose Edit > Paste, or press Ctrl-V (Cmd-V) on the keyboard.

✔ Tips

■ If you copy some HTML source code from another program, such as the Source view of a Web browser, and paste it into a Dreamweaver page in Design view, the HTML appears on the page, with tags and all. That's because while what you've pasted in is HTML markup, Dreamweaver is trying to be smarter than you—it's assuming that markup is what you want to display. If that's not what you want, but rather you want the *result* of the markup to display in your page, just switch to the Code view in Dreamweaver before you paste. The HTML code will paste into the page, and when you switch back to the Design view, it will display the proper formatting.

■ Dreamweaver offers Undo and Redo commands in the Edit menu, which can often be very useful for fixing mistakes or repeating operations. You can also use the keyboard shortcuts Ctrl-Z (Cmd-Z) for Undo and Ctrl-Y (Cmd-Y) for Redo.

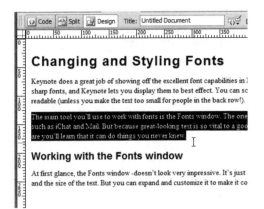

Figure 4.2 Begin dragging and dropping text by selecting it.

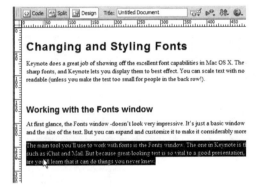

Figure 4.3 When you release the mouse button, the text moves to where you dropped it.

Dragging and Dropping Text

If all you want to do is move some text from one place on a page to another, it's often faster to drag and drop the text.

To drag and drop text:

1. Select the text you want to move (**Figure 4.2**).

2. Move the cursor over the selected text. The cursor will change from an I-beam to an arrow.

3. Click and hold your mouse button over the selected text, and drag it to its new location, releasing the mouse button when the cursor is where you want the text (**Figure 4.3**).

   The text moves to its new home.

✔ Tip

- To duplicate the text, hold down the Ctrl (Option) key while dragging-and-dropping. A copy of the text appears when you re–lease the mouse button.

Using Paste Special

New to Dreamweaver 8, the Paste Special command in the Edit menu gives you a variety of options that control the way formatted content is pasted into Dreamweaver's Design view.

You will probably use the Paste Special command most often when pasting in text from Microsoft Word or Excel, in order to maintain the formatting that the text had in those programs (**Figure 4.4**). Text pasted in from Excel can appear in Dreamweaver as a formatted table, which saves you a lot of time and effort.

The Paste Special options are:

◆ **Text only** pastes just the text; paragraph marks and all formatting are stripped from the text (**Figure 4.5**).

◆ **Text with structure** pastes the text and maintains the structure (notably paragraphs tabs, and lists), but eliminates other text formatting (**Figure 4.6**).

◆ **Text with structure plus basic formatting** keeps the text and text structure, and keeps bold and italic formatting (**Figure 4.7**).

◆ **Text with structure plus full formatting** preserves the text, structure, and styles from the original document (**Figure 4.8**).

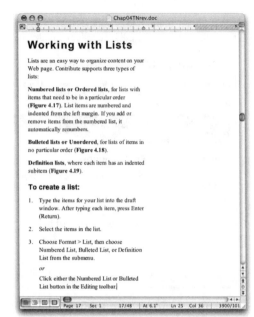

Figure 4.4 Paste Special does a great job of maintaining the formatting from Microsoft Word documents.

Figure 4.5 This is the "Text only" version of the text from Figure 4.4, with paragraph marks and formatting stripped out.

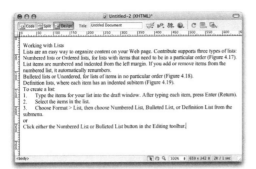

Figure 4.6 With the "Text with structure option," the text in paragraph marks are there, but there's no character formatting.

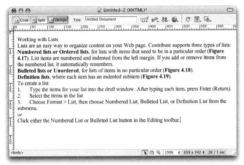

Figure 4.7 The "Text with structure plus basic formatting" option maintains bold and italic formatting.

Figure 4.8 The final option, "Text with structure plus full formatting," maintains all the formatting from the Word document.

To use Paste Special:

1. Select the text you want to cut or copy.

   The text will usually be in a different application than Dreamweaver.

2. Cut or copy the text.

3. Switch to Dreamweaver, and click to set the insertion point where you want the text to appear.

4. Choose Edit > Paste Special, or press Ctrl-Shift-V (Cmd-Shift-V).

   The Paste Special dialog appears (**Figure 4.9**).

5. In the dialog, click the radio button next to the paste option you want.

6. Click OK.

   The text pastes in according to the option you selected.

✔ Tips

■ If you use the "Text with structure plus basic formatting" or "Text with structure plus full formatting" choices, you can also paste graphics into Dreamweaver along with the formatted text.

■ You can copy and paste graphics from most applications into Dreamweaver, but if you want to paste a graphic along with formatted text, you must use Paste Special.

Figure 4.9 Choose the option that you want from the Paste Special dialog.

Applying Headings

After paragraphs, headings are the most important structural element on most Web pages. Headings point your site's visitors to essential information on the page, and they separate sections of the page. Think of headings as being similar to headlines in a newspaper.

Text you enter into Dreamweaver begins with no heading; Dreamweaver refers to this text as None in the Property Inspector. As soon as you press Enter (Return), Dreamweaver wraps the text in paragraph tags, and the text becomes paragraph text.

HTML has six sizes of headings, plus paragraph text, as shown in **Figure 4.10**. These headings don't have a fixed point size, unlike headings in say, Microsoft Word or Adobe InDesign. Instead, they are sized relative to one another and the size of the paragraph text, and the size that the user sees depends on the settings in the user's Web browser. By default, headings are usually displayed in boldface.

You can change the look of headings (their size, font, color, and so forth) using CSS, which will be covered in Chapter 5.

✔ Tip

■ You can only have one size of HTML heading in a particular element. You can work around this limitation with CSS styles.

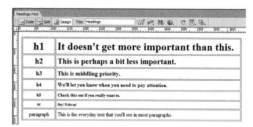

Figure 4.10 Here are examples of the six Heading sizes, plus Paragraph, which is usually used for body text.

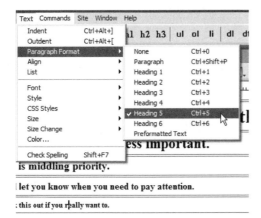

Figure 4.11 Choose the heading size you want from the Paragraph Format submenu.

Figure 4.12 Another way of choosing the heading size is to use the Format pop-up menu in the Property Inspector.

To apply a heading:

1. Click in the line you want to change.

   Note that you don't have to select text; because a heading is a block style, it affects the entire paragraph the cursor is in.

2. Choose Text > Paragraph Format > Heading x, where x is the heading size you want (**Figure 4.11**).

   or

   Press Ctrl-1 for Heading 1, Ctrl-2 for Heading 2, and so on. On the Mac, press Cmd-1 for Heading 1, Cmd-2 for Heading 2, and so on.

   or

   Choose a heading from the Format pop-up menu of the Property Inspector (**Figure 4.12**).

   or

   Click one of the heading buttons in the Text category of the Insert Bar (**Figure 4.13**).

   There are only buttons for Heading 1, Heading 2, and Heading 3, listed as h1, h2 and h3, respectively.

   The text changes to the heading you selected.

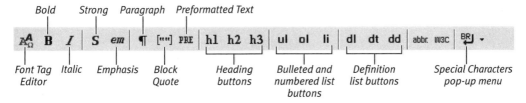

Figure 4.13 The Text category of the Insert Bar gives you buttons with many options, including ways to apply three heading sizes.

To turn text into paragraph text:

1. Click in the line you want to change.

2. Choose Text > Paragraph Format > Paragraph.

   or

   Press Ctrl-Shift-P (Cmd-Shift-P).

   Dreamweaver changes the text into a paragraph.

To remove heading formatting:

1. Click in the line you want to change.

2. Choose Text > Paragraph Format > None.

   or

   Press Ctrl-0 (Cmd-0). (Those are zeros, not the letter "O".)

   The Format menu of the Property Inspector changes to None, indicating that the text has no heading or paragraph style assigned to it.

Applying Character Formats

Character formatting is styling that you can apply to words and individual characters, rather than to blocks such as paragraphs. This formatting includes changing the font, font size, and font color.

Beginning with Dreamweaver MX 2004, and continuing in Dreamweaver 8, the program dispensed with the old method of applying these sorts of character formatting (which was to use the HTML `<font>` tag), in favor of using CSS styles. This change happened mostly behind the scenes in the Code view, so if you have been using Dreamweaver for quite some time, you may not have even noticed the change.

APPLYING CHARACTER FORMATS

Changing Fonts and Font Sizes

In Dreamweaver, you have the ability to set the typeface, or font, for any text on your page. But not all computers or Web browsers use the same fonts. If you specify a font that your site visitor doesn't have on his or her computer, chances are the content won't look the way you intend. Because neither you nor Dreamweaver can be sure what fonts will be available to your site visitors, Dreamweaver uses *font combinations* (also called *font groups*) to work around the problem. Font combinations allow you to provide options for the browser by creating multiple font choices. For example, a font combination could include Arial, Helvetica, and Geneva fonts, and the Web browser would render the page using the first choice available to the browser. If none of the fonts in the combination are installed, the browser will display the text using whatever font is set as the default in the browser's preferences. Dreamweaver comes with six predetermined font combinations, and you can add more as you need them. Each choice in the Font pop-up menu in the Property Inspector represents the first font in that font combination (**Figure 4.14**).

Although Dreamweaver is reminiscent of a word processor, it's really not one, and it has the font-handling characteristics of HTML and CSS. Dreamweaver allows users to apply several font sizes from the Font Size pop-up menu in the Property Inspector, which it implements as CSS styles (**Figure 4.15**). You also have the option of choosing the units of measurement used for font sizes (**Figure 4.16**).

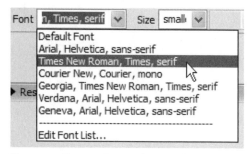

Figure 4.14 Choose a font combination from the Font pop-up menu in the Property Inspector.

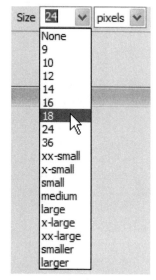

Figure 4.15 Choose a font size from the Size pop-up menu.

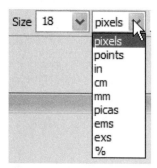

Figure 4.16 You can also choose the units of measurement for the font size.

To set a font:

1. Select the text you want to modify.

2. Choose a different font combination from the Font pop-up menu in the Property Inspector, or choose Text > Font, and then choose the font combination from the submenu.

   The text changes appearance.

✔ Tip

■ Dreamweaver's preset font combinations include fonts that are found on nearly every computer sold in the last several years. Most of these fonts are available for both Windows and Macintosh. For example, Arial, Courier, Georgia, Helvetica, Times New Roman, Verdana, and Trebuchet are all fonts that come standard on both platforms.

To set font size:

1. Select the text you want to modify.

2. Choose a different size from the Font Size pop-up menu in the Property Inspector.

3. Choose the unit of measurement you want from the Units pop-up menu, next to the Font Size pop-up menu.

   The text changes appearance.

✔ Tip

■ Some of the sizes listed in the Font Size pop-up menu in the Property Inspector are *relative* sizes, meaning they set a font size to be larger or smaller relative to the default font size.

CHANGING FONTS AND FONT SIZES

Making Your Own Font Lists

You can modify the preset font combinations, and you can also create new font combinations.

To edit the Font List:

1. Choose Text > Font > Edit Font List.

   The Edit Font List dialog appears (**Figure 4.17**).

2. To add a font combination, click the plus button, then click the arrow buttons next to the Available Fonts list and select fonts to move them to the Chosen Fonts list.

   or

   Select a font combination in the Font List, and click the minus button to remove it.

   or

   Use the arrow buttons above the Font List to move a selected font combination up or down in the list.

3. Click OK to save your changes.

✔ Tips

■ You can type the name of a font not on your system in the field below the Available Fonts list, then click the left-facing arrow button to add that font to the Chosen Fonts list. You might choose to add a font when you want to use one you know is available on the systems of users who will be visiting your site. For example, if your site will attract many Mac OS X visitors, you can use some of the OS X system fonts, such as Lucida Grande, that are common on the Mac but not on Windows.

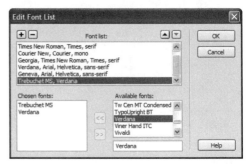

Figure 4.17 The Edit Font List dialog lets you define new font combinations.

■ If you add specialized fonts to your own font lists, you must remember that most users out on the Internet may not have access to those fonts. If you're designing a site for a specific client base, such as a corporate intranet, and you know that all of the machines that will be viewing the site will have your specialized fonts available, then go for it.

Color well

Figure 4.18 Click the color well in the Property Inspector to set the font color.

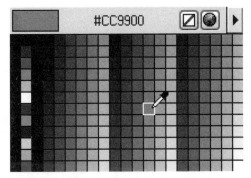

Figure 4.19 Use the eyedropper on the color picker to choose your new text color.

Changing Font Color

You can select text and change its color, which applies a CSS style to the text. You'll use the color well in the Property Inspector and the color picker to do the job.

To color text:

1. Select the text you want to color.

2. Click the color well in the Property Inspector (**Figure 4.18**).

   The color picker appears (**Figure 4.19**).

3. Click a color with the eyedropper to select it; it can be any color in the color picker or any color visible on your desktop or the page you are editing.

   When you select the color, the color picker closes and the text changes color.

Applying Text Styles

The most common text formatting is to make text bold or italicized, and of course Dreamweaver can do that. But it can also apply several other text styles, some of which are for specialized uses, as shown in **Figure 4.20** and **Table 4.1**.

Many of these text styles are meant for displaying programming or script code, so they won't be used at all on many sites. Others, such as Underline and Strikethrough, are deprecated in the HTML 4.01 standard, which means that they are obsolete and may not work in future browsers.

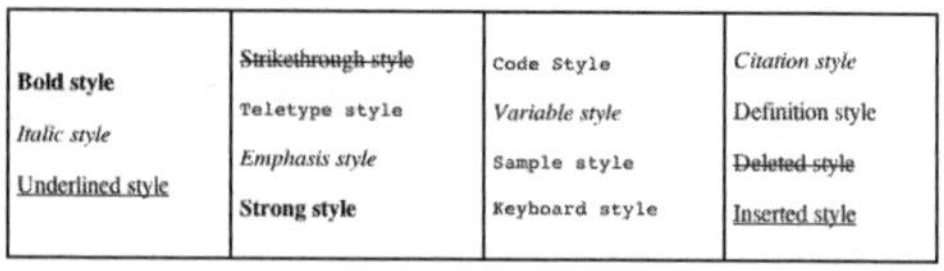

Figure 4.20 Dreamweaver offers a number of useful (and not so useful) text styles.

Table 4.1

Text Styles	
STYLE	DESCRIPTION
Bold	Makes text boldface.
Italic	Italicizes text.
Underline	Underlines text.
Strikethrough	Text is shown with a line through it.
Teletype	Reminiscent of an old typewriter. Usually shows text in a monospaced font such as Courier.
Emphasis	Italicizes text on screen. Causes screen readers to stress importance in speech.
Strong	Bolds text on screen. Causes screen readers to add additional importance to speech.
Code	Depicts programming code, usually in a monospaced font.
Variable	Marks variables in programming code. Usually displayed as italics.
Sample	Meant to display sample output from a computer program or script. Usually displayed in a monospaced font.
Keyboard	Meant to depict text a user would type on the keyboard. Usually displayed in a monospaced font.
Citation	Used to mark citations and references. Usually displayed as italics.
Definition	Used to mark the first, defining usage of a term in a document. Usually displayed as italics (Safari on the Mac displays this as regular text).
Deleted	Marks deleted text. Shown the same as strikethrough.
Inserted	Marks inserted text. Shown the same as underlined.

To apply a text style:

1. Select the text you want to change.

2. Choose Text > Style, then choose the style you want from the submenu.
   The text's appearance changes.

✔ Tip

■ Actually, by default Dreamweaver does not use the traditional <b> and <i> HTML tags for bold and italic, respectively. Instead it uses <strong> and <em> (for emphasis). The latter tags are preferred as part of best practices, because they are better handled by screen readers used by visually impaired users. If you want to switch Dreamweaver back to using <b> and <i>, choose Edit > Preferences (Dreamweaver > Preferences), and in the General category of the Preferences dialog, deselect "Use <strong> and <em> in place of <b> and <i>."

Using Preformatted Text

Browsers usually ignore invisible formatting that doesn't affect page content, such as tabs, extra spaces, extra line feeds, and the like. If you need to display text exactly as entered, however, you can use the Preformatted paragraph format, which wraps the text in the `<pre>`…`</pre>` tags and makes browsers display all of the text characters.

Originally, preformatted text was meant to display tabular data in rows and columns, such as the output of a spreadsheet. In order to make the information line up, browsers display preformatted text in a monospaced font such as Courier (**Figure 4.21**).

To apply preformatting:

1. Select the text you want to change.

2. From the Format pop-up menu of the Property Inspector, choose Preformatted.

   or

   In the Text category of the Insert Bar, click the Preformatted Text button (**Figure 4.22**).

   or

   Choose Text > Paragraph Format > Preformatted text.

   The text changes appearance.

Planet	Orbital period (years)	Day (days)	Moons
Mercury	0.241	58.6	none
Venus	0.615	-243	none
Earth	1.00	1.00	1
Mars	1.88	1.03	2
Jupiter	11.86	0.414	63
Saturn	29.46	0.426	49
Uranus	84.01	0.718	27
Neptune	164.79	0.671	13
Pluto	248.5	6.5	1

Figure 4.21 Preformatted text lines up neatly, as with this table.

Preformatted Text button

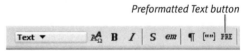

Figure 4.22 Apply the style with the Preformatted Text button.

Adding Line Breaks

Just as in a word processor, you press Enter (Return) in Dreamweaver to create a new paragraph. This is fine when you want to actually create a new paragraph, but not so great when you just want to move the cursor down a line, as you might want to do when entering an address. That's because Web browsers (and Dreamweaver) insert a blank line above and below a paragraph, so if you make each line of the address its own paragraph, it looks goofy (**Figure 4.23**).

Untitled-1*
Code
Split
Design
Title:
HomeCook.info
123 Main Street
Napa, CA 95111

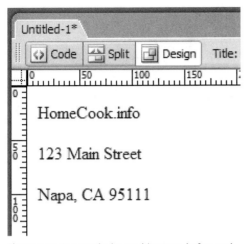

Figure 4.23 Paragraphs have whitespace before and after them, which isn't really appropriate for things like addresses.

What you want to do is add a *line break*, which moves the cursor down one line without creating a new paragraph. In the code, Dreamweaver adds the HTML `<br />` tag to the end of the line.

To insert a line break:

- At the end of the line you want to break, press Shift-Enter (Shift-Return).

  or

  At the end of line you want to break, in the Text category of the Insert Bar, select Line Break from the Characters pop-up menu.

  The text changes (**Figure 4.24**).

Untitled-1*
Code
Split
Design
Title:
HomeCook.info
123 Main Street
Napa, CA 95111

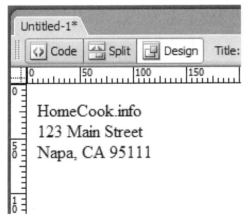

Figure 4.24 After you replace the paragraph tags with line breaks, the address looks better.

✔ Tip

- Line breaks are invisible characters in both Dreamweaver and Web browsers, but you can make them visible in Dreamweaver if you want. Choose Edit > Preferences (Dreamweaver > Preferences), then click the Invisible Elements category. Click the check box next to "Line breaks," then click OK. Dreamweaver then displays line breaks in the Design view (**Figure 4.25**).

HomeCook.info
123 Main Street
Napa, CA 95111

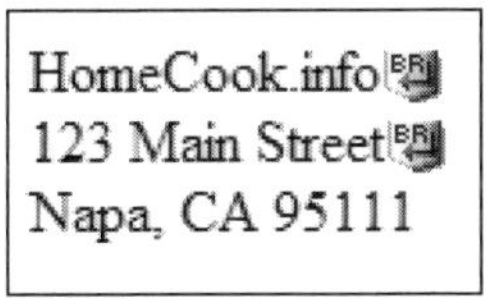

Figure 4.25 With the appropriate preference enabled, you can see the invisible line break characters.

Indenting Text

You won't indent text in Dreamweaver as you would with a word processor. The most common kind of indenting, indenting the first line in a paragraph, is usually done with a tab in a word processor, but tabs have no effect in HTML. Instead, you can use the text-indent CSS style rule. See Chapter 5 for more about using CSS.

You can add whitespace to text—and simulate a tab—with non-breaking spaces. See "Inserting Special Characters," later in this chapter.

When you are indenting paragraphs to set them apart from preceding and following paragraphs, Dreamweaver uses the HTML <blockquote> tag. This indents both the left and right margins of the block quoted paragraph. You aren't limited to paragraphs; you can block quote any block element, such as headings.

To block quote text:

1. Click in the paragraph or other block element you want to indent.

2. Click the Indent button on the Property Inspector (**Figure 4.26**).

   or

   In the Text category of the Insert Bar, click the Block Quote button.

   or

   Choose Text > Indent or press Ctrl-Alt-] (Cmd-Opt-]).

   The text changes (**Figure 4.27**).

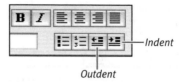

Figure 4.26 Use the Indent button to apply a block quote to your text.

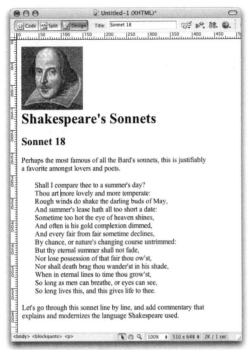

Figure 4.27 The block quote nicely sets off the sonnet from the commentary text.

✔ Tips

- To add more indenting, click the Indent button on the Property Inspector again. This nests the `<blockquote>` tags.

- The CSS `margin` style rule is a much more flexible way to indent block elements. See Chapter 5.

To remove block quoting:

1. Click in the paragraph or other block element you want to indent.

2. Click the Outdent button on the Property Inspector.

   or

   Choose Text > Outdent or press Ctrl-Alt-[(Cmd-Opt-[).

   The text changes.

Aligning Text

Dreamweaver can align text with the left margin, right margin, or center of the page. You can also justify text, which adds space as needed between words so that both the left and right margins are aligned.

To align text:

1. Click inside the paragraph you want to align.

2. Click one of the alignment buttons in the Property Inspector (**Figure 4.28**).

   After you click the button, it appears highlighted, so you know what alignment has been selected.

   or

   Choose Text > Align > Left, Center, Right, or Justify.

   or

   Use one of the keyboard shortcuts listed in **Table 4.2**.

✔ Tip

- You can also use Cascading Style Sheets to align text. See Chapters 5 and 6.

Table 4.2

Alignment Shortcut Keys		
SHORTCUT KEY (WINDOWS)	**SHORTCUT KEY (MAC)**	**WHAT IT DOES**
Ctrl-Alt-Shift-L	Cmd-Opt-Shift-L	Left alignment
Ctrl-Alt-Shift-C	Cmd-Opt-Shift-C	Center alignment
Ctrl-Alt-Shift-R	Cmd-Opt-Shift-R	Right alignment
Ctrl-Alt-Shift-J	Cmd-Opt-Shift-J	Full justification

Figure 4.28 The text alignment buttons in the Property Inspector.

Lucy Kaplansky Discography
1. The Tide (1994)
2. Flesh and Bone (1996)
3. Ten Year Night (1999)
4. Every Single Day (2001)
5. The Red Thread (2004)

Lucy Kaplansky Discography
1. The Tide (1994)
2. Flesh and Bone (1996)
3. Cry Cry Cry (1998) w/Richard Shindell, Dar Williams
4. Ten Year Night (1999)
5. Every Single Day (2001)
6. The Red Thread (2004)

Figure 4.29 Numbered lists automatically renumber if you insert a new item between two existing items.

Global Survival Kit

- Metal box
- Survival knife
- Compass
- Fire starter
- Water bag
- Water purification tablets
- Rescue whistle
- Fishing and foraging kit

Figure 4.30 Bulleted lists are single-spaced and indented.

Working with Lists

Lists are an easy way to organize content on your Web page. Dreamweaver supports three types of lists:

Numbered lists or Ordered lists, for lists with items that need to be in a particular order (**Figure 4.29**). List items are numbered and indented from the left margin. If you add or remove items from the numbered list, it automatically renumbers.

Bulleted lists or Unordered, for lists of items in no particular order (**Figure 4.30**).

Definition lists, where each item has an indented subitem (**Figure 4.31**).

Continues on next page

Excerpts from *The Devil's Dictionary*, by Ambrose Bierce
Originally published 1911 (copyright expired)

CHILDHOOD , n.
    The period of human life intermediate between the idiocy of infancy and the folly of youth -- two removes from the sin of manhood and three from the remorse of age.
DAWN , n.
    The time when men of reason go to bed. Certain old men prefer to rise at about that time, taking a cold bath and a long walk with an empty stomach, and otherwise mortifying the flesh.
DELIBERATION , n.
    The act of examining one's bread to determine which side it is buttered on.
NONSENSE , n.
    The objections that are urged against this excellent dictionary.
SCRIBBLER , n.
    A professional writer whose views are antagonistic to one's own.

Figure 4.31 Definition lists have the definitions indented under the definition terms. The definition terms don't have to be all uppercase—they just happen to be in this figure.

To create a list:

1. Type the items for your list into the window. After typing each item, press Enter (Return).

2. Select the items in the list.

3. Choose Text > List, then choose Unordered List, Ordered List, or Definition List from the submenu.

   or

   Click either the Unordered List or Ordered List button in the Property Inspector.

   or

   Click one of three buttons in the Text category of the Insert Bar: *ul* for Unordered List, *ol* for Ordered List, or *dl* for Definition List.

   The text changes to the kind of list you chose.

✔ Tips

■ At the end of your list, you can turn off the list function either by pressing Enter (Return) twice or by clicking the appropriate list button in the Property Inspector.

■ There are three other buttons in the Text category of the Insert Bar that you can use to apply list tags to text. The *li* button marks text as a *list item*; the text must be within a bulleted or numbered list. The other two buttons are used for definition lists. The *dt* button marks text as a *definition term*, and the *dd* button marks text as a *definition description*.

■ Because the Text category of the Insert Bar was originally designed to help you work in Code view, some of the list buttons will cause the Dreamweaver window to change to Split view, so you can see the code and design panes at the same time. If you want to avoid code altogether, use the Property Inspector or the menu bar to format your lists.

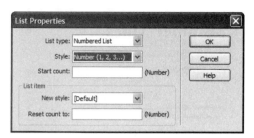

Figure 4.32 In the List Properties dialog, you can change the way lists are numbered and bulleted.

Setting List Properties

You can change numbered list and bulleted list properties in Dreamweaver. Choose between five types of numbering, as shown in **Table 4.3**. For bulleted lists, you can choose either a round bullet (the default) or a square bullet. There are no properties to set for a definition list.

To set list properties:

1. Click in the list you want to change to place the insertion point.

2. Choose Text > List > Properties.
   The List Properties dialog appears (**Figure 4.32**).

3. Do one or more of the following:
   ▲ In the "List type" pop-up menu, select Bulleted List, Numbered List, or Directory List ("definition list" is called "Directory List" in this dialog for some reason).
   ▲ In the "Style" pop-up menu, select one of the Bulleted List or Numbered List styles.
   ▲ Use the "Start count" text box to set the value for the first item in the numbered list.

4. Click OK.

✔ Tip

■ You may notice that there is a fourth choice in the "List type" pop-up menu, called Menu List. That choice creates an unusual type of list that is based on the <menu> tag. That tag was deprecated (that is, recommended that it not be used), when HTML 4.01 was standardized several years ago. We suggest that you avoid the use of the Menu List option.

Table 4.3

List-Numbering Options	
LIST NAME	**EXAMPLE**
Number	1, 2, 3, 4 …
Roman Small	i, ii, iii, iv …
Roman Large	I, II, III, IV …
Alphabet Small	a, b, c, d …
Alphabet Large	A, B, C, D …

Nesting Lists

You can indent lists within lists to create *nested lists*. Because nested lists do not have to be of the same type, you can create, for example, a numbered list with an indented bulleted list, and you can have multiple levels of nested lists within one overall list (**Figure 4.33**).

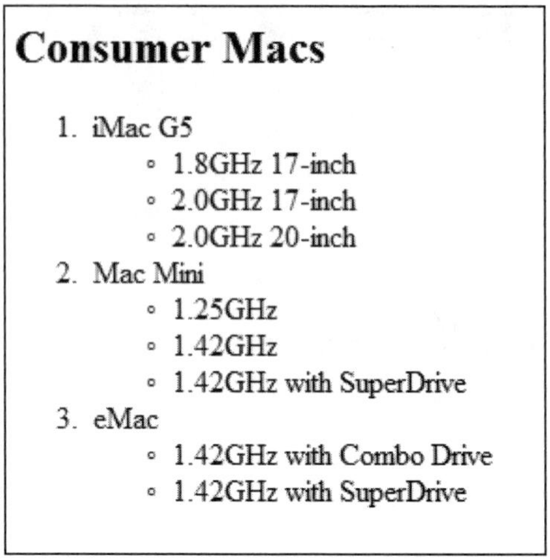

To create a nested list:

1. Click the end of a line within an existing list to place the insertion point.

2. Press Enter (Return).

   Dreamweaver creates another line of the list.

3. Press Tab.

   Dreamweaver creates a new indented sublist of the same type as the parent list. For example, if the parent list is a numbered list, the new sublist will also be a numbered list.

4. (Optional) If you want the sublist to be a different type of list than the parent list, click the Numbered List or Bulleted List button in the Property Inspector.

5. Type the list item.

6. Press Enter (Return).

   Dreamweaver creates a new sublist item.

7. To return to the original list, use the up or down arrow keys to move the insertion point into one of the items in the original list, or click to place the insertion point where you want it.

Consumer Macs

1. iMac G5
   - 1.8GHz 17-inch
   - 2.0GHz 17-inch
   - 2.0GHz 20-inch
2. Mac Mini
   - 1.25GHz
   - 1.42GHz
   - 1.42GHz with SuperDrive
3. eMac
   - 1.42GHz with Combo Drive
   - 1.42GHz with SuperDrive

Figure 4.33 You can nest bulleted lists inside numbered lists.

✔ Tips

- You can also click the Outdent button in the Property Inspector to merge the sublist back into the main list.

- Use the List Properties dialog to format sublists as well as lists.

- If you try to create a sublist within a list that is in a table by pressing Tab, Dreamweaver will jump to the next cell, rather than indenting and creating a nested list. One workaround is to create the nested list outside of the table, cut it, then paste it in the table cell where you want it to go.

Figure 4.34 Insert unusual characters from the Special Characters pop-up menu in the Text category of the Insert Bar.

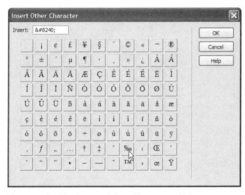

Figure 4.35 The Insert Other Character dialog provides the rest of the special characters Dreamweaver can insert.

Inserting Special Characters

You can add special characters, such as the Euro, copyright, or trademark symbol, to your page in Dreamweaver without having to remember their bizarre HTML equivalents or odd keyboard combinations. In Dreamweaver, relief is just a menu choice away.

To insert a special character:

1. Click in the page to place the insertion point where you want the special character to appear.

2. In the Text category of the Property Inspector, choose the character you want from the Special Characters pop-up menu (**Figure 4.34**).

   or

   Choose Insert > HTML > Special Characters, then choose the special character you want from the submenu.

   or

   If the character you want doesn't appear in the menu, choose Other Characters from the pop-up menu in the Insert Bar, or choose Other from the Insert > HTML > Special Characters submenu. The Insert Other Character dialog appears (**Figure 4.35**).

3. Click the character you want to use, then click OK to close the dialog.

   Dreamweaver inserts the special character on your page.

About Non-Breaking Spaces

An oddity about HTML is that it ignores multiple spaces. One of the special characters you can insert is the *non-breaking space*, which is useful for adding multiple consecutive spaces, and also for nudging text and even images. Dreamweaver uses the HTML code for a non-breaking space (which is ` `) between paragraph tags so that blank lines appear in Web browsers, like so:

```
<p> </p>
```

If you want multiple spaces between words, insert one or more non-breaking spaces. The easiest way to do this is to press Ctrl-Shift-Space (Cmd-Shift-Space), but you can also use the Special Characters pop-up menu in the Text category of the Insert Bar or the Insert > HTML > Special Characters submenu.

Dreamweaver by default ignores multiple spaces, but you can change this behavior and force the program to insert multiple non-breaking spaces in the code. Choosing Edit > Preferences (Dreamweaver > Preferences), choose the General category, and then select the check box next to "Allow multiple consecutive spaces."

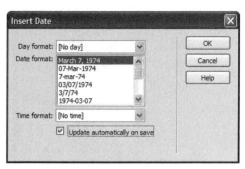

Figure 4.36 Dreamweaver lets you insert dates into your pages in a variety of formats.

Adding Automatic Dates

Dreamweaver can insert the current date and time in a variety of formats into your Web page. You can choose whether or not to add the day of the week.

To insert the current date:

1. Click in your page to place the insertion point where you want the date to appear.

2. Choose Insert > Date.

   The Insert Date dialog appears (**Figure 4.36**).

3. Do one or more of the following:

   ▲ If you want the name of the day to appear, use the "Day format" pop-up menu to set the appearance of the day of the week.

   ▲ Make a selection from the "Date format" list.

   ▲ If you want the time to appear, choose the 12-hour or 24-hour format from the "Time format" list.

   ▲ Select "Update automatically on save," if you want that to happen. This is very useful if you want visitors to your site to know when the page was last updated.

4. Click OK.

   Dreamweaver inserts the date (and any additional items you chose) into your page.

Adding Horizontal Rules

A *horizontal rule* is a line that runs across the page, creating a division between parts of the document (**Figure 4.37**). By default, a horizontal rule in Dreamweaver is the width of the page, is 1 pixel high, and has a small drop shadow. You can change these properties if you want.

To insert a horizontal rule:

1. Click in the page to place the insertion point where you want the horizontal rule to appear.

2. Choose Insert > HTML > Horizontal Rule.

   A line appears as wide as the page.

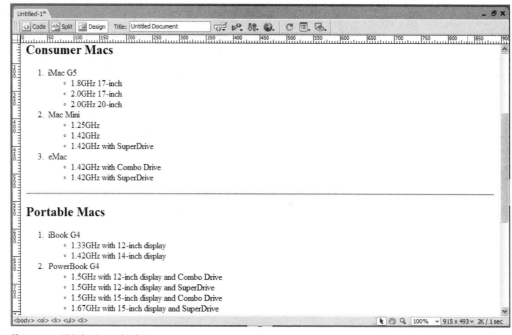

Figure 4.37 This horizontal rule separates two sections of the page.

To modify a horizontal rule's properties:

1. Click the horizontal rule to select it.

The Property Inspector changes to show the Horizontal Rule properties (**Figure 4.38**).

2. Do one or more of the following:

▲ Type a number in the W (for Width) field, and choose either "pixels" or "%" from the pop-up menu. Choosing "pixels" creates a fixed-width line; choosing "%" creates a line that expands or contracts depending on the width of the site visitor's browser window.

▲ In the H (for Height) text box, type a number for the horizontal rule. This height is measured in pixels.

▲ From the Align pop-up menu, choose Default, Left, Center, or Right. The Left and Right choices are only going to be useful if the width of the horizontal rule is less than the width of the page.

▲ The Class pop-up menu allows you to apply a CSS style to the horizontal rule.

▲ If you select the Shading check box, the line appears as an outline, rather than as a solid line.

✔ Tip

■ Horizontal rules are a leftover from the early days of HTML. Use them sparingly, if at all, because they tend to make a page look dated.

Figure 4.38 You can change the width and height of a horizontal rule in the Property Inspector.

Finding and Replacing

Dreamweaver's Find and Replace feature can save you a lot of time, because you can automatically find and change text on a single page, in pages within a folder, on pages you select, or throughout your site. You can choose to change text in the Design view, or search and change just in the Code view.

Imagine that you have a company's site with dozens of pages devoted to singing the praises of their premier product, the amazing WonderWidget. Then one day you get a call from your client letting you know that because of a trademark dispute, they have to rename the product WonderThing. Rather than opening each page and making one or more changes on each of them, just put Dreamweaver's Find and Replace feature to work, and you'll be done in just a few minutes.

The Find and Replace window

The Find and Replace window, which you open by choosing Edit > Find and Replace, or by pressing Ctrl-F (Cmd-F), will be the tool you use for changing text, as shown in **Figure 4.39**. Let's look at some of the parts of this window.

◆ The **Find in** pop-up menu allows you to tell Dreamweaver the *scope* of the search. You can choose to find text in the Current Document (the default); Selected Text; Open Documents; in a Folder you select; in Selected Files in Site; or in the Entire Current Local Site.

◆ The **Search** pop-up menu lets you choose what kind of search you want to do. You can choose Text; Text (Advanced), which gives you additional search options; Source Code, which allows you to search in the HTML; or Specific Tag, which searches the contents of HTML tags that you select. The latter two options will be covered in the next section.

◆ The **Find** field is where you enter the text you wish to find.

◆ The **Replace** field is where you enter the text you want to replace the found text.

◆ The **Save Query** button allows you to save searches for later use. This is great for instances where you create complex queries, so you don't have to do all the work to set up the search again.

◆ The **Load Query** button allows you to retrieve a saved search.

◆ The **Search Options** let you constrain your searches. "Match case" returns results with the same uppercase and lowercase as the text you entered in the Find field. "Match whole word" only finds the text if it matches one or more complete words. "Ignore whitespace" tells Dreamweaver not to pay attention to additional spaces, tabs, and non-breaking spaces. It's on by default, and it's usually best to leave it on. Finally, "Use regular expression" (covered later in this chapter) lets you use wildcard characters to construct extremely complex searches.

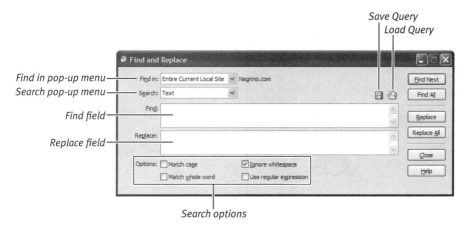

Save Query
Load Query

Find in pop-up menu
Search pop-up menu
Find field
Replace field
Search options

Figure 4.39 The Find and Replace dialog provides a lot of power for making quick changes on a single page, or throughout your site.

FINDING AND REPLACING

Finding Text with a Simple Search

Simple searches work pretty much the same way that they do in a word processor. Just enter the text you want to find and the text that you want to replace it with, and away you go. Of course, you don't have to replace text; if you want you can just use the Find and Replace dialog to find text in one or more files.

To find text:

1. Choose Edit > Find and Replace, or press Ctrl-F (Cmd-F).

The Find and Replace dialog appears.

2. From the Find in pop-up menu, choose one of the options for the scope of your search.

3. From the Search pop-up menu, choose Text.

4. In the Find field, type the word or phrase that you're looking for.

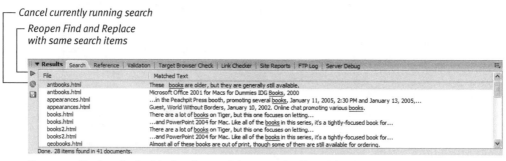

Cancel currently running search

Reopen Find and Replace with same search items

Figure 4.40 The Search tab of the Results panel shows you the file name and matched text when you click the Find All button.

5. Click the Find Next button.

Dreamweaver finds and highlights the found text. If the scope of the search included more than one page, Dreamweaver opens the first file the text was found within, and highlights the text. If the text isn't found, you'll get a message to that effect at the bottom of the Find and Replace dialog.

or

Click the Find All button.

Dreamweaver does the search, closes the Find and Replace dialog, and opens the Search tab of the Results panel (**Figure 4.40**).

6. If you clicked Find All in step 5, double-click one of the search results in the Results pane to open it and highlight the found text.

✔ Tips

■ If you select some text before you bring up the Find and Replace dialog, the text automatically appears in the Find field, as long as you selected fewer than 255 characters.

■ You can do a quick find on the current page by selecting some text and choosing Edit > Find Selection, or by pressing Shift-F3 (Cmd-Shift-G). Dreamweaver will highlight the next occurrence of the text you selected.

■ You can click the green triangle button in the Results panel to reopen the Find and Replace dialog with the same search terms.

■ If you have a search that's running for a very long time, you can cancel it by clicking the octagonal red Cancel button in the Results panel.

■ You can clear the search results in the Results panel by right-clicking in the panel and choosing Clear Results from the resulting shortcut menu.

To find the next result:

◆ Choose Edit > Find Next, or press F3 (Cmd-G).

Dreamweaver finds and highlights the next result of the search, without reopening the Find and Replace dialog.

To find and replace text:

1. Choose Edit > Find and Replace, or press Ctrl-F (Cmd-F).

The Find and Replace dialog appears.

2. From the Find in pop-up menu, choose one of the options for the scope of your search.

3. From the Search pop-up menu, choose Text.

4. In the Find field, type the word or phrase that you're looking for.

5. In the Replace field, type the replacement word or phrase.

6. Click the Find Next button.

When Dreamweaver finds the text, it is highlighted.

7. Click the Replace button.

Dreamweaver replaces the found text with the contents of the Replace field.

or

Click Replace All.

Dreamweaver warns you that you cannot undo changes made in unopened files. Of course, you can undo changes in any open documents by choosing Edit > Undo. If you still want to make the changes, click Yes.

Dreamweaver searches through the entire scope of the search, replacing all occurrences of the found text. When it is done, you'll see a message telling you how many changes it made.

✔ Tips

■ Use a Replace operation to expand abbreviations and save time while you're creating pages. For example, let's say that you're creating a Web site about JavaScript. Rather than typing JavaScript again and again while writing the site, just type "JS," then before you upload the site, do a Find and Replace, changing every occurrence of "JS" to "JavaScript." You can do the same thing with company or people's names, or almost any text that you repeat a lot.

■ Dreamweaver does not update the Search tab of the Results panel when you perform Replace operations.

■ If you get a bunch of search results, but you only want to make replacements in some of those results, you can do that, and save a bunch of time in the process. Rather than opening each page separately and applying the replacement, do it all in one swoop by using the Results panel and the Find and Replace dialog together. First, click the green triangle in the Results panel, which reopens the Find and Replace dialog. In the Results panel, Ctrl-click (Cmd-click) the results where you want to make replacements. Those lines will highlight. Then switch back to the Find and Replace dialog, and click Replace (*not* Replace All). The files that are modified are marked by a green dot next to their names in the Results panel.

Tag pop-up menu

Figure 4.41 The Text (Advanced) option allows you to search for text within HTML tags.

Performing Advanced Text Searches

An advanced text search allows you to do a more precise search by looking for text within (or outside of) particular HTML tags. You can further fine-tune the search by specifying particular attributes of the HTML tags.

Perhaps the most common example of why you would want to use such a search lies in the title of your Web pages. Whenever you create a new page in Dreamweaver, the page automatically gets the title "Untitled Document." If you forget to enter titles, you could end up with a bunch of pages on your site with the same "Untitled Document" name (it's easy to do: while writing this section, I found and fixed a page on my personal site that had been titled "Untitled Document" for four years!). A basic search and replace won't help, because "Untitled Document" is within the `<title>` tag of the pages, and a basic search only searches the body of a document. An advanced text search, which combines text and HTML searches, is the solution.

To perform an advanced text search:

1. Choose Edit > Find and Replace, or press Ctrl-F (Cmd-F).

   The Find and Replace dialog appears.

2. From the Find in pop-up menu, choose one of the options for the scope of your search.

3. From the Search pop-up menu, choose Text (Advanced).

   The dialog changes, and adds the option to search tags (**Figure 4.41**).

Continues on next page

4. In the Find field, type the word or phrase that you're looking for.

5. Choose either Inside Tag or Not Inside Tag from the pop-up menu next to the + and - buttons.

   Inside Tag refers to text that is enclosed within a container tag, such as <p>...</p>.

6. Choose an HTML tag from the Tag pop-up menu.

7. (Optional) If you want to narrow the search further by limiting the search to a particular attribute of the tag you chose in step 6, click the + button. If you do not, skip to step 12.

   The attribute line is added to the dialog (**Figure 4.42**).

   An example of an attribute would be the width attribute of the <table> tag.

8. (Optional) From the first pop-up menu in the attribute line, choose With Attribute or Without Attribute.

9. (Optional) Choose the attribute you want from the next pop-up menu.

   Dreamweaver will only show the attributes for the tag you chose in step 6.

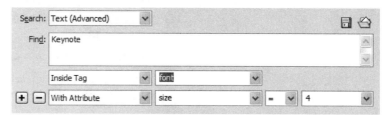

Figure 4.42 You can narrow your search further by adding one or more attributes to the tag search.

10. (Optional) Set a comparison in the next pop-up menu, choosing from = (equals), < (less than), > (greater than), or != (not equals). These only work if the attribute's value is a numeric amount, such as the `size` attribute of the `<font>` tag, i.e., `<font size="4">`.

11. (Optional) In the next field (which is also a pop-up menu), type the value of the attribute. This can be a number or text.

or

Choose [any value] from the pop-up menu. This is useful when you want all tags with a particular attribute, but you don't care what the value of the attribute is.

12. If you want to replace the found text, type the replacement word or phrase in the Replace field.

13. Depending on what you want to do, click Find Next, Find All, Replace, or Replace All.

✔ Tip

- For more information about the different HTML tags and their attributes, choose Window > Reference, then choose O'Reilly HTML Reference from the Book pop-up menu of the Reference tab of the Results panel.

PERFORMING ADVANCED TEXT SEARCHES

Finding and Replacing in Source Code

Dreamweaver's ability to find and replace within the HTML source code is extremely powerful. You can look for text within particular tags, and you can even look within particular tags for specific attributes. You can also find text relative to other tags. For example, you can change specified text within a <table> tag, and leave everything else alone. If you like, you can even use Find and Replace to replace, delete, or change tags and attributes.

Searching and replacing inside source code is much like regular text searches, except that you'll be working in the Code view.

To find and replace in source code:

1. Choose Edit > Find and Replace, or press Ctrl-F (Cmd-F).

   The Find and Replace dialog appears.

2. From the Find in pop-up menu, choose one of the options for the scope of your search.

3. From the Search pop-up menu, choose Source Code (**Figure 4.43**).

4. In the Find field, type the word or phrase that you're looking for.

5. In the Replace field, type the replacement word or phrase.

6. Depending on what you want to do, click Find Next, Find All, Replace, or Replace All.

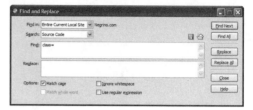

Figure 4.43 Choose Source Code to search the HTML in Code view.

Finding and Replacing with a Specific Tag

A specific tag search lets you find and modify HTML tags. This has many uses; for example, many people are now converting old sites that used `<font>` tags to CSS. You can use a specific tag search to strip out all those old tags. Or you can change the now-passé `<b>` and `<i>` tags to their more modern equivalents, `<strong>` and `<em>`.

The key to the specific tag search is the Action menu, which specifies what replacement action Dreamweaver will carry out on the tags found in the search. See **Table 4.4** for a list of the actions available.

To find and replace within a specific tag:

1. Choose Edit > Find and Replace, or press Ctrl-F (Cmd-F).

The Find and Replace dialog appears.

2. From the Find in pop-up menu, choose one of the options for the scope of your search.

Continues on next page

Table 4.4

Action Menu Options	
ACTION	**DESCRIPTION**
Replace Tag & Contents	Replaces the tag and everything within the tag with the contents of the With field that appears to the right of the Action pop-up menu. This can be either plain text or HTML.
Replace Contents Only	Replaces the contents of the tag with the contents of the With field.
Remove Tag & Comments	Deletes the tag and all of its contents.
Strip Tag	Removes the tag, but leaves any content within the tag.
Change Tag	Substitutes one tag for another.
Set Attribute	Changes an existing attribute to a new value, or adds a new attribute.
Remove Attribute	Removes an attribute from a tag.
Add Before Start Tag	Inserts text or HTML before the opening tag.
Add After End Tag	Inserts text or HTML after the closing tag.
Add After Start Tag	Inserts text or HTML after the opening tag.
Add Before End Tag	Inserts text or HTML before the closing tag.

3. From the Search pop-up menu, choose Specific Tag.

The Find and Replace dialog changes to show the tag functions (**Figure 4.44**).

4. Choose the tag that you want from the tag pop-up menu that appeared next to the Search pop-up menu.

You can either scroll the pop-up menu to find a tag, or you can type the first letter of the tag in the box. Dreamweaver will automatically scroll the list.

5. (Optional) If you want to narrow the search to a particular attribute of the tag that you selected, click the + button, then choose values for that attribute, as discussed previously in this chapter.

If you want to narrow the search further, you can do so by clicking the + button and adding attributes.

6. Choose from the Action pop-up menu, then (depending on the action you chose) set any required values.

7. Depending on what you want to do, click Find Next, Find All, Replace, or Replace All.

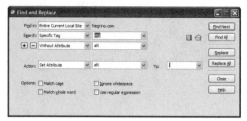

Figure 4.44 When you are searching within a specific tag, you can add attributes for that tag, and you can also specify actions that you want to perform on the found tag.

Using Regular Expressions for Searching

A *regular expression* is a pattern, written using special symbols, which describes one or more text strings. You use regular expressions to match patterns of text, so that Dreamweaver can easily recognize and manipulate that text. Like an arithmetic expression, you create a regular expression by using *operators*, in this case operators that work on text, rather than numbers.

The operators in a regular expression (see **Table 4.5**) are like the wildcard symbols that you may have seen in find and replace features in other programs, such as word processors, except that regular expressions are much more powerful. They can also be complex and difficult to learn and understand, so if Dreamweaver's other finding and replacing methods are sufficient for you, you may not need to bother with regular expressions.

Learning regular expressions is beyond the scope of this book, but we'll show you how to use one in an example. Let's say that you want to find all of the HTML comments throughout your site. You can use this simple regular expression:

```
<!--[\w\W]*?-->
```

Continues on next page

Let's break that expression down. You read a regular expression from left to right. This one begins by matching the beginning characters of the HTML comment, <!--. The square brackets indicate a range of characters; for example, [a-z] would match any character in the range from a to z. In this case, the range includes two regular expression operators: \w means "any single letter, number, or the underscore," and \W means "any character other than a letter, number, or underscore." Taken together as a range, [\w\W] means "any range of characters." The * means "the preceding character (in this case, everything found by the contents of the square brackets) zero or more times" and the ? means "the preceding character zero or one time." Taken together, they match a comment of any length. The regular expression ends by matching the closing characters of an HTML comment, -->.

To search with a regular expression:

1. Choose Edit > Find and Replace, or press Ctrl-F (Cmd-F).

   The Find and Replace dialog appears.

2. From the Find in pop-up menu, choose one of the options for the scope of your search.

3. From the Search pop-up menu, choose any of the options.

   In this case, since we're looking for HTML comments, you should choose Source Code.

4. Enter the regular expression in the Find field (**Figure 4.45**).

Figure 4.45 You can add regular expressions to both the Find and Replace fields.

5. Select the check box next to "Use regular expressions."

When you choose "Use regular expressions," it disables the "Ignore whitespace" search option, because they are mutually exclusive.

6. (Optional) Enter text or a regular expression in the Replace field.

7. Depending on what you want to do, click Find Next, Find All, Replace, or Replace All.

✔ Tip

- There's a lot to say about regular expressions, certainly enough to fill an entire book or twelve. If you're interested in learning more, check out *Mastering Regular Expressions*, by Jeffrey Friedl (2002, O'Reilly & Associates). For a lighter read, try *Teach Yourself Regular Expressions in 10 Minutes* by Ben Forta (2004, Sams). There are also many Web sites that provide regular expression tutorials, which you can find with a Google search.

USING REGULAR EXPRESSIONS FOR SEARCHING

Table 4.5

Regular Expression Special Characters	
CHARACTER	MATCHES
\	Escape character; allows you to search for text containing one of the below special characters by preceding it with the backslash
^	Beginning of text or a line
$	End of text or a line
*	The preceding character zero or more times
+	The preceding character one or more times
?	The preceding character zero or one time
.	Any character except newline
\b	Word boundary (such as a space or carriage return)
\B	Non-word boundary
\d	Any digit 0 through 9 (same as [0-9])
\D	Any non-digit character
\f	Form feed
\n	Line feed
\r	Carriage return
\s	Any single white space character (same as [\f\n\r\t\v])
\S	Any single non-white space character
\t	Tab
\w	Any letter, number, or the underscore (same as [a-zA-Z0-9_])
\W	Any character other than a letter, number, or underscore
[abcde]	A character set that matches any one of the enclosed characters
[^abcde]	A complemented or negated character set; one that does not match any of the enclosed characters
[a-e]	A character set that matches any one in the range of enclosed characters
[\b]	The literal backspace character (different from \b)
{n}	Exactly n occurrences of the previous character
{n,}	At least n occurrences of the previous character
{n,m}	Between n and m occurrences of the previous character
()	A grouping, which is also stored for later use
x|y	Either x or y

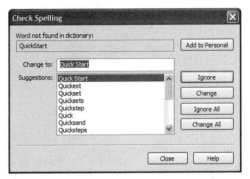

Figure 4.46 Click Add to Personal in the Check Spelling dialog to add an unknown word to Dreamweaver's personal dictionary.

Checking Spelling

No word processor comes without a spelling checker these days, and neither does Dreamweaver. You can check the spelling on the currently open page and add words to Dreamweaver's spelling checker in a personal dictionary.

To spell-check your page:

1. Choose Text > Check Spelling, or press Shift-F7 (same on Windows and Mac).

   If Dreamweaver finds a word it believes is spelled incorrectly, the Check Spelling dialog opens (**Figure 4.46**). Otherwise, you'll get a dialog that says "Spelling check completed."

2. Click Add to Personal if the word Dreamweaver found is correct and you want to add it to your personal dictionary so that Dreamweaver doesn't flag it as an error again.

   or

   Click Ignore to tell the spelling checker to ignore this instance of the word, or Ignore All to ignore the word throughout the document.

   or

   Select a replacement from the Suggestions list, or type the replacement in the Change to text box. Then click the Change button, or click Change All to replace the word throughout the document.

3. When the spelling check is finished, click Close.

CHECKING SPELLING

STYLING PAGE CONTENT

5

You want your Web site to look inviting, colorful, and organized, right? You need style! With styles, your site doesn't just look good—you get other benefits as well. Your site is easier to maintain and update, it downloads faster and uses less bandwidth, and it's more accessible to every type of browser. In this chapter you'll get a basic understanding of Cascading Style Sheets, better known as CSS. Then we'll get into the details of how Dreamweaver uses the CSS Styles panel and the CSS Rule Definition dialog to give you control over creating and applying styles to your pages.

Understanding CSS

Cascading Style Sheets are all about style, looks, and presentation. CSS properties and rules give you an amazing array of control over foregrounds, backgrounds, colors, fonts, positions, alignments, margins, borders, lists, and other aspects of presentation.

Appendix C contains a complete list of CSS properties. That list is amazing in its scope, but it can be a little overwhelming as well. Dreamweaver organizes all the properties listed in Appendix C into a couple of manageable interfaces: the CSS Styles Definition dialog and the CSS Styles panel. With these two features, you can control every style aspect of every element on your page. From your document's body to its divs, paragraphs, lists, tables, and links, to using spans to style individual words or even individual letters, it's all handled with the CSS Styles panel or the CSS Styles Definition dialog.

Content vs. presentation

Content is king, the saying goes, because users seek content when they come to your site. Content is the actual information in the headings, paragraphs, lists, divs, tables, forms, images, blockquotes, links, and other HTML elements you use on a page. With no styling, content looks something like an outline (**Figure 5.1**).

Figure 5.1 A page with no styles shows content and working links, even though it isn't beautifully arranged.

Figure 5.2 Add styles to the same page to determine rules for layout, background, fonts, margins, and other presentation features.

The unstyled content should be useful and informative, even if it doesn't look like much. That's because some users are getting only the text content; for instance, those with screen readers, PDA browsers, cell phone browsers, or text-only browsers. Some of these also get images, but not all, so be careful to never require images on your pages.

Once you add presentation rules in a style sheet, you have the layout, color scheme, font choice, background, and other "pretties" that make a Web page look good in a standard browser (**Figure 5.2**). The content itself hasn't changed. What has changed is the way the content is presented on the page. With different presentation, that is, different styles, the same content could look entirely different.

The power of CSS derives from the separation of content from presentation. You can make the content look like anything you want simply by changing the way it is styled and presented.

Setting CSS Preferences

When you're first learning CSS, you'll want to set your preferences so that Dreamweaver gives you the maximum help:

◆ In the General category, be sure you've selected "Use CSS instead of HTML tags" (**Figure 5.3**).

◆ In the CSS Styles category (**Figure 5.4**), setting the styles to use *shorthand* is optional. Shorthand saves on bandwidth when downloading style sheets as default values are omitted. For the most dependable results, don't use shorthand.

For the "When double-clicking in CSS panel" preference, it's easy to rely on "Edit using CSS dialog" while you learn about styles. If you find you prefer to edit using the Properties pane, you can change it later.

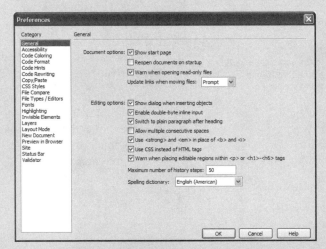

Figure 5.3 Set Dreamweaver General Preferences to use CSS instead of HTML tags.

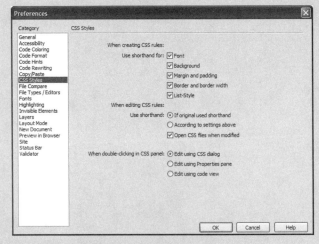

Figure 5.4 The CSS Styles Preferences should be set based on how you like to work.

Setting CSS Preferences

Anatomy of the CSS Styles Panel

In Dreamweaver 8, the CSS Styles panel has been extensively reworked and revised, so it's worth taking the time to familiarize yourself with it even if you're a long-time Dreamweaver user. And if you're new to Dreamweaver, take the time now because the CSS Styles panel will become a good friend.

The illustration (below left) shows the CSS Styles panel in All mode, with the All Rules and Properties panes displayed. The Properties pane is in Category view.

The illustration on the bottom right shows the CSS Styles panel in Current mode, with the Summary, Rules, and Properties panes displayed. The Properties pane is in Set view.

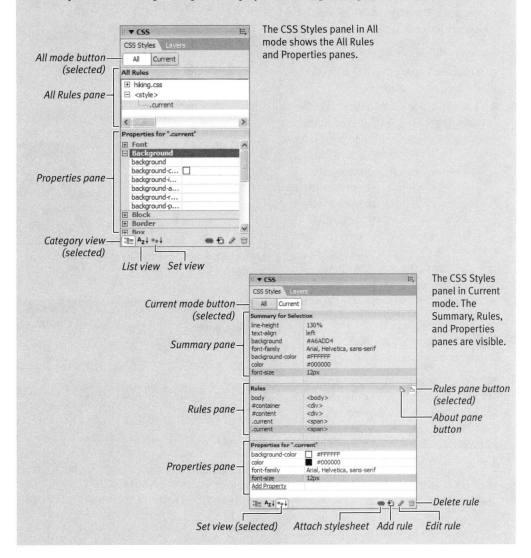

The CSS Styles panel in All mode shows the All Rules and Properties panes.

All mode button (selected)

All Rules pane

Properties pane

Category view (selected)

List view   Set view

The CSS Styles panel in Current mode. The Summary, Rules, and Properties panes are visible.

Current mode button (selected)

Summary pane

Rules pane

Properties pane

Rules pane button (selected)

About pane button

Delete rule

Set view (selected)   Attach stylesheet   Add rule   Edit rule

Creating a Style Rule for a Tag

A style rule begins with a *selector*. A selector can be a tag, an `id`, or a `class`. Everything you do to create new styles, apply styles, and edit styles starts with creating a rule.

To create a style rule for a tag:

1. With a page open in Dreamweaver, click the New CSS Rule button 🗂 in the CSS Styles panel. The New CSS Rule dialog appears (**Figure 5.5**).

2. Complete the following:

   ▲ **Selector Type:** Choose Tag (redefines the look of a specific tag).

   ▲ **Tag:** Dreamweaver makes its best guess (based on your current selection or cursor placement when you clicked the New Style button) as to what tag you wanted this style to apply to. That tag automatically appears in the Tag field. If that tag isn't the one you wanted, select it using the pop-up menu (**Figure 5.6**).

   ▲ **Define in:** Select "This document only" to add the style to just the document you have open. The other options available here will be covered later in this chapter.

3. Click OK, and the CSS Rule definition dialog appears (**Figure 5.7**).

4. Set properties in the eight categories as desired. Which category contains which field is covered in "Dreamweaver CSS Categories," next. If you want to see how something looks without dismissing the dialog, click Apply.

5. Click OK, and the new rule will now be in effect.

Figure 5.5 If a tag is selected in the document, it may automatically appear in the Tag field in the New CSS Rule dialog.

Figure 5.6 Any tag can be styled—just select the one you want.

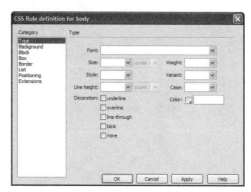

Figure 5.7 Font rules are set in the Type category and the colors picked here are foreground (text) colors.

✔ Tips

- New rules can also be created by selecting text in the document window and choosing Text > CSS Styles > New.

- There's a lot more to the New CSS Rule dialog, but don't fret; its other options will be covered later in this chapter.

- Not familiar with classes and ids? What you'll need to know is covered in the sidebar "Choosing Between Classes and IDs," later in this chapter.

- This example creates an *internal* style: one where the style information is included inside the Web page itself. Internal styles are useful for testing, but in the long run, you'll want to make all your styles *external*, that is, in their own file. How to do that will be covered later in this chapter.

Choosing Between Divs and Spans

Divs and *spans* are generic containers. Div is short for *division*. A div is meant to hold a section of a page that you use and style as a block. Use divs to organize content into meaningful containers. You might structure your page with a div for the masthead, a div for the navigation, a div for the content, and a div for the footer. The way you choose to position the divs creates your layout. Divs for smaller blocks of content can be nested inside other divs. In **Figure 5.8**, for example, the highlighted div #photofeature is inside the div #content, which is inside the div #container.

Span elements are for inline use. A span, for example, can enclose a letter, word, or phrase. With a style rule attached to the span, you achieve a distinctive presentation for an inline element.

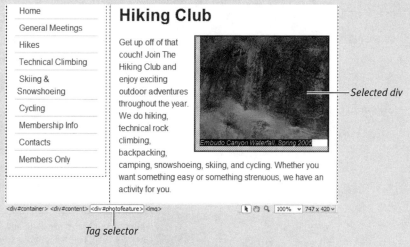

Figure 5.8 Divs can be nested, positioned, and styled individually. The tag selector indicates a named div with a # symbol, such as <div#photofeature>.

Dreamweaver CSS Categories

Dreamweaver uses the CSS Rule definition dialog to break down CSS into various categories. Below, you'll find each of the categories in the CSS Rule definition dialog, along with what you can find in that category. If you want more details about valid values for each field, check out Appendix C.

Type (Figure 5.7)

◆ Font

◆ Size

◆ Style

◆ Line height

◆ Decoration

◆ Weight

◆ Variant

◆ Case

◆ Color

Background (Figure 5.9)

◆ Background color

◆ Background image

◆ Repeat

◆ Attachment

◆ Horizontal position

◆ Vertical position

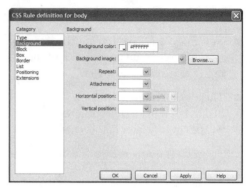

Figure 5.9 Always give a page a background color, even if you're using a background image.

Figure 5.10 Set rules for spacing and alignment of text in the Block category. Text indent affects first line only—yes, you can indent paragraphs with CSS!

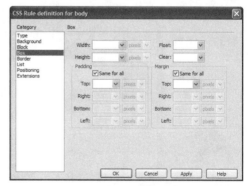

Figure 5.11 Set rules for width and height in the Box category. Margin and padding are both transparent, which means that a background shows through either.

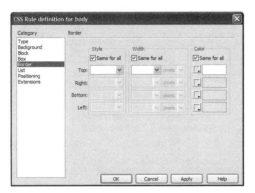

Figure 5.12 Set rules for borders in the Border category. Uncheck "Same for all" to style borders individually.

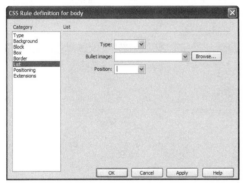

Figure 5.13 Set rules for list type and position in the List category. If you want an image instead of a standard bullet, specify it here.

Block (Figure 5.10)

◆ Word spacing

◆ Letter spacing

◆ Vertical alignment

◆ Text align

◆ Text indent

◆ Whitespace

◆ Display

Box (Figure 5.11)

◆ Width

◆ Height

◆ Float

◆ Clear

◆ Padding (Same for All, Top, Right, Bottom, Left)

◆ Margin (Same for All, Top, Right, Bottom, Left)

Border (Figure 5.12)

◆ Style (Same for All, Top, Right, Bottom, Left)

◆ Width (Same for All, Top, Right, Bottom, Left)

◆ Color (Same for All, Top, Right, Bottom, Left)

List (Figure 5.13)

◆ Type

◆ Bullet image

◆ Position

Positioning (Figure 5.14)

◆ Type

◆ Width

◆ Height

◆ Visibility

◆ Z-index

◆ Overflow

◆ Placement (Top, Right, Bottom, Left)

◆ Clip (Top, Right, Bottom, Left)

Extensions (Figure 5.15)

◆ Page break (Before, After)

◆ Cursor visual effect

◆ Filter visual effect

✔ Tips

■ Page break properties are used in style sheets for print.

■ The eight categories of style definitions in the CSS Rule definition dialog cover nearly every CSS property included in Appendix C. Even more impressive is that you can apply any of the properties in any of the eight categories to *any element* in your document. Backgrounds, for example, can be used in the body element, but can also be used with div, class, table, blockquote, span, acronym, quote, form, paragraphs, or any other element.

Figure 5.14 Set position in the Positioning category. The z-index refers to the stacking order when more than one layer occupies the same position. Clip refers to material that might overflow the size set for width and height.

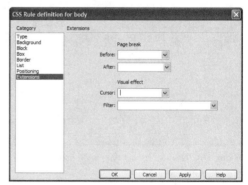

Figure 5.15 Set extensions in the Extensions category. Internet Explorer for Windows is the only browser that supports the Filter extensions.

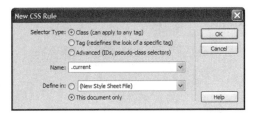

Figure 5.16 A class selector name is preceded by a period when creating a new style.

Creating a Custom Class

Redefining the style for a tag gives you considerable control, as HTML has a tag for nearly any type of text you need to format. And yet, there are times when you want to create a style rule for something that doesn't already have a logical tag as a label. You can do that with a `class`. You get to create a custom name for the style when you create a class.

To create a class:

1. With a page open in Dreamweaver, click the New CSS Rule button in the CSS Styles panel. The New CSS Rule dialog appears (**Figure 5.16**).

2. Set the Selector type to Class (can apply to any tag), and set the Name to a name of your own choosing, preceded by a period (.). This is your new `class` name.

3. Click OK, and the CSS Rule definition dialog appears.

4. When you've completed filling out the CSS Rule definition dialog, click OK to accept your changes.

✔ Tips

■ Don't create classes to describe text when there are already logical tags that do the job. For example, don't create a class to make text big and bold and use it as a heading. HTML already provides six heading tags (h1, h2, h3, h4, h5, and h6). Simply redefine one of the existing heading tags to suit your purpose. Remember, you want to use HTML to create a logical structure for your content, and CSS to style the structured content.

■ Pick a `class` name that will serve you over time. A name that describes a purpose rather than a particular property works best. For example, if you wanted to highlight certain vocabulary words in red, you could name a class either .red or .vocab. If you redesigned the site later and change the color scheme, the name .red might not make sense any longer, but .vocab would still have meaning.

Choosing Between Classes and IDs

You can identify a particular element on a page by assigning it a name. Named elements can then be targeted with CSS rules. The two available methods for assigning names in CSS are with *classes* and *ids*.

A class is reusable. Many different elements on a page can be assigned to the same class. For example, in a blog you might create a class style called `blogentry` and assign it over and over again to every blog entry. Or there might be several vocabulary words on a page assigned to the class `vocab`.

An id, on the other hand, can only be used once per page. Since ids are unique, they are used for all sorts of things in addition to CSS rules, such as JavaScripts and link destinations. IDs are very useful in CSS when assigned to divs. Giving a div a named id enables you to write CSS rules for a specific block of content with regard to its position, background, margins, and other properties.

In the CSS Styles panel, you see the names of any id or class style rules you add to your style sheet (**Figure 5.17**). In the style sheet a hash or pound sign (#) precedes an id selector. A period (.) precedes a `class` selector.

Figure 5.17 A complete style sheet contains ids (#navlist), restyled tags (td), classes (.small), and pseudo-class selectors (a:visited).

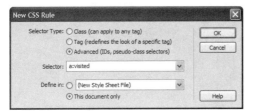

Figure 5.18 The pseudo-class selectors are available from a pop-up menu for Advanced selector types.

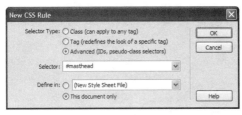

Figure 5.19 A selector based on an id must begin with a pound sign (#).

Creating Advanced Selectors

Elements in HTML can nest. Inside the body might be a div named content, with a div named newitem nested inside that. Each of these nested elements exists in a parent-child relationship that allows CSS properties to be inherited. The child elements are *descendants* of the parent elements and inherit properties from them.

Descendant elements can be pinpointed precisely to create extremely selective selectors. Take the lowly list item, or li. If you redefine the li tag, you style every list item anywhere in the body. However, if you have div named content, and a li within that, you can write a style for the selector #content li. Instead of styling every li anywhere in the document, it will only style each li inside the content div.

Dreamweaver calls *contextual* selectors like this *advanced*. There's more about advanced selectors in the "Advanced Terminology" sidebar, later in this chapter.

To create an advanced style:

1. With a page open in Dreamweaver, click the New CSS Rule button ▣ in the CSS Styles panel. The New CSS Rule dialog appears (**Figure 5.18**).

2. Set Selector Type to Advanced (IDs, pseudo-class selectors). For Selector, one of the pseudo-class selectors may appear in the dialog by default. Select a pseudo-class selector from the pop-up menu or type a selector of your own choosing in this field by doing one of the following:

   Type a pound sign (#) and the id name to style a named section of the page—usually a div (**Figure 5.19**).

   or

Continues on next page

Type a pound sign (#), the id name, and a space before the pseudo-class selector to style only those navigation links in a particular named section of the page (**Figure 5.20**).

or

Type a pound sign (#), the id name, a space, and an HTML tag to style an element found only in the named section of the page (**Figure 5.21**).

or

Type a group of selectors, separated by a comma and a space, to assign the same style properties to every selector in the group with a single rule (**Figure 5.22**).

3. Click OK, and the CSS Rule definition dialog appears.

4. When you've completed filling out the CSS Rule definition dialog, click OK to accept your changes.

✔ Tips

■ Rules for the pseudo-classes won't work reliably with the cascade unless you define them in the following order: a:link, a:visited, a:hover, a:active. A way to remember the L-V-H-A order is the memory device LoVeHAte.

■ If you use the Insert Div Tag button from the Insert Bar (found in both the Common and Layout categories) to insert a div, Dreamweaver offers you the chance to create a new advanced style for the div immediately (**Figure 5.23**). Click the New CSS Style button in the Insert Div Tag dialog to define properties for the new div.

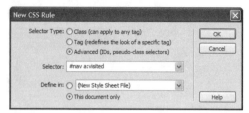

Figure 5.20 Type in the Selector field to create selectors that fit your document.

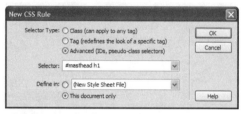

Figure 5.21 A contextual selector lets rules apply to only tags within certain named divs.

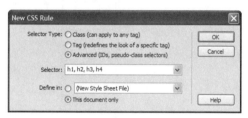

Figure 5.22 Every tag in this group list of selectors will follow the same style rule.

Figure 5.23 Dreamweaver politely suggests that you create a new style for a new div as soon as you insert it in your document.

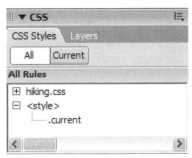

Figure 5.24 When you're in All mode in the CSS Styles panel, any external style sheets are listed by file name, while internal styles are shown in `<style>`.

Advanced Terminology

Advanced selectors are extremely powerful, so specific vocabulary exists to describe them.

Pseudo-classes are so named because pseudo-states don't actually exist in the document. The user must do something to create the pseudo-class, such as visit a link, hover over a link, or even hover over a visited link.

Comma-separated lists of selectors (p, td, li) are called *group* selectors.

Selectors such as #nav li or #content p are known as *contextual* selectors (or *descendant* selectors). These selectors are the workhorses of CSS because they allow you to write specific rules for text based on the element in context (or the element from which it descends). The selector #content p styles only the p elements in the #content div. The selector #footer p styles only the p elements in the #footer div. So while you may have paragraphs in your content area and paragraphs in your footer area, there is no reason why they have to share the same presentation rules.

Working with the CSS Styles Panel

The CSS Styles panel (Window > CSS Styles) shows all the styles affecting a document or a selected style. You can apply, modify, delete and do other style-related tasks right in the CSS Styles panel without having to open the CSS Rule definition dialog. If you need an overview of what's where in the panel, look back at the "Anatomy of the CSS Styles Panel" sidebar, earlier in this chapter.

To work in All mode:

1. In your document, click All at the top of the CSS Styles panel (**Figure 5.24**). All the styles affecting the document appear: any linked or imported external style sheets as well as any styles in only the open document. An external style sheet is indicated by a file name, for example, `hiking.css`. Styles internal to this document only are in the `<style>` category.

   Click the plus (+) (Windows) or the disclosure triangle (Mac) to expand a category if it isn't already expanded.

   Continues on next page

2. Examine the rules for individual styles by highlighting a specific style and doing one of the following:

Click the Show category view icon at the lower-left of the CSS Styles panel ▤. Properties for the selector appear in categories in the Properties pane at the bottom (**Figure 5.25**). Click the plus (+) or the disclosure triangle (Mac) to expand any category.

or

Click the Show list view icon at the lower-left of the CSS Styles panel ᴬᶻ↓. Properties for the selector appear as a list in the Properties pane at the bottom (**Figure 5.26**).

or

Click the "Show only set properties" icon at the lower-left of the CSS Styles panel ⁺⁺↓. Set properties for the selector appear in the Properties pane (**Figure 5.27**).

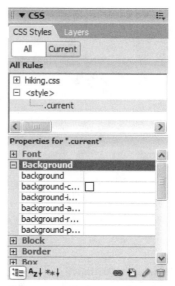

Figure 5.25 Expand a style sheet name to see all the style rules. The Category view of the Properties pane shows categories, which must be expanded to examine properties.

Figure 5.26 Pick a specific style from the list and its properties are shown in the Properties pane. In List view, the Properties pane shows a list of all the properties for a selected style.

Figure 5.27 In Show only set properties view, the Properties pane eliminates everything from view except the set properties for the selected style.

3. To add a new property directly in the CSS Styles panel, click the icon for "Show only set properties" ***↓**, then click Add Property. An editable field appears with a pop-up menu listing every possible property (**Figure 5.28**).

4. To modify a property, click on the property value. An editable field appears (**Figure 5.29**). Type any change and press Return (Enter).

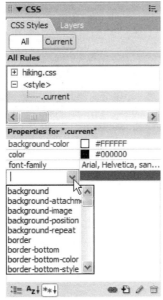

Figure 5.28 To set a new property while in the Property pane, choose from the list.

Figure 5.29 Any property value is editable in the Property pane.

To work in Current mode:

1. In your document, do one of the following:

   Place the cursor in an element in the document window.

   or

   Select an element using the tag selector at the lowerleft of the document window (**Figure 5.30**).

2. Click Current at the top of the CSS Styles panel (**Figure 5.31**). The Summary for Selection pane appears.

3. In the middle pane, you can choose whether to show information about the selected property (About, Figure 5.31), or show the cascade of rules for the selected tag (Rules, **Figure 5.32**). Click on a property highlighted in the Summary for Selection list, and then choose either the About or Rules button on the right.

   At the bottom, the Properties list shows the properties and their values.

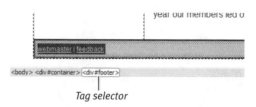

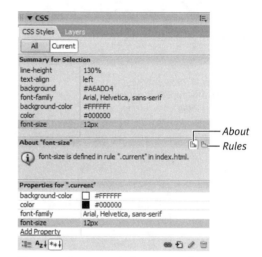

Tag selector

Figure 5.30 Elements you want to style can be selected in the document window with the tag selector.

— About
— Rules

Figure 5.31 Current mode focuses on only the currently selected style.

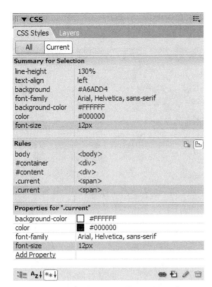

Figure 5.32 You can see information about the selected property, or see the cascade of rules that apply to the selected tag.

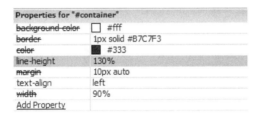

Figure 5.33 In Current mode, you can see inherited styles affecting a selector. The style is shown with a strikethrough if it doesn't apply to the current selection.

4. If properties for the selected element were overridden by rules for other selectors, Dreamweaver indicates this with a strike-through of the property name (**Figure 5.33**). Use the mouse to hover over the property showing a strikethrough and a pop-up tip appears explaining why this property is not applied.

✔ Tips

- Verify how styles are implemented on your pages by previewing them in a variety of browsers. More than one style rule can affect a particular page element. Sometimes the style rules conflict and you get unexpected results.

- When things don't look as expected in the browser, troubleshoot style rules using Current mode in the CSS Styles panel. The Properties pane provides valuable help to spot style conflicts.

- Inheritance information in the About pane of the CSS Styles panel in Current mode is also useful when troubleshooting conflicting style rules.

Applying Styles

Most styles take effect immediately in the current document and in any other documents linked to an external style sheet. If you redefine a tag, for example, acronym, then any time you use the acronym tag, the style is applied. Pseudo-class selectors such as a:link also are immediately applied to the selected elements in any linked documents.

Other styles are different—your document doesn't use them until you add them to an element. For instance, after you define a style rule for a class, you must then apply that class to text in the document, and the same goes for ids.

To apply a style to a class:

1. In a document, select the text to which you want the style to apply.

   or

   Place the cursor anywhere in a paragraph to apply the class to the entire paragraph.

   or

   Select a tag with the tag selector at the lower left of the document window.

2. Do one of the following:

   In the CSS Styles panel, select All mode, then right-click the name of the style you want to apply, and choose Apply from the contextual menu (**Figure 5.34**).

   or

   In the Property Inspector, choose the style you want to apply from the Style pop-up menu (**Figure 5.35**).

   or

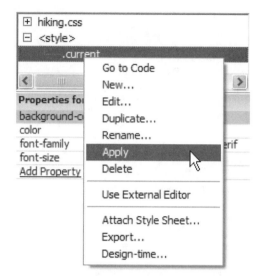

Figure 5.34 Use the contextual menu to apply a class style rule.

Figure 5.35 Use the Style pop-up menu on the Property Inspector to apply a class style rule.

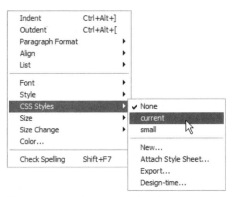

Figure 5.36 A third way to apply a class style rule is to choose the menu Text > CSS Styles and then choose from the submenu.

In the document, right-click the selected text, then in the pop-up menu, choose CSS Styles and then the style you want to apply.

or

Choose Text > CSS Styles, and in the sub-menu choose the style you want to apply (**Figure 5.36**).

External, Internal, and Inline: Look Ma, It's the Cascade

Styles can be external, internal, or inline. An external style resides in a separate style sheet file, one with a name that usually ends in .css. An internal style lives inside each individual Web page that needs it, located within style tags inside the document's head. And finally, there are inline styles; they live within the HTML tags themselves, and only apply to whatever's inside that tag.

Style rules *cascade*. This means that while multiple styles can cover a particular element, there are rules to determine which style takes precedence. The order of the cascade is first external, then internal (meaning in the document head), and then inline. When style rules conflict, the laws of the cascade determine how the conflict is settled.

In general, the closer a rule is to the element getting styled, the more power the rule has in the battle of conflicting style rules. The whole idea is a lot easier to understand with a specific example.

Let's look at the selector p. Suppose in your external style sheet you redefined p to be black, Arial, and 100% in size. Every p element in your document will be black, Arial, and 100%. No conflict there.

Into your conflict-free life comes a need to have *just one document* that uses your attached external style sheet display paragraphs that are black, Arial, and 90% in size. You know how to create a style for just one document, and you write an internal style making the p 90%. Now you have a conflict. Is a p element going to follow the rule in the external style or the rule in the internal style? The cascade goes from external to internal, so the internal rule is closer and has the power to overrule the external rule in this conflict. Conflict solved. Any p element in this one document will be 90% in size.

But you want one paragraph to be red, not black. So you write a class rule and apply it inline to the paragraph. Now you have an inline style and a new conflict. The cascade goes from external to internal to inline, so the inline style has the power to overrule both the internal rule and the external rule. Conflict solved. Any p element in this one class will be red.

To remove a style from a class:

1. Select the text to which the class was applied. The tag selector in the lower left of the document indicates the presence of a class with a period; for example, `<p.current>` means that the `current` class has been applied to this `<p>` tag (**Figure 5.37**).

2. Do one of the following:

   In the Property Inspector, choose None from the Style pop-up menu.

   or

   In the document, right-click the selected text. In the pop-up menu, choose CSS Styles and then None (**Figure 5.38**).

   or

   Choose Text > CSS Styles, and in the submenu choose None.

3. The class is no longer applied to the selected text. However, the style is still available in the style sheet.

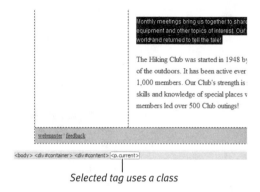

Selected tag uses a class

Figure 5.37 It's easy to identify elements with classes applied in the tag selector bar. The element has a period in the name, for example `<li.current>`.

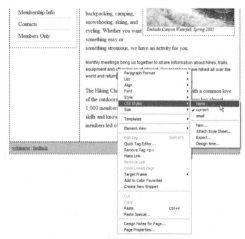

Figure 5.38 Removing a class is as simple as choosing None from the CSS Styles submenu.

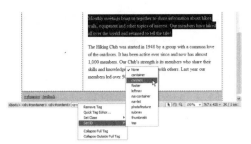

Figure 5.39 Even the tag selector has a pop-up menu, giving you an easy way to add an id.

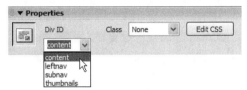

Figure 5.40 The Property Inspector can be used to add an id, but only for divs.

To apply a style to an id:

1. In a document, select the text or tag to which you want to add an id.

2. Do one of the following:

   In the CSS Styles panel, select All mode, then right-click the name of the style you want to apply, and select Apply from the context menu (Figure 5.34).

   or

   Right-click the element in the tag selector, and choose Set ID from the contextual menu (**Figure 5.39**).

   or

   If the selected element is a div, use the Property Inspector to choose an id to apply from the pop-up menu (**Figure 5.40**).

3. Check the tag selector to verify that the id has been applied by looking for the name of the tag followed by a # followed by the name of the id.

✔ Tips

- When you remove a class from the selected text, it's still available to be applied elsewhere. Removing the class from the tag doesn't remove the rule itself from your page.

- If you select some text that isn't inside a container (a paragraph or div, for example), and apply a style, Dreamweaver will wrap a new span tag around that text and apply the new style to the span.

- If the pop-up menu in the Property Inspector doesn't show the id you want, it may be because that id is used elsewhere on the page. An id must be unique on the page, so if you want to move it from one place to another, remove it from the first place before attempting to apply it to the second.

Creating Styles with the Property Inspector

For users who are upgrading from an older version of Dreamweaver, it's the most natural thing in the world to use the Property Inspector to create styles. You can still style text with the Property Inspector in Dreamweaver 8, but there are a few things to keep in mind.

The old way of using Dreamweaver added dozens, perhaps hundreds, of font tags to a page with the Property Inspector. Getting rid of all those bandwidth-eating font tags is a good thing. Nowadays, the Property Inspector won't generate font tags if your Preferences are set to Use CSS instead of HTML tags (see Figure 5.3). Instead, it creates styles.

This sounds good, but there's a problem: the Property Inspector only writes *internal* styles. There's nothing wrong with internal styles, if that's what you want. You may want to design a page using internal styles and export the styles when you're finished. Keep in mind that this is what's happening, and you're good to go.

To create styles with the Property Inspector:

1. Open a new, blank document, or a document with content but with no styles yet applied.

2. Click the Page Properties button on the Property Inspector. The Page Properties dialog appears (**Figure 5.41**).

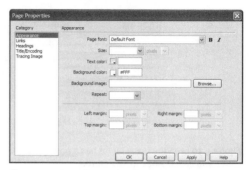

Figure 5.41 Page Properties for Appearance determine backgrounds, fonts, colors, and margins.

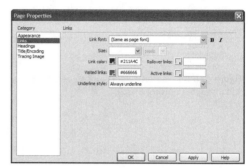

Figure 5.42 Page Properties for Links set up fonts, colors, and sizes for links.

Figure 5.43 Page Properties for Headings set up fonts, colors, and sizes for headings.

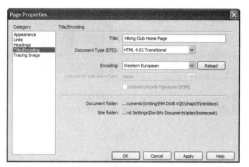

Figure 5.44 Page Properties for Title/Encoding determine title, document type, and language encoding.

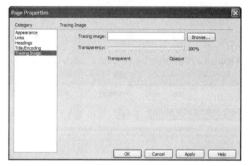

Figure 5.45 Page Properties for Tracing Image set up a tracing image.

- Names in the Page Properties dialog are not always standard CSS selector or property names. For example, in the Links category, Rollover links correspond to the CSS pseudo-class selector a:hover and Underline style corresponds to the CSS property text-decoration.

3. The Page Properties dialog contains five categories. You can set properties as desired in the following:

Appearance: Set appearance properties for the body, including page font, size, text color, background color, background image. If you use a background image, you should also set how it repeats. Margins are set individually for top, right, bottom, and left.

Links: Set link font, size, link color, visited links, rollover links, active links, and select underline style from the pop-up menu (**Figure 5.42**).

Headings: Set a heading font, and choose a size and color for each heading (**Figure 5.43**).

Title/Encoding: Type a page title. Choose Document Type (DTD) from the pop-up menu. Leave Encoding alone unless you know what you're doing and are creating pages in multiple languages (**Figure 5.44**).

Tracing Image: Browse to locate the tracing image and set the degree of transparency (**Figure 5.45**). Tracing images were covered in Chapter 3, "Building Your First Page."

4. Click Apply to see how your changes look, and then OK to accept your changes.

✔ Tips

- The styles and properties you set are stored internally in this document only. You can inspect them in Code view. The Document Type appears in the first line of code. The language encoding appears in a meta element in the head. The styles are enclosed in a style element in the head. If you set a tracing image, it appears in Design view.

To create classes with the Property Inspector:

1. Open a document and select the text or tag to be styled.

2. On the Property Inspector, set new values for any or all of the following: Font, Size, and Color. For color, use the Color Picker to choose a color for the selected text (**Figure 5.46**).

Figure 5.46 Write class rules for Font, Size, and Color with the Property Inspector. Here, Color is being set.

3. Dreamweaver creates a class with a generic name, and that class is applied immediately to the selected text. The new class appears in the Style pop-up menu on the Property Inspector (**Figure 5.47**). The class is applied with a span tag to inline text (**Figure 5.48**). If the selected text is a complete element, such as a paragraph, the class is applied to the element's tag.

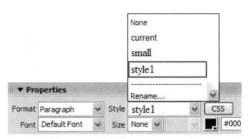

Figure 5.47 The Style pop-up menu on the Property Inspector lists available class rules. Choose a class from this menu to apply it.

✔ Tip

- In step 2, don't change the Format or Style value or you'll be changing your selection instead of creating a new class.

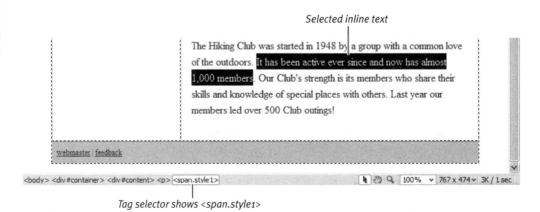

Selected inline text

Tag selector shows <span.style1>

Figure 5.48 To apply a class to an inline element, such as a sentence, word, or letter, Dreamweaver uses a span element.

Figure 5.49 Right-click any style to reveal the Edit menu choice.

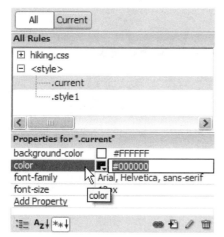

Figure 5.50 Edit any property value directly in the Properties pane.

Modifying a Style

Changing a style is quick and easy. You're already familiar with the CSS Rule definition dialog and the CSS Styles panel, and you can modify styles using either one.

To modify a style with the CSS Rule definition dialog:

1. Open a document. In the CSS Styles panel, click All mode, choose a style, and then do either of the following:

   Right-click the style name and choose Edit from the pop-up menu (**Figure 5.49**).

   or

   Click the Edit Style button at the lower right of the CSS Styles panel.

2. The CSS Rule definition dialog appears. Make changes as desired.

3. Click OK to accept your changes.

To modify a style with the CSS Styles panel:

1. Open a document. In the CSS Styles panel, choose a style in either All or Current mode. Properties for the selected style appear in the Properties pane.

2. Click a value in the Properties pane. An editable field appears (**Figure 5.50**).

3. Change as desired, and press Enter (Return) to complete your changes.

Renaming Styles

The names Dreamweaver assigns to class styles for you aren't particularly helpful or meaningful. It's a good idea to give class styles a descriptive name of your own choosing. You may also find you need to rename a class because your site has changed.

To rename a style:

1. Open a document, and select the class to rename.

2. In the Property Inspector, choose Rename from the Style pop-up menu (**Figure 5.51**). The Rename Style dialog appears (**Figure 5.52**).

3. If the class you want to rename is not selected in the Rename Style field, use the pop-up menu to choose it. Type a name in the New name field, and click OK to accept.

4. If the style you chose is used in multiple places, or it's in an external style sheet that can affect multiple pages, you'll be prompted as to whether you want to make this change everywhere (**Figure 5.53**). If you want this, click Yes.

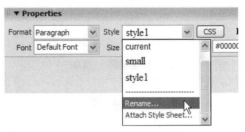

Figure 5.51 Select Rename from the Styles pop-up menu to give a style a new name.

Figure 5.52 Type the new name in the field to rename your style.

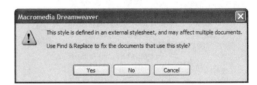

Figure 5.53 If you want, Dreamweaver will update the name everywhere in your site after you rename a style.

Deleting Styles

When you delete a style from a style sheet, the formatting of any element to which it was applied immediately changes. If the style was applied as a `class`, references to the `class` still exist in the document, even though the style is no longer available.

To delete a style:

1. Open a document, and in the CSS Styles panel, choose the style name to delete.

2. Click the Delete CSS Rule button in the lower right of the panel 🗑. Note that you don't have to click OK or accept anything—it just disappears immediately.

DELETING STYLES

Working with Font Groups

Font groups determine which fonts a browser displays on your Web page. A browser uses the first font in the group that is installed on the user's system. If none of the fonts in the group are installed, the browser displays the text as specified by the user's browser preferences.

To modify a font group:

1. Open a document in Dreamweaver.

2. Choose Text > Font > Edit Font List.

   or

   Choose Edit Font List from the Font pop-up menu in the Property Inspector.

   The Edit Font List dialog appears (**Figure 5.54**) and displays three categories of information:

   Font list: Displays current font groups.

   Chosen fonts: Displays fonts in the chosen group.

   Available fonts: Displays all the fonts available on your system. The font selected is displayed in the text field below.

3. Do any of the following:

   ▲ To add or remove fonts from a font group, click the arrows button (◁ or ▷) between the Chosen fonts list and the Available fonts list.

   ▲ To add or remove a font group, click the Plus or Minus button (⊞⊟) at the top of the dialog.

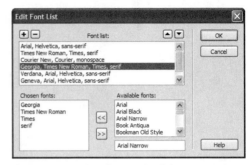

Figure 5.54 Use the Edit Font List dialog to create, modify, or remove font groups.

WORKING WITH FONT GROUPS

▲ To add the name of a font that is not installed on your system, type the font name in the text field below the Available fonts list and click the ⊡ button to add it to the group.

▲ To move a font group up or down in the list, click the arrow buttons (⊡⊡) at the top of the dialog.

4. Click OK to accept your changes.

✔ Tips

■ To avoid surprises, it's good practice to stick with the commonly available fonts for most text. If you really need to use a fancy, decorative font for short bits of text, you may be better off making an image of the text and placing it as a graphic.

■ It's good practice to add either the generic serif or sans-serif font choice at the end of every font group you create. If the user doesn't have any of your specified fonts, you'll at least still have a say over whether the font is serif or sans-serif.

■ We would love to add something here like, "You can be assured that people with *this* browser and *this* operating system will have *these* fonts"—but we can't. New browser versions get shipped that don't include the same fonts the older versions did. The same goes for operating systems. And then, of course, people can always delete or disable their existing fonts. The font groups that ship with Dreamweaver, as a general rule, are very likely to be dependable. And of course, always end your font list with either serif or sans-serif for best results.

Fonts and Operating Systems

Not all computer systems have the same fonts. For example, a common sans-serif font on Windows systems is Arial. A similar sans-serif font on Macintosh systems is Helvetica. Many Linux systems have Helvetica, but not all. All these systems have some default sans-serif font, however.

When choosing font groups, select fonts that share similar characteristics and try to cover all the bases in terms of operating systems. Then add either the generic serif or sans-serif choice at the end, just in case none of your preferred choices are available.

Why add a font you don't even have to your font group? One reason is that you expect a lot of your viewers to have a particular font (even though you don't have it).

Creating an External Style Sheet

Up to now, this chapter has covered how to create internal styles, but we also mentioned that internal styles may not always be the right choice. Here's how to create a new external style sheet, either from scratch or using one of the many *design files* that are included in Dreamweaver as a starting point.

To create a new external style sheet based on a design file:

1. From Dreamweaver's menu, choose File > New. The New Document dialog appears (**Figure 5.55**).

2. If it wasn't chosen by default, select the category "CSS Style Sheets" to see a long list of style sheets display in the center column (**Figure 5.56**). Choose any of these to see a preview and description in the right column.

3. If you see a design you like, click Create. A new untitled style sheet document will open that contains the rules defined in the style sheet you selected. Save this file with a name that ends in .css.

To create a new external style sheet from scratch:

1. Choose File > New. The New Document dialog appears (Figure 5.55).

2. In the New Document dialog, select Basic page for the Category, CSS for the page type, and click Create. A new blank style sheet opens in Code view (**Figure 5.57**). Save this file with a name that ends in .css.

   or

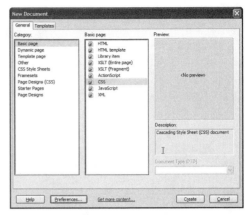

Figure 5.55 The New Document dialog lets you create many different types of files.

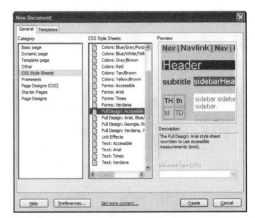

Figure 5.56 Dreamweaver comes with plenty of CSS designs for you to use as starting points.

Figure 5.57 A blank CSS document, ready for you to add your rules.

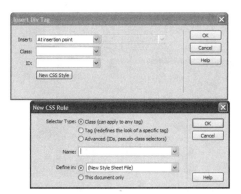

Figure 5.58 The Insert Div Tag dialog opens the New CSS Rule dialog.

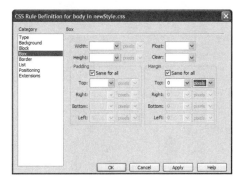

Figure 5.59 If you said you wanted a new style sheet file, here's where it's actually created.

1. With a document open, click the Insert Div Tag button in the Common or Layout category of the Insert Bar, and the Insert Div Tag dialog displays. Click New CSS Style, and the New CSS Rule dialog opens (**Figure 5.58**).

2. Enter any `class`, `tag`, `id`, or `pseudo-class` selector that you'd like in your new CSS file. Set Define in to "(New Style Sheet File)" and click OK. The Save Style Sheet File As dialog appears (**Figure 5.59**).

3. Choose a file name that ends in .css, and click Save. The CSS Rule Definition dialog appears (**Figure 5.60**). Add the rules you want (as described earlier in this chapter), click OK, and you'll be back at the Insert Div Tag dialog, with your new style sheet (including any rules you set) open in Code view behind the current document.

✔ Tip

■ If you've created a new style sheet using the Insert Div Tag dialog, your new style sheet is automatically attached to your document. If you created the new style sheet any other way, you'll have to attach it manually. That's covered in "Attaching a Style Sheet," next.

Figure 5.60 Now that you've created a new style sheet file, you need to add rules to it.

CREATING AN EXTERNAL STYLE SHEET

Attaching a Style Sheet

It doesn't do you any good to create a style sheet if your Web pages don't know about it. In order for a Web page to use an external style sheet, that style sheet has to be *attached* to the Web page.

To attach a style sheet:

1. Click the Attach Style Sheet icon at the bottom of the CSS Styles panel ⊕.

   or

   Right-click in the CSS Styles panel and choose Attach Style Sheet (**Figure 5.61**).

2. The Attach External Style Sheet dialog appears (**Figure 5.62**). Click the Browse button to bring up the Select Style Sheet File dialog (**Figure 5.63**). Navigate to the style sheet you just created, select it, and click OK.

3. Back in the Attach External Style Sheet dialog, select Add as Link if it isn't already chosen, and click OK to attach the style sheet. If your style sheet includes any rules that affect the active document, you'll see those changes reflected immediately.

Figure 5.61 There are at least two ways to attach a style sheet from the CSS Styles panel.

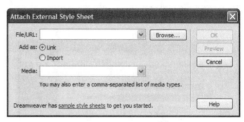

Figure 5.62 Choose which style sheet you want to attach to your Web page, and how you want to attach it.

Figure 5.63 Choose which style sheet file to attach by browsing for it.

Figure 5.64 And here are all the styles your Web page can now access.

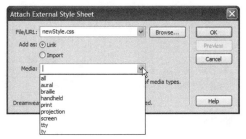

Figure 5.65 If you want your style sheet to only apply when the page is printed, here's where to set that.

✔ **Tips**

■ Looking at the All Rules pane of the CSS Styles panel (**Figure 5.64**), you'll notice that your style sheet is now included, and all of its properties can be viewed.

■ You're offered a choice of using *link* or *import* to attach your style sheet. Each has its advantages: link works in more browsers, for instance, while import allows you to nest style sheets (i.e., you can attach a style sheet using import, and then that style sheet can include an import of another style sheet, and so on).

■ You can use both link and import in the same document. That's a handy way to use two style sheets, where the link attaches a bare-bones style sheet and the import attaches a more complex style sheet that older browsers (such as Netscape Navigator) can't handle.

■ When attaching a style sheet, you're also offered a choice of Media. Those choices include all, aural, braille, handheld, print, projection, screen, tty, and tv (**Figure 5.65**). It's also acceptable to use no media type at all; in that case, the style sheet applies to all media types. And finally, you can also enter in a list of media types (comma-separated) if you want your style sheet to apply to some media types but not others.

■ If you use set the media type for your style sheet, you can test it by choosing View > Style Rendering and picking which media type to view. When you do this, though, remember that few browsers offer full support for media types.

Moving Internal Styles to External

There are a number of reasons why your pages might have internal styles instead of using an external style sheet: possibly they're from an older site (when that was more common), or possibly you used internal styles to test your layout. But now your internal style sheet is ready to live on its own, so your styles need to come out of your Web page and into a stand-alone file.

To export styles:

1. With the Web page open that contains the styles you want to export, choose File > Export > CSS Styles (**Figure 5.66**). The Export Styles As CSS File dialog appears (**Figure 5.67**).

2. You should be prompted with the correct place to save your file. Come up with a good name (ending in .css) and click Save.

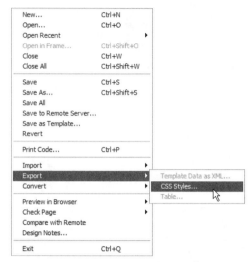

Figure 5.66 You can export the CSS styles out of a Web page and into an external file.

Figure 5.67 Here's where you name that external CSS file.

MOVING INTERNAL STYLES TO EXTERNAL

Figure 5.68 When your styles are exported and then attached, you'll have two of every rule.

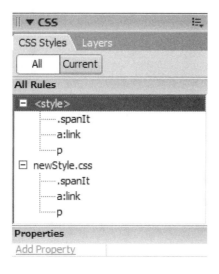

Figure 5.69 You can then delete the internal styles, leaving only the external.

3. Follow the directions given earlier in this chapter in "Attaching a Style Sheet" and use link or import to attach the new style sheet file to your current Web page. Look in the CSS Styles panel, and you should notice that all your styles are now duplicated (**Figure 5.68**)—don't fret, that's what should happen.

4. Select the `<style>` line in the panel, and click the Delete Embedded Stylesheet icon 🗑 at the bottom of the panel (**Figure 5.69**). This removes the internal styles from your Web page.

✔ Tips

- If you're not seeing duplicates in Step 3, make sure that you're in All (Document) Mode and that both sets of rules have been expanded.

- If you're the careful type, use the "Show only set properties" button to see rules for each style, and then compare each internal style against the external style before deleting the internal style.

POSITIONING PAGE CONTENT

In Chapter 5, you saw how to use CSS (Cascading Style Sheets) to style text. There's a whole lot more that CSS can do besides make your words look pretty—style sheets can also be used to precisely position elements on your page.

This chapter covers the how-tos of positioning plus how to use Dreamweaver's layout tools in a way that suits your work style. You'll also get a look at some of the great new features in Dreamweaver 8 that help you use CSS for layout and positioning elements. We'll wrap it all up with a historical overview of how older versions of Dreamweaver used to recommend that you position elements on your page and why those approaches just aren't the right choices any longer.

CSS Layout Basics

When CSS first started becoming popular (that is, when enough browsers supported it consistently), its primary use was for styling text, and Web designers were thrilled to say goodbye to the font tag. It's just as possible to use CSS to define how your page is laid out, and thankfully, browsers and their market share have now gotten to the point where it's feasible to make the switch.

The box model

When you're talking about positioning elements with CSS, you immediately run into the term *the box model*. Here's a quick overview of what you'll need to know to be able to use CSS for positioning.

When working with CSS and layout, you're creating boxes (almost always done by adding a div) and positioning them on your pages. Each box contains several elements (**Figure 6.1**): its margin, border, padding, and content. Using CSS, you can set rules for each element. Additionally, you can (for example) set different rules for the top, right, bottom, and left sides of an element.

Let's say that you want to put a line above and below your text. You can set the border around your text (that is, to the tag that contains your text) to 1px black solid just for the top and bottom. If you don't set the other sides, they'll be set to 0 by default.

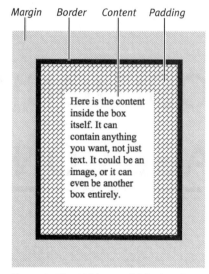

Figure 6.1 The CSS box model, broken down into parts.

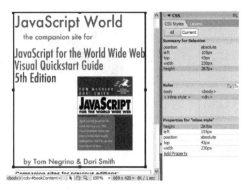

Figure 6.2 An example of an absolutely positioned box with set dimensions.

Positioning your boxes

Now that you've created boxes on your page, you want to place them. In order to do that, you need to understand two new concepts: *position* and *float*.

The position of a box can be *static*, *relative*, *inherit*, *absolute*, or *fixed* (**Figure 6.2**).

◆ **Static:** The simplest position is static; it just means that the box ends up wherever it would normally end up, all on its own. Any left or top offsets you give it are ignored.

◆ **Relative:** The next simplest is relative, which is just like static except that you can set its left and top positions.

◆ **Inherit:** Inherit is used when you want a box to automatically inherit the properties of its parent (that is, its container). Wherever that box happens to be, it just takes on the position rules based on its container.

◆ **Absolute:** Absolute and fixed are similar, in that both can specify exactly where on your page you want the box to appear. The difference between the two involves their frame of reference: an absolutely positioned box is positioned in reference to its container. If you have an absolutely positioned box placed 100 pixels from the top of a page, and another absolutely positioned box inside that box that is also set to be 100 pixels down, the interior box will be 200 pixels down, not 100—because its frame of reference is to the box that it's inside.

◆ **Fixed:** Fixed positioning, on the other hand, is based on the page itself. If you set a box to be fixed at 100 pixels down, it will always be there, even if you scroll the page. When you scroll, that box will move down with you so that it's always 100 pixels down from the top of the visible page.

Floating your boxes

Alternatively, a box can be set to float, such that its contents stick to one side of its containing element or another (**Figure 6.3**). The values for float are *left*, *right*, *none*, and *inherit*.

◆ **Left:** A box that is floated to the left causes everything else on the page (everything that isn't explicitly told to be somewhere else, that is) to wrap around it to the right.

◆ **Right:** Just like left, a box floated to the right causes everything else to wrap around it on the left.

◆ **None:** This is the default, but it's sometimes useful to be able to explicitly tell a box, no, don't float (usually when trying to work around browser bugs).

◆ **Inherit:** If you do want a box to inherit the float value of its container, just say so explicitly by setting float to inherit.

✔ Tips

■ What's described here is how browsers are supposed to handle positioning and floating boxes, and all of the browsers released in the last few years handle it well. Older browsers may have varying degrees of difficulty with these concepts. As always, we recommend testing your site in as many browsers (and versions and platforms) as possible.

■ This is just a quick and dirty definition. Many pages (and possibly some entire books) have been written on the intricacies of the box model.

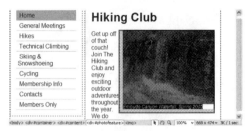

Figure 6.3 This graphic and its caption are both floated to the right.

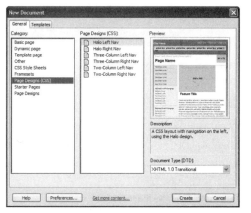

Figure 6.4 The familiar New Document dialog contains handy CSS page designs to get you started.

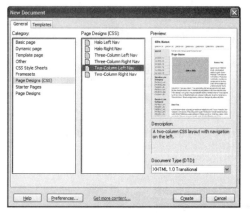

Figure 6.5 You can look at the Preview column to decide which of the designs you want to use as the basis for your page.

Using Design Files

Initially, you might think that it's difficult to get started using CSS for positioning, but thankfully, Dreamweaver has included something to make getting started easy as can be: using Dreamweaver *design files*. These files are flexible, professionally developed templates that are available to use as a starting point.

To use a Dreamweaver design file:

1. From Dreamweaver's menu, choose File > New. The New Document dialog appears (**Figure 6.4**).

2. If it wasn't chosen by default, select the category "Page Designs (CSS)," and six designs will be listed in the center column: Halo Left Nav, Halo Right Nav, Three-Column Left Nav, Three-Column Right Nav, Two-Column Left Nav, and Two-Column Right Nav. Choose any of these to see a preview in the right column (**Figure 6.5**). Directly below the preview is a short description of the design.

Continues on next page

3. If you see a design you like, click Create. A new untitled Dreamweaver document opens in the chosen design, and the Save As dialog appears (**Figure 6.6**).

4. Choose a name for your new file and click Save. The Copy Dependent Files dialog appears (**Figure 6.7**). If the design file you chose has dependent files that go with it, here's your chance to get them all in one fell swoop. Click Copy to accept them.

5. You now have a template for your site that's entirely CSS-based (**Figure 6.8**). You can now modify both the page and the accompanying CSS files.

Figure 6.6 Save the file to begin.

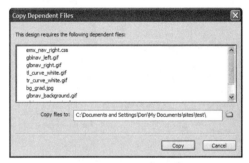

Figure 6.7 Then copy over the dependent files in order to have the complete look.

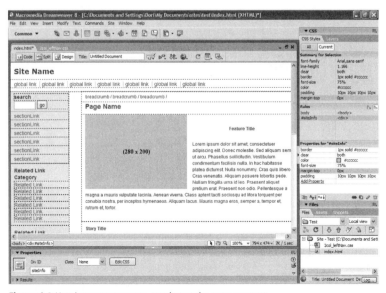

Figure 6.8 Here's your new page, ready to take your content.

✔ Tips

■ Even if none of the included design files suits your taste, take a look at them and check out how they work. They're a good way to learn how to use CSS to position elements on a page.

■ Want someone else to do the layout work for you, and the included design files aren't what you're looking for? Check out `http://www.positioniseverything.net/`, a great site with plenty of different layouts (**Figure 6.9**). Choose view source for a page you like, select all, and copy. Then go back to Dreamweaver, create a new blank HTML page, switch into Code view, and paste. You'll have everything you need. As the site itself says, "The source code for each demo has all the relevant CSS embedded in the head section. Please feel free to take, use, and if need be, abuse all code found on this site."

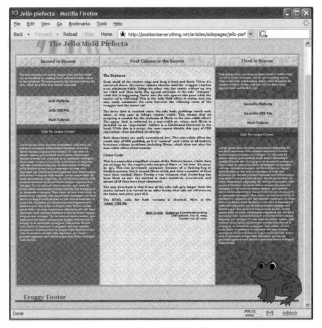

Figure 6.9 The colors might be loud, but the three-column layout works well.

Laying Out Your Page

Here's where things get interesting: now that we've got the theory, it's time to put it into practice. Chapter 5 covered the basics of creating style sheets and divs and attaching style sheets, so if you need a refresher, take a look at those sections again.

Before you start laying out your page, you need to think about what you want on that page and where you want it to go. As discussed back in Chapter 2, the best way to do that is with pencil and paper. That should tell you what styles you'll need: for instance, a header, footer, content area, navigation area, and lastly, a container to hold all of them. Once you've sketched it all out, create a new style sheet (as covered in Chapter 5) and add those styles in as previously described.

Now you're ready to start. We'll work from a blank Web page and a complete style sheet.

To lay out your page:

1. Add a div to your page by clicking the Insert Div Tag button in the Common category on the Insert Bar 🖾. The Insert Div Tag dialog appears (**Figure 6.10**). From the ID pop-up menu, select the appropriate style—here, it's container.

Figure 6.10 Start your new page off by adding your first div.

Figure 6.11 And here it is on your page, with the standard dummy text.

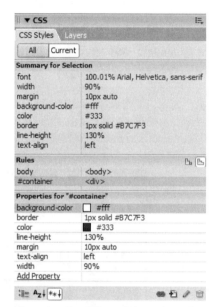

Figure 6.12 The CSS panel shows the style rules and properties.

Figure 6.13 When a div has a background, it shows up automatically.

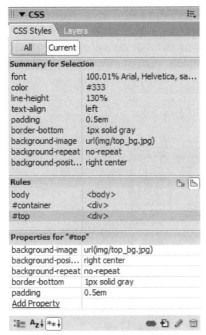

Figure 6.14 Using the top style gives the div a background image.

Figure 6.15 Placing the logo on the header makes the div the correct height.

2. Click OK to accept. The Web page now shows the new div container (**Figure 6.11**). Because the container id was previously set up in the style sheet, it already has the properties we know we'll need: in this case, the margin is set to 10px and the border is set to be a solid 1 pixel in a nice shade of light blue (**Figure 6.12**). Because we're using ids (as opposed to classes), we know that the name is unique on the page. And because of that, the term "container" can now mean both the div named container and the style named container.

3. The next div to add (as described above) is the page header, which here has the id top (**Figure 6.13**). It goes inside the container div (actually, everything on the page will). The header's background graphic automatically shows up because top's properties (**Figure 6.14**) include background-image.

4. Drag the logo over from the Assets panel to give the page header the desired height (**Figure 6.15**). HTML defaults to putting it on the far left of the div, so it doesn't need any positioning changes to be in the right place for this example.

Continues on next page

5. Add the two main parts of the page: navcontainer and content (**Figure 6.16**). The navcontainer style (**Figure 6.17**) will contain the future navigation area, and so, is floated to the left and assigned a fixed width of 160 pixels. The content style (**Figure 6.18**) has a left margin of 200 pixels, which moves it away from navcontainer.

Figure 6.16 Two more parts of the page have been added: the navcontainer and content divs.

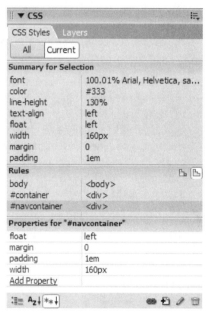

Figure 6.17 The navcontainer style floats the navigation to the left with a width of 160 pixels.

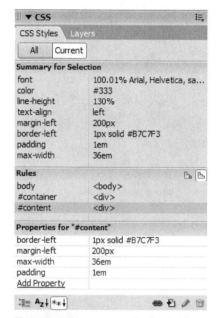

Figure 6.18 The content style contains the body of the page, pushed 200 pixels to the right.

Figure 6.19 The two previously covered divs now contain navlist and photofeature, respectively.

6. Each of those two main parts has a child element: in this case, navlist and photofeature, so it's time to add them (**Figure 6.19**). The navlist style (**Figure 6.20**) will contain the future navigation, which will consist of styled list elements. The photofeature style (**Figure 6.21**) includes both the photograph and the caption, so it's not just floated to the right; it also has a text color and font style.

Continues on next page

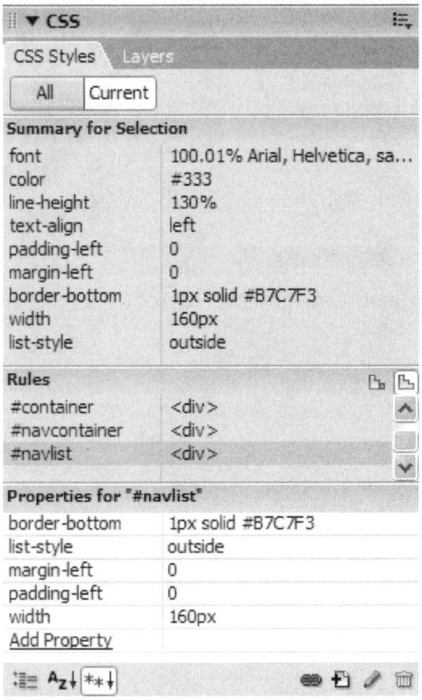

Figure 6.20 The navlist style will contain the future navigation bar.

Figure 6.21 The photofeature style will contain not just the image but also the caption, floating them both to the right.

7. Add an image and caption to the photofeature div (**Figure 6.22**), and you'll notice something interesting: that div now extends outside the area of its parent div. Don't fret; that's okay.

8. Add footer to the page (**Figure 6.23**), and its style properties (**Figure 6.24**) move it to the bottom after everything else. Now, all that's left is to add your text and navigation links, and your page is done.

Figure 6.22 The content and caption have been added here, and they're doing just what they've been told to do.

Figure 6.23 The footer goes at the bottom of the page.

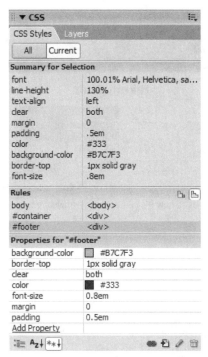

Figure 6.24 Here are the footer properties. The footer is not fixed in a particular place, so the page can be a variable length.

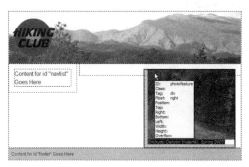

Figure 6.25 Hovering over a div gives you useful information about that element.

✔ Tips

■ Dreamweaver automatically adds the text 'Content for id "idName" Goes Here' whenever you create a new div. You'll want to delete that, but don't do it immediately. It can be hard to click inside an empty div, so leave that text there until you've added something inside.

■ As you add divs to the page and assign ids to them, you'll notice that the list of divs shown in the Insert Div Tag ID pop-up menu gets shorter and shorter. That's because Dreamweaver knows that each id must be unique on the page, and once you've assigned it to a div, it's no longer available for use. If you make a mistake and apply the wrong id somewhere, you'll need to remove it from the first usage before you can assign it to its correct element.

■ If you hover over an element on the page (as in **Figure 6.25**), a pop-up tip appears giving you information about that element. In this case, you can see that it's a div, that its name is photofeature, and that it's floated to the right.

Using the Visual Aids

Laying out pages with CSS can be frustrating because it can sometimes be difficult to tell which elements are where and why. Thankfully, Dreamweaver has a few handy features that make creating CSS-based layouts much simpler. Dreamweaver refers to these as Visual Aids.

Figure 6.26 shows our example CSS-based page with all visual aids turned off. It's fine, but if we had a problem, it would be difficult to tell where each div begins and ends. That's where the visual aids shine.

The visual aids can be found on the right side of the Document toolbar 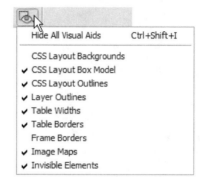. Although it looks like a button, that little downward facing arrow means that it's actually a pop-up menu. If you click on it, you'll get the options seen in **Figure 6.27**. Or, you can choose View > Visual Aids, and then select any of the menu options (**Figure 6.28**).

To turn each visual aid on or off, choose it from the menu to toggle its checkmark, or you can choose Hide All (Ctrl-Shift-I or Cmd-Shift-I) to turn them all off temporarily. For day-to-day use, we recommend keeping CSS Layout Backgrounds turned off, and CSS Layout Box Model and CSS Layout Outlines on.

Figure 6.26 The page looks nice, but it doesn't give any clues as to how it's laid out in Dreamweaver.

Figure 6.27 Here's the visual aids menu and your choices.

Figure 6.28 Or, you can get to it via the menu bar.

Figure 6.29 CSS Layout Backgrounds are gaudy but useful.

Figure 6.30 The CSS Layout Box Model shows you the exact limits of the currently selected element.

Figure 6.31 CSS Layout Outlines give you a subtle way of telling your elements apart.

Here's a rundown of the CSS-related items in these menus:

◆ **CSS Layout Backgrounds:** Put on your sunglasses and turn on CSS Layout Backgrounds (**Figure 6.29**). With this aid, Dreamweaver assigns a different background color for every layout block. If you've already set a background color, that will go away, as will background images—note that while you can see the header logo, you can't see the header background graphic.

Dreamweaver's documentation describes the color choices as "visually distinctive," but we prefer to not beat around the bush: we just call them loud and bright. Sorry, but there's no way to change the color choices. On the other hand, the garishness makes it very clear which div is which.

◆ **CSS Layout Box Model:** You've seen the Layout Box Model aid (**Figure 6.30**) used previously in this chapter. When enabled, it shows just the selected element, including its margin, borders, and padding. If you recall from Figure 6.18, the content div had a 1 pixel solid light blue left border, a 200 pixel left margin, and a padding of 1 em. When this visual aid is enabled, each of these is shown visually and uniquely on the document along with the dimensions of the div.

◆ **CSS Layout Outlines:** The CSS Layout Outlines option simply puts a dashed line around the border of each layout block (**Figure 6.31**). Again, you've seen it throughout most of this chapter. It can be tricky to see what your borders are set to when this is on, and you should also keep in mind that the dashed line includes the padding but excludes the margins.

Using Design-Time Style Sheets

It's common when working with CSS-based layouts that you want something to display in a particular way while you're designing—but *only* while you're designing, that is, during *design time*. You can tell Dreamweaver to use certain style sheets only at design time, and even to turn off certain style sheets only at design time.

As with the previous visual aids, you wouldn't want your real Web site to look like that, but it's handy while trying to do those last few tweaks or track down a problem. If you want something that Dreamweaver's built-in visual aids don't provide, Design-time style sheets allow you to create your own.

```
 1   /* CSS Document */
 2
 3   p {
 4       display:block;
 5   }
 6
 7   h1 {
 8       background-color: orange;
 9   }
10
```

Figure 6.32 This very simple style sheet gives us extra information in Dreamweaver.

CSS Layout Blocks

Dreamweaver uses what it refers to as *CSS layout blocks*, which are one of the following:

◆ A div without display:inline.

◆ An element with display:block.

◆ An element with position:absolute.

◆ An element with position:relative.

CSS layout blocks are used by the visual aids and design time style sheets to help designers understand how the parts of a CSS-based layout work together on your page.

For instance, say you have a design time style sheet that assigns position: relative to all of your links (that is, to all *a* tags). When you then turn on CSS Layout Backgrounds, all of your links will be their own bright color, allowing you to easily pick them out.

Figure 6.33 Design-time style sheets can be chosen here.

Figure 6.34 Or they can be chosen from the CSS panel.

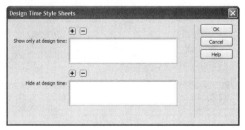

Figure 6.35 But either way, you end up at the Design Time Style Sheets dialog.

To show a Design-time style sheet:

1. Create and save a new style sheet containing the style rules that should display only inside Dreamweaver. **Figure 6.32** shows an example that contains two simple rules: p is set to `display:block` and h1 gets a background color of `orange`. See the "CSS Layout Blocks" sidebar for an explanation of why you'd want to modify the p tag.

2. To choose a Design-time style sheet, either choose Text > CSS Styles > Design-time (**Figure 6.33**), or right-click inside the CSS Styles panel and choose Design-time from the contextual menu (**Figure 6.34**). The Design Time Style Sheets dialog appears (**Figure 6.35**).

Continues on next page

3. To add a style sheet that shows only at design time, click the upper plus button ⊞. The Select File dialog appears (**Figure 6.36**). Navigate to your new style sheet, choose it, and click OK.

4. Back in the Design Time Style Sheets dialog, your new style sheet is now listed next to Show only at design time. If it's correct, click OK.

5. The Web page now appears with some slight changes (**Figure 6.37**): the h1 title now has an orange background, and paragraphs can now be identified using the CSS Layout Box Model visual aid. If we use the CSS Layout Backgrounds visual aid (**Figure 6.38**), paragraphs are now clearly distinct from other elements on the page.

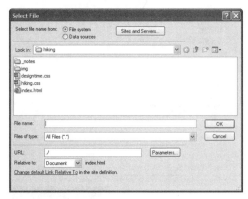

Figure 6.36 The Select File dialog lets you choose your Design-time style sheet.

Figure 6.37 Now the h1 is all lit up.

Figure 6.38 And paragraphs are delineated when the background visual aid is used.

Hiking Club

Figure 6.39 Style sheets can also be hidden, as seen on this plain page.

To hide a style sheet at design time:

◆ Follow steps 2 through 4 from "To show a Design-time style sheet" earlier, but click the lower plus button ⊞ instead. Select a style sheet to hide, and click OK.

In **Figure 6.39**, the main style sheet for the page has been hidden. This allows you to see the page without the effect of styles, or to see the page with some styles but not others. This can be a big help when trying to track down CSS-related issues.

To remove a Design-time style sheet:

1. Bring up the Design Time Style Sheets dialog as described earlier. Select the style sheet to remove and click the minus button ⊟ above the style sheet name. If you have multiple style sheets to remove, continue to delete them in this way.

2. Click OK to accept, and your Web page will display closer to the way it will appear on the Web.

✔ Tips

■ Design-time style sheets are an extremely powerful tool when used in conjunction with Dreamweaver's CSS Layout Blocks.

■ Despite how it looks, your document is not actually being changed. Design-time style sheets are not really added to or removed from your Web page: Dreamweaver handles it all internally.

■ Don't forget that you also have the Style Rendering toolbar (covered in Chapter 1), which you can use to display your page as it would appear with print style sheets, handheld style sheets, projection style sheets, and so on. You can also use the Style Rendering toolbar to turn off the display of style sheets altogether.

Using the Grid

If you want items on a page to line up, a handy way to do it is to use the grid—a feature you may well be familiar with from other applications such as Photoshop. If you're used to it elsewhere, it's easy; if you're not, here's a quick overview.

The grid overlays graph paper-like lines on your Web page, making it easy to see if elements on the page are horizontally or vertically aligned. Nothing on your page is actually changed, and the lines are only visible inside Dreamweaver. If you choose to have elements on your page *snap to the grid*, whenever you move an element close to a grid line, it will "jump" (or snap) to match up with it. This way, you know for sure that your elements are perfectly aligned.

To turn the grid on or off:

◆ To toggle the grid display, choose View > Grid > Show Grid (**Figure 6.40**), or click the View Options menu button on the Document toolbar (**Figure 6.41**) and choose Grid, or press Ctrl-Alt-G (Cmd-Option-G). Your document displays the grid if it wasn't already displayed (**Figure 6.42**), and vice versa.

Figure 6.40 You can get to all the grid options from the menu.

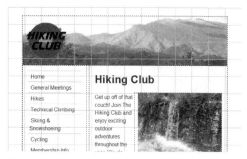

Figure 6.41 And you can turn them on or off from the View Options menu.

Figure 6.42 Here's our usual page with the grid visible.

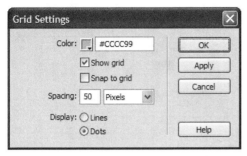

Figure 6.43 If you don't like the grid defaults, the settings can be changed.

To change the grid settings:

1. Choose View > Grid > Grid Settings (Figure 6.40). The Grid Settings dialog appears (**Figure 6.43**).

2. From this dialog, you can change the color, the spacing, and whether the grid displays as lines or dots. You can also use this as a way to set the Show grid and Snap to Grid options at the same time. If you want to check how a setting looks, click Apply. When you like your results, click OK, and if the grid is set to show, your document appears with your chosen grid style. If the grid is not set to show, the settings will still be changed, and will display their new values the next time you show the grid.

To make elements snap to the grid:

1. Choose View > Grid > Snap to Grid (Figure 6.40), or check the Snap to grid check box in the Grid Settings dialog (Figure 6.43), or press Ctrl-Alt-Shift-G (Cmd-Option-Shift-G).

2. Move an absolutely positioned page element. It snaps to line up with the grid if you move the element within a few pixels of a grid line.

USING THE GRID

189

Using Guides

Like grids, guides are another tool commonly found in other design applications. Guides can do almost everything grids can, and a whole lot more. For instance, guides can be locked into place, guides can be set to percentages of the page, and not only can elements snap to guides, but guides can be set to snap to elements.

To turn guides on or off:

◆ To toggle the display of guides, choose View > Guides > Show Guides (**Figure 6.44**), or click the View Options menu button on the Document toolbar (**Figure 6.45**) and choose Guides, or press Ctrl-; (Cmd-;).

To add a guide to your page:

1. Click the cursor in either the horizontal or vertical ruler, and drag into the document. The guide appears along with a tip that displays the number of pixels that the guide is currently away from the edge of the document (**Figure 6.46**).

2. When the guide is where you want it, release the mouse. The line remains, but the tip goes away.

Figure 6.44 As you could with the grid, you can get to many guide options in the menu.

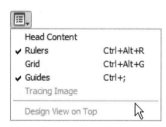

Figure 6.45 You can turn guides on and off from the View Options menu.

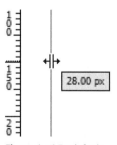

Figure 6.46 By default, guides are measured in pixels.

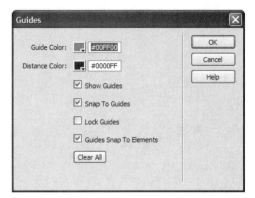

Figure 6.47 Use the Guides dialog to change any of its settings.

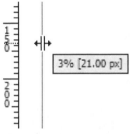

Figure 6.48 If you want a percentage instead of pixels, hold down the Shift key.

To edit guide settings:

1. Choose View > Guides > Edit Guides (Figure 6.44), and the Guides dialog appears (**Figure 6.47**).

2. From here, you can set:
   - ▲ The guide and distance colors.
   - ▲ Whether guides should show.
   - ▲ Whether elements should snap to guides, guides snap to elements, both, or neither.
   - ▲ Whether guides are locked.

   You can also use it to clear all the current guides by clicking the Clear All button.

3. When your changes are complete, click OK.

✔ Tips

■ To move a guide, move the mouse over the guide. When the cursor changes, click the guide and drag it to its new location.

■ To remove a guide from your page, move the guide off the document. Mac users will see a little "puff of smoke" animation—sorry, Windows users! You can also remove all the guides at once (without the animated effect) by choosing View > Guides > Clear Guides (Figure 6.44) or by clicking Clear All in the Guides dialog (Figure 6.47).

■ To inspect the current position of a guide, hover the cursor over the guide, and a tip showing the position appears.

■ To position a guide based on the percentage distance of the document rather than pixels, hold down the Shift key while moving the guide (**Figure 6.48**). The tip displays the current location in both pixels and percentages when you're moving it and also when you check the guide's position later.

Continues on next page

USING GUIDES

- To see how far a guide is from the sides of your document, hold down the Ctrl (Cmd) key. Lines appear showing the distance in pixels (and percentage, if set in the previous tip) to the edges of the document (**Figure 6.49**). If you have multiple guides on your page, the distance shown will be from guide to guide or from guide to edge.

- Guides can be locked on your page so that they can't be moved. To do this, choose View > Guides > Lock Guides (Figure 6.44) or use the Guides dialog (Figure 6.47). It's a toggle, so just do it again to unlock your guides.

- Rulers have to be visible for you to add guides, but you can view, move, and delete guides even when the rulers are hidden.

- Guides can be used to simulate dimensions of standard browsers. Choose View > Guides and pick one of the standard sizes from the bottom of the menu (Figure 6.44). This creates both vertical and horizontal guides on your page. Be careful, though, as you can still move them accidentally, and then they aren't much use at giving you your dimension hints. This is the one exception to the previous tip: you can create guides with this method even when the ruler is hidden.

- As with the grid, you can choose to snap elements to your guides—but you can also choose to snap guides to your elements. Choose either View > Guides > Snap To Guides, View > Guides > Guides Snap To Elements, or even both (Figure 6.44). Or, you can set them in the Guides dialog (Figure 6.47).

- If you double-click a guide, the Move Guide dialog appears (**Figure 6.50**). Use this dialog to set the guide to a precise position in pixels, inches, centimeters, or percentages.

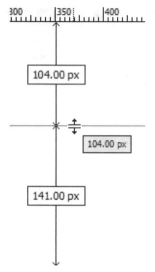

Figure 6.49 Holding down the Ctrl (Cmd) key gives you the distance between the document edge and the guide.

Figure 6.50 Double-click a guide to get to the Move Guide dialog.

Figure 6.51 You can zoom in on a particular part of the screen.

```
   6%
  12%
  25%
  50%
  66%
✓ 100%
 150%
 200%
 300%
 400%
 800%
1600%
3200%
6400%
────────────
 Fit Selection
 Fit All
 Fit Width
```

Figure 6.52 Pick a particular magnification level to make everything larger or smaller.

Zooming In On Your Page

Yes, it's another feature borrowed from standard design applications, just like the grid and guides. New in Dreamweaver 8, the Zoom feature lets you design your pages more precisely. And as with the grid and guides, you'll need to be in Design view to use it.

To zoom into your page:

◆ Select the Zoom tool 🔍 from the status bar at the bottom right of your document, and your cursor changes to a magnifying glass with a plus 🔍. While in zoom mode, you can do either of two things:

▲ Click and drag to draw a box over the area you want to zoom in on (**Figure 6.51**). That rectangle expands to take up the entire document window.

▲ Click the spot on the page you want to magnify. Continue to click it until you get the magnification level you want.

or

Press Ctrl-= (Cmd-=) until you've reached the level you want.

or

Select a magnification level from the Zoom pop-up menu in the status bar (**Figure 6.52**).

or

Type your desired magnification level into the Zoom text box in the status bar `100% ▾`.

or

Continues on next page

Select View > Magnification and pick a magnification level (**Figure 6.53**).

or

Select an element on the page, and then choose View > Fit Selection (Figure 6.53).

or

Select an element on the page, and then choose Fit Selection from the Zoom pop-up menu in the status bar (Figure 6.52).

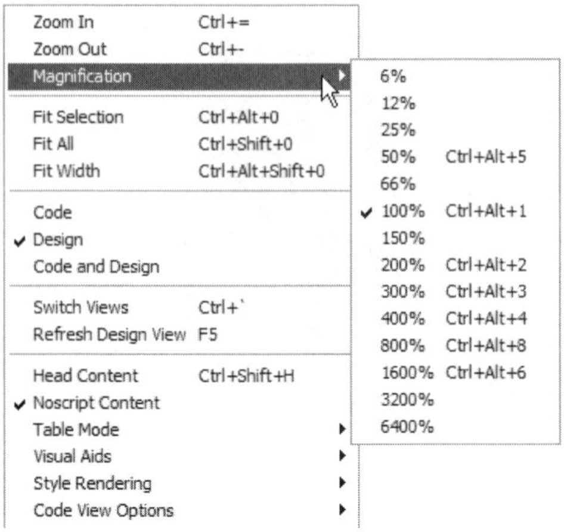

Figure 6.53 You can also get to the magnification levels from the menu.

To zoom out from your page:

◆ Select the Zoom tool from the status bar at the bottom right of your document. Press Alt (Option) and the cursor changes to a magnifying glass and a minus. Click on the page to zoom out.

or

Press Ctrl-- (Cmd--) until you've reached the level you want.

or

Select View > Magnification and pick a magnification level (Figure 6.53).

or

Choose View > Fit All or View > Fit Width (Figure 6.53).

or

Choose Fit All or Fit Width from the Zoom pop-up menu in the status bar (Figure 6.52).

✔ Tips

- To edit your page in Zoom mode, select the pointer in the status bar and click inside the page.
- To pan your page after you've zoomed in, select the hand icon in the status bar, and then drag the page to move around.

```
592w
536 x 196   (640 x 480, Default)
600 x 300   (640 x 480, Maximized)
760 x 420   (800 x 600, Maximized)
795 x 470   (832 x 624, Maximized)
955 x 600   (1024 x 768, Maximized)
544 x 378   (WebTV)

Edit Sizes…
```

Figure 6.54 Dreamweaver comes with pre-set window sizes for the most commonly used monitors.

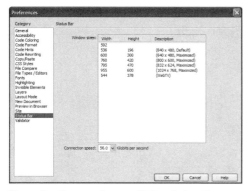

Figure 6.55 You can view or edit the window sizes in the Status Bar category of Dreamweaver's Preferences.

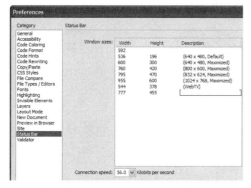

Figure 6.56 New sizes can be added just by clicking in the first unused line and typing the appropriate dimensions.

Setting Page Dimensions

It's handy to be able to easily set guides to show the dimensions of common browsers, but it's not quite the same as seeing how your design actually appears in a window of that size. That's where setting page dimensions comes in.

To resize the window to a preset size:

◆ Click the Window Size pop-up menu in the status bar, and select one of the listed sizes (**Figure 6.54**). Your document window resets itself to that size.

To edit the preset window sizes:

1. Click the Window Size pop-up menu in the status bar, and select Edit Sizes. The Status Bar preferences display appears (**Figure 6.55**).

   or

   Open Dreamweaver's preferences and select the Status Bar Category.

2. Click in any of the fields and write over the current value to replace it. To add a value, click in the first unfilled line (**Figure 6.56**). To delete a value, clear the entire line by deleting the contents of each field.

   Continues on next page

3. Click OK to accept. The new size now appears in the Window size pop-up menu (**Figure 6.57**).

✔ Tips

- You can resize the window to a fixed width (leaving the height alone) by entering only a width value. To make the window resize to a fixed height, enter only the height.

- You can't resize a document on Windows if it's maximized.

- While it looks like you can sort the values in the Status Bar preferences, you actually can't.

- Sadly, if you enter a new window size, it doesn't get added as a new possible value for creating guides—it's only for resizing.

- While you're in the Status Bar preferences, take the chance to reset the Connection speed if it's not appropriate for you or your audience. That number is what Dreamweaver uses to calculate page download time, which is shown on the far-right end of the status bar.

592w	
536 x 196	(640 x 480, Default)
600 x 300	(640 x 480, Maximized)
760 x 420	(800 x 600, Maximized)
795 x 470	(832 x 624, Maximized)
955 x 600	(1024 x 768, Maximized)
544 x 378	(WebTV)
777 x 455	My design size
Edit Sizes…	

Figure 6.57 And here's my new window size.

Figure 6.58 When drawn, layers look like a simple box on the screen.

Figure 6.59 When you select a layer, it has selection and resize handles.

Old Time Dreamweaver

Once upon a time, it was difficult to make a Web page look just the way you wanted it to look because browsers had very little support for layout. Dreamweaver worked hard to make positioning possible despite the poor browser support, and the primary way Dreamweaver did this was with what it calls *layers*. The remainder of this chapter covers them.

It's important to note that Dreamweaver's layers are not the same thing as the HTML `layer` tag. The `layer` tag was implemented in Netscape 4 and only Netscape 4. Neither earlier versions of Netscape, nor later versions of Netscape, and no other browser ever included it—so don't even bother with it.

Given the capabilities of Dreamweaver 8, and the browsers available at the time Macromedia shipped it, Dreamweaver's layers are in nearly the same shape as that of the HTML `layer` tag: obsolete, and not for use going forward. However, you may have older sites that were set up with layers, so it's worth learning a little about how they work.

Layers for layout

You can create a layer by going to the Layout category of the Insert Bar, clicking the Draw Layer button 🗔, and then drawing a box in the document window (**Figure 6.58**). Each box you draw is absolutely positioned on your Web page, with a fixed height and width and a fixed position from the top and left edges of the page.

The layers can be selected, moved, and resized by clicking on the border of a layer. Once a layer is selected, you can see its selection handle and resize handles (**Figure 6.59**).

Don't Do It!

We might be coming off a little heavy-handed here, but it's from experience: don't use layers. Just don't. If you have a site that uses layers, it's worth taking the time to carefully convert it to use block positioning layout, divs, and CSS.

Layers themselves, along with converting layers to tables and vice versa, are remnants of an older, sadder time. Dreamweaver leaves them in for historical reasons, but if you're just starting out, they're the wrong way to go.

Once you've added your layers to your page, they can be used in the same way divs were described above—you can add text, images, or whatever you'd like to your layers.

Styles for layers are internal, and each layer has a separate set of rules of its own—usually with meaningful names like Layer1 and Layer2. If you want to see which layer you're working on, move the cursor over the layer, and a tip appears giving the id, size, and position of that layer (**Figure 6.60**).

Layers can overlap other layers if you define them to do so (**Figure 6.61**). If you don't want them to overlap, you can check the Prevent overlaps box in the Layers tab of the CSS panel (**Figure 6.62**). That panel also contains the visibility indicator: a blank space, or an open or closed eye, on the left side of the panel. If the eye is open, that layer is visible. If the eye is closed, that layer is hidden. If the column is blank, the layer inherits its parent's visibility (layers which have the document as their parent will be visible). The right column of the table is the Z-index of the layer. Wherever two layers overlap, the one with the higher Z-index displays. The numbers don't have to be sequential; for instance, if you want something to always display, give it a huge Z-index such as 5000.

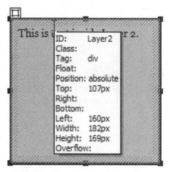

Figure 6.60 Hovering over a layer gives you the layer's name, size, and position.

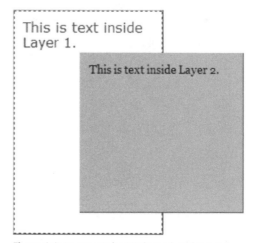

Figure 6.61 Layers can be overlapped, and you can tell Dreamweaver which goes on top.

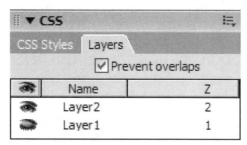

Figure 6.62 The Layers tab of the CSS panel lets you show and hide layers as well as set the Z-index.

Figure 6.63 Converting layers to tables is found under the Modify menu.

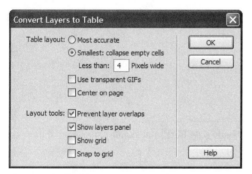

Figure 6.64 The Convert Layers to Table dialog lets you set several options, and Dreamweaver obeys some of them.

Converting layers to tables

You could use layers just like divs, and given that the layer tool actually creates divs, that would be somewhat equivalent. But the real point of layers was to be able to lay out pages visually in the days before divs had widespread browser support. So, that was the next step: converting layers to tables. This is where things get ugly fast.

To convert a layer-based page to tables:

1. Choose Modify > Convert > Layers to Table (**Figure 6.63**). The Convert Layers to Table dialog appears (**Figure 6.64**).

2. The Convert Layers to Table dialog gives you a number of choices:

   ▲ Whether you want your new table to be as close as possible to the original, or as small as possible, which collapses empty cells. If you choose the latter, you have the option of choosing how small cells must be before they're collapsed.

   ▲ You can choose if you want to use transparent GIFs. If you do this, the bottom row of your table consists of spacer GIFs, forcing your new table into strictly sized columns.

   ▲ You can choose if you want your new table to be centered on the page.

Continues on next page

- ▲ You're given a choice of whether or not you want to prevent layer overlaps, but it doesn't matter what you pick; Dreamweaver doesn't care. If you turn this option off *and* turn off the Prevent overlaps choice on the Layers tab of the CSS panel, and then try to convert a page that contains overlapping layers, you'll still get **Figure 6.65**, which tells you that you can't convert this page. If that's your situation, move your layers until they no longer overlap (**Figure 6.66**).

- ▲ You're given a choice of whether or not you want the Layers tab of the CSS panel to show after the conversion. If you turn this on, the Layers tab and CSS panel will be open when the conversion is done. If you turn it off, and the Layers tab was previously open, the CSS panel group collapses. If you turn it off and the Layers tab isn't currently open, nothing happens.

- ▲ You also have a choice of showing the grid, and of whether you want to snap your new table cells to that grid. You can choose one, both, or neither.

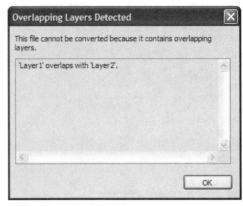

Figure 6.65 Whether you care or not, Dreamweaver won't let you convert your layers to a table if there are any overlaps.

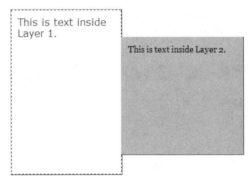

Figure 6.66 Here's our simple page before the conversion.

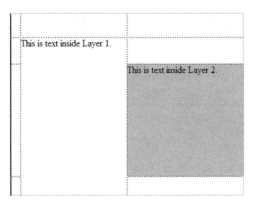

Figure 6.67 And here's our page after the conversion, not looking quite the same—the fonts, padding, and borders were lost.

3. Click OK to accept, and your page will be re-created in tables (**Figure 6.67**). Except... it doesn't really work correctly. For instance:

▲ In the original layered version, the left-hand layer had 10 pixels of padding, a dashed red border, and the text was in a large red serif font. In the new tables version, all of that is gone.

▲ The right-hand layer also had padding and a specific font, and neither of those carried over—but the colored background did.

▲ If you look at the source code, the rules that were created for the two layers still exist, even though they aren't used any more.

✔ Tips

■ You can't convert just some of the layers on a page. The conversion process converts all layers on the page.

■ We're not sure why anyone would want to check the Show layers panel box. After all, once you've converted from layers to tables, the Layers tab isn't of any further use to you!

■ There really is no excuse to create new pages with this method: you can start and end with tables if that's what works for your site, or you can start and end with divs, but there is no reason to start with layers and end with tables.

OLD TIME DREAMWEAVER

Converting tables to layers

Okay, you're convinced—tables aren't the way to do layout any more, and you want to convert all your pages to CSS and divs. Great!

And then you remember that back in Figure 6.63 there was another option: Modify > Convert > Tables to Layers. Well, this is going to be easy, you think: after all, layers are just a sort of div, right? Not so fast, there.

To convert tables to layers:

1. Choose Modify > Convert > Tables to Layers (Figure 6.63). The Convert Tables to Layers dialog appears (**Figure 6.68**).

2. The Convert Tables to Layers dialog is similar to the Convert Layers to Table dialog, but it has considerably fewer options:

   ▲ You can choose whether or not to check Prevent layer overlaps, but whether or not you check this, none will be created.

   ▲ The Show layers panel choice makes considerably more sense here than it did going the other way around.

   ▲ And again, you can choose to take this opportunity to Show grid and Snap to grid.

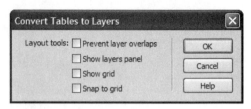

Figure 6.68 You can also convert tables to layers, although you shouldn't.

Figure 6.69 Here's a straightforward page designed with tables.

Figure 6.70 But that page doesn't quite make the transition to layers very well.

3. Click OK when you're ready to see the mess that ensues. For instance, the HomeCook site (**Figure 6.69**) looks fine in tables; after its conversion to layers (**Figure 6.70**), it appears rather odd:

▲ The HomeCook text in the header has moved up to the top of the screen, while the tagline below it has stayed in place.

▲ All the font styles have been lost.

▲ Font colors have been lost in some places but retained in others.

▲ The bullet points next to the navigation items are gone, and the navigation no longer goes all the way over to the left margin.

▲ The colored vertical bar on the right side that contains reviews now has varying widths.

And so on. The new version also contains 22 layers, each of which has its own style rule including fixed size and position on the page.

✔ **Tip**

■ If you have a page that contains both tables and other elements, converting that page to layers moves everything (not just the tables!) into layers.

WORKING WITH LINKS

Links are what make the Web, well, *webby*—the interconnections between pages and sites are a fundamental part of why the Web is different from print. Without links coming in to your site, no one will ever find it. And without links going out from your site, it's a dead end. Dreamweaver makes it easy to add links to your site.

There are a number of different kinds of links: some links are internal to a page, some internal to a site, and some links go to another server altogether. This chapter will cover all of these, along with targets, image links, and email links.

Creating Text Links

If you can drag your mouse from here to there, you can create a link inside Dreamweaver. All you have to do is decide what on the page you want to be the link, and where you want that link to point.

Because creating links is such a large part of developing a Web site, there are multiple ways to create links. You can figure out which method works best for you.

To create a text link:

1. Select some text on the page to be the link. **Figure 7.1** shows that the title "HomeCook.info" has been selected.

2. In the Property Inspector, click on the Point to File icon ⊕. An arrow will appear, and that arrow can be dragged into the Files panel. Drag it to the file you want, and release the mouse.

   or

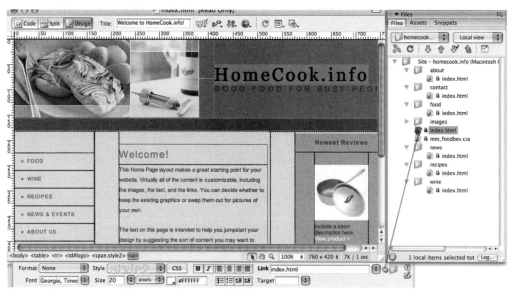

Figure 7.1 Drag the Point to File icon, and the arrow will follow to the selected link file.

CREATING TEXT LINKS

Figure 7.2 You can also select a link file from the Select File dialog.

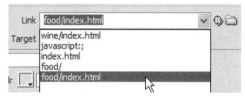

Figure 7.3 Or use this pop-up menu in the Property Inspector.

Figure 7.4 Finally, you can type the link file name in the Hyperlink dialog.

In the Property Inspector, click on the Browse for File icon 🗀. The Select File dialog will appear (**Figure 7.2**). Choose the file you want and click OK.

or

In the Property Inspector, click in the Link text field and type in the name of the file you want to link to.

or

In the Property Inspector, click on the pop-up menu to the right of the Link text field, and choose from the list of recently used links (**Figure 7.3**).

or

In the Insert Bar, click on the Hyperlink button 🖾. The Hyperlink dialog will appear (**Figure 7.4**). Type in the name of the file to link to, or click the Browse For File icon to select a file. Click OK when you're done.

✔ Tip

■ If you want to remove a link, click inside the text you want to de-link, click on the *<a>* in the tag selector, and then clear the Link text field in the Property Inspector.

The Different Types of Links

When you create a link from one Web page to another, there are three possible types of links you can add: absolute, document relative, or site root relative. **Figure 7.5** shows the file list from www.homecook.info, a fairly typical site, with a number of files inside various folders. **Figure 7.6** shows another way of looking at the same information.

◆ **Absolute:** The index.html file contains a link to http://www.dori.com/index.html, which is another site altogether. This is an absolute link. The link starts with the explicit name of a server where the file can be found. It's also correct for the link to just go to either http://www.dori.com/ or http://www.dori.com; in both cases, the link will take you to the default file for that domain (in this case, index.html).

◆ **Document Relative:** The index.html file also contains a link to the index.html file inside the about folder. To tell the browser how to navigate from one to the other, the link is about/index.html. That link is *relative* to the document it's being called from: the server knows based on that link that it needs to find a folder named about at the same level as the index.html file, and inside that folder, a file named index.html.

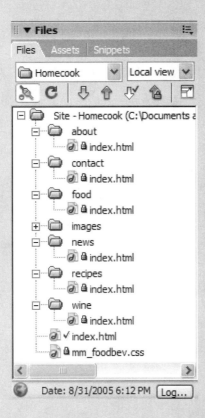

Figure 7.5 Here's a list of folders and files (as seen in the Files panel) from a site of medium complexity.

If about/index.html linked back to index.html, it would link to ../index.html. Once again, the server starts looking for the next file at the same level as the current file, and those two periods tell the server to go *up* a level—back to www.homecook.info. And from there, it's easy to find the index.html file. A file two levels deep would link to the main index page by linking to ../../index.html. It goes up two levels of folders before looking for a particular file.

Document relative links are especially useful when you're testing on your local machine—the browser can get from one page to another just based on the location of the current document.

◆ **Site Root Relative:** Another way to reference files within the same site is by referencing them by where they are within the site, that is, relative to the root of the site, not the current document. The root of the site is always identified with a forward slash: /. With a site root relative link, the page at /food/index.html would link to /index.html. You no longer need to tell the server to go up a level or two; instead, you just tell it to start at the root and look for that particular file.

Site root relative links are useful when you're creating site-wide Library items. For instance, the left-hand menu in Figure 7.1 contains links to /about/index.html and /food/index. html. With site root relative links, you know that those links work everywhere on the site, no matter what page contains that menu. Library items will be covered in Chapter 13.

Links to external sites must be absolute links. Links within a site can use either document relative or site root relative links or a combination of the two. Which a site uses by default is set in Dreamweaver's preferences (see "Changing Link Relative To").

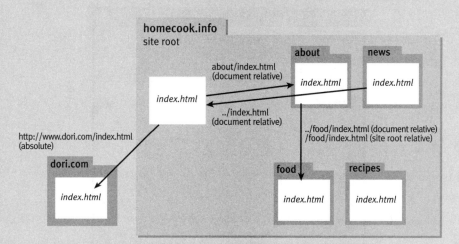

Figure 7.6 The about, news, food, and recipes folders (or directories) are all contained within the site root folder.

Changing Link Relative To

It's awkwardly named, but it's useful: you can change the *Link Relative To* (that is, whether the link is document relative or site root relative) for either a single file, or for the site as a whole. As mentioned in "The Different Types of Links" sidebar, your links can either be document-relative or site root-relative, or even a mix of those on each page.

To change the "Link Relative To" for a link:

1. In the Property Inspector, click on the Browse for File icon ⬜. The Select File dialog will appear (Figure 7.2).

2. Near the bottom of the dialog, there's a pop-up menu with the label "Relative to." From that pop-up, you can switch between Document and Site Root (**Figure 7.7**), and the URL for the link will change.

3. Click OK to save your changes.

Figure 7.7 Use the Select File dialog to make your link site or document relative.

To change the "Link Relative To" for a site:

1. In the Property Inspector, click on the Browse for File icon 📁. The Select File dialog will appear (Figure 7.2).

2. Near the bottom of the dialog, there's a link that says "Change default Link Relative To in the site definition." If you click on the link (the part that's blue and underlined), you'll end up at the Advanced tab for the Site Definition for your site, with the Local Info category chosen (**Figure 7.8**). From here, you can choose either radio button next to "Links relative to," where the choices are Document or Site root. This will change the link that you're currently modifying, and the default for future links, but it will not change any other existing links on the page or site.

3. Click OK to save your changes.

✔ Tip

■ You can also follow the directions (found in Chapter 2) for editing the Site Definition. If you click on the Advanced tab and choose the Local Info category, you'll end up in the same place.

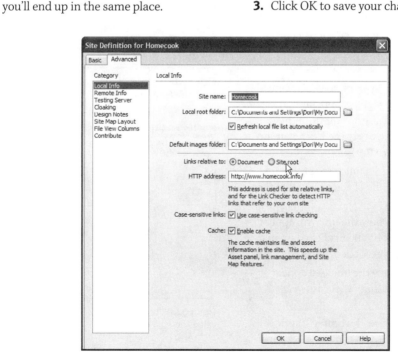

Figure 7.8 Or you can set the "Links relative to" for the entire site.

Formatting Links

One of the most common uses of CSS is to change the way links are displayed in the browser. Want your links to only be underlined when the cursor is over them? Want the background or text color to change when a visitor clicks? Or maybe you just want something other than your visitor's default colors? That's all CSS, and Dreamweaver can handle that. As covered in Chapter 5, you'll need to know if your site is going to use internal or external styles.

To format links:

1. Click on the New CSS Rule button at the bottom of the CSS panel ☐. The New CSS Rule dialog will appear.

2. If you want to set a style that will apply to all links (whatever their state), or to set the default appearance for links, choose "Tag (redefines the look of a specific tag)" for the Selector Type, and for Selector, choose *a*.

   or

   For the Selector Type, choose "Advanced (IDs, pseudo-class selectors)," and for Selector, choose any option from the pop-up menu: *a:link*, *a:visited*, *a:hover*, or *a:active* (**Figure 7.9**).

   ▲ *a:link* is the default state of the link, seen when none of the other states are in use.

   ▲ *a:visited* is how the link will appear after the link has been clicked on and the linked page loaded.

   ▲ *a:hover* is how the link will appear while the visitor's cursor is over the link.

   ▲ *a:active* is how the link will appear while the visitor is clicking that particular link.

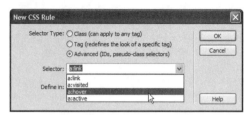

Figure 7.9 The New CSS Rule dialog lets you choose which rule you're going to define.

Figure 7.10 When you want a new style sheet, you can create that file here.

Figure 7.11 After you create the rule, define its values here.

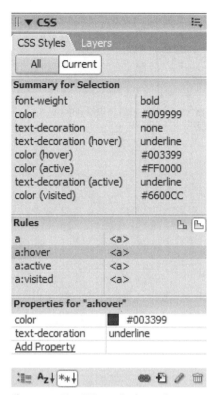

Figure 7.12 The CSS panel, after various *a* rules have been defined. New properties can be set from here, also.

3. For Define in, there are at least two options: New Style Sheet File or This document only. If the current document links to any style sheets, their names are included in the pop-up menu. Choose whichever is appropriate for this site, and click OK.

4. If you chose to create a new style sheet, you'll see the Save Style Sheet File As dialog (**Figure 7.10**). Choose where to save it and what to name it, and click Save.

5. The CSS Rule Definition dialog will appear (**Figure 7.11**). You can create the specific rules you want for links either here or directly in the CSS panel (**Figure 7.12**).

✔ Tips

■ If you don't set styles for your links, they are likely to display underlined and blue (unvisited) and purple (visited)—but you can't be sure of that.

■ Figure 7.12 shows some of the most common rules for CSS-formatted links: bold font-weight, and no underline except when the cursor is over the link.

The Style of Links

How to style links has been an ongoing controversy over the years: should a Web designer ever mess with a user's defaults? Should links always be underlined? Should links always, sometimes, or never say, "Click here"?

The answers, as with so much about Web design, depend on who's visiting your site. If you've got a traditional e-commerce site geared towards average surfers, you'll probably want to make things as simple and straightforward as possible. If you've got a cutting-edge art gallery site that attracts people who are used to fashion-forward sites, you can be a little more daring. If you aren't sure which way to go, figure out what sites attract visitors like yours, and style your links similarly.

There's one rule that's always true: be consistent across your site. No one should ever have to learn a new navigation style on every page.

Targeting Links

Sometimes you want a link to go to a new window, or to an existing window other than the one you're clicking on. That's done by giving the link a *target*, which is the name of the window in which you want the new page to load.

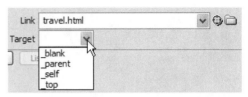

Figure 7.13 Set a link's target in the Property Inspector with this pop-up menu.

To give a link a target:

1. Follow the steps above to create a link, and then click on the *<a>* in the tag selector.

2. Directly below Link in the Property Inspector is a text field named Target where the target is entered. Alternatively, you can just click on the pop-up menu to the right of the field to choose the target.

3. If you're working on a site without frames, you have four choices: _blank, _parent, _self, and _top (sites with frames are different and will be covered in Chapter 11). Choose one from the pop-up, and the target field will show your choice (**Figure 7.13**).

   • blank: Open a new, blank window.

   • parent: If the current window was opened by a previous link to a blank target (that is, the current window is a newly opened window), open this link in the previous window. If the current window wasn't opened that way, what happens depends on the user's browser—but usually, it will just open in the current window.

   • self and top: For non-framed sites, these are both equivalent to not using any target at all.

✔ Tips

- To remove a target, just click in the target text field in the Property Inspector and erase its content.

- The underscore before the name of a target is there to tell the browser that this is a special type of target and not just the name of another window. You'll learn about named windows in Chapter 11.

Figure 7.14 The Named Anchor dialog lets you create a new anchor on your page.

Figure 7.15 The part of the page shown here has two anchors: the selected one is blue, and the unselected one is yellow.

✔ Tips

- While you do see that anchor on the page in Dreamweaver, it's not going to be there when you or anyone else sees the page in a browser—it's just there for your editing convenience, and it's one of the few ways in which Dreamweaver isn't 100% WYSIWYG. Hate seeing them? From the menu bar, choose View > Visual Aids > Invisible Elements to toggle the visibility of these icons on or off.

- There are many ways to delete a named anchor. One way is to click on the anchor icon and delete it. Or, in the Property Inspector, clear the Named Anchor name field.

Adding Named Anchors

Normally, when a new Web page is displayed, it does so showing the very top of a page. Adding an *anchor* to a link allows you to choose to display the page starting at a given point on a page. In order to use an anchor, you'll need to create at least two things: the anchor itself, and then the link to that anchor.

To create an anchor:

1. Open your document, and click in the spot in the file where you want the named anchor to be.

2. On the Insert Bar, click on the Named Anchor button 🐚, and the Named Anchor dialog will appear (**Figure 7.14**).

3. Choose a name for the anchor that will be unique for this page. Remember also that this anchor is going to be part of a URL, so it can only contain characters that are valid: no spaces, ampersands, question marks, etc.

4. Click OK. In the spot where you created the new anchor, an anchor icon will appear (**Figure 7.15**). If you click on that anchor, the tag selector will show the anchor with its name, and the Property Inspector will allow you to modify the name (**Figure 7.16**).

Figure 7.16 The Property Inspector for a named anchor.

To link to an anchor on the same page:

◆ Follow the directions from "Creating Text Links" earlier in this chapter, but drag the Point To File icon ◉ to the Named Anchor icon on the page. The selected text will now be linked to the new anchor.

✔ Tip

■ It's possible that the Point To File icon and the Point To File arrow can end up going to different spots on the page. The one that matters, in this case, is the icon itself, *not* the tip of the arrow.

To link to an anchor on another page:

◆ If the two files are open in different windows, place the windows such that you can see both the link source and the link destination. Then, follow the directions for linking to an anchor on the same page, but drag the icon to the separate page.

or

If you're using Dreamweaver's tabbed interface, you won't be able to see both the link source and the destination at the same time, so you'll have to add the anchor part of the link manually. Follow the directions from "Creating Text Links" earlier in this chapter, and when that's complete, click in the Link field in the Property Inspector and add a # followed by the anchor name to the end of the existing link. So if you want to link to the `chap07` anchor on the `dw8vqs.html` page, your link would be to `dw8vqs.html#chap07`.

Adding Links to Graphics

Making a graphic a link isn't all that different from creating a text link. The main difference is that the link and target fields on the Property Inspector are in a different area, so you might not see them at first glance. Additionally, you don't get the handy pop-up menu on the Link field, so you can't just reuse one of the links you've recently made.

To add a link to a graphic:

1. Select the image in the document window.

2. Using the Property Inspector (**Figure 7.17**), click on the Point to File icon ⊕ next to the Link field. An arrow will appear, and that arrow can be dragged into the Files panel. Drag it to the file you want, and release the mouse.

✔ Tips

■ As mentioned above in "Creating Text Links," there are many ways to create links. Over time, you'll find the one that works best for you.

■ It's very common that images in the top-left corner of a Web page link back to a site's home page; common enough that if you don't do this, your site's visitors may be confused. Unless there's a good reason why you shouldn't do this for a site, set this up as the default.

■ You can make individual parts of an image link to different Web pages. That's done with *image maps*, and they're covered in Chapter 8.

Figure 7.17 For images, the Link and Target fields aren't where you might expect them to be on the Property Inspector.

Adding Email Links

If you want your site's visitors to be able to contact you, you'll need to add a link that allows people to send you email.

To add an email link:

1. Click the spot on the page where you want to add an email link.

2. On the Insert Bar, click on the Email Link button , and the Email Link dialog will appear (**Figure 7.18**).

3. Fill in the text field with the text you want to display in the Web browser, and fill in the E-Mail field with the email address. Click OK when you're done.

Figure 7.18 The Email Link dialog lets you set both the link (the email address) and the text that will be displayed on the Web page.

✔ Tips

■ Dreamweaver doesn't do any kind of error checking to make sure that the email address is in a valid format, so be careful when you're entering it.

■ Putting an email address on a Web site can lead to that address getting all kinds of garbage or spam. There are a variety of ways to protect your email address. The simplest is just to encode it—put it into a format such that the browser can understand it, but a spider sent out by a spammer can't. To learn more about this, search on Google for "email" + "obfuscator."

INCLUDING IMAGES AND MEDIA

8

Image and media files convey an important amount of the message of your Web site. Depending on your site, you may even get most of your message across with pictures and moving media, such as video and animation. Most sites, however, use images to supplement the text, which is the main source of information and interest to your site's visitors.

On the other hand, we've all seen Web sites that suffer from graphic overkill. There's a balancing act between sites that use graphics to enhance the message and those that use images to bludgeon the visitor into submission. Just think of all the sites that you've seen that use images of green text on a red background, for instance, or the sites that are so proud of their "fabulous" graphic look that they relegate the text to microscopic type.

Dreamweaver has many abilities to place and modify images, as well as to control how text wraps around images. The program also does a great job of adding dynamic media to your pages, such as Flash animations and movie files, such as QuickTime and Windows Media. In this chapter, we'll cover how you can use Dreamweaver to add graphics and media files to your Web pages. You'll get to use your talents to add images to express and enhance your site's message.

Adding Images

Dreamweaver can place images on your Web page that come from your local hard disk or that are already on your Web site. By default, Dreamweaver 8 now prompts you to add *alternate text* to the image, which is text that is read aloud by screen reader software used by the visually disabled. If you have existing images on your pages that don't have alternate text, it's easy to add. You can, of course, easily delete images from your page.

To add an image to your page:

1. Click to place the insertion point in the document where you want the image to appear.

2. In the Common category of the Insert Bar, click the Image button (**Figure 8.1**).

   or

   Choose Insert > Image, or press Ctrl-Alt-I (Cmd-Opt-I).

   or

   Drag the icon of an image file from the Windows or Macintosh desktop into your document. If you choose this method, skip to Step 4.

   The Select Image Source dialog appears (**Figure 8.2**).

   By default, the dialog will be set to the images folder of your local site folder.

3. In the dialog, navigate to and select the file that you want to insert.

   A preview of the image appears in the Select Image Source dialog, with information below the image including the image's size in pixels, its graphic format, its file size, and the estimated time for the file to download (based on the Connection Speed pop-up menu in the Status Bar category of Dreamweaver's Preferences).

Image button

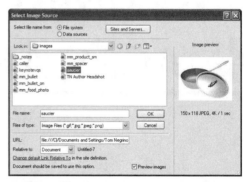

Figure 8.1 Begin inserting an image by clicking the Image button on the Insert Bar.

Figure 8.2 Navigate to the image you want in the Select Image Source dialog.

Figure 8.3 Dreamweaver lets you know that it will use an absolute file reference, rather than a relative reference to the image file, until you save the document.

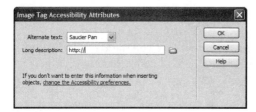

Figure 8.4 Enter alternate text for use by screen reader software used by the visually disabled.

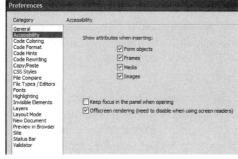

Figure 8.5 The image appears in the document.

Figure 8.6 You can set Accessibility settings in Dreamweaver's Preferences dialog.

4. Click OK (Choose).

If you have not already saved the document, Dreamweaver displays an alert letting you know that it can't use a document-relative path, and that it will use an absolute file reference until you save the file (**Figure 8.3**).

5. Click OK to dismiss the alert.

The Image Tag Accessibility Attributes dialog appears (**Figure 8.4**). This is the dialog you will use to add alternate text.

6. In the Alternate text text box, type the alternate text you want to use for the image.

7. (Optional) In the Long description text box, add a URL that leads to a page with a detailed description of the image.

8. Click OK.

The image appears on your page (**Figure 8.5**).

✔ Tips

■ In some browsers, an image's alternate text appears when you hover the mouse pointer over the image on the page.

■ The Image Tag Accessibility Attributes dialog only appears if the option for images has been set in the Accessibility category of the Preferences dialog (**Figure 8.6**). Because using alternate text is one of the commonly accepted Web best practices, the option is turned on by default. If you don't want Dreamweaver to prompt you for alternate text every time you insert an image, clear the Images check box in Preferences.

■ If you click Cancel in the Image Tag Accessibility Attributes dialog, the image appears on your page without alternate text. You can always add alternate text later using the Property Inspector.

About Graphic Formats

There are three main still (as opposed to moving) image formats used on the Web: JPEG, GIF, and PNG. If you are not already familiar with these formats, here's a quick rundown, in the order in which they were originally developed:

◆ **GIF,** which stands for Graphics Interchange Format, is a lower resolution graphics format with only eight bits of color information, which means that a GIF file can only contain up to 256 colors. GIFs are usually used for line drawings, flat cartoons, logos, and the like; in other words, images that don't need thousands or millions of colors (as would, for example, a photograph). There are two nice things about the GIF format. One is that it allows for *transparency*, which allows you to set one or more colors in the GIF file to be the same as the background color of the page. This allows for irregularly shaped objects to appear on your page and appear to be other than a rectangular image. The other useful feature of this format is the ability to add simple animation to images. A particular GIF file can contain multiple frames, and the file automatically steps through the frames to produce a rudimentary animation, like a flipbook.

◆ **JPEG,** which stands for Joint Photographic Experts Group, is a format that was developed specifically to handle photographic images. A JPEG file can use 24 bits of color information, which allows it to offer millions of colors. The JPEG format is "lossy," which means that it uses compression to reduce the file size. The look of the image depends on the amount of compression used to record it. High levels of compression will result in noticeable image degradation, because image information is actually being thrown away in order to reduce the file size. However, you can realize a significant reduction in file size at moderate levels of compression, with little or no visible effect, especially at the relatively low resolutions provided on Web pages. Unlike the GIF format, a JPEG file can contain neither transparency nor animation.

◆ **PNG,** or Portable Network Graphics, was created to replace the GIF format with an image format that didn't require a patent license to use (the owner of the GIF patent began enforcing the patent in 1995 and demanding royalty payments from software companies whose software created GIF files). PNG also improves upon GIF's 256-color limitation; a PNG file supports millions of colors and much better transparency options (but PNG does not offer animation). Macromedia Fireworks uses PNG as its native file format, and of course Dreamweaver fully supports the PNG format. Some very old Web browsers (for example, Internet Explorer 3) don't support PNG graphics, but there are so few of these browsers still in use that you generally shouldn't worry about it.

To add alternate text to an existing image on your page:

1. Click on an image to select it.

2. In the Alt text box in the Property Inspector (**Figure 8.7**), type the alternate text, then press Enter (Return).

   Dreamweaver adds the alternate text to the image.

To delete an image:

1. Click on an image to select it.

2. Press Backspace (Delete).

   The image disappears from the page.

✔ Tip

■ You can cut, copy, or paste images as you would with text.

Figure 8.7 You can also add alternate text in the Property Inspector.

Inserting Images from the Assets Panel

Any images that you've used on your site will be listed in the *Assets panel*, which is a tab in the same panel group as the Files panel. The Assets panel has buttons running down its left side that show you different asset categories (**Figure 8.8**). The first of these categories is Images. When you click the Images button in the panel, you get a list of all the images in your site. Clicking an item in the list shows you a preview of the image in the Assets panel's preview pane, allowing you to easily browse through the images. You can browse any of the other asset categories in the same fashion.

To insert an image from the Assets panel:

1. Click in your document to set the insertion point where you want the image to appear.

2. If it's not already showing, click the tab for the Assets panel, or choose Window > Assets, or press F11 (Opt-F11).

3. Click the Images button in the Assets panel.
   The images in your site appear in the Asset list.

4. Click on the image you want to insert.
   A preview of the image appears in the Assets panel's preview pane.

5. Click the Insert button at the bottom of the Assets panel.
   or
   Drag the image from the Asset list into the document.
   or
   Right-click the image you want in the Asset list, then choose Insert from the resulting shortcut menu.
   The image appears in your document.

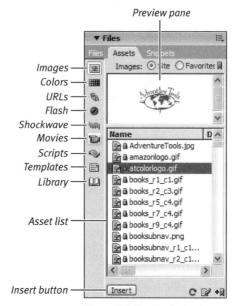

Preview pane

Images —
Colors —
URLs —
Flash —
Shockwave —
Movies —
Scripts —
Templates —
Library —

Asset list —

Insert button —

Figure 8.8 Choose the image that you want to work with in the Assets panel.

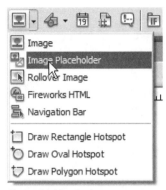

Figure 8.9 Use the Images pop-up menu on the Insert Bar to insert an image placeholder.

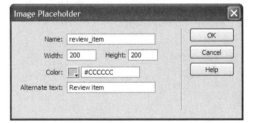

Figure 8.10 Use the Image Placeholder dialog to specify the placeholder's parameters.

Adding Image Placeholders

When you first work on a page, you'll often be creating pages without all of the finished elements, such as the text and images. That shouldn't stop you from working on the page's design, of course. You can always copy and paste, "The quick brown fox…" or similar text as a placeholder for the text that's to come, and Dreamweaver gives you the ability to insert image placeholders, as well. The placeholder lets you allot the space on the page for a future image, allowing you to position and size the placeholder and finish your design before you have all the content. When you are ready to turn the placeholder into the final image, all you have to do is double-click on the placeholder.

To insert an image placeholder:

1. Click in your document to set the insertion point where you want the image placeholder to appear.

2. Choose Insert > Image Objects > Image Placeholder.

    or

    In the Common category of the Insert Bar, choose Image Placeholder from the Images pop-up menu (**Figure 8.9**).

    The Image Placeholder dialog appears (**Figure 8.10**).

3. Fill out the Width and Height fields for the image placeholder (the units are pixels).

    The Name and Alternate text fields are optional; if you fill them out, the text will appear in the Property Inspector in the Name and Alt text boxes. You cannot use spaces in the Name field.

    The default color for an image placeholder is a light gray; if you want to change that color, click in the color well and choose a new color from the resulting color picker.

    Continues on next page

4. Click OK.

The new image placeholder appears in your document (**Figure 8.11**).

To replace the placeholder with an image:

1. Double-click the image placeholder.

The Select Image Source dialog appears (Figure 8.2).

2. Select the file that you want to insert.

3. Click OK (Choose).

The Image Tag Accessibility Attributes dialog appears.

4. In the Alternate text text box, type the alternate text you want to use for the image.

5. Click OK.

The image appears on your page.

✔ Tip

■ If you are also responsible for creating the images on your site, and you own Macromedia Fireworks, when you select an image placeholder you'll see a button in the Property Inspector that has the Fireworks logo and the word Create (**Figure 8.12**). Clicking this button launches Fireworks and creates a new image with the same dimensions as the placeholder. After you finish making the image in Fireworks, save the image in your site. You are then returned to Dreamweaver. The new image is inserted automatically in your document, replacing the image placeholder.

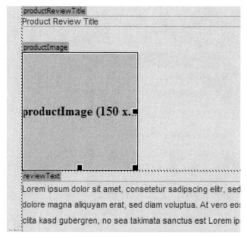

Figure 8.11 The image placeholder appears in the document, with its name and size (these are cut off if the image isn't big enough).

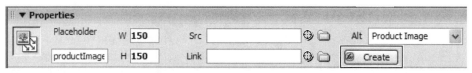

Figure 8.12 Click the Create button in the Property Inspector when an image placeholder is selected to launch Macromedia Fireworks so that you can replace the placeholder with a finished graphic.

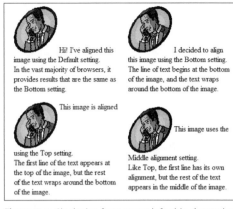

Figure 8.13 Clockwise from upper left, this shows the effects of the Default, Bottom, Middle, and Top vertical alignments.

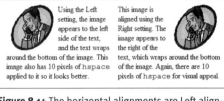

Figure 8.14 The horizontal alignments are Left alignment (left) and Right alignment (right).

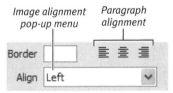

Figure 8.15 Don't confuse the paragraph alignment and image alignment settings in the Property Inspector.

■ When you use the Property Inspector to align images, Dreamweaver applies an alignment property to the `<img>` tag. While that's acceptable, you can also use CSS to align images, as described in Chapter 5.

Aligning Images

As with text, images can be aligned to the left, middle, or right side of a page. You also have some control over how text wraps around images.

Unless you've explicitly set up some way of laying out pictures and text (such as using CSS to position page elements, or using an invisible table), images appear *inline*, that is, in the flow of the text on the page. Because images are usually larger than the accompanying text, inline image settings can cause text to wrap in ways you might not expect.

There are four settings in the Property Inspector that you can use for vertical alignment: Default, Bottom, Middle, and Top (**Figure 8.13**). Two settings control horizontal alignment: Left and Right (**Figure 8.14**).

Make sure that you don't confuse the image alignment settings and the paragraph alignment settings (Left, Middle, and Right) that are also in the Property Inspector. The former apply to just images, and the latter apply to entire paragraphs.

To set image alignment:

1. Click to select the image you want to align.

2. In the Property Inspector, choose the alignment option you want from the Align pop-up menu (**Figure 8.15**).
   The image aligns as you command.

✔ Tips

■ The Property Inspector offers you four other alignment options: Baseline, TextTop, Absolute Middle, and Absolute Bottom. These are obsolete properties that don't work in all browsers. Don't use them.

Setting Image Properties

Besides alignment, there are several other properties that you can set for images using the Property Inspector (**Figure 8.16**):

◆ **Name** lets you name the image. This name is used to refer to the image in scripts, and you must enter a name for scripts to be able to manipulate the image, as you might want to do for a roll-over. You cannot use spaces or punctuation in an image name.

◆ **W** (for Width) is the width of the image in pixels.

◆ **H** (for Height) is the height of the image in pixels.

◆ **Src** (for Source) shows the path to the image file on your site.

◆ **Link** shows the destination if the image has a link to a URL.

◆ **Alt** shows the alternate text for the image.

◆ **Class** shows the CSS class, if any, that has been applied to the image.

◆ **Edit** is a group of tools that allows you to make adjustments to the image.

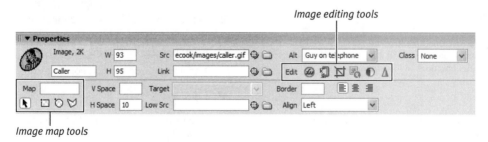

Image editing tools

Image map tools

Figure 8.16 You can make a variety of adjustments to an image in the Property Inspector.

◆ **Map** is a field and four tools that allow you to name and add an image map to the image. See "Creating Image Maps" later in this chapter for more information.

◆ **V Space** allows you to put vertical margins, in pixels, above and below the image.

◆ **H Space** allows you to put horizontal margins, in pixels, to the right and left of the image.

◆ **Target** specifies the frame or window in which the destination of a link should load. The pop-up menu next to the Target field shows the names of all the frames in the current frameset. There are also four other target possibilities. The _blank target loads the linked file into a new browser window. The _parent target loads the linked file into the parent frameset, the window of the frame that contains the link, or the full browser window. The _self target loads the linked file into the same frame or window as the link. This is the default choice. The _top target loads the linked file into the full browser window and removes all frames.

◆ **Low Src** allows you to specify a lower resolution image that will appear in the browser until the full image has finished loading. With the widespread use of broadband connections, this option has fallen out of favor.

◆ **Border** allows you to add a colored border, in pixels, around the entire image.

To set image properties:

1. Click to select the image to which you want to apply one or more properties.

2. In the Property Inspector, apply the property you want.

   The property is immediately applied.

✔ Tips

■ If you don't want to apply an interactive effect like a rollover to an image, you can leave its Name field blank.

■ The pop-up menu next to the Alt field has one choice, <empty>. You can use this attribute for images, such as spacer GIFs, that don't need to be read by screen readers for the visually disabled. Because accessibility guidelines state that all images should have alternate text, it's a good idea to apply this attribute to any images that are literally just taking up space.

■ Though you can add whitespace around images using the V space and H space properties, you'll have more control (and have valid XHTML pages) if you use CSS to provide margins for images.

■ You should also use the CSS border properties, rather than the Border option in the Property Inspector. You'll have more control over the kind and color of the border.

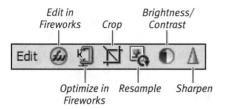

Edit in Fireworks *Crop* *Brightness/ Contrast*

Optimize in Fireworks *Resample* *Sharpen*

Figure 8.17 The Property Inspector gives you access to a variety of image editing tools.

Editing Images

When you're working with images on your site, you'll often want to tweak them to improve their looks. You could use an external image editing program, such as Adobe Photoshop or Macromedia Fireworks to do the job, but it's more convenient to work right in Dreamweaver for simple changes. For extensive modifications, you'll still need an external image editor, however.

The Property Inspector gives you six buttons that allow you to edit an image (**Figure 8.17**). Two of the buttons, Edit and Optimize in Fireworks, hand the image off to Fireworks (if you own it) for editing and optimization for the Web. Using these buttons is covered in Chapter 14, "Working with Other Applications."

The other four buttons let you make quick image adjustments right in Dreamweaver. They are: Crop, which lets you trim away portions of an image; Resample, which adds or subtracts pixels from an image that has been resized (this reduces the image size for better download performance); Brightness and Contrast, which allows you to correct images that are too dark or too light; and Sharpen, which changes the contrast of the edges inside an image, making it appear to be more in focus.

✔ Tips

- You can only edit JPEG and GIF image files with Dreamweaver's built-in tools.

- If you select an image and the image editing tools are grayed out, it's probably because you enabled Check In/Check Out for your site, and you need to check out the file for editing. For more about Check In/Check Out, see Chapter 16.

- To halt the editing process after you begin it and leave the image unchanged, press the Esc key.

To crop an image:

1. Select the image that you want to crop.

2. In the Property Inspector, click the Crop button.

   or

   Choose Modify > Image > Crop.

3. Dreamweaver puts up an alert dialog letting you know that the changes you will be making to the image are permanent, but that you can still use Undo to back away from the changes. Click OK.

   A crop selection box with eight resize handles appears within the image. Parts of the image outside of the crop selection box are dimmed (**Figure 8.18**).

4. Click and drag the crop selection box to move it around the image, and resize the box by dragging any of its selection handles, until you have the portion of the image you want to keep inside the box.

5. To complete the crop, press Enter (Return).

   or

   Double-click inside the crop selection box. Dreamweaver trims the image.

To resize and resample an image:

1. Select the image that you want to change.

2. Using the image's resize handles, make the image larger or smaller.

   or

   Use the W or H text boxes in the Property Inspector to resize the image numerically.

   The image resizes, and the Resample button in the Property Inspector becomes available for use.

Figure 8.18 The part of the image outside the selection rectangle will be cropped out.

EDITING IMAGES

Figure 8.19 Drag the sliders in the Brightness/Contrast dialog to change the intensity of the image.

3. In the Property Inspector, click the Resample button.

or

Choose Modify > Image > Resample.

Dreamweaver resamples the image. On many images, the effect is quite subtle.

To adjust the brightness and contrast of an image:

1. Select the image that you want to adjust.

2. In the Property Inspector, click the Brightness and Contrast button.

or

Choose Modify > Image > Brightness/Contrast.

The Brightness/Contrast dialog appears (**Figure 8.19**).

3. If it isn't already checked, select the Preview check box.

This makes adjusting the image a little slower, but it allows you to see the effects of your changes on the image as you make them.

4. Move the Brightness and the Contrast sliders until the picture looks the way you want it.

or

Enter a numeric value in the text boxes next to Brightness and Contrast. The sliders begin in the middle of the range, and the acceptable range for each slider is from -100 to 100.

5. Click OK.

To sharpen an image:

1. Select the image that you want to sharpen.

2. In the Property Inspector, click the Sharpen button.

   or

   Choose Modify > Image > Sharpen.
   The Sharpen dialog appears (**Figure 8.20**).

3. If it isn't already checked, select the Preview check box.

   This makes sharpening the image a bit slower, but it allows you to see the effects of your changes on the image as you make them.

4. Move the Sharpness slider until the picture looks the way you want it.

   or

   Enter a numeric value in the text box next to Sharpness. The slider begins at zero and goes to 10.

5. Click OK.

✔ Tip

- Use a light hand when using the Sharpen tool. Over-sharpening an image often makes it look unnatural, with edges in the picture that look too prominent, or even oddly outlined (**Figure 8.21**).

Figure 8.20 Sharpening an image often brings out important detail that isn't as noticeable in the unsharpened image.

Figure 8.21 Over-sharpening an image (bottom) can make items in the image look weird.

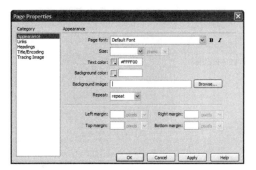

Figure 8.22 Use the Page Properties dialog to insert a background image.

Adding a Background Image

Most pages use a solid color or no color as their background, but sometimes you may want to use an image as the background of your page. This image will underlie all of the text and other images on your page. Though background images are a bit of a dated look, they can still be used on modern pages, if you use them well.

Dreamweaver 8 creates background images by creating a CSS rule to redefine the <body> tag. You can do this by creating the rule manually (see Chapter 5 for details on how to do that), but it's easier to use the Page Properties dialog.

To add a background image to your page:

1. Open the page to which you want to add the background image.

2. In the Property Inspector, click the Page Properties button.

   or

   Choose Modify > Page Properties, or press Ctrl-J (Cmd-J).

   The Page Properties dialog appears (**Figure 8.22**).

3. In the Appearance category of the dialog, click the Browse button next to "Background image."

   The Select Image Source dialog appears.

4. Navigate to and select the image you want to use as the background image, then click OK (Choose).

   Continues on next page

5. From the Repeat pop-up menu in the Page Properties dialog, choose how you want the image to be repeated on the page (if it is smaller than the page):

   ▲ **repeat** tiles the image across and down the page, filling the page.

   ▲ **repeat-x** tiles the image across the top of the page.

   ▲ **repeat-y** tiles the image down the left edge of the page.

   ▲ **no-repeat** places the image on the page just once, in the upper-left corner of the page.

6. To see how the image will appear on the page, click the Apply button.

   The background image appears on the page (**Figure 8.23**).

7. Click OK.

✔ Tip

■ Before CSS, designers set background images by adding a `background` attribute to the `<body>` tag. If you are asked to work on older sites, one of the renovations you should make is to remove this old attribute and replace it with a CSS rule.

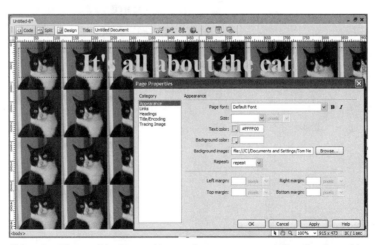

Figure 8.23 The small background image of my cat was repeated endlessly on this page by setting "repeat."

Figure 8.24 We'll turn this map of four Western states into an image map.

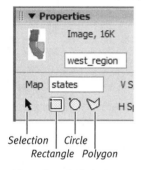

Selection | *Circle*
Rectangle | *Polygon*

Figure 8.25 Both the image and the image map have been named in this figure.

Creating Image Maps

It's easy to add a link to an image; just select the image and use the Link text box in the Property Inspector to define the link's destination. But what if you wanted to have different parts of an image link to different pages? You'll need an *image map*. With an image map, you can define areas of the image as *hotspots*, and each hotspot has its own link.

To create an image map:

1. Select the image you want to turn into an image map.

   In this example, we're using a map of Washington, Oregon, California, and Nevada (**Figure 8.24**). We'll add hotspots to each of the states.

2. In the Map text box of the Property Inspector, enter a name for the image map (**Figure 8.25**).

   The name cannot begin with a number and can only contain letters, numbers, or the underscore character.

3. Use the Rectangle, Circle, or Polygon tools to draw a hotspot over part of your image.

   The tool you use depends on the shape of the area that you want to make into a hotspot. For example, we used the Rectangle tool to create the hotspots for Washington and Oregon, and the Polygon tool to create the hotspots for California and Nevada.

Continues on next page

Dreamweaver shows the hotspot as a light blue area overlaid on your image (**Figure 8.26**). The blue highlighting won't show up on your Web pages.

4. When a hotspot is selected, the Property Inspector shows properties for the hotspot (**Figure 8.27**). Use the Link field to attach a link to the hotspot.

5. (Optional) Use the Target pop-up menu to target the destination of the link.

   If you need more information about the use of the Link or Target controls, see Chapter 7.

6. Enter the alternate text for the hotspot in the Alt field.

7. Repeat steps 3-6 for each of the other areas on the image you want to turn into hotspots.

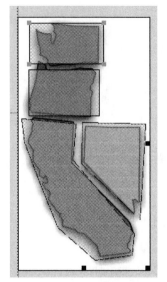

Figure 8.26 Each of the state images has been overlaid with a hotspot.

✔ Tips

■ To change the properties of a hotspot, use the hotspot selection tool to select the hotspot, then make changes in the Property Inspector.

■ You can resize and reshape hotspots; just select the hotspot with the hotspot selection tool, then click and drag one of the selection handles that appear at the corners of the hotspot.

■ Image maps have somewhat fallen out of favor recently; you see more sites using interactive Flash movies to provide users the benefits of clickable images.

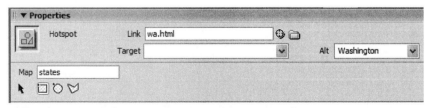

Figure 8.27 Add the link for a hotspot in the Property Inspector.

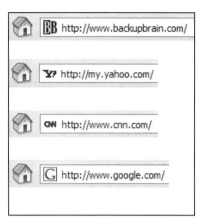

Figure 8.28 Here are the favicons for four different sites, as seen in Mozilla Firefox.

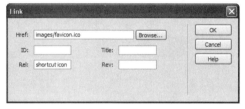

Figure 8.29 The Link dialog allows you to add the path to the favicon file and its alternate text.

Adding a Favicon

One of the little touches that will finish off your Web site is if you add a *favicon*, that little icon that appears in the address bar of a browser when your site loads (**Figure 8.28**). A favicon is another way to underscore your site's brand identification, and often represents the logo of the organization that runs the site. Favicons are only 16 by 16 pixels large, and virtually all modern Web browsers support them.

Before you can add a favicon to the index page of your site, you'll need to create one. There are dedicated favicon editing programs available for purchase, but we prefer to use one of the free online tools that converts a JPEG or GIF file into a favicon for you, such as the ones at www.chami.com/html-kit/services/favicon/, or http://tools.dynamicdrive.com/favicon/.

Once you have your favicon file, which must be named favicon.ico, you'll add it to your site's pages in Dreamweaver. You'll do that with the <link> tag, which, while more often used for linking CSS style sheets, works fine for this purpose, too.

To add a favicon to your page:

1. Obtain your favicon.ico file, and move it into your local site folder.

   Because it's an image, it makes sense to us to put the favicon file into the images folder, but you can put it anywhere you want in the local site folder.

2. Open the page to which you want to add the link to the favicon.

3. Choose Insert > HTML > Head Tags > Link. The Link dialog appears (**Figure 8.29**).

Continues on next page

4. In the Href text box, enter the path to the `favicon.ico` file.

or

Click the Browse button to open the Select File dialog. Navigate to the `favicon.ico` file and click OK (Choose).

5. In the Rel text box, type "shortcut icon" (don't include the quotes).

6. Click OK, then save the page by choosing File > Save.

After you next synchronize your local site to the remote site, the favicon will show up when you load the page in a Web browser.

✔ Tip

■ You must repeat the process of adding the link to the favicon on every page in your site. If your site uses templates, adding the link to a template file will automatically add it to all the pages based on that template. For more about using templates, see Chapter 13.

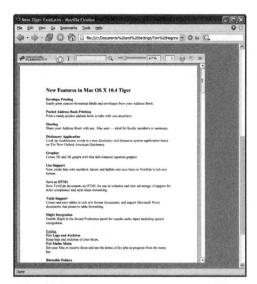

Figure 8.30 A FlashPaper file is great for displaying documents electronically.

Adding Flash, Shockwave, and FlashPaper

Because Macromedia is the maker of the Flash multimedia format, it should come as no surprise that Dreamweaver makes it easy to add many different varieties of Flash objects to your pages. The three kinds we'll discuss here are *Flash animations*, *Shockwave animations*, and *FlashPaper*. A Flash animation is a Flash file that has been optimized for playback on the Web. This kind of file has the .swf extension. You can play this animation in Dreamweaver, or in a Web browser. A Shockwave file is an animation format very similar to a Flash file, but it is created by Macromedia Director, rather than Macromedia Flash.

A FlashPaper document is a Flash file that has been optimized to display printed documents, in a similar manner to the Adobe Acrobat format (**Figure 8.30**). A FlashPaper file can be displayed by any Web browser that has the free Flash Player; Macromedia claims that more than 98% of Internet users have the Flash Player.

✔ Tip

- Files with the .fla extension are Flash document files that can only be opened in the Flash program itself. These sorts of files can't be played in Dreamweaver or Web browsers.

To insert a Flash or Shockwave animation:

1. Click to set the insertion point where you want the Flash or Shockwave animation to appear.

2. Choose Insert > Media > Flash, or press Ctrl-Alt-F (Cmd-Opt-F).

    or

    Choose Insert > Media > Shockwave, or press Ctrl-Alt-D (Cmd-Opt-D).

    The Select File dialog appears.

3. Navigate to the file you want, select it, and click OK (Choose).

    The Object Tag Accessibility Attributes dialog appears (**Figure 8.31**).

4. Enter alternate text in the Title field of the dialog.

5. Click OK.

    Dreamweaver inserts the animation file into your document as a placeholder.

✔ Tip

■ The Access Key and Tab Index fields in the Object Tag Accessibility Attributes dialog are used with forms. See the "Labeling Your Fields" sidebar in Chapter 10 for more information.

To play the animation placeholder in Dreamweaver:

1. Select the placeholder.

    Selection handles appear at the edges of the placeholder.

2. Click the Play button in the Property Inspector (**Figure 8.32**).

    Dreamweaver plays the animation file in the document window.

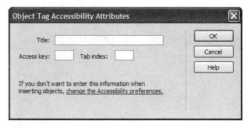

Figure 8.31 Add alternate text for the Flash or Shockwave file in the Object Tag Accessibility Attributes dialog.

Animation placeholder

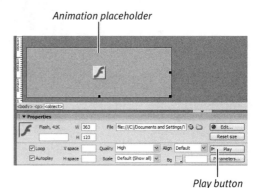

Play button

Figure 8.32 Use the Play button in the Property Inspector to preview your animation.

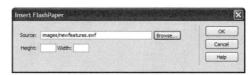

Figure 8.33 Define the location and size of the FlashPaper file in this dialog.

How FlashPaper Works

FlashPaper documents are converted into the Flash file format using a printer driver called the FlashPaper Printer that is installed when you install Macromedia Contribute 3 for Windows or Macintosh (Contribute is part of the Studio 8 package). The FlashPaper document can be aligned and resized within a Dreamweaver document as you would any other graphic image. Since it is Flash, it can be resized without a loss of quality.

Because the Flash file format is especially efficient, a FlashPaper document is usually smaller, often dramatically so, than the source document. For example, in tests that we ran, the FlashPaper version of an 8 Mb Adobe Acrobat (PDF) document was only 2.6 Mb in size. A 584 Kb Word document ended up as a 182 Kb FlashPaper file. There is a big benefit to smaller download sizes for documents, as it means more users will be likely to wait while the document downloads.

While you can use FlashPaper in place of a PDF file in many applications, FlashPaper is not a complete replacement for PDF files. PDF has many collaboration and security features that FlashPaper lacks, such as annotation, digital signatures, and encryption. But like PDF, FlashPaper allows you to search for text within the FlashPaper document. You can also select and copy text.

Another limitation is that you cannot edit a FlashPaper document. If you need to update the document, you must make changes to the document you originally converted, then convert it again to a FlashPaper document.

To add a FlashPaper document:

1. Click to set the insertion point where you want the FlashPaper document to appear.

2. Choose Insert > Media > FlashPaper.
   or
   In the Common category of the Insert Bar, choose FlashPaper from the Media pop-up menu.
   The Insert FlashPaper dialog appears (**Figure 8.33**).

3. Click the Browse button in the dialog.
   The Select File dialog appears.

4. Navigate to the file you want, select it, and click OK (Choose).
   You return to the Insert FlashPaper dialog.

5. (Optional) Set the Height and Width (in pixels) you want for the FlashPaper document.

6. Click OK.
   The Object Tag Accessibility Attributes dialog appears.

7. Enter alternate text in the Title field of the dialog.

8. Click OK.
   Dreamweaver inserts the FlashPaper file into your document as a placeholder.

✔ Tip

- You can view a preview of the FlashPaper file in Dreamweaver by selecting it and clicking the Play button in the Property Inspector, but you can only get the full functionality of FlashPaper by viewing it in a browser.

ADDING FLASH, SHOCKWAVE, AND FLASHPAPER

Inserting Flash Text

It's a fairly common thing to create things like text headlines in a graphics program such as Photoshop or Fireworks. By doing the text as a graphic, the designer has more flexibility and control over the use of fonts, text effects, and colors. Of course, you can't select the text, so it can't be copied, which is a drawback. Graphics also take longer to download than text. But the benefit of being able to get the exact look you need sometimes offsets those drawbacks.

Rather than using a separate graphics program to create text, Dreamweaver allows you to create graphical text as a Flash file, which the program refers to as *Flash text*. The Flash file is resizable without a loss of quality, and it is often smaller than an equivalent graphic rendered as a GIF or JPEG file, resulting in faster download times.

✔ Tip

- Dreamweaver can render any TrueType font on your system into Flash text, but it does not work with PostScript fonts.

Figure 8.34 You can partially preview the look of the Flash text while creating it in this dialog.

To add Flash text:

1. Click to place the insertion point where you want the Flash text to appear.

2. Choose Insert > Media > Flash Text.

   or

   In the Common category of the Insert Bar, choose Flash Text from the Media pop-up menu.

   The Insert Flash Text dialog appears (**Figure 8.34**). Many of the choices in this dialog are optional; at a bare minimum you will need to enter text in the Text field and choose the font and size.

3. In the Text field, type the text that you want to turn into Flash text. To start a new line, press Enter (Return).

   By entering the text first, you'll be able to see how the text will look in the font that you've chosen. This field, however, doesn't show you a preview of the font size, bold, italic, or text color.

4. From the Font pop-up menu, choose the font.

   Your entry in the Text field changes to reflect the font you chose.

5. In the Size field, enter the font size in pixels.

6. If desired, click either or both the Bold or Italic button.

7. By default, the text is left aligned. If you want center or right alignment for the Flash text, click the appropriate button.

   This alignment refers not to the alignment of the text on the page, but rather the alignment of text within the Flash graphic image you are creating.

8. If you want to change the text color, click the color well next to Color, then set the color from the resulting color picker.

   Continues on next page

INSERTING FLASH TEXT

9. If you want the Flash text to change color when the user positions the mouse cursor over the text, click the color well next to Rollover color, then set the color from the resulting color picker.

10. If you want the Flash text to be a link, enter the destination of the link in the Link field. Or, click the Browse button to select the link's destination.

11. Change the target of the link with a choice from the Target pop-up menu.

12. If you want to change the background color of the Flash text, click the color well next to Bg color, then set the color from the resulting color picker.

   You will usually want to change this color to match the background color of the page; if you do not, the background of the Flash text will be white.

13. In the Save as field, enter a name for the Flash text. If you want to save the Flash file in a particular place in your site (we usually save them in the images folder), click the Browse button to bring up a save dialog.

14. To see how your Flash text will appear, click the Apply button.

   The Flash text appears in the document window (**Figure 8.35**).

15. If you want to make further changes, do so in the Insert Flash Text dialog. Otherwise, click OK to save your changes and dismiss the dialog.

   The Flash Accessibility Attributes dialog appears (**Figure 8.36**).

16. Enter alternate text for the Flash text in the Title field.

17. Click OK.

Figure 8.35 After clicking the Apply button, the Flash text appears in the document window.

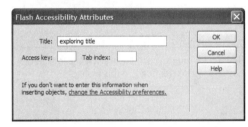

Figure 8.36 Enter the alternate text for the Flash text graphic in this dialog.

To edit Flash text:

1. Double-click the Flash text you want to change.

   The Insert Flash Text dialog appears.

2. Make changes in the dialog as needed, then click OK.

✔ Tips

- You can resize the Flash text by selecting it and dragging its selection handles. If you hold down the Shift key while dragging the lower-right handle, the image will resize proportionately.

- You can return the Flash text to its original dimensions by selecting it and clicking the Reset size button in the Property Inspector.

Adding Flash Buttons

If you want to add interactivity to your Web site, one way to do it is to create button images in a graphics program such as Fireworks or Photoshop, then apply rollover behaviors in either of those programs or in Dreamweaver. A rollover behavior will make the button's appearance change when the user puts his mouse cursor over the button. For more information about adding rollover behaviors, see Chapter 12.

Dreamweaver has a variety of attractive predesigned animated buttons created in Flash that you can place on your page with the Flash buttons feature. These buttons are small interactive Flash movies.

To add Flash buttons:

1. Click to place the insertion point where you want the Flash button to appear.

2. Choose Insert > Media > Flash Button.

   or

   In the Common category of the Insert Bar, choose Flash Button from the Media pop-up menu.

   The Insert Flash Button dialog appears (**Figure 8.37**).

3. Choose the style of Flash button you want from the scrolling Style list.

   When you select a style from the list, a preview of the button appears in the Sample section of the dialog.

4. Enter the text that you want to appear in the button in the Button text field.

5. Adjust the button text by choosing a font from the Font pop-up menu and choosing the font size with the Size text box.

Figure 8.37 It's easy to make great-looking animated buttons with the Flash Button tool.

Figure 8.38 When you click the Apply button, the Flash button (in this case the Show Cart button) appears in your document.

6. You will always want your Flash button to be a link, so enter the destination of the link in the Link field. You can also click the Browse button to select the link's destination.

7. Change the target of the link with a choice from the Target pop-up menu.

8. If you want to change the background color of the Flash button, click the color well next to Bg color, then set the color from the resulting color picker.

   You will usually want to change this color to match the background color of the page; if you do not, the background of the Flash button will be white.

9. In the Save as field, enter a name for the Flash button. If you want to save the Flash file in a particular place in your site (we usually save them in the images folder), click the Browse button to bring up a save dialog.

10. To see how your Flash button will appear, click the Apply button.

    The Flash button appears in the document window (**Figure 8.38**).

11. If you want to make further changes, do so in the Insert Flash Button dialog. Otherwise, click OK to save your changes and dismiss the dialog.

    The Flash Accessibility Attributes dialog appears.

12. Enter alternate text for the Flash text in the Title field.

13. Click OK.

To edit Flash buttons:

1. Double-click the Flash button you want to change.

   The Insert Flash Button dialog appears.

2. Make changes in the dialog as needed, then click OK.

Adding Flash Video

Flash video is a way of showing video on your Web site. Like other video formats, such as QuickTime, Windows Media, and RealVideo, Flash video can show you full-motion video in context on your Web page. But one of the big advantages of Flash video is that most browsers already have the Flash plug-in installed, so your video is likely to be viewable by more people.

Before you can put a Flash video file on your Web page, you must, of course, convert your video to the Flash video format, which has the .flv extension. Macromedia Studio 8 includes the Flash 8 Video Encoder, which can convert QuickTime, DV, MPEG, AVI, and Windows Media files into Flash video.

To insert a Flash video file:

1. Click to place the insertion point where you want the Flash video file to appear.

2. Choose Insert > Media > Flash Video.

   or

   In the Common category of the Insert Bar, choose Flash Video from the Media pop-up menu.

   The Insert Flash Video dialog appears (**Figure 8.39**).

3. From the Video type pop-up menu, choose either Progressive Download Video or Streaming Video.

   You will most often choose Progressive Download Video, which downloads the Flash video file to the user's hard disk and then plays it. The Streaming Video choice requires extra server-side software (Macromedia Flash Communication Server).

4. In the URL field, enter the path to the Flash video file. You can instead click the Browse button, which brings up the Select File dialog, which allows you to navigate to select the video file.

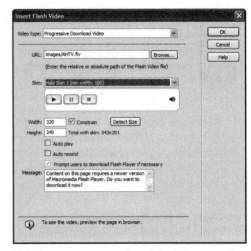

Figure 8.39 You get a preview of the different media controllers available to you for Flash video directly below the Skin pop-up menu.

✔ Tip

- There are many variables involved in converting one kind of video file to another, and a complete discussion is way beyond the scope of this book. Instead, we suggest that you begin learning more about Flash video on the Macromedia Web site at www.macromedia.com/devnet/flash/ articles/video_guide.html.

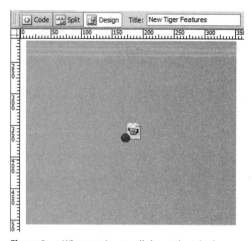

Figure 8.40 When you're set all the options in the Insert Flash Video dialog, a placeholder appears in the document window.

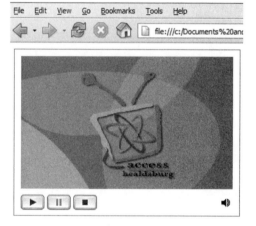

Figure 8.41 When you preview the Flash video in a Web browser, you can see and hear the video playing.

5. From the Skin pop-up menu, choose the kind of video controller you want to appear with the video.

6. Enter the Width and Height (in pixels) that you want to use to display the video.

   or

   Click the Detect Size button, which attempts to read the Flash video file and figure out what size it is. Depending on your video, this option may not work, but it is worth trying.

7. If you want the video to automatically begin playing when the Web page is loaded, select the Auto play check box.

8. If you want playback control to automatically return to the starting position after the video finishes playing, select the Auto rewind check box.

9. Click OK.

   A placeholder for the Flash video file appears on your page (**Figure 8.40**). You cannot play the Flash video file inside Dreamweaver. Instead, you must preview the page and the video in a Web browser (**Figure 8.41**).

To edit a Flash video file's properties:

1. Click to select the Flash video file.

2. In the Property Inspector, make the changes you want (**Figure 8.42**).

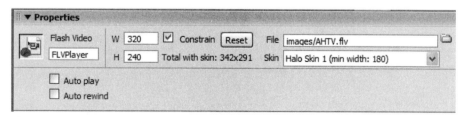

Figure 8.42 Adjust the settings for a Flash video file in the Property Inspector.

Adding QuickTime and Other Media

Figure 8.43 Dreamweaver puts a placeholder for the plug-in media file in the document window.

Video and audio files, with the exception of the various flavors of Flash media, are handled by Dreamweaver as *plug-in media*. That's because these files need plug-in software to be installed in a Web browser in order to be played. The most common plug-in media are QuickTime, Windows Media, RealAudio or RealVideo, and MP3 audio files.

To add plug-in media files:

1. Click to place the insertion point where you want the media file to appear.

2. Choose Insert > Media > Plugin.

   or

   In the Common category of the Insert Bar, choose Plugin from the Media pop-up menu.

   The Select File dialog appears.

3. Navigate to and select the media file you want, then click OK (Choose).

   A placeholder for the plug-in file appears on your page (**Figure 8.43**).

To preview your media file:

1. Select the placeholder for the media file.

2. In the Property Inspector, click the Play button.

   This may not work if Dreamweaver can't find the appropriate plug-in on your system. In that case, save the page and preview the file in a Web browser.

✔ Tip

■ Dreamweaver creates the placeholder file as a small square icon on the page. When you preview the file, that icon will be replaced by the media file controller, which has the playback controls. The small size of the icon won't allow you to use the media controller, so before you preview the file, click on the placeholder icon and use its selection handles to make it wide enough so that you can see the entire media controller.

To edit a plug-in file's properties:

1. Click to select the plug-in file.

2. In the Property Inspector, make the changes you want (**Figure 8.44**).

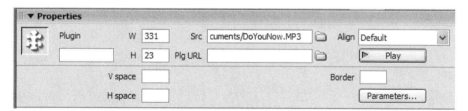

Figure 8.44 You can adjust the settings for a plug-in media file in the Property Inspector.

INSERTING TABLES

You will often use tables on Web pages to present *tabular information*—that is, data best presented in the form of rows and columns. You can also use tables for layout—that is, to align text and images on the page—but as you'll see later in the chapter, in most cases you should be using CSS for layout instead.

In this chapter, you'll learn how to create and format tables, ensure that tables and their content look the way you intend, work with Dreamweaver's many table tools, and you'll learn how to save time when you're using tables.

Moving Away from Tables for Layout

One of the most widespread uses for a table is as a layout device (sometimes called *layout tables*). You can create tables on your page, then use the table cells to contain the text and images on the page. Because you have good control over the size of the cells and the position of their boundaries, you can line up and lay out elements on the page with precision, though it often requires some extremely complex tables. By hiding the borders of the table cells, the site visitor doesn't notice the tables. This, up until the last few years, is how most nicely designed Web pages you've seen were created.

However, there are many problems with using tables for layout. First of all, the table has nothing to do with the *content* of the page (the information your visitor sees); all it does is affect the *presentation* of the content. One of the biggest benefits of CSS is that it *separates* content from presentation. As a result, you can completely redesign CSS-based sites largely by changing one file, the style sheet. If your presentation is mixed with your content, as it is with a table-based layout, it makes site redesigns difficult and expensive. Similarly, tables make it difficult to maintain visual consistency throughout a site (because the layout tables on different pages may not be the same).

So that's what is wrong with tables from the standpoint of the Web designer, but there are problems for the site visitor, too. Tables make the size of an HTML page unnecessarily large (costing you extra bandwidth charges), and site visitors must download the layout tables on every page they visit in the site (ditto). Pages load slower than with a CSS-based layout, and slow page loads drive visitors away. Table-based pages are also much more difficult to read by users with disabilities and by visitors using cell phones and PDAs.

Tables were necessary for good-looking Web sites back in 1997, because the Web browsers of the day had many limitations, not the least of which was that none of them supported the then-emerging CSS standards for layout. But all modern browsers have reasonably good support for using CSS for layout (though ironically, the most widely used browser as of this writing, Microsoft Internet Explorer 6 for Windows, lags well behind other browsers such as Mozilla Firefox, Apple Safari, and Opera). The vast majority of users of the Web now use Web browsers that can handle CSS-based layouts just fine.

As a result, you can (and should!) use Dreamweaver to build great-looking, CSS-based sites that are faster to load, accessible for everyone, and easier for you to redesign and maintain. To learn more about laying out your pages with CSS, see Chapter 6.

MOVING AWAY FROM TABLES FOR LAYOUT

Because table-based layout has been so pervasive for almost a decade, Dreamweaver still has tools that make it easy for you to create page layouts with tables. You'll find more about those tools at the end of this chapter in the "Using Table Layout Mode" section. We've covered these tools for completeness, even though we don't recommend that you use tables for layout. Also, we figure you may be coming here after reading some other books, such as *Creating a Web Page in Dreamweaver: Visual QuickProject Guide*, which solely uses the table-based layout method. If all you know is table-based layout, you might wonder why we didn't cover it, so we have briefly done that to avoid confusion between books that use older layout methods and this book.

By the way, even with sites that use tables for layout, you can still use CSS to style the text inside the tables. Some CSS markup is devoted to styling text, and some is devoted to positioning elements on the page. You can use the styling kind of CSS to make your text look good, even inside a table. You just shouldn't mix the positioning elements of CSS with tables; choose one method or the other for positioning elements on your pages.

MOVING AWAY FROM TABLES FOR LAYOUT

Creating a Table

Tables typically consist of one or more rows and one or more columns. Each rectangular area at the intersection of a row and column is called a *cell*. Cells contain the page's text or images, and items within a cell can't extend past the cell's boundaries.

You can insert a table anywhere on a page, even within another table (this is called *nesting* a table). By default, Dreamweaver creates tables with three rows and three columns, but you can easily change that format during the process of inserting the table. After you do make changes, Dreamweaver remembers them and uses them as the defaults for the next table you create.

To add a table to your page:

1. Place the insertion point where you want the table to appear.

2. On the Layout category of the Insert Bar, click the Table button (**Figure 9.1**).

or

Continues on next page

Table button

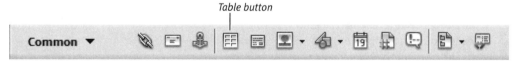

Figure 9.1 You'll use the Common category of the Insert Bar to add tables to your pages.

CREATING A TABLE

Choose Insert > Table, or press Ctrl-Alt-T (Cmd-Opt-T).

The Table dialog appears (**Figure 9.2**).

3. Enter the number of rows you want in the table, and press Tab.

4. Enter the number of columns you want in the table, and press Tab.

5. In the "Table width" text box, enter a number that will either be in pixels or a percentage of the page width, then choose the units from the pop-up menu to the right of the text box (**Figure 9.3**).

6. Set one or more (or none) of the following (see the "Anatomy of a Table" sidebar for explanations of the settings):

   ▲ Enter a figure in the "Border thickness" text box for the size of the border, in pixels, that will be displayed between cells.

   ▲ Enter a figure in the "Cell padding" text box for the amount of space, in pixels, between the content in the cells and the cell border.

   ▲ Enter a figure in the "Cell spacing" text box for the number of pixels of space between cells.

7. In the Header section, choose the kind of header you want: None, Left, Top, or Both. The icons for the headers tell you what each choice looks like.

8. (Optional) In the Accessibility section, enter a caption for the table, then choose how you want the caption to be displayed by choosing from the "Align caption" pop-up menu. Your choices are Default, Top, Bottom, Left, or Right. Caption text will appear in all browsers. If you enter text in the Summary text box, that text will appear only in screen readers for the visually disabled.

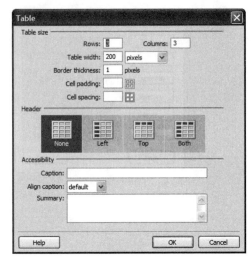

Figure 9.2 The Table dialog lets you get started building a table.

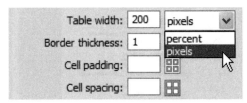

Figure 9.3 You can set the width of your table either in pixels or as a percentage of the browser page width.

Figure 9.4 The green dimension lines tell you the width of the table in pixels. The dimension lines above each column do not show pixel widths in this figure because the columns are set to be a percentage of the table width.

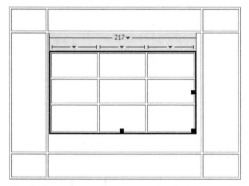

Figure 9.5 You can nest a second table inside any cell of an existing table.

9. Click OK.

The table appears in your page (**Figure 9.4**). When a table is selected, as in the figure, or when the insertion point is in a table cell, Dreamweaver shows green dimension lines above the table. The top line shows the width of the table in pixels. Each column also has a dimension line, which shows the width of the column in pixels if you have set a fixed width for the column. Columns with widths relative to the table width show dimension lines (so you can easily see each column) without pixel values. These dimension lines appear only in Dreamweaver's Design view, not in a Web browser.

✔ Tips

- To insert a table within a table, place the insertion point inside a cell of an existing table, then choose either of the methods in step 2. The new table appears inside the first table (**Figure 9.5**).

- You don't have to get the number of rows and columns right the first time; you can always add or subtract them later. See the sections "Adding Rows and Columns" and "Deleting Table Elements" later in this chapter.

- If you don't want to see the dimension lines above tables, you can turn them off by choosing View > Visual Aids > Table Widths, which removes the checkmark from the menu item.

- Table captions appear above or below (or next to) the table, and are actually part of the table. When you move the table, the caption moves with it. To edit a caption, select it and type over the existing text. To change the alignment of the caption, place the insertion point in the caption, then right-click and pick one of the choices from the Align submenu in the resulting shortcut menu.

CREATING A TABLE

Anatomy of a Table

Besides rows and columns, tables have several other attributes that affect how they look. You'll find controls for these items in the Property Inspector when you have selected a table.

Border thickness is the width of the border around the table, in pixels (**Figure 9.6**). Dreamweaver sets it to one pixel by default, which results in a thin border. If the border thickness is set to a nonzero amount, you will also see a border between table cells. You'll often see the border thickness set to zero on pages that are using tables for page layout and the designer doesn't want you to see borders. Borders with zero thickness appear in Design view with dotted borders.

Cell padding is the amount of space, in pixels, between a cell's borders and its content (**Figure 9.7**). Use this setting to give cell content more breathing room within cells. If you don't specify a number here, most browsers use a default value of one pixel.

Cell spacing is the amount of space between each table cell, also measured in pixels (**Figure 9.8**). If you don't specify a number here, most browsers use a default value of two pixels. Wide cell spacing gives the table a look that is very 1996, so use this setting with care.

Border color is the color of the border around the table and between the table's cells.

Background color is the color of the cell's contents (though you can set the color of text in the cell separately). You can also use the Text Color attributes to color text within the cell.

Background image allows you to use an image, rather than just a color, as the background for a table.

Table header tags part of the table as a header. The header is formatted as bold and centered, but more important, it has the `<th>` HTML tag, which allows screen readers used by visually disabled users to correctly read the table. It's better to use a table header tag in Dreamweaver than to manually make cells bold and centered.

Sales Territory	1st Quarter	2nd Quarter
North	$2,700	$2,850
East	$3,700	$4,200
South	$2,200	$2,100
West	$2,900	$3,200

Sales Territory	1st Quarter	2nd Quarter
North	$2,700	$2,850
East	$3,700	$4,200
South	$2,200	$2,100
West	$2,900	$3,200

Sales Territory	1st Quarter	2nd Quarter
North	$2,700	$2,850
East	$3,700	$4,200
South	$2,200	$2,100
West	$2,900	$3,200

Figure 9.6 The same table with a border thickness of zero pixels (top), one pixel (middle), and 10 pixels (bottom). Cell padding and cell spacing are set to zero.

Sales Territory	1st Quarter	2nd Quarter
North	$2,700	$2,850
East	$3,700	$4,200
South	$2,200	$2,100
West	$2,900	$3,200

Figure 9.7 Cell padding has been set to 5 pixels, which gives more whitespace around the table contents.

Sales Territory	1st Quarter	2nd Quarter
North	$2,700	$2,850
East	$3,700	$4,200
South	$2,200	$2,100
West	$2,900	$3,200

Figure 9.8 Cell spacing of 5 pixels creates a wide border between cells—a dated look.

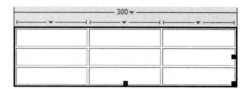

Figure 9.9 You can tell this table is selected because it has a thick border around its edges with resize handles.

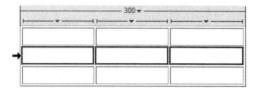

Figure 9.10 When you move the cursor to the left edge of a table and the pointer changes to an arrow, you can click to select the whole row.

Selecting Table Elements

To work effectively with a table, you'll need to know how to select its elements. You can select an entire table; one or more rows and columns; an individual cell or multiple cells; and nonadjacent cells, rows, or columns.

To select the entire table:

◆ Click the table's upper-left corner.

or

Click the bottom or the right edge of the table.

or

Click in the table, and then choose Modify > Table > Select All.

A border with resize handles appears around the table (**Figure 9.9**). Dimension lines also appear.

✔ Tip

■ Clicking any interior cell border also selects the entire table.

To select an entire row:

1. Place the pointer at the left edge of a row. The pointer becomes an arrow.

2. Click to select the entire row (**Figure 9.10**). You can click and drag to select multiple rows.

The cell borders for the selected row highlight.

To select an entire column:

1. Place the pointer at the top edge of a column.

The pointer becomes an arrow.

2. Click to select the entire column (**Figure 9.11**).

You can click and drag to select multiple columns.

or

Click the triangle in the dimension line above any column to display a pop-up menu, then choose Select Column (**Figure 9.12**).

The cell borders for the selected column highlight.

To select a single cell:

◆ Click and drag in the cell.

or

Click in the cell, then choose Edit > Select All, or press Ctrl-A (Cmd-A).

or

If the cell is empty, triple-click inside the cell.

The cell highlights to show it has been selected.

To select multiple adjacent cells:

◆ Click in the first cell you want to select, and drag to the last cell.

or

Click in the first cell you want to select, hold down Shift, and then click in the last cell. All the cells in between will also be selected. You can also Shift-click in this manner to select rows or columns.

To select nonadjacent cells:

◆ Ctrl-click (Cmd-click) in the first cell, hold down Ctrl (Cmd), and then click the other cells you want to select (**Figure 9.13**). You can also Ctrl-click (Cmd-click) to select nonadjacent rows or columns.

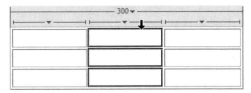

Figure 9.11 The pointer also changes to an arrow above columns. Click to select the column.

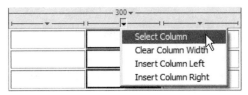

Figure 9.12 If you prefer, you can use the pop-up column menu to select the column.

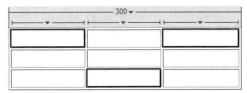

Figure 9.13 By Ctrl-clicking (Cmd-clicking), you can select nonadjacent cells.

Sales Territory	Q1	Q2	Q3	Q4
North	$2,700	$2,850		
East	$3,700	$4,200		
South	$2,200	$2,100		
West	$2,900	$3,200		

Figure 9.14 If you wanted to select the cells under Q3 or Q4, it could be difficult to do so because they are so small.

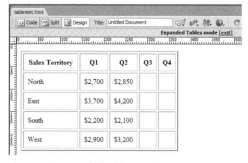

Figure 9.15 Click the Expanded button in the Layout category of the Insert Bar to enter Expanded Tables mode.

Figure 9.16 Expanded Tables mode makes all the tables in the document bigger, so you can select table elements easier. Note the indicator bar at the top of the document window that tells you that you're in a special mode.

Using Expanded Tables Mode for Selecting

When you're selecting tables and table elements, it can sometimes be difficult to select the particular part you're after, especially if some of the table cells are narrow horizontally or vertically (**Figure 9.14**). To make things easier on you, Dreamweaver offers *Expanded Tables mode*, which temporarily adds a border (if there is none) and increases the cell padding and cell spacing. These changes aren't permanent, and don't show up in a Web browser.

To enter Expanded Tables mode:

1. Choose View > Table Mode > Expanded Tables Mode.

   or

   In the Layout category of the Insert Bar, click the Expanded button (**Figure 9.15**).

   or

   Press F6.

   The Design view switches to Expanded Tables mode (**Figure 9.16**), changing the appearance of all the tables in the document.

   An indicator bar appears at the top of the document window to let you know you're in the Expanded Tables mode.

2. Select and edit table elements as you like.

✔ Tip

- Remember that Expanded Tables mode is not a WYSIWYG (What You See Is What You Get) view, as is the standard Design view. Always switch out of Expanded Tables mode before you do any serious page layout or formatting.

To exit Expanded Tables mode:

◆ Choose View > Table Mode > Expanded
Tables Mode.

or

In the Layout category of the Insert Bar,
click the Standard button.

or

Click the [exit] link in the Expanded
Tables mode indicator bar.

or

Press F6.

Adding Rows and Columns

You may find you need to add additional content to your table. Dreamweaver allows you to add rows or columns to your table, either singly or in multiples.

To insert a single row in a table:

1. Place the insertion point in a table cell.

2. In the Layout category of the Insert Bar, click either the Insert Row Above or Insert Row Below button (**Figure 9.17**). A new row will appear above or below the row where the insertion point is.

   or

   Choose Insert > Table Objects > Insert Row Above.

   or

   Choose Insert > Table Objects > Insert Row Below, or press Ctrl-M (Cmd-M).

   or

Continues on next page

Insert Row Above

Insert Column to the Left

Insert Row Below

Insert Column to the Right

Figure 9.17 You'll use the Layout category of the Insert Bar to make changes to tables.

ADDING ROWS AND COLUMNS

Right-click in the cell, and choose Insert Row from the shortcut menu. This adds a row below the row where the insertion point is.

The row appears in your table (**Figure 9.18**).

✔ Tip

■ If the insertion point is in the last cell of the table, pressing Tab adds a row to the bottom of the table.

To insert a single column in a table:

1. Place the insertion point in a table cell.

2. In the Layout category of the Insert Bar, click either the Insert Column to the Left or Insert Column to the Right button. A new column will appear to the right or left of the column where the insertion point is.

   or

   Choose Insert > Table Objects > Insert Column to the Left.

   or

   Choose Insert > Table Objects > Insert Column to the Right.

   or

   Right-click in the cell, and from the resulting shortcut menu choose Table > Insert Column. This adds a column to the left of the column where the insertion point is.

   The column appears in your table.

Sales Territory	Q1	Q2	Q3	Q4
North	$2,700	$2,850		
East	$3,700	$4,200		
South	$2,200	$2,100		
West	$2,900	$3,200		

Figure 9.18 A new row has appeared in the middle of this table.

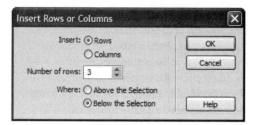

Figure 9.19 Use the Insert Rows or Columns dialog to add multiple rows or columns to a table in one operation.

To insert multiple rows or columns into a table:

1. Place the insertion point in a table cell.

2. Right-click, and then choose Table > Insert Rows or Columns from the short-cut menu.

   or

   Choose Modify > Table > Insert Rows or Columns.

   The Insert Rows or Columns dialog appears (**Figure 9.19**).

3. Select either the Rows or Columns radio button.

4. Enter the number of rows or columns you want to add. You can either type a number into the text box, or use the arrow buttons next to the text box to increase or decrease the number.

5. Next to Where, click the appropriate button to select the location of the new rows or columns.

   The rows or columns appear in your table.

ADDING ROWS AND COLUMNS

Merging and Splitting Cells

Dreamweaver lets you combine two or more adjacent cells into one larger cell, or split a single cell into two or more cells.

To merge cells:

1. Select the cells you want to merge.

2. Choose Modify > Table > Merge Cells, or press Ctrl-Alt-M (Cmd-Opt-M).

    or

    Right-click, and then choose Table > Merge Cells from the shortcut menu.

    The cells merge (**Figure 9.20**).

✔ Tip

■   You can merge an entire row or column into one cell.

To split cells:

1. Place the insertion point in the cell you want to split into two cells.

2. Choose Modify > Table > Split Cell, or press Ctrl-Alt-S (Cmd-Opt-S).

    or

    Right-click, and then choose Table > Split Cell from the shortcut menu.

    The Split Cell dialog appears (**Figure 9.21**).

3. Choose whether to split the cell into rows or columns.

4. Enter the number of new rows or columns for the split.

5. Click OK.

    The cell divides into two or more cells (**Figure 9.22**).

✔ Tip

■   Even if you select multiple cells, Dreamweaver can split only one cell at a time.

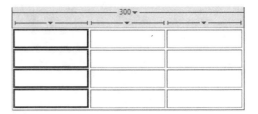

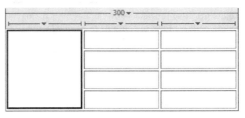

Figure 9.20 The four cells at the left edge of this table (top) have been merged into one cell (bottom).

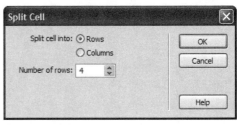

Figure 9.21 You can use the Split Cell dialog to divide cells into multiple rows or columns.

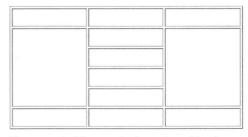

Figure 9.22 In this example, the center cell has been split into four cells.

MERGING AND SPLITTING CELLS

Figure 9.23 Use the Property Inspector to change the width and height of a table numerically.

Resizing Table Elements

You can resize tables horizontally or vertically, and also make columns wider and rows taller. You can also specify the width and height of tables, rows, and columns numerically.

To resize an entire table:

1. Click the bottom or the right edge of the table. The table will be selected, and a border with resize handles appears around it.

2. Drag one of the resize handles. To widen the table, drag the handle on the right edge of the table; to make the table taller, drag the handle on the bottom edge of the table; and to make the table grow in both directions simultaneously, drag the handle at the bottom-right corner of the table. Holding down the Shift key as you drag will maintain the proportions of the table.

To resize a table numerically:

1. Click the bottom or the right edge of the table to select it.

2. In the Property Inspector, enter a number in the W (for width) field (**Figure 9.23**). In the pop-up menu next to the field, choose either %, which makes the table width a percentage of the overall width of the page, or pixels, to set an absolute size for the table width.

3. Enter a number in the H (for height) field. In the pop-up menu next to the field, choose either % or pixels.

4. Press the Tab key or click in the document window to apply your changes.

✔ **Tip**

■ You can mix different units for the width and height of a table. So, for example, you can specify that the table's width is 50% of the page width, and set it to be 350 pixels tall.

To resize columns:

1. Select the column you want to resize.

2. Drag the column's right border to make the column wider.

   or

   In the Property Inspector, type a number in the W (for width) field (**Figure 9.24**). The width unit is in pixels. Alternatively, click the triangle in the dimension line above the column and choose Clear Column Width from the resulting pop-up menu; this makes the column resize to fit the contents.

To resize rows:

1. Select the row you want to resize.

2. Drag the bottom border of the row to make the row taller.

   or

   In the Property Inspector, type a number in the H (for height) field (**Figure 9.25**). The height unit is in pixels.

✔ Tips

- If you set a width in percentage for a table, the table resizes based on the width of the user's browser window. This may really change the look of your table. You should make sure that you preview the page in a Web browser and resize the browser window to see the effect.

- Tables always stretch to fit the content inside the table.

- Text inside cells usually wraps to fit the width of the cell. To force the cell to expand to the width of the text, you can turn off text wrapping on a cell-by-cell basis. Click in the cell, and then in the Property Inspector, click the "No wrap" check box.

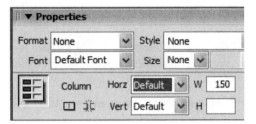

Figure 9.24 When you select a column, the Property Inspector changes and you can numerically set the column's width.

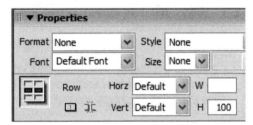

Figure 9.25 Selecting a row allows you to numerically set the row's height.

- Don't be misled into thinking you have ultimate control over row height and column width, and therefore control over what your site visitor sees. Different browsers display content differently, and short of previewing your site with every browser ever made on every computer platform, there's no way to be absolutely certain that your site visitor will see exactly what you intended.

RESIZING TABLE ELEMENTS

Clearing and Converting Table Values

When you have a table selected, there are six buttons in the Property Inspector that can be very handy and save you a bunch of time (**Figure 9.26**). These buttons clear the width and height values for the table, or convert table units from percent to pixels or vice versa.

Clear Column Widths and Clear Row Heights are great for collapsing a table to fit its contents. Convert Table Widths to Pixels and Convert Table Heights to Pixels let you change widths or heights from relative to fixed measurements. Convert Table Widths to Percent and Convert Table Heights to Percent does the opposite, converting a fixed size table to a relative one.

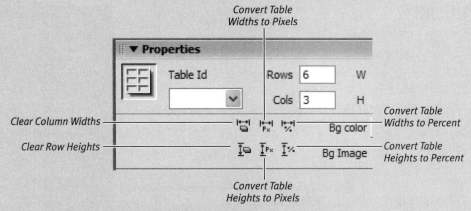

Figure 9.26 Use these six buttons in the Property Inspector to quickly clear width and height values, or convert tables to and from fixed widths.

Deleting Table Elements

If you want to remove tables, rows, or columns, you can make short work of the task.

To delete a table:

1. Select the table by clicking its right or bottom edge. A border with resize handles appears around the table.

2. Press Backspace (Delete).

To delete rows:

1. Select one or more rows.

2. Press Backspace (Delete).

   or

   Choose Modify > Table > Delete Row, or press Ctrl-Shift-M (Cmd-Shift-M).

   or

   Right-click the row, and then choose Table > Delete Row from the shortcut menu.

   The row disappears from the table.

To delete columns:

1. Select one or more columns.

2. Press Backspace (Delete).

   or

   Choose Modify > Table > Delete Column or press Ctrl-Shift-minus key (Cmd-Shift-minus key).

   or

   Right-click the row, and then choose Table > Delete Column from the shortcut menu.

   The columns disappear from the table.

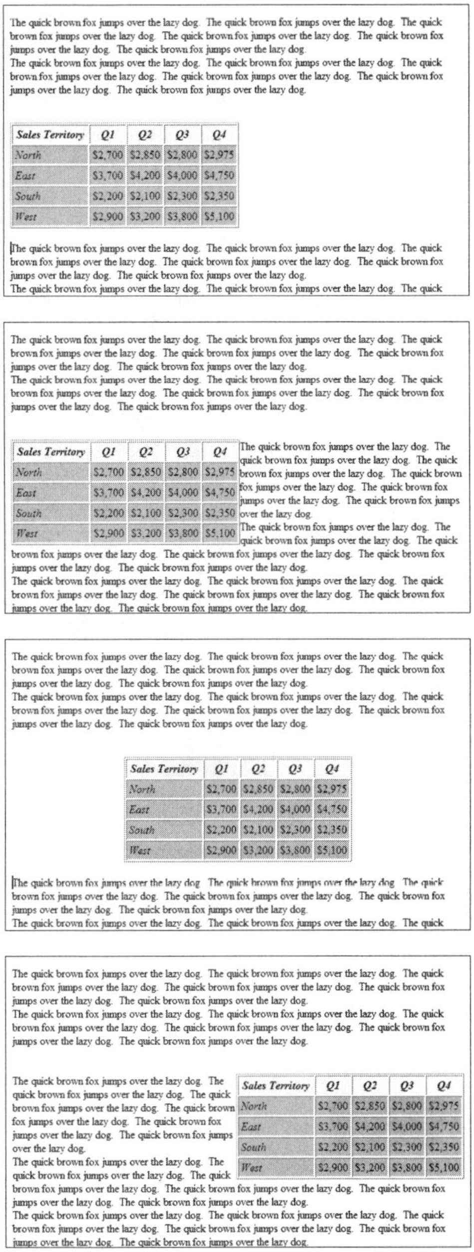

Figure 9.27 The effects of different types of table alignment. From top to bottom, Default, Left, Center, and Right alignments.

Specifying Table Alignment

When you have a table and text together, you can set the alignment of the table, in some cases wrapping the text around the table (**Figure 9.27**). You can choose from four different alignments:

◆ **Default** uses the browser default alignment for tables (usually it places the table to the left side of the page). This setting prevents text from wrapping around the table to the right.

◆ **Left** places the table to the left side of the page, and allows text to wrap around the right side of the table.

◆ **Center** centers the table on the page, with no text wrapping.

◆ **Right** places the table to the right side of the page, and allows text to wrap around the left side of the table.

Use the Property Inspector to set table alignment. This applies HTML attributes to the `<table>` tag, which is acceptable, but not really compliant with best practices. Instead, you should specify table alignment with a CSS style. See Chapter 5 for more information.

To set table alignment:

1. Select the table you want to align.

2. In the Property Inspector, choose the alignment you want from the Align pop-up menu.

   The table moves to the alignment you selected.

Setting Cell Properties

Alignment of the text or images inside of a cell requires using the Property Inspector to set *cell properties* for each cell. You can use these alignment cell properties to set both the horizontal and vertical alignments. You can also set cell properties for the background color of the cell, and also set the color of the cell border.

To set cell alignment:

1. Place the insertion point in the cell you want to format.

2. In the Property Inspector (**Figure 9.28**), from the "Horz" pop-up menu choose Default, Left, Center, or Right (**Figure 9.29**).

   The Default choice usually gives the same visual result as Left.

Figure 9.28 Use the Property Inspector to set horizontal and vertical alignment for cell contents.

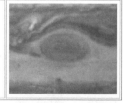

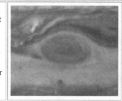

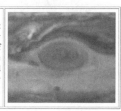

Figure 9.29 Horizontal text alignment within a cell. From top to bottom, Left (the default), Center, and Right text alignment.

This spectacular Hubble Space Telescope color picture of Mars at its 2001 opposition was created by combining several monochrome images taken at different wavelengths, then using a computer to assign color values to individual pixels.

This spectacular Hubble Space Telescope color picture of Mars at its 2001 opposition was created by combining several monochrome images taken at different wavelengths, then using a computer to assign color values to individual pixels.

This spectacular Hubble Space Telescope color picture of Mars at its 2001 opposition was created by combining several monochrome images taken at different wavelengths, then using a computer to assign color values to individual pixels.

Figure 9.30 Vertical text alignment within a cell. From top to bottom, Top, Middle (the default), and Bottom alignment.

3. From the "Vert" pop-up menu choose Default, Top, Middle, Bottom, or Baseline (**Figure 9.30**).

The Default choice usually gives the same visual result as Middle. Baseline sets the cell alignment to match the baseline of the text within the cell, and is usually used to align images and text that are inside the same cell. Baseline usually gives the same visual result as Bottom.

To set a cell background or border color:

1. Place the insertion point in the cell you want to format.

2. In the Property Inspector, click the color well next to Bg to bring up the color picker and select the cell's background color.

The cell's background color changes.

3. In the Property Inspector, click the color well next to Brdr to bring up the color picker and select the cell's border color.

The cell's border color changes.

Sorting Table Content

It's not uncommon to enter data into a table, then add more data, and then want to sort the whole thing. You asked for it, Dreamweaver can do it. The program sorts by the content of any column in your table, either numerically or alphabetically, in ascending or descending order, and can sort on two successive criteria.

There are some limitations to Dreamweaver's sorting abilities. You cannot sort merged cells, and Dreamweaver doesn't have the ability to sort part of a table, so you can't, for example, have the program ignore the merged cells you used for your table's title. Dreamweaver displays an error message if you try to sort a table containing merged cells.

Another problem is that the sorting algorithm Dreamweaver uses isn't terribly smart. For example, you can sort numerically, but Dreamweaver doesn't understand dates in tables, so you're liable to get sorts like this:

3/19/99

3/25/77

3/3/02

Dreamweaver sorted the dates numerically, reading left to right, which resulted in an incorrect sort.

Despite these restrictions, table sorting in Dreamweaver is useful—you just have to be aware of the limitations.

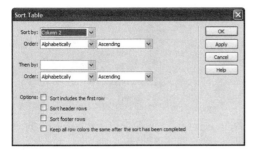

Figure 9.31 The Sort Table dialog lets you sort the contents of your table either alphabetically or numerically.

To sort a table:

1. Place the insertion point in any cell of the table you want to sort.

2. Choose Commands > Sort Table.
   The Sort Table dialog appears (**Figure 9.31**).

3. From the "Sort by" pop-up menu choose the column you want to use to sort the table.

4. In the Order pop-up menu on the left, choose whether to sort the column alphabetically or numerically.

5. In the Order pop-up menu on the right, choose whether to sort the column in ascending or descending order.

6. If you want to sort on a second set of criteria repeat steps 3 through 5 with the "Then by" set of pop-up menus.

7. Make any selections from the Options list.
   By default, the "Sort includes the first row" option is not selected. This is because the first row of a table is frequently a header row. If your table doesn't seem to be sorting properly, check this option.

8. Click OK.
   Dreamweaver sorts your table according to the criteria you selected.

✔ Tips

- Dreamweaver can't sort on rows, just columns.

- If you want a merged row at the top of your table, do the sort first, and then merge the cells.

- Be careful when you're sorting numbers. If you accidentally leave the sort on Alphabetically, you'll get an alphanumeric sort (1, 10, 2, 20, 3, 30) instead of a numeric sort (1, 2, 3, 10, 20, 30).

SORTING TABLE CONTENT

Formatting Tables

Dreamweaver comes with 17 preset table formats, which apply fonts, cell borders, and cell-background colors to tables to provide a more attractive look and make the table data more readable (**Figure 9.32**). These formats are similar to features of Microsoft Excel's AutoFormat option for worksheets.

If you like the look of one of the preset formats, you can apply it to your table with just a few clicks, and move on to other work. But if you want to customize the formatting further, you can do that, too.

Because the table formatting gets applied to the entire table, you'll be best off if the table already contains all of its data (or at least has its complete structure) before you start formatting it. Otherwise, you might have to reapply the formatting if you add or subtract rows or columns.

You can also use a CSS style to format a table, with the table's look being defined by instructions in a CSS style sheet. You can choose to have the table style apply to all tables in your document (if you use the style sheet to redefine the `<table>` tag), or you can create a custom CSS class for a particular kind of table you want to use, and apply the style to the table with the Property Inspector.

Sales Territory	Q1	Q2	Q3	Q4
North	$2,700	$2,850	$2,800	$2,975
East	$3,700	$4,200	$4,000	$4,750
South	$2,200	$2,100	$2,300	$2,350
West	$2,900	$3,200	$3,800	$5,100

Figure 9.32 Using contrasting colors in rows can often make tables more readable.

To apply table formatting:

1. Place the insertion point inside the table you want to format.

2. Choose Commands > Format Table. The Format Table dialog appears (**Figure 9.33**).

3. From the scrolling list, choose a format. A sample of the format appears in the dialog, next to the list.

4. If you are pleased with the look of the format you chose, skip to Step 9.

5. (Optional) To modify the row colors, choose First and Second colors by clicking in either of the color wells to bring up the color picker. Then choose how you want the rows to alternate colors by choosing from the Alternate pop-up menu.

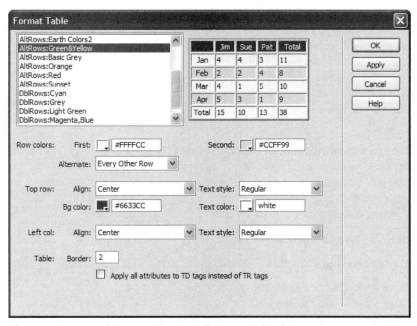

Figure 9.33 Use one of the preset formats in the Format Table dialog as is, or customize it to create your own format.

FORMATTING TABLES

6. (Optional) You can format the top row differently from the rest of the table; this is often done for a table header. Choose how you want to align the top row text by picking from the Align pop-up menu, then choose Regular, Bold, Italic, or Bold Italic from the "Text style" pop-up menu. You can also set the background color of the table or the text color of the top row by clicking in the respective color well to bring up the color picker.

7. (Optional) You can also format the text in the left column. Choose the text alignment from the Align pop-up menu, then choose the text style.

8. (Optional) To set the width of the border (in pixels), enter a number in the Border text box.

9. Click OK.

Dreamweaver applies the format to the table (**Figure 9.34**).

✔ Tips

■ The preset formats only work on one table at a time. If you have nested tables, you'll need to apply a preset format to each table separately.

■ You can't create and save a custom table format in the Format Table dialog, but you can certainly create, format, and save an empty table for later use. Just create and format the table, select it, then save it as a snippet. See Chapter 13 for more about creating snippets.

To apply a CSS style to a table:

1. Select the table you want to format.

2. In the Property Inspector, choose the style you want from the Class pop-up menu (**Figure 9.35**).

The table takes on the formatting from the CSS style you chose.

Sales Territory	Q1	Q2	Q3	Q4
North	$2,700	$2,850	$2,800	$2,975
East	$3,700	$4,200	$4,000	$4,750
South	$2,200	$2,100	$2,300	$2,350
West	$2,900	$3,200	$3,800	$5,100

Figure 9.34 The customized format, as applied to the table.

Figure 9.35 Apply a CSS style to a table in the Property Inspector.

FORMATTING TABLES

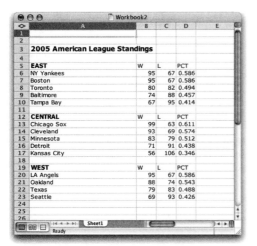

Figure 9.36 Tabular data to be imported into Dreamweaver will often start out as a Microsoft Excel worksheet.

Importing and Exporting Tabular Data

Because tables are best used for tabular data, it stands to reason that Dreamweaver has an easy way to import such data (from database programs or Microsoft Excel, for example) and turn it into a table. This data needs to be in the form of a *delimited text file*, that is, a file that includes the data, separated by some character, such as a tab, a comma, or another delimiter.

To explain how a delimited file works, imagine that you have some data that would be displayed well in a table, such as baseball standings. Each row of the table with the standings contains information on a team, and the different columns of the table contain the team's name, number of wins, number of losses, and winning percentage, as in the example (shown in Excel) in **Figure 9.36**. To use this Excel data in Dreamweaver, you first need to export the data out of Excel as a delimited file, which is easy; you simply save a copy of the file in the "Text (Tab delimited)" format. This saves the data in the Excel worksheet as a plain text file. Each column of data is separated by a tab character, and each row of the data ends with a return character. Dreamweaver can then read in this delimited text file and convert it into a table.

Dreamweaver can also do the reverse trick of turning the data in a table into a delimited text file. This allows you to export table data to Excel or a database program for further processing, or you can take a table on a Web page and move it to a word processor or page layout program such as Adobe InDesign.

Continues on next page

To import tabular data into a table:

1. Place the insertion point where you want the table to appear.

2. Choose File > Import > Tabular Data.

or

Choose Insert > Table Objects > Import Tabular Data.

The Import Tabular Data dialog appears (**Figure 9.37**).

3. Click the Browse button to select the delimited data file.

The Open dialog appears.

4. Navigate to the data file, select it in the Open dialog, then click Open.

The name of the data file appears in the Import Tabular Data dialog's "Data file" text box.

5. From the Delimiter pop-up menu, choose the delimiter character used in the data file.

Your choices in this pop-up menu are Tab, Comma, Semicolon, Colon, and Other. If the data file uses an unusual delimiter character, choose Other and type that character into the text box next to the Delimiter pop-up menu.

6. In the "Table width" section, choose "Fit to data" if you want the table width to be just as wide as the data, or "Set to" if you want the table to be a fixed width. If you choose the latter option, enter a number in the text box and choose the units from the pop-up menu (either percent or pixels).

7. As you prefer, enter values for cell padding, cell spacing, and the table border. You can also choose to format the text in the top row of the table (which is usually a header of some sort). Your choices are no formatting, bold, italic, or bold italic.

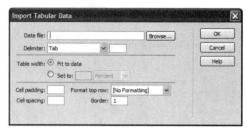

Figure 9.37 Use the Import Tabular Data dialog to select the delimited text file and format the table you are about to create.

Figure 9.38 The formatted table, built from the imported data, appears in your document.

Figure 9.39 Use the Export Table dialog to save the data from a Dreamweaver table as a delimited text file.

✔ Tip

■ If you only want to export a portion of a table, for example the top ten rows, select those rows, copy them, then paste them into a different part of the document, where they will create a new table. Export the new table as a delimited text file, then delete the new table.

8. Click OK.

Dreamweaver reads the delimited text file and inserts it into your page as a formatted table (**Figure 9.38**).

✔ Tip

■ If the table imports incorrectly, chances are that the data file uses a delimiter different from the one you chose in step 5. You will have to delete the incorrect table and import it again with the correct setting.

To export a Dreamweaver table's data to a delimited file:

1. Place the insertion point in any cell of the table.

2. Choose File > Export > Table.

   The Export Table dialog appears (**Figure 9.39**).

3. From the Delimiter pop-up menu, choose the delimiter character you want to use in the exported text file. Your choices are Tab, Space, Comma, Semicolon, or Colon.

4. From the "Line breaks" pop-up menu, choose the operating system that is the destination for the text file. Your choices are Windows, Mac, or UNIX.

   The reason for this option is that each of the platforms has a different way of indicating the end of a line of text.

5. Click Export.

   The Export Table As dialog appears.

6. Give the file a name, navigate to where you want to save it, and click Save.

   Dreamweaver saves the table data as a delimited text file.

Using Table Layout Mode

Because tables have such a rich history with Web designers as a primary layout tool (even though they have now fallen out of favor for that purpose), Dreamweaver offers *Table Layout mode*, which allows you to draw layout tables and table layout cells directly in the document window. Dreamweaver then builds the (usually very complex) table required to implement the layout you drew.

In Table Layout mode, you can simply draw a layout table on the page, then draw layout cells within the layout table. Alternatively, you simply draw the layout cells on the page; Dreamweaver then automatically creates the layout table to contain the layout cells. Oddly, this latter method is the one that you will use most often. The layout cells will hold your content; after you've created them, you will fill in the cells with text and images. It's easy to move, resize, and modify the layout cells. Because you're using the tables you create as layout devices, Dreamweaver sets the border widths for the layout table to 0, so that the borders don't appear. Cell padding and cell spacing are also set to 0, so you can place objects precisely next to one another.

As in Extended Tables mode, the document window changes while you're in Table Layout mode, to let you know that you have options that are not normally available. Layout tables appear on screen with a tab identifying them (this tab doesn't appear in a Web browser).

Layout Table

Layout *Layout Table Cell*

Figure 9.40 Enter Table Layout mode by clicking the Layout button on the Insert Bar.

To create a layout table:

1. On the Insert Bar, switch to the Layout category (**Figure 9.40**).

2. Click the Layout button on the Insert Bar.

   An indicator bar appears at the top of the document window to let you know you're in Layout mode.

3. Click the Layout Cell button on the Insert Bar.

   When you move the mouse pointer back over the document window, you will see that the cursor has changed to a crosshair.

4. Click and drag anywhere in the document window to draw the layout cell.

   The layout cell appears in the document window as you drag. When you release the mouse button, Dreamweaver encloses the layout cell that you drew within a layout table (**Figure 9.41**). The area of the layout table outside of the layout cell will be gray.

Continues on next page

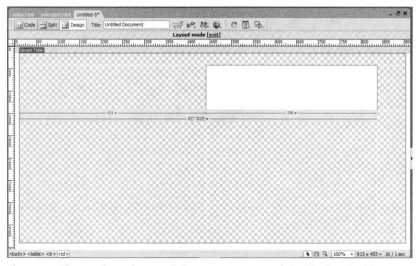

Figure 9.41 After you draw a layout cell, Dreamweaver surrounds it with a layout table.

5. You'll probably want more than one content area inside your layout table, so click the Layout Cell button again and draw your second layout cell. Repeat for as many content areas as you need.

6. To enter content in the layout cells, click inside a cell and type or insert an image in the usual fashion. Repeat until you are done (**Figure 9.42**).

7. To exit Layout mode, click the Standard button on the Insert Bar.

or

Click the [exit] link in the indicator bar at the top of the document window.

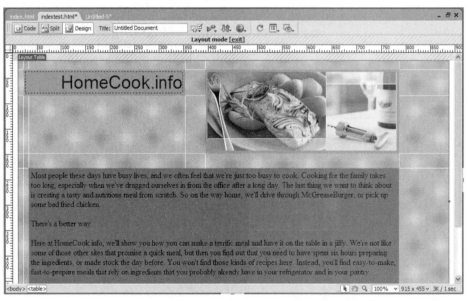

Figure 9.42 This alternative layout for the HomeCook.info site uses three layout cells, which I've filled with text and an image.

✔ Tips

■ Annoyingly, Dreamweaver exits draw Layout Cell mode whenever you are finished drawing a cell, requiring another click on the Insert Bar's Layout Cell button for each cell. To draw multiple cells in a row, hold down the Ctrl (Cmd) key while dragging out cells.

■ Layout cells cannot overlap.

■ The Layout Table button in the Insert Bar is most useful when you want to create a nested layout table inside another layout table.

■ You cannot draw a table over anything that is already on the page. If you try, the cursor will turn into the circle-with-a-slash symbol, indicating that the operation is forbidden. Since you'll be using layout tables for layout, I suggest that you create them on new blank pages. You can also create them at the bottom of your document, after any content that is already on the page.

■ You can resize and modify layout cells in the same way that you do any other table cell. Click inside a cell to select it, then resize it by dragging one of the cell's resize handles, or for more precision, resize it numerically in the Property Inspector. Change the cell's properties with the Property Inspector.

■ To move a layout cell, click and drag one of the edges of the cell, but make sure not to accidentally grab one of the cell's resize handles.

USING TABLE LAYOUT MODE

Using Forms and Fields

A lot of Web sites exist just to provide information and entertainment to site visitors. But if you want your site to get information back from your visitors, you'll need some way to let them interact with you and your site. To do that, you'll need to add a form.

A form contains fields, and those fields can be anything from a simple check box to a group of radio buttons, or a single or multi-line text entry area. And of course, you'll want some sort of "OK" or "Submit" button so that your visitors will know how to send you their completed form. Look at the Forms category of the Insert Bar (**Figure 10.1**), and you'll see that it contains everything you need to add any kind of form and field to your site.

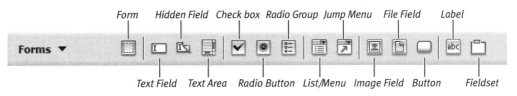

Figure 10.1 The Forms category of the Insert Bar contains all the fields you might want to add to your form.

Adding a Form to a Page

You could start creating a page by throwing fields onto it, but when your visitor clicks Submit, the browser won't know what to do with the data. That's where you need a form—it tells the browser that all this information is part of one package, and it tells the browser what it should do with all of the information that it's gathered.

To add a form to a page:

1. Choose where on your Web page you want your form, and click the form button ▢ on the Insert Bar. A red box will appear on your page (**Figure 10.2**).

2. If that box hasn't been automatically selected, select it, and you'll see the options you can change for your new form in the Property Inspector (**Figure 10.3**). The ones that apply solely to forms are:

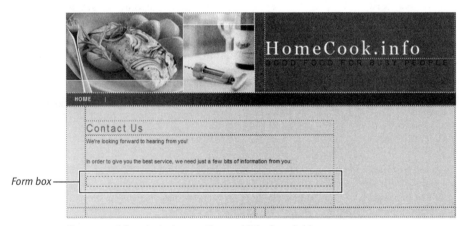

Form box ⎯

Figure 10.2 A form looks bare until you add the form fields.

Figure 10.3 The Property Inspector is where you set a form's name, action, and method.

The Uncovered Fields

There are two form fields in the Insert Bar that aren't covered in this chapter:

- **Jump Menus:** These will be covered in Chapter 12, *Using Behaviors and Navigation Objects*.

- **File field:** If you need to upload a file to a server, you'll want to use this type of form field. It's fairly self-explanatory, but you'll need to talk to your server administrator about how they've set up their server to accept files.

▲ **Form name:** If you're going to be doing any JavaScript validation of your form, it's a good idea to give it a name. In addition, some CGIs (which stands for Common Gateway Interface) need their associated forms to have a particular name.

▲ **Action:** This is the program on the Web server that is executed when the form is submitted. You'll need to get the name of this from your system administrator or hosting provider. It's also commonly referred to as a System CGI.

▲ **Method:** The most common options are GET and POST. POST passes the form data as part of the header of the request to the server. GET passes the data as part of the URL of the request to the server. Because of this, and because GET has a length limitation, POST is what you'll usually want.

▲ **Enctype:** This field describes the enclosure type being sent to the server. The default is `application/x-www-form-urlencoded`. The only time you'll want to use `multipart/form-data` is if you're asking your visitors to upload a file.

✔ Tips

- No, that red border around the form won't actually display on your site. It's just there in Dreamweaver so that you'll know where the form begins and ends.

- Make sure that all your form fields are inside your form; if they are not, their contents won't be sent to the server. It's a good idea to put the entire page inside the form.

- If you try to add a form field to a page that doesn't have a form, you'll be asked if you want to add a form tag. You might think from this that it's not worth bothering to add a form tag manually first, but it is. You'll have better control over where the form is placed, and what ends up going inside it.

ADDING A FORM TO A PAGE

Adding Text Fields

The simplest type of form field you can have is a simple, single-line text field. Your average form will have several of them, allowing people to enter anything from their name to their phone number to their shoe size.

Figure 10.4 The first text entry field added to the form.

To add text fields:

1. Choose where in your form you want your text field to appear (by clicking in the document), and click the text field button 🔲 on the Insert Bar. The new text field will appear on your page (**Figure 10.4**).

2. If the text field hasn't been automatically selected, select it, and you'll see the options you can change for your new field in the Property Inspector (**Figure 10.5**). From there, you can change the fields:

   ▲ **TextField:** This field contains the name of the field, which can be used by JavaScript behaviors and by CGI scripts on the server.

   ▲ **Char width:** This is the width of the text input area on your page. The larger this number, the wider the space it needs. And as it's the number of characters allowed, the larger the font you've set (usually with CSS), the wider the space will be.

Figure 10.5 Set a text field's properties via the Property Inspector.

▲ **Max Chars:** This is the maximum number of characters that someone visiting your site can enter into this field. For instance, you might want to limit a phone number to ten characters, or a credit card to 16.

▲ **Type:** This has three values: *Single line*, *Multi line*, and *Password*. Multi line will be covered in the next section, "Adding a Text Area." The only difference between Single line and Password is what the user sees when they enter something into this field: if the type is Password, no matter what your visitor types, it will appear as black dots. The correct value will be sent back to the server, though.

▲ **Init val:** The initial value of the field. This text is displayed when the page is loaded.

✔ Tip

■ There's another type of field that's similar to a text field called a *hidden field*. It's used when there's information that a CGI needs to get from a form, but which a user doesn't enter—so the field itself contains a value, but isn't seen in the document. Adding a hidden field is virtually identical to adding a text field: just click on the hidden field button 🖾 in the Insert Bar (obviously, where it's put on the Web page doesn't matter) and then set the value and unique field name in the Property Inspector.

Labeling Your Fields

When you click on a button in the Insert Bar to add a form field to your page, the Input Tag Accessibility Attributes dialog may appear (**Figure 10.6**). This dialog allows you to set certain attributes that can enhance accessibility. These fields are:

◆ **Label:** Figure 10.6 shows a label of "First Name: " being entered. Figure 10.4 shows the result: that text is displayed just to the left of the new text field.

◆ **Style:** There are three style options: *Wrap with label tag*, *Attach label using 'for' attribute*, and *No label tag*. If you choose *Wrap with label tag*, Dreamweaver will (as you might guess) surround your new `<input>` tag with a `<label>` tag:

```
<label>First Name: <input type="text" name="textfield" /></label>
```

If you choose *Attach label using 'for' attribute*, Dreamweaver will write the `<label>` tag based on what you enter for *position* (covered below):

```
<label for="textfield">First Name: </label><input type="text" name="textfield"
  id="textfield" />
```

Unfortunately, Dreamweaver doesn't offer full WYSIWYG support for this option—you can then change the `name` and `id` attributes of your new text field (by changing the TextField), but the `label`'s `for` attribute, which should change to match, doesn't. There isn't any way to change it short of going into the markup and changing it by hand.

If you choose *No label tag*, the text you enter will appear, but it'll be just that: text.

The `<label>` tag helps make your site more accessible in two ways: it tells voice browsers that this is the text associated with this field, and it allows users with certain browsers (such as Firefox) to click on the text label as an alternative to only clicking inside a check box. This gives your visitor a larger space in which to click. Accessibility is important, and using the `<label>` tag helps make your site more accessible—but if you want to use it with Dreamweaver's Design mode, stick with the *Wrap with label tag* option.

◆ **Position:** The label for a form field can be either before or after the field. For text fields, you'll usually see the label before the field. For check boxes, you'll usually see the label afterwards. The default value of the position changes depending on the type of field (**Figure 10.7**).

◆ **Access key:** Some browsers allow users to enter keyboard shortcuts to select form fields. If you want this option, enter the keyboard shortcut for the field here. For instance, if I entered *g* in Figure 10.7, the user with Internet Explorer for Windows could click that check box by pressing Alt-G.

◆ **Tab Index:** If you want users to be able to tab from form field to form field in a particular order, you'll want to assign each field a tab index. This is the numbered order in which the user can tab through your form's fields. It's especially useful to set this when your form fields are inside table cells, as the default can be quite different from what you actually want to occur. The numbers need to be between 0 and 32767, and they don't have to be in sequence: you can make your fields be (for instance) 100, 200, and so on, leaving room for future changes to your form.

If you don't use labels, access keys, or tab indices, and are annoyed at seeing this dialog come up every time you add another form field, you can get rid of it by clicking on the link at the bottom. This opens Dreamweaver's preferences, and turning off "Show attributes when inserting Form objects" will make the dialog go away for good. If you later decide you want it back, go back into Preferences, choose the Accessibility category, and you can turn it back on again.

You can also add a label afterwards by clicking the label button on the Insert Bar, but it doesn't do what you expect. Instead of bringing up the Input Tag Accessibility Attributes dialog, Dreamweaver instead adds a `<label>` tag around whatever you have selected and throws you into Split mode. If you are markup-phobic, stick with adding labels along with their associated fields.

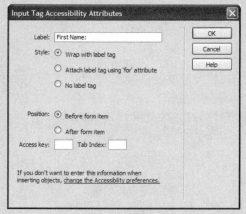

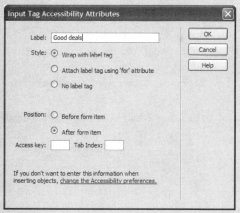

Figure 10.6 To enable your site to be accessible, set the label attributes here. The default position for a text field label is before the form item.

Figure 10.7 For a check box, the label's default position is after the form item.

Adding a Text Area

It's possible that you want your visitors to enter more than just a single line of text—maybe they have a lot to say, or you just want to have a free-form area in which to enter their comments. If that's the case, you'll want to use a text area.

To add a text area:

1. Choose where in your form you want your text area to appear, and click the text area button ▣ on the Insert Bar. The new text area will appear on your page (**Figure 10.8**).

2. If the text area hasn't been automatically selected, select it, and you'll see the options you can change for your new field in the Property Inspector (**Figure 10.9**). From there, you can change the same values that you could for text fields, with some small differences:

   ▲ **Num Lines:** This is the number of lines that you want the field to take up on the page. If you only want a single line, use a text field instead.

   ▲ **Wrap:** The choices here are *default*, *wrap*, *logical*, and *physical*. Stick with default, as the other options don't work cross-browser and cross-version.

Figure 10.8 A text area lets your visitors enter multiple lines of text, and will scroll when necessary.

Figure 10.9 Use the Property Inspector to set the dimensions and initial value of the text area.

Contact Us
We're looking forward to hearing from you!

In order to give you the best service, we need just a few bits of information from you:

First Name:
Last Name:
Please enter your comments here:

Email:

I am interested in learning more about:
☐ Recipes
☐ Wine
☐ Cookware
☐ Cooking News
☐ Good Deals

Figure 10.10. Check boxes are an easy way to get exact information from your site's visitors.

Adding Check Boxes

Check boxes are one of the most commonly used form fields, and you're likely to want several on your forms. They're particularly useful when you want specific responses from your site visitors, and you don't want them to have to enter data into text fields (and possibly misspell their entry).

To add a check box:

1. Choose where in your form you want your check box to appear, and click the check box button ☑ on the Insert Bar. A new check box will appear on your page (**Figure 10.10**).

2. If the check box hasn't been automatically selected, select it, and you'll see the options you can change for your new field in the Property Inspector (**Figure 10.11**):

   ▲ **Checkbox name:** This is the name of the field, and will be used by any JavaScript validation as well as any server-side CGI.

   ▲ **Checked value:** This is the value that's passed to the server (and JavaScript client-side code) when the user has checked the check box.

   ▲ **Initial state:** This refers to the appearance of the check box when the page is first loaded—is the box checked or unchecked?

✔ Tip

■ Just a reminder: the difference between check boxes and radio buttons is that for a group of radio buttons, only a single option can be picked. When you have a group of check boxes, however, each check box has no relationship to the other check boxes, so you can select multiple check boxes.

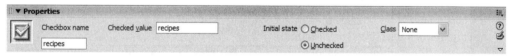

Figure 10.11 Set the name and value of the check box in the Property Inspector, along with the checked status of the box when the page is loaded.

Adding a Fieldset

A *fieldset* is HTML's way of grouping fields on your form together to add additional meaning for the user. While how a fieldset will display on a Web page depends on the browser being used: Dreamweaver's Design view shows it as a thin gray line around a fieldset's contents. Compare Figure 10.10 with **Figure 10.12**: it's easier to see that those check boxes are grouped together, and all have a similar function.

To add a fieldset:

1. Choose where in your form you want your fieldset to appear, and click the fieldset button ☐ on the Insert Bar.

2. The Fieldset dialog will appear (**Figure 10.13**), asking you to enter a *legend*—that's the text that will appear at the beginning of the fieldset (Figure 10.12). Enter that text, click OK, and the fieldset box will appear.

3. If you're adding a fieldset to an existing form, drag the related fields into the fieldset. If it's a new form, click inside the fieldset and create its fields.

✔ Tips

- If the fieldset contains no form fields, the legend will appear inside the box. When form fields are added, the legend will be displayed as part of the box.

- If you're dragging fields inside the fieldset, be careful when selecting—you'll want to make sure (for example) that all of a label is selected.

Figure 10.12 Adding a fieldset to your form helps group together related form fields, making your form easier for your visitors to understand.

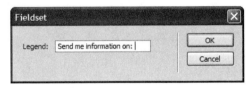

Figure 10.13 Enter the legend text into the Fieldset dialog.

- You can't change a fieldset or a legend via the Property Inspector. If you want to modify either, the legend can be changed by modifying the text in the document window, and the fieldset can be changed by going into Code view.

- A fieldset can contain any type of form fields, not just check boxes.

ADDING A FIELDSET

Figure 10.14 The Radio Group dialog lets you enter all of your radio buttons in a single dialog.

Adding a Radio Button Group

Radio buttons don't exist by themselves— they always come in a group. And of that group, only one option can be chosen: your visitors can pick rock *or* paper *or* scissors.

To add a radio button group:

1. Choose where in your form you want your radio button group to appear, and click the radio group button 🖳 on the Insert Bar.

2. The Radio Group dialog will appear (**Figure 10.14**), asking you to enter several fields:

   ▲ **Name:** A radio group needs a name that associates all of the radio buttons together. In this example, your visitor is choosing whether or not to subscribe to a newsletter, so the name is "newsletter."

   ▲ **Radio button label:** Each radio button needs a label to distinguish it from its neighbors. In this example, the labels are "Yes" and "No."

   ▲ **Radio button value:** Each radio button needs a value, which will be passed back to the server CGI and/or JavaScript. The values here are, again, "Yes" and "No."

   ▲ **Lay out using:** Radio buttons are normally aligned vertically, so here you make your choice of how you want that layout to be done in the HTML markup. Your choices are "Line breaks" and "Table." Line breaks will almost always be sufficient.

Continues on next page

The Radio Group dialog starts with two fields, which you can overwrite to say whatever you want. If you want to add more radio buttons, click the + on the left side. If you want to delete buttons, in the list, select the one you want to remove, and click on the -.

To rearrange the order of buttons, in the list, select the name of the button to move, and then click the up/down arrows to move that button.

3. Click OK to accept your entries, and your new radio button group will be added to your document (**Figure 10.15**).

Figure 10.15 Here's your radio group. Only one item can be clicked.

✔ Tips

■ If you want your buttons to all be on the same line (as in this example), select "Lay out using Line Breaks," and then remove the line breaks. Sadly, Dreamweaver doesn't include an option of "just leave them on the same line, okay?"

■ There's also an option on the Insert Bar to add a single radio button: ⬤. It's unlikely, though, that you'll ever want to have only a single radio button on a page. If you add a single radio button to an existing radio group, be sure to copy the name of the group exactly into the Property Inspector (**Figure 10.16**). In fact, your best bet is to click one of the existing radio buttons, copy the name from the Property Inspector, click the new radio button (if it already exists; add it if it doesn't), and then paste the name in from the clipboard.

■ If you want one of your radio buttons to be set as checked, click on that button in your document, and then change the Initial state in the Property Inspector from Unchecked to Checked.

■ Dreamweaver will happily let you set multiple radio buttons with their initial state checked even though browsers won't display it that way. Be careful that you're only setting zero or one radio button to be checked.

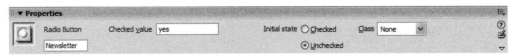

Figure 10.16 When setting the properties for an individual radio button, be careful in setting the name of the group—it has to match other radio buttons to work correctly.

Figure 10.17 You'll enter all the values for pop-up menus and scrolling option lists in the List Values dialog.

Figure 10.18 The new pop-up menu is now on your form.

Adding a List/Menu

Another common form element is what's referred to in the forms category of the Insert Bar as a *list/menu*. It's actually the two forms of the HTML `select` tag: either a pop-up menu or a scrolling list of options. If it's the latter, you can decide whether the user can click on a single option or on multiple options.

To add a pop-up menu:

1. Choose where in your form you want your pop-up menu to appear, and click the list/menu button 📟 on the Insert Bar.

2. The List Values dialog will appear (**Figure 10.17**). Enter your desired options. The Item Label is what appears in the pop-up, and the Value is what's sent to the server-side CGI/JavaScript.

3. Click OK, and your new pop-up will appear on your page (**Figure 10.18**).

4. If the pop-up menu hasn't been automatically selected, select it, and you'll see the options you can change for your new field in the Property Inspector (**Figure 10.19**):

   ▲ **List/Menu:** This is the field name that will be passed back to the server-side CGI/JavaScript when it processes the form.

   ▲ **Type:** The choices are Menu or List; for a pop-up menu, choose Menu.

   ▲ **Initially selected:** You can choose one of the menu options to be the default that's shown when the page loads.

   Continues on next page

Figure 10.19 Change the pop-up menu into a scrolling option list in the Property Inspector.

▲ **List Values:** Clicking this button causes the List Values dialog (**Figure 10.20**) to reappear.

To add a scrolling option list:

1. Follow steps 1-3 above to create a pop-up menu, and select the pop-up menu.

2. In the Property Inspector (**Figure 10.21**), change Type to List. You'll notice that even though you've changed the type to list, your field still displays as a pop-up menu.

3. Change the Height to show the number of items you want displayed at any one time in the scrolling list. Changing this causes the field to display as a scrolling list (**Figure 10.22**).

4. If desired, change the Selections option to allow multiple choices. When you do this, visitors to your site will be able to pick several options in the scrolling list at one time.

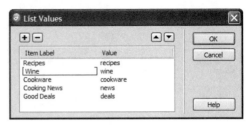

Figure 10.20 You can return to the List Values dialog to view or change the items by clicking the List Values button in the Property Inspector.

✔ Tip

■ If you leave the Height set to 1, and change Selections to "Allow multiple," you'll also see your pop-up menu change to a scrolling list. But a scrolling list with a height of one isn't much of a scrolling list—it's too difficult for your users to see what's available.

Figure 10.21 If you change from a pop-up menu to a scrolling list, you'll get a couple of new options in the Property Inspector.

Figure 10.22 And here's the new scrolling list next to a pop-up menu.

Styling Forms

How forms should be styled is a matter of hot debate among leading Web designers: are tables acceptable, or should you try and stick to CSS-only solutions?

The grim reality is that it's unlikely that you'll get 100% of what you want from CSS, which is why we've used tables in this example—browsers such as Microsoft Internet Explorer 6 for Windows still can't do what's required. On the other hand, a simple form with a simple layout such as this one still comes across differently in browsers, even with the entire layout designed with tables. Looking at **Figures 10.23**, **10.24**, and **10.25**, you can see that each browser has its own quirks, and no two look exactly the same.

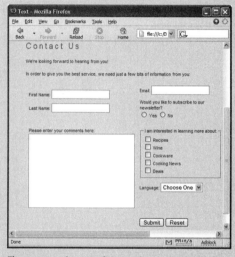

Figure 10.23 Our new form, as it appears in Firefox on Windows.

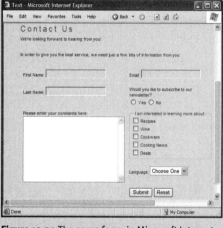

Figure 10.24 The same form, in Microsoft Internet Explorer for Windows. You can't see it in black and white, but the text field backgrounds are yellow and the fieldset legend is blue, while the other two browsers show them as white and black.

Figure 10.25 And finally, the same form in Safari on the Mac. Even when you use CSS to style form fields in a certain way, Safari will often use its own Mac-like fields instead.

Adding a Button

A form on your site doesn't do you much good unless you can get the information that's entered into it, and that's the primary use of a button. A Submit button triggers the action specified in the form tag (described earlier in this chapter). Another type of button is the Reset button, which allows a user to go back to a form's original state.

To add a button:

1. Choose where in your form you want your button to appear, and click the button icon 🖵 on the Insert Bar. The default value—the Submit button—will appear on your document (**Figure 10.26**).

2. If the button hasn't been automatically selected, select it, and you'll see the options you can change for your new button in the Property Inspector (**Figure 10.27**):

   ▲ **Button name:** This is the name of the button; generally, you'll use "Submit" to specify that it's a Submit button, and "Reset" to show that it's a Reset button (**Figure 10.28**).

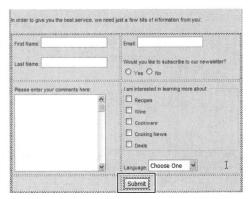

Figure 10.26 Add a Submit button to your Web form so you can receive your visitor's completed form.

Figure 10.27 The buttons you'll usually use are Submit and Reset; this one's a Submit button.

Figure 10.28 A button can be changed to a Reset button using the Property Inspector.

✔ Tip

- There is actually one other type of button: an image button. It is created by clicking the image field button 🖻 on the Insert Bar. You'll be prompted to browse for an image file in your site, and the image will then appear in your document. When a visitor comes to your site and completes the form, clicking on that image will trigger an immediate submission of the form.

▲ **Value:** This is the message that will be displayed on the Submit button itself. It's common for it to say "Submit," but it can also say, "Place order," "OK," or whatever you think your users will understand.

▲ **Action:** There are three possible actions. *Submit form* and *Reset form* do what you'd expect. *None* creates a generic button, which can later be set to trigger a JavaScript action (covered in Chapter 12).

Submit/Reset or Reset/Submit?

If you want to start a fight in a group of designers, just ask which order your Submit and Reset buttons should be in. There are two vocal schools of thought, and they tend to break down into Windows advocates versus Mac advocates.

In a nutshell, Windows users expect to find the OK/Submit button as the first button in a group, while Mac users are accustomed to always seeing it as the right-most button. As shown in **Figures 10.29** and **10.30**, interface designers who work on cross-platform applications are able to change the order depending on the user's platform. While this is the same General Preferences dialog on both platforms, notice that where Mac and Windows users click to accept their changes is very different.

If you're working on a Web site you don't have that flexibility, but you should be aware that visitors to your site will have expectations about how your forms should work—and at least some of those expectations will disagree with yours. We're not going to make the call here as to which is preferable; that call should be made based on your visitor logs and your own personal preferences.

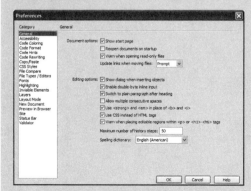

Figure 10.29 Dreamweaver's General Preferences on Windows show the buttons as OK, Cancel, and Help at the bottom right.

Figure 10.30 The General Preferences on the Mac have Help at the bottom left, and Cancel and OK at the bottom right.

ADDING FRAMES

Normally a Web page fills an entire browser window. However, a browser window can be split into two or more smaller individual panes called *frames*. Each frame contains an individual Web page.

Frames are used to define areas of a page, such as a navigation bar or a masthead, that remain constant as the user moves through the site. They are also used to define content areas where the content changes each time a navigation link is clicked. Frames allow you to have a site where the navigation part of the window only loads a single time (reducing your bandwidth needs), but the content part of the window changes whenever the user requests a new page.

In this chapter you'll learn how to create framed layouts, insert individual Web pages into the frames, and manage the navigation for a framed site.

How Frames Work

When you look at a framed site, you are actually seeing multiple pages (**Figure 11.1**). You've seen the site in Figure 11.1 before, but not in frames. At first glance you might not notice the site is framed. But once you start scrolling you'll realize the difference. Notice the scrollbar in Figure 11.1. See how it starts about halfway down the side of the page? That's because there are actually three framed pages shown, and only the frame on the lower right has a scrollbar.

The arrangement of the individual frames is determined by the *frameset document*. The frameset document contains one or more *frameset* tags, which set up the number of frames, how they will be arranged, and which individual Web pages will be displayed when the page is opened for the first time.

Figure 11.1 The HomeCook.info site in a framed layout looks much like the other layout.

No matter how many frames a browser window displays, there is usually only one frameset document for a site. A Web page with three frames actually needs four separate documents to display correctly: the frameset document and the three individual documents that fill the three frames.

A frameset divides a window into either columns or rows, but not both at once. Luckily, framesets can be *nested*, or put one inside another. A frameset of columns can be nested in a row of another frameset. Or, a frameset of rows can be nested in a column of another frameset. In Figure 11.1, the frameset has two rows. The top row holds the site identification. The bottom row splits into two columns with a nested frameset. One column holds the navigation, and the other holds the content. The content frame is the one with the scrollbar.

The frameset document is invisible to the user. It sets up the arrangement of the visible pages shown in the frames. The user sees the results of the frameset document, but not the actual frameset document itself.

But wait, there's an accessibility issue. Not all browsers work with framesets. Therefore, each frameset document contains a *noframes* section. Use the `noframes` section to provide basic information in case the user's browser cannot display frames. Links to your content pages are an example of good information to include in a `noframes` section. That way every user can find your valuable content.

Dreamweaver lets you set up the frameset and then work on the individual Web pages for the frames separately. Or you can work on the individual Web pages while they are displayed in the frameset. Both are perfectly valid choices; for instance, an individual might manage a site with only a few pages inside the frameset, while a larger site might have numerous people handling different content pages.

HOW FRAMES WORK

Should You Use Frames?

Using frames is often a poor choice for layout. Although frames do have some advantages, they're outweighed by the disadvantages, to the point that few professional/commercial sites now use frames. For every advantage of frames, there are usually ways to achieve the same effect without frames.

The most common reason for using frames is navigation. A navigation bar displayed in a frame is always visible no matter how much you scroll in other frames.

Some disadvantages of using frames are:

◆ Not all browsers provide good frame support. Cellphone browsers, PDA browsers, and browsers for users with disabilities have problems with frames. A `noframes` section helps, but it's a poor substitute for the good browsing experience you hope users have at your site.

◆ It's not possible to bookmark framed pages. The URL of a framed page doesn't appear in the browser's address bar.

◆ It's difficult to get graphic elements to line up precisely between frames.

◆ Testing the navigation is time-consuming.

◆ Search engines may not be able to properly navigate and index a framed site.

◆ Visitors who come to your site via search engines will load an unframed page, as search engines will send visitors to your content pages and skip your navigation. To work around that requires some way to get to the "real" version—the content page they want, inside the proper frameset.

Some advantages of using frames are:

◆ Static frames such as navigation bars or graphical banners don't have to be reloaded each time the content changes, making your site load faster.

◆ Each frame has its own scrollbar and can be scrolled individually.

Sometimes frames are the best layout choice in spite of their disadvantages. When that is the case, be extra careful to:

◆ Provide helpful `noframes` content, such as a list (with links) of your content pages.

◆ Use the `title` attribute to give each frame a descriptive name. This helps with frame identification and navigation. See *Creating a Frameset* for details.

◆ Provide a friendly way for visitors arriving from a search engine to get into your framed site.

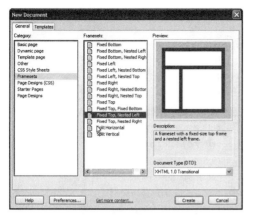

Figure 11.2 Dreamweaver's New Document dialog has numerous predefined Framesets.

Figure 11.3 The Frame pop-up menu lets you select each frame to give it a title attribute.

Creating a Frameset

Dreamweaver comes with several predefined framesets that include the most commonly used frame layouts. For example, the HomeCook.info site needs a top frame for the masthead, a left frame for the navigation, and a right frame for the changing content. Dreamweaver has a predefined frameset that fits these specifications.

If you like, you can instead create a custom frameset from scratch, by manually drawing frames into a page. Dreamweaver gives you the tools to create and resize frames.

To use a predefined frameset:

1. Choose File > New.

   or

   Click the Framesets link in the "Create from Samples" section of the Dreamweaver Start Page.

   The New Document dialog appears.

2. Select Framesets from the Category list (if you used the Start Page, this was already done for you).

3. In the Framesets column, select a layout.

   For example, you can choose Fixed Top, Nested Left (**Figure 11.2**). This layout uses a frameset with two rows. A second frameset with two columns is nested in the bottom row.

4. Click Create.

   Dreamweaver opens the new framed window, and the Frame Tag Accessibility Attributes dialog appears, if you have your Preferences set for Frames Accessibility (**Figure 11.3**). (You do have Preferences set for Frames Accessibility, right?)

   Continues on next page

In the dialog, select each frame from the Frame pop-up menu and give a descriptive `title` attribute to each frame by typing it into the Title field.

In Figure 11.3, we replaced the default suggestion for mainFrame with the more descriptive title "content." A good `title` for the topFrame is "site identification." A good `title` for the leftFrame is "site navigation." Remember, `title` attributes help users whose browsers can't display frames understand and navigate your site, so be informative.

✔ Tip

- You can also create a frameset using the Layout category of the Insert Bar. Use the Frames button there to choose the frameset layout you want (**Figure 11.4**).

To create a custom frameset:

1. Create a new HTML document by choosing File > New, then double-clicking Basic Page in the resulting New Document dialog.

2. Choose View > Visual Aids > Frame Borders (**Figure 11.5**).

   This turns on a dotted border around the frame edges.

3. Click and drag the dotted border to insert frames. The cursor changes to a double-headed arrow cursor to drag (**Figure 11.6**).

   If you drag from the top or bottom, the document splits horizontally. If you drag from the left or right, the document splits vertically. If you drag from a corner, the document splits into four frames.

✔ Tip

- You can also add frames to a frameset by choosing Modify > Frameset > Split Frame Left, Split Frame Right, Split Frame Up, or Split Frame Down.

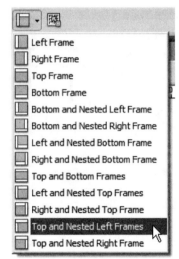

Figure 11.4 The Insert Bar has numerous predefined framesets as well.

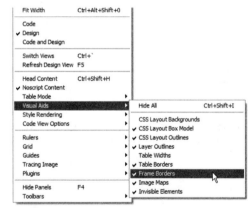

Figure 11.5 One of the Visual Aids you can view is Frame Borders.

To delete a frame from a frameset:

1. Choose View > Visual Aids > Frame Borders (Figure 11.5).

2. Click and drag the dotted border to the edge of the document window to delete a frame.

   or

   Click on the frame border and drag it until it meets another frame border.

Double-headed arrow cursor

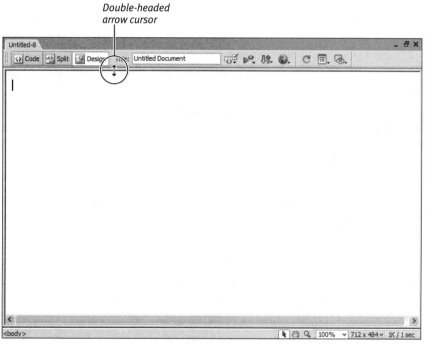

Figure 11.6 The dotted line around the outside of the document window indicates the frame borders. Drag to create frames.

Frame Name vs. Frame Title

Frame navigation won't work unless you can point to a frame by name. (See "Targeting Frames with Links" a little later in this chapter.) Every frame needs a name. Dreamweaver assigns a default name based on location or assumed purpose, for example, topFrame, leftFrame, mainFrame.

The *Frame name* displays at the left on the Property Inspector when a frame is selected. If you don't like Dreamweaver's choice of name, you can type a different one in the Frame name field. If you use a name of your own choosing, there are a few rules:

◆ No spaces are allowed in a frame name.

◆ The name must begin with a letter or number.

◆ It's okay to mix uppercase and lowercase letters.

Frame names work behind the scenes to make the frameset function. They don't make any difference to your users.

Frame titles, on the other hand, do make a difference to at least some of your users. As we mentioned previously, the title attribute provides important identification and navigation help for users with certain types of browsers. Dreamweaver doesn't presume to suggest a title attribute text for you. Instead, it prompts you for it in the Frame Tag Accessibility Attributes dialog. This is your one chance to enter title information if you work only in Design view.

The rules are different for title attribute text. More than one word, spaces, even sentences can go into a title attribute. For example, the title attribute for the topFrame might be something like "Site identification and a link back to the home page."

Look at the markup for topFrame to see where name and title are used:

```
<frame src="masthead.html" name="topFrame" scrolling="No" noresize="noresize"
id="topFrame" title="site identification and a link back to the home page" />
```

Everything in that code snippet can be modified from the Property Inspector except title. That's why you need to grab your chance to write a great blurb for the title text when the Frame Tag Accessibility Attribute dialog prompts you for a title.

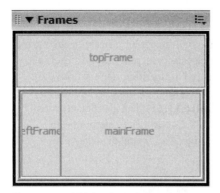

Figure 11.7 A thick border indicates the selected frameset.

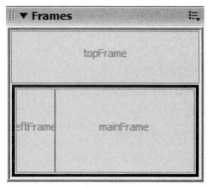

Figure 11.8 The nested frameset in the bottom row is outlined with a thick border, indicating that it is selected.

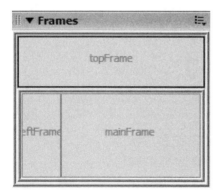

Figure 11.9 The black border indicates the selected frame. Note that the border for a frame is not quite as thick as the border for a frameset.

Using the Frames Panel

You've probably noticed by now that Dreamweaver has a panel for everything. Frames are no exception. If the Frames panel isn't visible, choose Window > Frames to bring it into view.

It's a good idea to keep the Frames panel in view when working with a framed site. It gives you a miniature view of the frames within a frameset. It also gives you an easy way to select either an individual frame or an entire frameset.

To select frames and framesets with the Frames panel:

1. In the Frames panel, click the outermost border around the frameset (**Figure 11.7**).

   The selected frameset will display a thick black border.

2. Do one of the following:

   ▲ To select a nested frameset, click the white border around the frameset (**Figure 11.8**).

   The selected frameset will display a thick black border.

   or

   ▲ To select an individual frame, simply click inside the frame (**Figure 11.9**).

   The selected frame will display a thick black border.

✔ Tips

■ When you select a frame in the Frames panel, the corresponding frame is selected in the document window. A dotted border highlights the selected frame in the document window. (**Figure 11.10**) The tag selector displays the appropriate element—in this example it's `<frame#topFrame>`.

■ When you select a frameset in the Frames panel, the corresponding frameset is selected in the document window. A dotted border highlights the frameset (**Figure 11.11**). The Tag Selector displays the appropriate element—in this example, it's `<frameset><frameset>`.

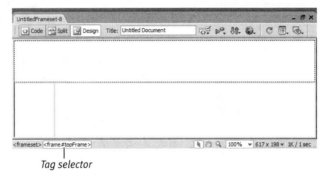

Tag selector

Figure 11.10 In the document window, the selected topFrame is indicated by a dotted border.

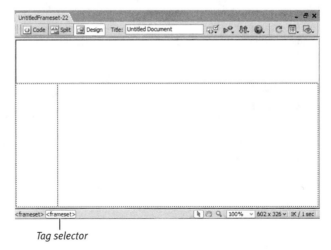

Tag selector

Figure 11.11 The dotted border indicates that the nested frameset in the bottom row is selected.

To adjust rows or columns of the frameset:

1. Select the frameset in the Frames panel.

2. Make adjustments with the Property Inspector (**Figure 11.12**).

   The Property Inspector displays options for Border, Border width, and Border color. You can also set either the row height or column width, depending on which is selected. Enter in a value, and choose pixels, percentage, or relative units.

   If the selected frameset contains rows, the rows are miniaturized on the Property Inspector. The selected row is indicated in a dark gray. Clicking a row in this miniature display on the Property Inspector selects it. Set the Row Value (that is, the height) for each row as needed.

   If the selected frameset contains columns, the columns are miniaturized on the Property Inspector (**Figure 11.13**). The selected column is indicated in a dark gray. Clicking a miniature column in this display on the Property Inspector selects it. Set the Column Value (that is, the width) for each column as needed.

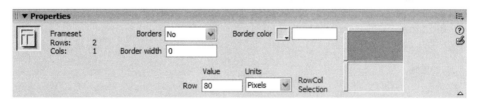

Figure 11.12 The Property Inspector shows a miniature frameset with rows when a frameset with rows is selected. Options to adjust the frameset are displayed.

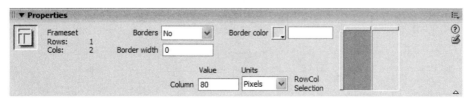

Figure 11.13 The Property Inspector with a column frameset selected. You see a miniature frameset indicating which column your adjustments will affect.

✔ Tips

- Row height and column width can be set in exact units (pixels), as a percentage of the frameset, or as relative. If you choose relative, the row or column will take up whatever space is available. Relative rows and columns can shrink or grow, depending on the size of the browser window. Relative units are considered the most accessible.

- As you work with frames, you'll see that Dreamweaver provides many visual cues, such as dotted borders around selected framesets in the document window and thick borders around selected framesets in the Frames panel. These visual cues are important to watch because it is easy to accidentally change something you don't intend to change in a complicated frameset if you don't pay attention to the selected element. They also help you make sure you have the right element selected when it comes time to save your work. Remember that these visual cues won't show up in the Web browser.

- Selecting a frame or frameset in the Frames panel is not the same as placing an insertion point in a frame by clicking within a frame in the document window.

To adjust frame properties:

1. Select the frame you want in the Frames panel.

2. The Property Inspector displays properties for that frame (**Figure 11.14**). Make changes in one or more of the properties:

   ▲ **Frame name** gives a needed identifier to the frame (see the sidebar "Frame Name vs. Frame Title"). Each frame must have a name. If you create a custom frameset, you need to supply the name for the frameset yourself. (Dreamweaver supplies a default name for each frame in the preset framesets.) A name that helps you make sense of your layout such as leftFrame, navFrame, or menuFrame is what you want here. No spaces are allowed in the name.

   ▲ **Src** is the URL of the page that will initially be displayed in the frameset. Setting this field is covered below in "Inserting Pages Into Frames."

   ▲ **Scroll** options are No, Auto, and Default. *No* means that frame will not have a scrollbar ever, even if not all the contents of the frame are visible. *Auto* means a scrollbar will appear automatically if the contents of the frame are larger than the frame can display. *Default* is the browser's default, which is usually Auto. Scrollbars can be horizontal or vertical, depending on which is needed to see all the contents of a frame.

Continues on next page

Figure 11.14 With a frame selected, the Property Inspector displays options for adjusting and naming the frame.

▲ Normally a frame can be resized in the browser. Checking the **No resize** check box means that there will be no way to resize a frame in the browser. If you leave it unchecked, users can drag the frame borders in the browser window. This is useful for users who prefer to have especially small or especially large browser windows.

▲ **Margin width** and **Margin height** refer to the margin surrounding an individual frame.

▲ **Borders**, which can be set at the frameset level, can also be set individually for each frame.

▲ **Border color** allows you to set the color for the frame borders. Click the color well to bring up a color picker to help you set the color.

✔ Tips

■ If you click inside a frame in the document window, the Property Inspector displays the standard text properties for that frame's document. To change the properties of the frame itself, use the Frames panel to select the frame.

■ Monitor size and screen resolution can vary widely among users. Some users must enlarge the text with the browser controls in order to read it. It is a good idea to test your framed site with various browser configurations. Only testing will show you whether scrollbars or resizing are needed so that all your content is viewable.

■ Size issues can also lead to printing problems in some situations. You may need to provide special printer-friendly pages for a framed site.

■ One of the reasons that frames got such a bad reputation was due to the tacky look of sites after frame border colors were applied. If you're considering changing your framed site's border colors, please reconsider unless you've got a darned good reason.

Figure 11.15 This individual HTML page will be placed in the topFrame of the frameset.

Figure 11.16 This individual HTML page will be placed in the leftFrame of the frameset.

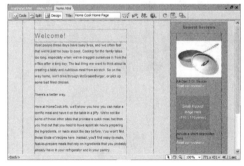

Figure 11.17 This individual HTML page will be placed in the mainFrame of the frameset.

Inserting Pages into Frames

Now that you've got your frames set up, you'll need to create pages to fill every frame. These pages are normal Web pages in every way except that they contain just a part of what will appear in the overall window. To prepare the HomeCook.info example, it took four individual pages: masthead.html (**Figure 11.15**), menu.html (**Figure 11.16**), home.html (**Figure 11.17**), and the frameset document.

To add a prepared page to a frame:

1. Click anywhere in the frame.

2. Choose File > Open in Frame.
   The Select HTML File dialog appears.

3. Browse to select the file you want to insert, then click OK (Choose).

Continues on next page

4. Repeat the steps to add files to other frames (**Figure 11.18**).

5. When every frame has its opening file, choose File > Save Frameset.

The inserted files are now the **Src** documents for the various frames in the frameset.

For more about saving framesets, see "Saving Framesets and Frames."

✔ Tip

- Naming a "home" page is slightly different with framed sites. You'd normally name the home page index.html. But in a framed site, you need that file name for the frameset. With a framed site, think of the initial set of files displayed when the frameset opens as Home. The page in Figure 11.17 is named home.html because it's in the opening content frame before any links are clicked.

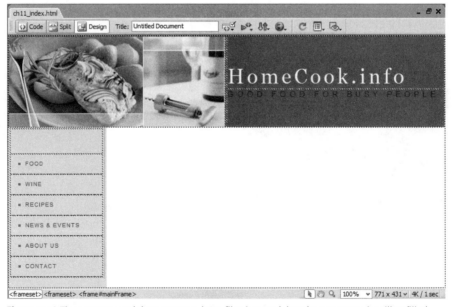

Figure 11.18 The topFrame and the leftFrame have files inserted, but the mainFrame is still unfilled.

To create a page in a frame:

1. Click anywhere in the frame.

2. Insert text and images with your normal Web content creation verve (**Figure 11.19**). If you need a refresher, take a peek at Chapter 3, "Building Your First Page" or Chapter 4, "Adding Text to Your Pages."

3. Choose File > Save Frame.

   For more about saving frames, see "Saving Framesets and Frames."

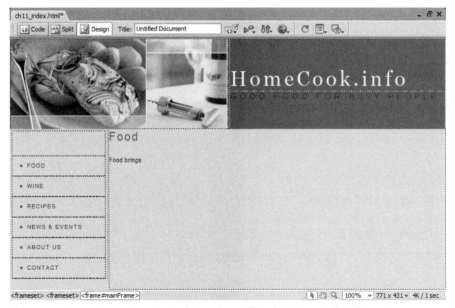

Figure 11.19 You can type or insert material in a framed file while it is part of the frameset.

Saving Framesets and Frames

As soon as you create a frameset it's selected in the document window. But if you've been working with frames and files, it can get tricky to know just what file you're working on. Sometimes the option to save that you want is grayed out. This could mean that the file was already saved. If you know it wasn't, then recheck all the visual clues to figure out what you have selected. Be sure you have the frame or frameset you intend to save selected.

To save a frameset:

1. To select the frameset, click the outer border of the frameset in the Frames panel.

   The thick border indicates the selected frameset, as in Figure 11.7.

2. Choose File > Save Frameset.

   If the frameset document has never been saved before, you'll be prompted to give the file a name. The frameset document is the file that is opened when a visitor first arrives at a URL, so frameset files are often saved as index.html.

   or

   Choose File > Save All.

This saves the frameset and all other open files at once. If this is the first time you are saving the files, Dreamweaver will prompt you to name each file prior to saving it.

or

Choose File > Save Frameset As.

This prompts you to save the frameset with a different name from the one you might already be using, and it is useful for making a backup or saving a copy.

✔ Tip

■ Double-check the document window to verify that the frameset you want to save is what's selected. Dotted borders outline the selected frameset (**Figure 11.20**). The tag selector at the bottom of the window displays <frameset>.

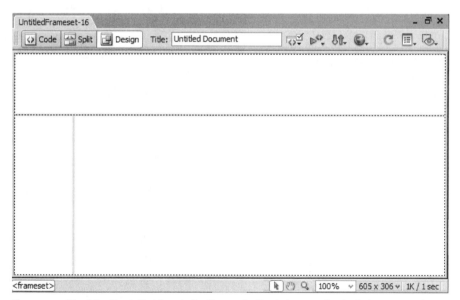

Figure 11.20 Check for the dotted lines indicating a selection to be sure about what you are saving.

To save a frame:

1. Click anywhere in an individual frame.

2. Several File menu options related to frames are now available:

   ▲ Choose File > Save Frame to save the currently selected frame.

   ▲ Choose File > Save Frame As to save the current frame with a different name.

   ▲ Choose File > Save Frame As Template. This will create a template you can use to create similar pages (see Chapter 13, "Make Life Easier: Using Templates, Libraries, and Snippets").

✔ Tip

■ If you're working on an internal content page of your site while typing in a frame in the frameset document window, be careful when you save. You only want to save the file in the frame, not the entire frameset. If you inadvertently save the frameset, you'll be accidentally changing the Src file in the frameset document to that of the file you just saved—probably not what you wanted.

Page Title and Frame Title

Every document you create in Dreamweaver has a Title field in the toolbar at the top of the document window. The frameset page title may be the only title a user ever sees for your framed site, so make it count. However, it's a good idea to give each individual document in the site a title, too.

We need a little semantic clarification here, because there are title elements, and then there are title attributes. You first heard about title elements in Chapter 3, "Building Your First Page." There you learned how to create the document title in the Title field at the top of the window. This is the title that appears in the title bar of a Web browser when the page is loaded.

In this chapter, we talk a lot about title attributes for frames. Now, title attributes are very important, but they're not the same thing as the title elements that give a document a title.

Attributes describe elements. An element is made with an HTML tag. If you wrap some text with an HTML tag, you've got an element. HTML elements are things like paragraphs, lists, images, headings, and frames. All those elements have attributes like size, color, border, margin, and possibly title. A title attribute tells you some characteristic about its element. In this chapter, title attributes give information about the frame element.

If all this semantic talk is too much for you, remember this: if Dreamweaver gives you a chance to put a title anywhere, do it!

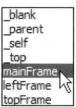

Figure 11.21 When you create a link while working in the frameset document, Dreamweaver provides the Target options in the Property Inspector.

Targeting Frames with Links

You probably surfed the Web for all of a minute and a half before you first realized that if you click on a link the current page goes away and a new page fills the window. That's a great system—except for framed sites. Often, when a link is clicked in one frame, the new file should open in some other frame entirely. You can make that happen by using a *target* attribute in the link. The `target` names the frame where the new file will open. Yep, that's why you named the frames.

To make a target link while working in the frameset:

1. Open the frameset with the page where you want the link visible.

2. Highlight the text for the link.

3. The Property Inspector link options appear.

   Browse for the file you want the link to open.

   or

   Click the Point-to-File icon and point to a file in the Files panel to create the link.

   Choose the target frame from the Target menu (**Figure 11.21**). Dreamweaver already knows which frames are in the frameset.

4. Choose Save > Frame to save your changes.

To make a target link while working on an individual page:

1. Open the page where the link will be.

2. Highlight the text for the link.

3. The Property Inspector link options appear.

   Browse for the file you want the link to open.

   or

   Click the Point-to-File icon and point to a file in the Files panel to create the link.

   Type the frame name in the Target field (**Figure 11.22**). Spelling and capitalization must be exactly right.

4. Save your changes.

✔ Tip

■ While it's definitely handy to have the pop-up menu of frame targets right there in the Property Inspector when making links in the frameset document window, it's not without peril. Inadvertent improper saves can play havoc with the frameset. If you create the individual pages for the site independently, outside of the frameset document, you do have to do a bit of extra typing to get the Target field filled in. However, when you save an individual page, you can't possibly save anything besides the individual page.

Figure 11.22 When you create a link in an individual document, you must manually type the target in the Target field of the Property Inspector.

Working with Frames and CSS

You won't use CSS to lay out a framed site, but what about for everything besides layout? CSS will work just fine with framed sites to control the various display properties of the individual pages.

In Chapter 5, "Styling Page Content," you learned how to attach a style sheet to a document. To use CSS with a framed site, you simply attach a style sheet to every individual page that will be inserted in your frameset.

TARGETING FRAMES WITH LINKS

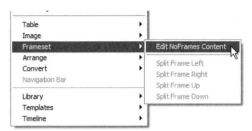

Figure 11.23 To set what will be displayed for non-frames-supporting browsers, choose Edit NoFrames Content from the Frameset submenu of the Modify menu.

Figure 11.24 The Edit NoFrames Content command brings up an empty NoFrames Content document.

Figure 11.25 Site information and links are added to the NoFrames Content document.

Adding noframes Content

A growing number of wireless users who access the Web with phones, PDAs, or pocket PCs can't view frames. Nor can users with disabilities who have specialized browsers. These folks need noframes content—unless you want them all to go away and leave your site alone, never to return.

The content in a noframes element could be an entire alternate Web page, providing all the information a frames-capable user would find in the framed site. A less ambitious noframes element might contain an invitation to the user to click through to a site navigation page or a site index page so that the content you offer could still be accessed.

Search engines also make use of noframes content. Use it to describe the site's key information and provide links for the search engine robots (or other users) to follow.

To add noframes content:

1. Select the frameset in the Frames panel.

2. Choose Modify > Frameset > Edit NoFrames Content (**Figure 11.23**).

3. A blank page appears in the document window, replacing the framed pages (**Figure 11.24**).

Type or paste the noframes content in this blank window (**Figure 11.25**).

4. To return to the frameset, choose Modify > Frameset > Edit NoFrames Content again.

✔ Tip

■ If you preview your site in a regular browser (which has no trouble displaying frames), you won't see the noframes content.

Working with Iframes

An *iframe* is an inline frame or an inline subwindow. In much the same way that you can insert an image into a page of text, you can insert an iframe. The iframe element inserts an entire miniature view of an HTML page into another page. This is handy when you want some small bit of content to come from somewhere else, in a page that otherwise isn't framed. For instance, those ubiquitous Google AdSense ads you see on many sites are done with iframes.

Dreamweaver isn't equipped to create iframes fresh out of the box, but you can get an extension to add the capability. For instance, one named iFrame Suite contains five extensions for working with iframes. It, along with other extensions related to iframes, are available at the Macromedia Exchange at www.macromedia.com. Appendix B, "Customizing and Extending Dreamweaver," has more information about how to install and use extensions.

USING BEHAVIORS AND NAVIGATION OBJECTS

12

Dreamweaver provides a number of JavaScript functions you can add to your pages easily. No prior knowledge of JavaScript is required to use them. Macromedia calls these JavaScript actions *behaviors*. Behaviors can add interactivity to your site. Many times the behavior is triggered by some action of the user; for example, the behavior will happen when the user clicks a link or hovers over a link. Other behaviors happen without any overt action from the user, such as a browser check for a needed plug-in as a page loads.

You add many behaviors with the Behaviors panel. There are also some behaviors available in the Insert Bar menu. And finally, Dreamweaver imports behaviors from other Macromedia Suite 8 software, such as Fireworks.

In this chapter you'll learn how to use behaviors to add rollovers, open new windows, check for plug-ins, validate forms, insert jump and pop-up menus, and add navigation bars. **Table 12.1** gives a full list of the available behaviors.

Table 12.1 The behaviors available through Dreamweaver. Only the most commonly used are covered in this chapter, but you can add any of these to your page.

Dreamweaver Behaviors	
BEHAVIOR	**DESCRIPTION**
Call JavaScript	Specify that a custom JavaScript should execute for a specific event. You can write the custom JavaScript yourself, or use one from the many available JavaScript libraries.
Change Property	Change the value of an object's properties. Only certain properties can be changed, and only in certain browsers.
Check Browser	Check the user's browser brand and version. Do this if you want to send the user to a page prepared especially for a certain browser.
Check Plugin	Send visitors to specific pages based on whether they have certain plug-ins installed. This only works in certain browsers.
Control Shockwave or Flash	Control whether to play, stop, rewind, or go to a frame in a Macromedia Shockwave or Macromedia Flash SWF file.
Drag Layer	Set up movable elements that users can drag. Attach this behavior to the document to make interactive puzzles, games, or sliders.
Go To URL	Open a new page in a specified window or frame or change the contents of two or more frames with one click.
Jump Menu	Create or edit a Jump Menu. Normally, you create a Jump Menu using Insert > Form Objects > Jump Menu, and merely use the Behaviors panel to edit it.
Open Browser Window	Open a URL in a new window. You can set the properties for the new window.
Play Sound	Play a sound for an event such as a page loading, a mouse moving over a link, or a mouse click.
Popup Message	Create a JavaScript alert with the message you specify, usually a brief informative statement.
Preload Images	Preload images that won't be seen right away, for example, images for rollovers. That way, there's no wait to see the image when the action is triggered.
Set Nav Bar Image	Edit the properties of navigation bar images. Normally, you create the nav bar using Insert > Image Objects > Navigation Bar. Use the Behaviors panel to control the display and actions of images in a navigation bar.
Set Text of Frame	Change the text display in a frame to the new content and formatting you specify. The new content can include text, HTML, and JavaScript functions.
Set Text of Layer	Replace the content and formatting of an existing layer with new content. The new content can include text, HTML, and JavaScript functions.
Set Text of Status Bar	Put a message in the browser's status bar.
Set Text of Text Field	Replace the content of a form's text field with new content. The new content can include text or JavaScript functions.
Show-Hide Layers	Show, hide, or restore the default visibility of one or more layers.
Show Pop-Up Menu	Create or edit a Dreamweaver pop-up menu or open and modify a Fireworks pop-up menu you've inserted in a Dreamweaver document.
Swap Image	Swap one image for another to create rollover effects or even swap more than one image at a time.
Swap Image Restore	Restore the last set of swapped images to their previous source files. If you leave the Restore option selected when you attach a Swap Image action, this action gets automatically added.
Validate Form	Check the contents of specified text fields to be sure the user has entered the proper type of data. You can also check whether the user entered something in a required field.

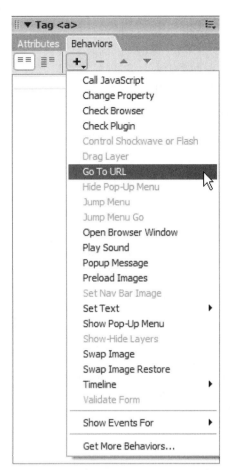

Figure 12.1 The Behaviors are shown in black if they are available for the particular element you chose, and in gray if they aren't. You can't select a grayed-out behavior.

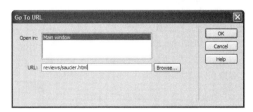

Figure 12.2 The Go To URL dialog is nice and simple. If you're using frames, frame names appear in the Open in box.

Using the Behaviors Panel

In order to add interactivity to your site, you'll want to add *behaviors* to the objects on your pages, such as images and links. You'll use the Dreamweaver Behaviors panel to add, modify, and remove behaviors. Objects can have multiple behaviors attached, so you'll also need to know how to rearrange their order.

To add a behavior:

1. If the Behaviors panel is not visible, choose Window > Behaviors (Shift-F4).

2. Select an object on the page such as an image or a text link.

3. Click the plus button ⊞ on the Behaviors panel to see the list of available actions for the selected object (**Figure 12.1**). If a choice is grayed out, that action is not available for the object selected. Click to choose an action.

4. The dialog for the chosen action opens (**Figure 12.2**). Enter the requested information in the dialog.

Continues on next page

5. The default event for that action is displayed in the events column on the left-hand side of the Behaviors panel (**Figure 12.3**). If you want a different event, select it from the pop-up menu in the events column (**Figure 12.4**) by clicking on the default.

To edit a behavior:

1. Select an object with a behavior attached.

2. Double-click the behavior name in the behaviors column of the Behaviors panel.

or

Select the behavior name and press Enter (Return). The dialog window for the behavior will open.

3. Change any parameters and click OK.

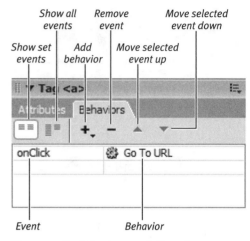

Figure 12.3 The Behaviors panel shows the event handler and the behavior name.

Figure 12.4 If you want to change the event handler, click the event. An arrow appears, and clicking it brings up the pop-up menu.

USING THE BEHAVIORS PANEL

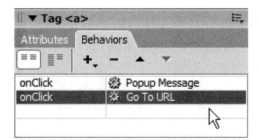

Figure 12.5 Any behaviors attached to an element execute in the order they are listed in the Behaviors panel.

To change the order of behaviors:

◆ If more than one behavior is attached to an object, the behaviors run in the order listed in the Behaviors panel, from the top to the bottom (**Figure 12.5**). Select an action and use the up ▲ or down ▼ arrow to change the order.

To delete a behavior:

1. On your Web page, select an object with an attached behavior.

2. In the Behaviors panel, select the name of the behavior you want to delete.

3. Click the minus button ▬.

   or

   Press Delete.

✔ Tips

■ You can extend Dreamweaver by adding additional behaviors from the Macromedia Exchange. See "Finding and Installing Extensions" in Appendix B for more information about extending Dreamweaver.

■ JavaScripts you write yourself can be inserted in Dreamweaver. To learn more about JavaScript, check out another of our books: *JavaScript for the World Wide Web: Visual QuickStart Guide (Fifth Edition)* (Peachpit Press).

Events and Browsers

JavaScript includes many *event handlers* such as onClick or onDblClick, as seen in Figure 12.4. The name of the event handler is usually pretty descriptive of the user event involved.

Not every browser understands every event. Dreamweaver gives you a say as to the browsers you want to choose events for (**Figure 12.6**). For instance, Set Nav Bar Image is available when you pick Netscape 6, but not when you choose HTML 4.01. Choose Show Events For in the Behaviors panel list of actions to specify your choice of browser or browsers.

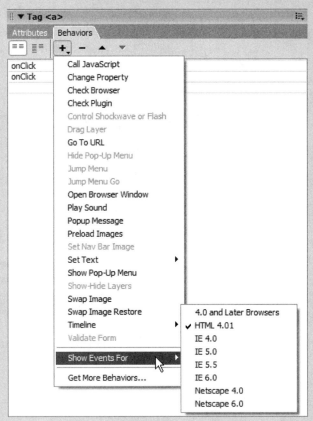

Figure 12.6 When you select Show Events For, you can choose from a list of browsers.

Events can only be applied to certain tags. See **Table 12.2** for specific event names and associated tags.

Table 12.2 Not all events available in Dreamweaver are listed. Some event handlers available in JavaScript are not available in Dreamweaver.

Dreamweaver Event Handlers		
EVENT	TRIGGERED WHEN	ASSOCIATED WITH
onAbort	The user stops the browser from completely loading the object	document, images
onBlur	A field loses focus	form fields
onChange	The user changes a default value on the page	form fields
onClick	The user clicks an object	links, form
onDblClick	The user double-clicks an object	links, images
onFocus	A field gains focus	form fields
onHelp	The user clicks F1 or something labeled Help	links, images
onKeyDown	The user presses a key on the keyboard	form fields
onKeyPress	The user presses any key	form fields
onKeyUp	The user releases a key	form fields
onLoad	When a page, frameset, or image finishes loading	document, images
onMouseDown	The user presses the mouse button	links, images
onMouseMove	The user moves the mouse	links, images
onMouseOut	The user moves the mouse off a selected object	links, images
onMouseUp	The user releases a mouse button	links, images
onMouseOver	The user points the mouse at an object	links, images
onReset	The user clicks a form reset button	forms
onResize	The user resizes the browser window	document
onScroll	The user scrolls up or down	document
onSelect	The user selects text in a form field	form fields
onSubmit	The user clicks the Submit button in a form	forms
onUnload	The user leaves a page	document

EVENTS AND BROWSERS

Adding Rollovers

Web users love *rollovers*, also called mouseovers. There's something endlessly pleasing about running a mouse over a page and watching things change. A color changes, an image changes, an image somewhere else on the page changes or pops up. What fun! Web users also expect rollovers—if they move their mouse over an image and nothing happens, they'll assume that it's not a link and move on to something else.

To add a rollover:

1. Prepare two images, such as those in **Figures 12.7** and **12.8**, for the rollover's Up and Over states.

2. Position the insertion point in the document where you want the rollover to appear.

3. On the Common tab of the Insert Bar, click the arrow beside the image icon (**Figure 12.9**).

4. Select Rollover Image.

   or

   Select Insert > Image Objects > Rollover Image.

5. The Insert Rollover Image dialog appears (**Figure 12.10**). Fill out the fields:

   ▲ **Image name:** This is the name that JavaScript will use internally to refer to this image.

   ▲ **Original image:** The Up state of the image, which is what will display when the page is loaded.

Figure 12.7 An example of an Up state image.

Figure 12.8 An example of an Over state image.

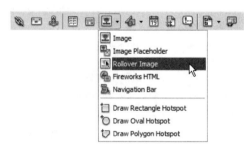

Figure 12.9 The image icon on the Common tab of the Insert Bar has a pop-up menu with several options.

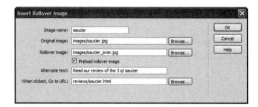

Figure 12.10 Specify the original image and the rollover image to insert a rollover image.

ADDING ROLLOVERS

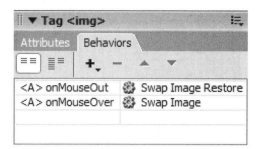

Figure 12.11 Be sure the Swap Image Restore behavior is added along with the Swap Image behavior.

Image States

To understand rollovers, buttons, and navigation bars, you need to know something about image states. An image state corresponds with a mouse event. The most common image states are:

◆ **Up** This image appears when the page first loads. It's the default image, in that it's what is displayed unless the user is interacting with this image.

◆ **Over** This image appears when the user moves the mouse over the image.

◆ **Down** This image appears when the user clicks the image. Down state images are often used in navigation bars to indicate the current page.

◆ **OverWhileDown** This image appears when the user moves the mouse over an image after clicking.

Most rollovers only use the Up and Over states.

▲ **Rollover image:** The Over state of the image, which is what will display when the user's cursor is over the image.

▲ **Preload rollover image:** This should be selected so the Over version of the image is in the browser's cache when it's needed. Don't make the users wait for the Over image to download—they might think the page isn't working and give up on your site.

▲ **Alternate text:** This is the alternate information for users with non-graphical browsers.

▲ **When clicked, Go to URL:** This is the URL of the Web page you want to open when the user clicks the image.

6. Click OK to accept the changes.

7. Check the default event in the Behaviors panel to be sure it's the one you want (**Figure 12.11**).

✔ Tips

■ Dreamweaver won't display the rollover. You must preview the page in a browser to see it.

■ Select the behavior in the Behaviors panel if you want to change the mouse events or edit the parameters of the Insert Rollover Image dialog.

■ To create multiple rollovers, use the Set Nav Bar Image behavior instead, as described in the next section.

ADDING ROLLOVERS

Adding Navigation Bars

A Dreamweaver navigation bar consists of a set of images that change in response to a user action. Before you use the Insert Navigation Bar command, you must prepare the image sets for each individual image (or button) that will appear in the navigation bar. If you want to use four image states, you'll need four images for each button similar to the four variations on the FOOD button you see in **Figure 12.12**.

To add a navigation bar:

1. Select the insertion point in the document window where the navigation bar goes.

2. Select Insert > Image Objects > Navigation Bar.

   or

   Select Navigation Bar from the pop-up menu next to the Image icon in the Common tab of the Insert Bar.

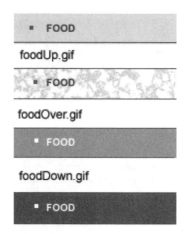

Figure 12.12 Save image variations with names that relate to the image state they represent.

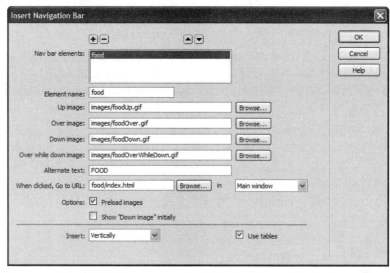

Figure 12.13 Those helpful image names come in handy when you're trying to manage four images for each button.

3. The Insert Navigation Bar dialog will open (**Figure 12.13**), and display the following fields:

▲ **Nav bar elements:** Don't enter anything here. As you add each element to your nav bar, this list grows automatically.

▲ **Element name:** This is the unique name that identifies the object. JavaScript objects must have unique names. On a nav bar, it makes sense to use a name that's the same or similar to the menu choice on the button. Remember, no spaces are allowed in the name.

▲ **Up image:** This is the Up (default) version of the image.

▲ **Over image:** This is the over version of the image.

▲ **Down image:** This image is displayed when the user clicks on the image.

▲ **Over while down image:** This version of the image appears when the user moves the mouse after clicking on the image.

▲ **Alternate text:** This is what displays for users with non-graphical browsers.

▲ **When clicked, Go to URL:** This is the page the user sees when the menu is clicked. Specify the window in which you want the URL to open. If you're using frames (See Chapter 11, "Adding Frames"), put the name of one of the frames here. If you're not using frames, leave it at "Main window."

Continues on next page

▲ **Options:** Always check Preload images. Show "Down image" initially would be selected on an individual page-by-page basis only if you're using the down version of the image to indicate the current page. When this option is selected, an asterisk appears after the element in the Nav bar elements list.

▲ **Insert:** This pop-up menu lets you choose either a horizontal or vertical layout for the nav bar.

▲ **Use tables:** If this check box is selected, the nav bar will use a table layout.

4. Click the plus button to add other elements and complete the dialog for each new element.

5. When you're done adding elements, click OK to accept your entries.

6. Check the default actions in the Behaviors panel to be sure they're the ones you want.

✔ Tips

■ If you want a navigation bar with only Up and Over image changes, leave the "Down image" and "Over while down image" fields blank.

■ Remember, alternate text appears when the image isn't visible. Write text that replaces the image effectively. If the button says "FOOD," for example, it's a good idea to use the word "FOOD" as the alternate text.

■ You can save some time if you copy and paste your navigation bar onto other pages. If you want to change the parameters for the navigation bar on individual pages, use the Modify > Navigation Bar command or the Set Nav Bar Image behavior.

■ You can save even more time by making your navigation bar into a reusable library item. (See Chapter 13, "Making Life Easier: Using Templates, Libraries, and Snippets," for more about library items.) You can't customize a library item on individual pages.

Modifying a Navigation Bar

No matter how often you think that you've got it just right when you first create your navigation, something's going to come along and make you change it. Some changes will be to the navigation bar itself, and some changes will be for only the images in the bar. How they're each changed differs slightly.

To modify a navigation bar:

1. Select the navigation bar in the document.

2. Select Modify > Navigation Bar. The Modify Navigation Bar dialog opens (**Figure 12.14**).

3. Make your changes as needed. This dialog's parameters are just like those in the original Insert Navigation Bar dialog.

Figure 12.14 Some of the choices from Figure 12.13 are no longer available when you use the Modify Navigation Bar dialog.

To modify images in a navigation bar:

1. Select one of the image elements in your navigation bar and double-click one of the Set Nav Bar Image actions in the Behaviors panel (**Figure 12.15**).

2. The Set Nav Bar Image dialog opens (**Figure 12.16**). This dialog looks similar to the Insert Navigation Bar dialog, but there are some major differences. You're only dealing with a single object from the nav bar, and you have tabs for basic and advanced modifications.

   On the Basic tab, you can modify any of the parameters for Element name, image URLs, Alternate text, and the URL for the page to open. The Options let you set the image to be in the Down state initially.

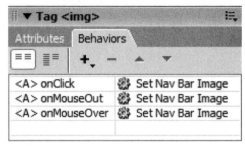

Figure 12.15 Double-click any behavior in the Behaviors panel to edit it. Alternatively, select it and press Return (Enter) to edit.

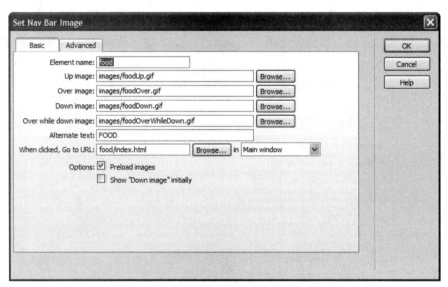

Figure 12.16 The Basic tab of Set Nav Bar Image dialog deals with just the specific button.

MODIFYING A NAVIGATION BAR

With the Advanced tab (**Figure 12.17**), use nav bar image actions to swap additional images elsewhere on the page with "Also set image."

For example, an image of an entrée might appear somewhere on the page when the FOOD button is in the Over state, or an image of a wine bottle might appear somewhere on the page when the WINE button is in the Over state. This type of fancy footwork—called a *disjoint rollover* in Dreamweaver—allows you to have multiple images that change due to a single event.

✔ Tip

■ A default opening image must be in place in the document before you can use the Advanced tab in the Set Nav Bar Image dialog to create a swap image behavior.

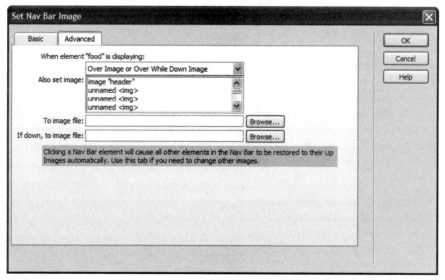

Figure 12.17 The Advanced tab has options to change other images besides just the selected button.

Opening a New Browser Window

It isn't a good idea to open a new browser window unless you really, really need one. Some users may not realize that a new window opened. Users may become lost or confused by the grayed-out Back button. Users may not realize they must close the new window to get back to the original page. Certain browsers, particularly those used by people with accessibility needs, may not deal with new windows in a way that helps the user understand what's happening. Depending on the action you use to trigger the opening of the new window, some users may not see it at all. For example, setting a new window to open during an onLoad event is the trick to getting a pop-up ad in a user's face. Therefore, many users set their browsers so pop-up windows won't open, ever.

Given all that, when is a new browser window justified? Consider it if the content of the new window is a small example or elaboration on one idea. Small means smaller than a normal-sized browser window. Small also means small in concept: if the main content of your page is clear already, a new window can add a little something people can check if they're interested. For instance, a good use of a new window is to show an enlarged image of a product.

You should explicitly tell the user that their click will cause a new window to open: "Click the image to see a larger view! Opens in new window." Leave the decision about whether to click up to your users—don't blindside them with windows that automatically open without warning.

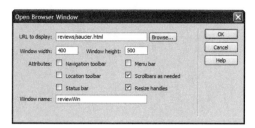

Figure 12.18 When you open a new browser window, you have all kinds of control over how that new window will appear.

To add the Open Browser Window action:

1. Prepare an HTML page or an image to appear in the new window.

2. Select an object such as a link or image in the document window.

3. In the Behaviors panel, click the plus sign **+.** to add a new behavior. Choose Open Browser Window from the pop-up menu, and the Open Browser Window dialog appears (**Figure 12.18**).

4. Fill out the following fields:

   ▲ **URL to display:** This is the HTML page or image that will appear in the new window.

   ▲ **Window width** and **Window height:** Set an exact pixel size for the new window.

   ▲ **Navigation toolbar:** Checking this box adds Back, Forward, Home, and Reload buttons.

   ▲ **Location toolbar:** Checking this box adds a location text box with the page URL showing.

   ▲ **Status bar:** Checking this box adds a display at the bottom of the browser window showing status information.

   ▲ **Menu bar:** Checking this box adds browser menu items, such as File, Edit, View, Go, and Help. This option only applies to Windows users; Mac users always have access to the menu.

   ▲ **Scrollbars as needed:** Checking this box adds scrollbars (either horizontal or vertical) only if needed. If unchecked, there will be no scrollbars. It's a good idea to always check this.

Continues on next page

OPENING A NEW BROWSER WINDOW

▲ **Resize handles:** Checking this box adds a gripper in the lower-right corner of the window for the user to drag, and a maximize button at the top of the window. If unchecked, the user can't resize the window by either method. This is another good attribute to routinely include.

▲ **Window name:** This is a required identifier needed by JavaScript. Remember, no spaces are allowed in this name.

5. Click OK to accept.

6. Check the default event. If it isn't the event you want, select another event from the pop-up menu.

✔ Tips

■ If the new window contains only an image, the pixel dimensions of the image and the pixel dimensions of the window aren't an exact match. For better control, many designers put the single image on an HTML page and link to the HTML page.

■ Dreamweaver can be extended with an action to add a "Close Window" script to an HTML page. It's a good idea to give users an obvious way to close the new window. See "Finding and Installing Extensions" in Appendix B for more information about extending Dreamweaver.

■ The event choices are determined by the targeted browsers. If an event you want is not available, check to see what's selected in the Show Events For submenu of the Add Events menu.

Figure 12.19 You can check for any plug-in, if you know the correct name for it.

Checking for Plug-ins

Check Plugin sends users to different pages depending on whether they have particular plug-ins. For example, if a user has Shockwave installed, you might send them to one page, otherwise, you might send them to a page where they get the same information but without Shockwave.

Most Dreamweaver behaviors are dependable cross-browser, but Check Plugin smacks into some browser issues. You can't detect plug-ins in Internet Explorer for Windows using JavaScript. Dreamweaver adds a VBScript plug-in detector when you select Flash or Director. This only works with Internet Explorer on Windows. There's no way to use Dreamweaver behaviors to check for plug-ins on Internet Explorer on Macintosh.

To add the Check Plugin action:

1. In the document window, use the tag selector to select either the document (the <body> tag) or a link (the <a> tag).

2. In the Behaviors panel, click the plus sign ✚ and select the Check Plugin action. The Check Plugin dialog opens (**Figure 12.19**) and shows the following:

   ▲ Choose a plug-in from the pop-up menu: Flash, Shockwave, Live Audio, Quick Time, or Windows Media Player.

   or

   ▲ Click the Enter radio button and type the name of a plug-in in the text box. The name must be exactly the same as the name in bold on the About Plug-ins page in a Netscape browser. To see the About Plug-ins page, enter about: plugins in Netscape's address field.

Continues on next page

- ▲ **If found, go to URL:** Enter the URL in this text box. This field is optional; if you leave it blank the user stays on the same page if the plug-in is detected.

- ▲ **Otherwise, go to URL:** Enter the alternate URL in the text box. If you leave this field blank, users *without* the plug-in will stay on the same page.

- ▲ **Always go to first URL if detection is not possible:** If detection is impossible, the user is sent to the URL in the "Otherwise, go to URL" box. If you select this check box, then the user instead goes to the first URL. If this is checked, users may be prompted by the browser to download the plug-in.

3. Click OK to accept changes.

4. Check the default event in the Behaviors panel to be sure it's the one you want.

✔ Tips

- ■ All Netscape browsers since version 2.0 can detect plug-ins. By "Netscape browser," we mean Netscape Navigator, Communicator, Mozilla, Firefox, and other browsers based on any of these.

- ■ Microsoft Internet Explorer for Mac does allow checking of plug-ins via JavaScript; however, Macromedia wrote their code to not allow it to work for this one browser. Why they did this, we don't know. We also don't know why Microsoft was able to put real plug-in detection into their Mac browser but not their Windows browser. If you're on a Mac, though, you should be using Safari or Firefox, in which case this would not affect you.

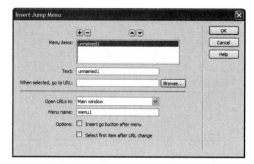

Figure 12.20 Here's a brand-new Insert Jump Menu dialog, ready for you to add as many items as you want.

Using Jump Menus

A jump menu is a pop-up menu listing links to documents or files. When a user chooses an item, they "jump" directly to the new URL.

Jump menus save space on the page. For example, to find a retailer in your area for a particular product, you might be asked to select your state or country. A list of states or countries could be very lengthy. Putting the links in a jump menu saves you from listing them in full as part of the page layout.

In addition to the required list of linked items, a jump menu can optionally include a menu selection prompt, such as "Select one," and a Go button.

To insert a jump menu:

1. Place the insertion point in the document.

2. Select Insert > Form > Jump Menu.

   or

   In the Form category of the Insert Bar, click the Jump Menu button.

   The Insert Jump Menu dialog appears (**Figure 12.20**). Fill it out as follows:

   ▲ **Menu items:** Don't type anything in this list. As you add items to the menu, they will automatically appear.

   Move items up or down in the Menu Items list by selecting one and using the up or down arrow to change its order.

   ▲ **Text:** Type the text you want for the menu item. You can type a prompt such as "Choose one" here. For text to be a prompt, leave the URL blank.

   ▲ **When selected, go to URL:** Browse or type the URL to go here.

Continues on next page

Continues on next page

- ▲ **Open URLs in:** Select the window where you want the URL to display. If you're using frames (See Chapter 11, "Adding Frames"), name one of the frames here.

- ▲ **Menu name:** Type a name in here for JavaScript to use; as always, it cannot contain any spaces.

- ▲ **Insert go button after menu:** Select this if you want a Go button. The Go button isn't required to make the menu work for users with JavaScript enabled in their browsers. If the user's browser doesn't use JavaScript or if the site uses frames, the Go button is needed.

- ▲ **Select first item after URL change:** If you use a prompt, select this.

3. Click OK to accept your changes., and the jump menu will show up on your page.

To edit a jump menu:

1. Double-click the Behavior name in the Behaviors panel. The Jump Menu dialog opens (**Figure 12.21**).

2. Make any changes as needed.

3. Click OK to accept the changes, and the revised jump menu will appear in your document.

To insert a jump menu Go button:

1. Select an insertion point in the document window. A jump menu must already exist in the document.

2. In the Behaviors panel, click the plus button ✚ and select Jump Menu Go. The Jump Menu Go dialog will open (**Figure 12.22**).

3. Select a menu for the Go button to activate. A Go button needs to be associated with a jump menu in order to work.

4. Click OK to create the button.

Figure 12.21 When you edit a jump menu, some of the original options are missing, particularly the "Insert go button after menu" choice.

Figure 12.22 The Jump Menu Go dialog attaches a Go button to an existing jump menu of your choice.

✔ Tip

- ■ A jump menu requires a form, which Dreamweaver adds automatically. You'll notice the red form indicator bordering the jump menu in the document window and you'll see a <form> tag in the tag selector bar.

USING JUMP MENUS

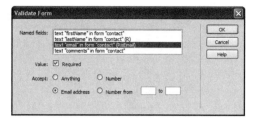

Figure 12.23 One form validation option is to require an email address from the user.

Validating Forms

Dreamweaver behaviors do some checks on how users complete forms. You can make certain fields required, check to make sure that a user has entered a value in a required field, or check to make sure that the user entered the correct type of information in a field.

With the Validate Form behavior you can set parameters for an entire form. You can also use the Validate Form behavior on individual fields. See Chapter 10, "Using Forms and Fields," for more information about making a form with Dreamweaver.

To validate a form:

1. In the document window, select the Submit button.

   or

   Select the `<form>` tag from the tag selector.

2. On the Behaviors panel, click plus **+.** and select Validate Form. The Validate Form dialog will open (**Figure 12.23**) and display the fields:

   ▲ **Named fields:** Select the first field in the box.

   ▲ **Required:** Select this if the user *must* enter data in this field in order for the form to be accepted.

   ▲ **Anything:** Check this radio button if any combination of text and numbers is acceptable.

   ▲ **Number:** Check this if you want the user to enter a zip code, phone number, or other strictly numerical data.

   ▲ **Email address:** Choose this if you want to check for an @ symbol within the entered data.

   ▲ **Number from:** Select this if you need to check for a number within a specified range.

Continues on next page

3. Select the remaining fields in the Named fields box and set the parameters for each until you have completed the dialog for each field in the form.

4. Click OK to accept your changes.

✔ Tips

■ You can also select an individual form field and add a validate form behavior. The dialog is the same but the event handler (that's the real name for those fields on the Behavior panel) is different. Check the Behaviors panel to be sure it's the correct event (onBlur or onChange) when setting validation parameters field by individual field. Be careful with this method, because it can get annoying to a user who wants to skip certain questions and come back to them later. Saving the validation for last, when the user finally clicks the Submit button, is a better idea.

■ When a user enters something incorrectly or neglects to fill in a required field, a JavaScript alert box similar to **Figure 12.24** pops up with a message about the error.

■ It's good practice to give users an explicit cue when a field is required. An asterisk next to a required field is a common visual cue, along with a note to the user that the asterisk denotes a required field. You may have colorblind users, so merely formatting the required field labels in a different color isn't considered adequate.

■ The Dreamweaver behaviors for validating forms are different from the server-side scripts used to handle submitted information. The same validity checks on user data you add with Dreamweaver should also be done with server-side scripts. Why both? The server-side checks are necessary because not everyone has JavaScript. The client-side JavaScript checks added here are also useful because they give faster feedback to users.

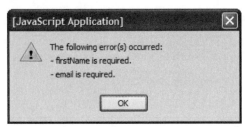

Figure 12.24 The user sees an alert if the form validation requirements aren't met.

VALIDATING FORMS

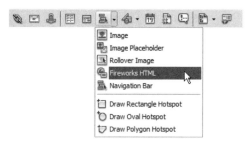

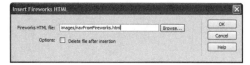

Figure 12.25 You can choose to add Fireworks HTML from the Image icon in the Common category of the Insert Bar.

Figure 12.26 Getting Fireworks HTML into Dreamweaver is as easy as pointing to the HTML file.

Inserting Fireworks Pop-Up Menus

If you own Fireworks 8, you can use it to create a pop-up menu. It's possible to create one without Fireworks (see the next section, "Inserting Dreamweaver Pop-Up Menus"), but Dreamweaver cautions you when you do that the pop-up menus created in Fireworks are easier to control and change.

If you create the pop-up menu in Fireworks and insert it into a Dreamweaver document, it's best to use the round-trip editing feature to edit the menu in Fireworks. You will be able to edit the pop-up menu in Dreamweaver, but if you do, you lose the ability to edit it in Fireworks later. Stick with Fireworks.

When you have the Fireworks pop-up menu completed, simply export it. Fireworks will create all the image and HTML files for you and add them to the Dreamweaver site root folder. With the files in your site folder, you're ready to insert the menu in Dreamweaver.

To insert a Fireworks pop-up menu:

1. Place the insertion point in the document where you want the menu.

2. Choose Insert > Image Objects > Fireworks HTML.

   or

   Select Fireworks HTML from the pop-up menu by the Image icon in the Common category on the Insert Bar (**Figure 12.25**).

   The Insert Fireworks HTML dialog will open (**Figure 12.26**).

   Continues on next page

3. Browse for or type the name of the Fireworks HTML file.

4. Select the "Delete file after insertion" option if you no longer want the Fireworks HTML to be stored as a separate file. Selecting this option won't affect the source PNG file associated with the HTML file, or your ability to use round-trip editing to edit the pop-up menu in Fireworks.

5. Click OK to insert your menu. All the HTML, image links, and JavaScript connected to the pop-up menu are inserted in the appropriate areas in the document.

✔ Tip

■ Deleting the HTML file after insertion has its pros and cons. You might want to keep it around to use elsewhere, or you might want to delete it to clean up after yourself. Either way, you can re-create it inside Fireworks, so if you delete it accidentally, it's not the end of the world.

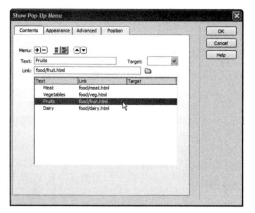

Figure 12.27 Use the Contents tab of the Show Pop-Up Menu dialog to define your menu choices.

Inserting Dreamweaver Pop-Up Menus

If you don't own Fireworks, all is not lost. You can still use Dreamweaver to insert a pop-up menu.

Pop-up menus are popular because they save space on the page and create a cleaner layout. The main site sections are shown with global navigation, but the subsection links don't appear until the mouse is over the main heading.

On HomeCook.info, the main site categories of food, wine, recipes, etc., have related sub-section pages. In the wine area, for example, there might be pages for red, white, and rosé wines, or domestic, imported, or regional wines, cooking wines, dessert wines—whew, you get the idea. If every possible link for the wine area was listed in the main menu, you'd have a messy and hard-to-use site. Multiply that by the links for food, recipes, news and the menu grows overwhelming. A pop-up menu is one way to solve that problem.

This behavior attaches to links, so have the global site navigation completed before you start adding subsection links.

To create a pop-up menu:

1. Select the relevant link for the pop-up menu.

2. In the Behaviors panel, click the plus ✚ and select Show Pop-Up Menu.

3. Dreamweaver tells you that pop-up menus work better when made with Fireworks. Click Continue, and the Show Pop-Up Menu dialog appears (**Figure 12.27**).

Continues on next page

4. Select the Contents tab.

▲ Three sets of icons follow the Menu option. The plus and minus buttons are the familiar icons to add or delete a menu item. The outdent ▤ and indent ▤ icons are used to create indented submenu items. Click the indent icon to begin a submenu and click the outdent icon when the submenu is complete. Use the familiar up and down arrows as needed to reorder the items in the menu list.

▲ **Text:** Type the text for the menu item in this field.

▲ **Target:** Select one, if needed. If you do nothing here, the link opens in the same window. If you're using frames, put the name of a frame here.

▲ **Link:** Type or browse to insert the URL in this field.

▲ Click the plus button next to the word "Menu" to add another item to your list, and repeat as needed.

5. Select the Appearance tab (**Figure 12.28**).

▲ Select Vertical menu or Horizontal menu for the menu layout from the pop-up menu.

▲ Specify a Font.

▲ Specify a font Size.

▲ Select the icons for Bold, Italic, Left Aligned, Centered, or Right Aligned as needed.

▲ Use the Color Picker to select Text and Cell colors for the Up state and the Over state.

▲ Check your choices with the miniature version of the menu.

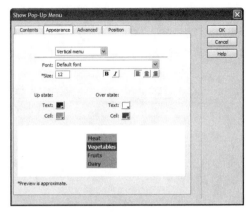

Figure 12.28 Use the Appearance tab to define your menu orientation and colors.

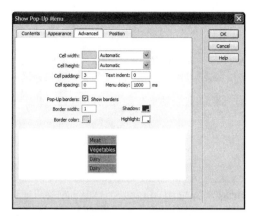

Figure 12.29 Use the Advanced tab to define the menu's table cells.

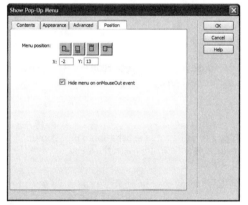

Figure 12.30 Use the Position tab to define the position of the pop-up.

6. Select the Advanced tab (**Figure 12.29**) if you need more precise layout.

   ▲ Enter Cell width in pixels or let the cells size themselves automatically depending on the contents.

   ▲ Enter Cell height in pixels or opt for automatic sizing.

   ▲ Enter Cell padding as desired.

   ▲ Enter Text indent as desired.

   ▲ Enter Cell spacing as desired.

   ▲ Enter a value in milliseconds for Menu delay. This is the delay between when the user mouses over the link and when the pop-up menu appears. One second equals 1000 milliseconds.

   ▲ In the Pop-Up borders area, indicate whether to Show borders. If you choose to show a border, then complete the remaining questions with a Border width and color choices for the borders.

   ▲ Check your choices with the miniature version of the menu.

7. Select the Position tab (**Figure 12.30**) to choose where the menu appears on the page.

   ▲ Select a Menu position for the pop-up menu from the preset options.

   ▲ Customize the preset menu position with values entered in the X (horizontal) and Y (vertical) coordinate fields. The custom coordinates count starts from the top-left corner of the menu.

   ▲ Be sure "Hide menu on onMouseOut event" is selected unless you want the pop-ups to continue to display after the user leaves that menu.

8. Click OK to accept your changes.

Continues on next page

9. Preview the file in your browser (**Figure 12.31**). If needed, make changes by double-clicking the Show Pop-Up Menu behavior in the Behaviors panel (**Figure 12.32**).

10. To add a pop-up menu for another of your global navigation links, select the appropriate link and repeat these steps.

✔ Tips

■ The JavaScript needed for a pop-up menu is so extensive, Dreamweaver saves it as an external file with a `.js` extension. You should see `mm_menu.js` in your site files. Remember, `mm_menu.js` needs to be uploaded to the server when you are transferring your files to the server or your menu won't work.

■ Be sure to test the appearance of pop-up menus in several different browsers and with as many operating systems as possible. There may be some variation in the way the menu displays in different situations. You'll probably want to do some fine-tuning and tweaking of parameters.

Figure 12.31 A pop-up menu has to be previewed in a browser. You can't test it in the Dreamweaver document window.

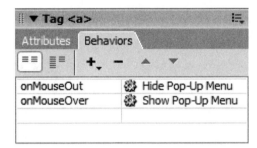

Figure 12.32 Be sure the behavior to Hide Pop-Up Menu gets added; otherwise, the menu just won't go away!

Making Life Easier: Using Templates, Libraries, and Snippets

The first thing you do when you begin a site in Dreamweaver is define a site root folder, as discussed in Chapter 2. You tell Dreamweaver where you're keeping all your site files. Dreamweaver rewards you for sharing the information by making all sorts of cool site-wide tools available to speed up your workflow and make your life easier. In seconds, Dreamweaver's site management tools can make changes to every file in your local site root folder—changes that would take you much longer done one file at a time.

We'll cover two of those timesaving whole-site tools, templates and libraries, in this chapter. In addition, you'll learn how to create timesaving bits of reusable code called *snippets*. You access templates and Library items from the Assets panel. Snippets have a separate panel.

Before getting into the details, some brief definitions are in order. *Templates* are like master page designs. They create a uniform page design for a site, while allowing certain material on each page to be customized for individual pages. *Library* items are not full pages, but reusable objects with text, code, images, or other elements that you insert in documents. For example, you can create a navigation bar as a Library item. Updating either a template or a Library item results in the automatic updating of any page in the entire site that is attached to the template or library. Snippets are custom-built code samples that you find useful and save for quick insertion. Changing a snippet doesn't have any site-wide effects.

They Can't Break Your Sites!

Pages made from templates are perfect for use in organizations that want relatively unskilled people to be able to make changes and updates to sites without the possibility of accidentally "breaking" the site. In fact, Macromedia has a program, Macromedia Contribute, that works hand-in-hand with sites built using Dreamweaver templates to allow people to add content and make changes to Web sites without being able to mess up the site's design elements. With Contribute, the site designer can assign site contributors to *user roles*, which specify the editing tasks the user is allowed. For example, you can have a user who can add and change text to a page, but can only style that text with CSS styles you supply, or you can prevent the user from styling text at all. You can also require that users send their changed pages to a supervisor for review before making the page live on the site. Many other permissions and restrictions are possible if people who work on your site use Contribute.

You'll find more information about using Dreamweaver to work with Contribute in Chapter 14, and if you want to know more about Contribute itself, we invite you to pick up *Macromedia Contribute 3 for Windows and Macintosh: Visual QuickStart Guide*, by Tom Negrino, also from Peachpit Press.

Creating a Template

Templates are perfect for many situations. For example, let's say you have a large site where many different individuals change content and add pages. Using a template provides control over the page layout and design by restricting changes only to certain *editable regions* on a page. Other areas on the page are *locked regions*, which can't be changed by people working on an individual page. Locked regions can only be edited in the original template file. This kind of control guarantees a consistent look and feel for a site, and prevents any accidental changes to locked regions.

When a change is made to a template, every page made from, or *attached* to, the template is automatically updated throughout the entire site. You can create a template from scratch, but it is simpler to use an existing page as a model for the template, and that's what we'll explain here.

Before you save a document as a template, make sure you've already included any needed `<meta>` tags, style sheets, behaviors, or other underlying parameters. These page elements are located in the locked regions of a template. There's no way to add things like style sheet links to individual pages made from a template—they must exist in the template already.

To create a template from an existing page:

1. Open the document you want to turn into a template.

2. Choose File > Save as Template.

   or

Continues on next page

Choose Make Template from the Templates pop-up menu of the Common category of the Insert Bar (**Figure 13.1**).

The Save As Template dialog appears, with the Site pop-up menu set to the current local site (**Figure 13.2**).

3. Enter the requested information in this dialog.

▲ **Existing templates:** You don't enter anything in this field. Dreamweaver lists any existing templates for the site automatically.

▲ **Description:** Type a brief description of the template.

▲ **Save as:** Type the name of the template.

4. Click Save.

If it doesn't already exist, Dreamweaver adds a `Templates` folder to your site files. Your new template will be inside this folder, with the file extension `.dwt`, indicating that the document is a Dreamweaver template.

✔ Tips

■ Templates are for local use; they're never loaded in a browser. The `Templates` folder and its `.dwt` files don't need to be uploaded to the server. Just upload the individual HTML pages made from the template. To make this easier, you can cloak the Templates folder, which prevents Dreamweaver from uploading it to the remote server. See "Cloaking Files," in Chapter 2, for more information.

■ It's possible to create a template from scratch. Choose File > New and select Template Page in the New Document window. Or you can start one using the New Template button in the Templates area of the Assets panel.

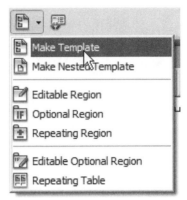

Figure 13.1 The pop-up menu for the Template icon in the Common category of the Insert Bar covers the basic commands you'll need.

Figure 13.2 Any page can be saved as a template. The name you type in the Save as field will be followed by the file extension `.dwt` in the Assets list.

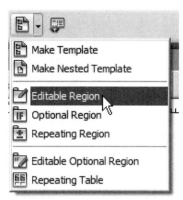

Figure 13.3 Use the pop-up menu for the Template icon in the Common category of the Insert Bar to designate editable regions in the template.

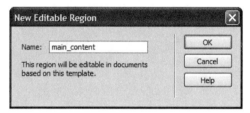

Figure 13.4 A short, descriptive name is best for a template region. Don't use spaces in the name; instead, use the underscore character, as shown.

Adding Editable Regions

Once you've saved the `.dwt` file, you will want to open it and define any regions you want to be editable. Regions on the page that you don't specifically mark as editable will be locked and can't be changed by anyone working on pages made from your template—hey, that's the whole point!

To add an editable region:

1. Open the template document.

2. Select the element to make editable, for example `<div>`, `<img>`, or `<td>`, with the tag selector in the document window.

   or

   Select the text to make editable. This choice is most useful when the text is within a div. Selecting the entire layer, rather than just the text within it, makes everything about the div editable, including its position. You probably don't want your users being able to change anything other than the text, so just select that text and it will be the only editable part of the div.

3. Choose Editable Region from the Templates pop-up menu in the Common category of the Insert Bar (**Figure 13.3**).

   or

   Choose Insert > Template Objects > Editable Region.

   The New Editable Region dialog appears (**Figure 13.4**).

4. Type a name for the region.

5. Click OK.

   Continues on next page

6. The editable region will be outlined in green in the document window. A tab at the upper left of the region displays the region name (**Figure 13.5**).

7. (Optional) Delete the text that was in the region and replace it with some general instruction regarding the region, for example, "This region is for main content." If you don't do this, it's okay—anyone making a page from the template can replace the text later.

Region name

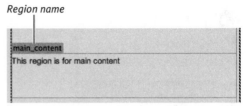

Figure 13.5 In the document window, the editable region is indicated with a visible tab giving the region name.

✔ Tips

■ You can make an entire table editable, or the table header, a table row, or individual cells within a table. But you can't put a table column or multiple noncontiguous table cells in a single editable region.

■ Don't use special characters in region names: no ampersands (&), single quote marks ('), double quote marks ("), or angle brackets (<) and (>).

■ Page titles are editable by default on pages that are created from templates.

ADDING EDITABLE REGIONS

Figure 13.6 To remove an editable region from a template, choose Remove Template Markup.

Removing Editable Regions

If you make a region editable and later decide you want to lock it instead, it's easy to remove the editable region.

To remove an editable region:

1. Click the tab in the upper left of the region to select the region.

2. Choose Modify > Templates > Remove Template Markup (**Figure 13.6**).

3. The region is locked.

Other Kinds of Template Regions

Dreamweaver can create more complex editable areas in addition to the basic editable region. These kinds of editable regions are used less frequently, but they're still useful when you need them. You probably noticed the options in the Templates pop-up menu in the Common category of the Insert Bar (Figures 13.1 and 13.3). They are:

◆ **Repeating Region:** Repeating regions can be duplicated by the user as often as needed. They're useful for things that vary from page to page, for example a chart of product colors or sizes, or a list of recipe ingredients. Repeating regions aren't editable until you define the editable areas of the region.

◆ **Optional Region:** You set conditions for optional regions, indicated by the word *if* in the tab showing the region name. Optional content can be either hidden or displayed, depending on whether the conditions are met. For example, let's say that you have a page of upcoming events. You have an image that says, "Coming Soon!" that you want to appear next to events that will occur in the next month. You can write code that checks the date, then displays the "Coming Soon!" image in an optional region when the code expression is true.

◆ **Editable Optional Region:** As with optional regions, you can decide whether or not to display content in these regions. Editable Optional Regions are, well, editable.

◆ **Repeating Table:** Repeating tables are actually repeating regions, but they automatically include table tags, so you can easily use them for tabular data.

Building Pages Based on a Template

Most of the time you will create new pages based on your template. This is the easiest and least confusing way to make templates work for you. It's also possible to take an existing page, say from an older site that you're completely redesigning, and apply a template to that page. That method is a bit trickier.

To make a new page from a template:

1. Choose File > New.

   The New Document dialog appears.

2. Click the Templates tab.

   The name of the dialog changes to "New from Template."

3. Select your site from the "Templates for" list. Any available templates for that site will display in the Site column.

4. Select the template you want from the Site column.

   A preview of the template will appear in the dialog (**Figure 13.7**).

5. Click Create.

   A new page, based on the template, appears.

6. Add content to the editable regions and save the new document with an appropriate file name and location in your site.

✔ Tip

- You can create a new page from a template faster once you get used to working with templates. In the Assets panel, click the Templates category, then right-click (Ctrl-click) on the template name and choose New from Template from the shortcut menu (**Figure 13.8**).

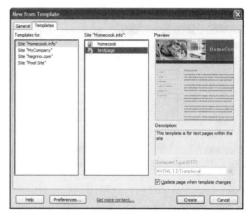

Figure 13.7 If you begin a new page from a template with the File > New command, you must choose the site, then the template.

Figure 13.8 Fewer steps are involved in starting a new page from a template if you right-click (Ctrl-click) the template name in the Assets panel.

Apply button

Figure 13.9 Modify an existing page to fit into a template page by selecting the template and clicking the Apply button.

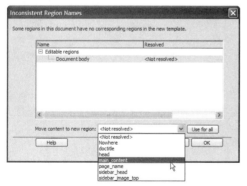

Figure 13.10 When retrofitting an existing page to work with a template, you must decide where to put the content. The pop-up menu shows possible regions.

✔ Tip

■ Dreamweaver expects the Templates folder to be at the top level of your site structure. Don't move it into a subfolder. If you do, Dreamweaver won't display the template files in your Assets panel or in the New Document template list.

To apply a template to an existing page:

1. Open the existing document to which you want to apply the template.

2. In the Assets panel, select the template you want and click the Apply button at the lower left (**Figure 13.9**).

    or

    Drag the template from the Assets panel to the document window.

    or

    Choose Modify > Templates > Apply Template to Page. The Select Template dialog appears. Click a template in the list to choose it.

    The Inconsistent Region Names dialog appears (**Figure 13.10**). This dialog allows you to tell Dreamweaver in which region of the new page it should place the document's existing content.

3. In the Inconsistent Region Names dialog, do the following:

    ▲ In the scrolling list, select an unresolved region.

    ▲ Use the "Move content to new region" pop-up menu to select an editable region for the content.

    If you choose Nowhere from the pop-up menu, the content will be removed from the document. If you click the "Use for all" button, all the unresolved content will be moved to the selected region.

4. Click OK.

5. The resulting document probably needs some cleaning up to work seamlessly with the template. For example, you may need to restyle some text, or move a bit of content manually. After that is completed, save as usual.

Modifying a Template

Templates give you tons of control over what can be edited and what can't. Sure, that's important. But what happens if you make lots of pages from your template and then something changes? Maybe you need to add a new item to the menu, or you need a new editable region on the page. The answer is that something really cool happens when a Dreamweaver template is modified: Dreamweaver automatically changes all the pages you've already made using that template. So you can make changes to just one page (the template) and have those changes automatically ripple through the site.

Normally, you'd start your modification directly in the template file. But you can also start from any document that is attached to the template. You can pick and choose the attached pages to which you want the changes to apply.

To modify a template file:

1. In the Assets panel, click the Templates button to display the templates, then double-click the template file you want to edit.

   or

   In the Assets panel, click the Templates button to display the templates, then highlight the template file and click the Edit button at the bottom of the panel.

   The template file opens in the document window.

2. Edit as desired, then choose File > Save, or press Ctrl-S (Cmd-S).

   The Update Template Files dialog appears. Each file attached to the template is listed in the dialog (**Figure 13.11**).

   If you click **Update**, every file attached to the template will update. If you click **Don't Update**, none of the files attached to the template will update.

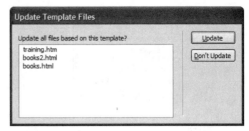

Figure 13.11 Here's the powerful part of using templates. Dreamweaver offers to update template-based pages when you change a template.

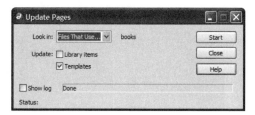

Figure 13.12 If you allow Dreamweaver to update template-based pages, it reports the results when it's finished.

You can't choose to modify just one page here (it's all or nothing), but it's possible to do that elsewhere. See the section below, "To modify an individual template-based page" for details.

3. Click Update.

The Update Pages dialog appears (**Figure 13.12**). Dreamweaver sorts through all the files in your site and makes the updates, showing you the progress in the Update Pages dialog.

This dialog also allows you to update all the pages in the site to their corresponding templates, or just update files based on a specific template. If you don't need any additional updates than the ones Dreamweaver already made, go to Step 7.

4. (Optional) From the "Look in" pop-up menu, choose Entire Site or Files That Use.

The first choice reapplies all the templates in the site to files made from those templates. The second choice, which is what you will want to do most of the time, just updates the pages based on the template you just edited.

When you make a choice from the "Look in" pop-up menu, the inactive Done button becomes active, and its label changes to Start.

5. (Optional) Make sure that the Templates check box is selected.

6. (Optional) Click Start.

When the process is complete, the Start button changes to Done and becomes inactive.

7. Click Close to dismiss the Update Pages dialog.

8. Close the template file.

MODIFYING A TEMPLATE

To modify a template attached to a current document:

1. With a document based on a template open, choose Modify > Templates > Open Attached Template.

   The template opens in a separate window.

2. Make your modifications as described in the previous section.

   When you save the template, you'll be prompted to update pages attached to that template, including the page you started with.

To modify an individual template-based page:

1. Change a template file as described above. In the Update Template Files dialog (Figure 13.11), click Don't Update.

2. Open a document attached to the same template.

3. Choose Modify > Templates > Update Current Page.

   The page updates with the changes you made to the template. No other pages in the site will update.

✔ Tips

- When your template links to a CSS file, all your template-based pages link to it as well. If you change your CSS rules, the pages created from the template will automatically reflect those changes in exactly the same way non-template-based pages reflect CSS changes.

- HTML pages changed by the update of a template file need to be uploaded to the server for the change to be visible to your site's visitors. The easiest way to do this is to synchronize the local and remote sites. See "Synchronizing the Local and Remote Sites" in Chapter 2 for more information.

MODIFYING A TEMPLATE

Creating a Library Item

For someone working alone, the restrictions imposed by using a template may be unnecessary or even annoying. For example, when you use templates, you have to set up the editable and locked regions, and then when you go to modify a page based on the template, you don't have access to page elements in the locked regions. These restrictions are great if you're a designer who is giving pages to co-workers to modify, but on sites where you want to exercise total control over editing every page, Library items offer some of the same timesaving abilities to update pages and maintain consistency as templates, but with far fewer restrictions.

Library items aren't full pages. They're small bits of text, images, or code that you insert when needed. Good material for a Library item might be a navigation bar, copyright notice, list of links, graphic masthead, or perhaps a search box. If you want to use something frequently, have it display consistently on any page, and update all instances of it at one time, a Library item fits the bill. And they're easy to create and use.

To create a Library item:

1. Open a document.

2. Select an element in the document <body>. It can be anything you want to reuse: text, tables, forms, navigation bars, images, or other elements.

3. Do one of the following:

   Choose Modify > Library > Add Object to Library.

   or

Continues on next page

In the Library category 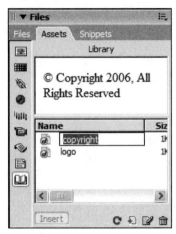 of the Assets panel, click the New Library item button.

or

Drag the selection into the Library category of the Assets panel.

4. The item appears in the Library category of the Assets panel (**Figure 13.13**). Type a name for the item.

In the document window, the item will be highlighted with a color, indicating that it's a Library item.

✔ Tips

■ The color used to highlight a Library item is yellow by default. If desired, this color can be changed in Dreamweaver's Preferences in the Highlighting category.

■ If it doesn't already exist, Dreamweaver creates a Library folder at the top level of your site. Library items are stored in this folder, with the file extension .lbi. The folder is for local use and doesn't need to be uploaded to the server.

Figure 13.13 Type a name for your new Library item here.

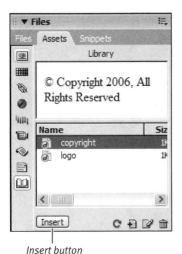

Insert button

Figure 13.14 A quick way to insert a Library item into a document is with the Insert button at the lower left of the Assets panel.

Using a Library Item

All you have to decide is where you want to use your Library items on your pages. The rest is easy.

To insert a Library item:

1. Position the insertion point in the document.

2. Drag the Library item from the Library category of the Assets panel into the document.

    or

    Highlight the Library item and click the Insert button at the lower left of the Assets panel (**Figure 13.14**).

    The Library item appears in the document.

To delete a Library item:

◆ From a document: select the Library item in the document window and press Backspace (Delete).

◆ From a site: choose the Library item in the Library category of the Assets panel and press Backspace (Delete). This step cannot be undone.

✔ Tip

■ Library items become part of the page's code and are subject to any CSS rules in style sheets linked to the page. For example, if your Library item contains a paragraph, and you have a CSS rule for the p selector, the inserted item will reflect the rule.

Editing a Library Item

You need to be a bit careful when you edit Library items, because when you change a Library item, Dreamweaver changes all instances of that item throughout all the pages of your site, in any documents that are not currently being edited. This can take some time if you have a large site, and you have to edit the item again to undo a mistake; the Undo command won't save you in this case. It's nothing to worry about; just be aware that changes can have far-reaching effects.

To edit a Library item:

1. Do one of the following:

   Double-click the item in the Library category in the Assets panel.

   or

   Highlight the item in the Library category in the Assets panel and then click the Edit button  in the lower right of the Assets panel.

   or

   Highlight the item in the document window. The Property Inspector shows information for the Library item (**Figure 13.15**). Click Open.

2. A window much like a document window appears, but it contains only the Library item (**Figure 13.16**).

3. Edit the item as needed.

Figure 13.15 When you select a Library item in the document window, you can use the Property Inspector to open the Library item.

Figure 13.16 An open Library item window is rather like a normal document window, except there's nothing there but the Library item.

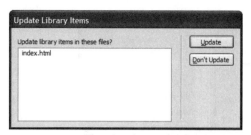

Figure 13.17 The benefit of using Library items comes from the ability to update any instances of the item in your site with one click of the Update button.

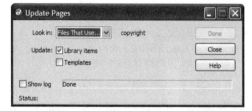

Figure 13.18 If you Update Library items, Dreamweaver reports on what it did.

4. Choose File > Save, or press Ctrl-S (Cmd-S). The Update Library Items dialog appears (**Figure 13.17**).

   ▲ **Update:** Updates every instance of the Library item used in your site.

   ▲ **Don't Update:** No Library items are updated.

   See the following section, "To update a Library item only in the current document," if you want to select individual pages to update.

5. Click Update to have Dreamweaver open the Update Pages dialog, run through all the files containing the Library item, update them, and report "Done" to you in the dialog when it's finished (**Figure 13.18**).

6. Click Close to dismiss the Update Pages dialog.

To update a Library item only in the current document:

1. Edit the Library item, then click Don't Update in the Update Library Items dialog (see the previous section, "To edit a Library item").

2. Open a document containing the Library item.

3. Choose Modify > Library > Update Current Page.

4. The Library item on this single page will update.

5. Save the document.

To rename a Library item:

1. Highlight the name of the Library item in the Library category of the Assets panel. Do one of the following:

   Right-click (Ctrl-click) and choose Rename from the shortcut menu.

   or

   Click on the item name, wait a second, and click it again.

   The Library item's name highlights and becomes editable (**Figure 13.19**).

2. Type the new name for the item.

3. The Update Files dialog appears (**Figure 13.20**). Click Update to change the name of the Library item on every page where it is in use.

✔ Tips

■ Library items can't contain any head elements, so you don't have access to the CSS panel when editing a Library item (internal CSS style sheets appear within the <head> tag).

■ Library items can't contain a <body> tag, so you don't have access to the Page Properties when editing a Library item.

■ HTML pages changed by the update of a Library item need to be uploaded to the server for the change to be visible to your site's visitors.

■ If a document is open when a Library item updates, you'll have to save the document manually. Updates save automatically in a closed document.

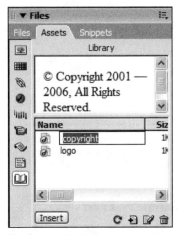

Figure 13.19 Need a better name for a Library item? You can change the name here.

Figure 13.20 When you change a Library item name, Dreamweaver asks you if you want to change all the instances of the item in the site to reflect the new name.

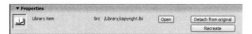

Figure 13.21 The Property Inspector can be used to detach a Library item from the source, or to re-create a Library item that's lost or missing.

Working on Library Items with the Property Inspector

As we mentioned in the previous section, "Editing a Library item," the Property Inspector offers some options for working on Library items. The previous section explained how to edit the Library item using the Open button, but there are two as yet unexplained buttons on the Property Inspector, Detach from original and Recreate.

Detaching a Library item doesn't remove the item from the page. It breaks the connection between the copy of the Library item on the current page and the original source in the site's Library folder. If you later update the original Library item, the current page's code won't be changed by the update.

Sometimes you can have a page that contains the code from a Library item that was removed from the site's Library folder (or never existed there). For example, let's say that you copied a page (that contained a Library item) from one of your sites to a different site. The site that now contains the page will not, of course, have a corresponding Library item in its Library folder. You can use the code in the current document to re-create the Library item in the new local site.

To detach the Library item:

1. Select a Library item in the document window.

2. On the Property Inspector, click Detach from original (**Figure 13.21**).

   Dreamweaver displays a dialog asking if you're sure you want to detach the item. Click OK. The link between the item on the page and the original in the Library is broken.

To re-create a missing or deleted Library item:

1. Open a document containing code for a Library item that is missing from the Library category of the Assets panel.

2. Highlight the item. The tag selector should display <mm:libitem>.

3. On the Property Inspector, click Recreate. The item will be re-created using the name it has on this page. The re-created item appears in the Library category of the Assets panel.

✔ Tips

■ If you detach a Library item from a page, the highlighting in the document window that indicated that the element was a Library item disappears along with the broken connection to the Library item source.

■ Right-clicking (Ctrl-clicking) on a Library item in the document window reveals a pop-up menu with the same options available on the Property Inspector to Open, Detach, or Recreate.

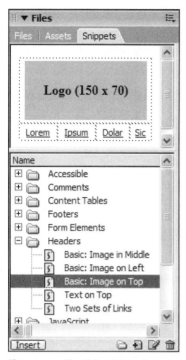

Figure 13.22 The Snippets panel comes preloaded with many useful snippets.

Figure 13.23 There's a brief description of a snippet to the right of its name.

Using Dreamweaver Snippets

The Snippets panel is used to store useful bits of code, or *snippets*, that can be inserted anytime, anyplace. In that way snippets are like Library items. But there's a big difference between snippets and Library items. If you change or update a snippet, there's no sitewide update to previously inserted versions of the snippet. There's no connection between the code in an inserted snippet and the original snippet.

Dreamweaver comes with many useful pre-built snippets already loaded and ready to use. You'll find them in the Snippets panel. If the Snippets panel is not already visible, choose Window > Snippets to bring it forward.

In the Snippets panel (**Figure 13.22**), the snippets that come with Dreamweaver are nicely organized into folders for you. Inside the folders you find individual snippets. Click on an individual snippet to see a preview in the preview pane at the top of the panel. You can also see a description of the highlighted snippet. If you work with a narrow window, as in Figure 13.22, you may have to scroll to the right with the horizontal scrollbar at the bottom of the Snippets panel to see the description. Expand the width of the panel (**Figure 13.23**) to read the description without scrolling.

You've probably already figured out that any custom snippets you save will appear in the Snippets panel, too. Your snippets and Dreamweaver's snippets are used in the same way. We'll explain how to save a new snippet first, and then how to use it.

To save a snippet:

1. Open a document containing the material you'd like to make into a snippet. Highlight the snippet (**Figure 13.24**). Be sure you get all the surrounding material needed by clicking the tag in the tag selector.

2. Click the New Snippet icon ⊞ in the bottom right of the Snippets panel. The Snippet dialog appears (**Figure 13.25**). Complete the following fields:

   ▲ **Name:** Type a name for the new snippet.

   ▲ **Description:** Type a description. This is helpful, but optional.

   ▲ **Snippet type:** Click Wrap selection if the snippet is meant to wrap around a selection. Click Insert block if the snippet is meant to be inserted as a block.

   If you choose Wrap selection, you will be asked to choose the parts of the snippet to Insert Before or Insert After the wrapped selection.

   ▲ **Insert code:** The code you high-lighted in the document is displayed here. This is an editable field.

   ▲ **Preview type:** Choose either Design or Code.

3. Click OK.

4. The snippet appears in the Snippet panel (**Figure 13.26**). The preview displays in the preview pane.

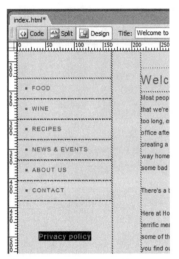

Figure 13.24 Select something on a page to save as a snippet.

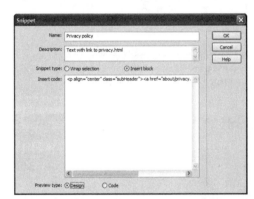

Figure 13.25 When you save your own snippets, you decide on a name, description, and other basics.

Figure 13.26 Snippets you save appear in the Snippets panel. You can drag them into existing folders or organize new folders of your own.

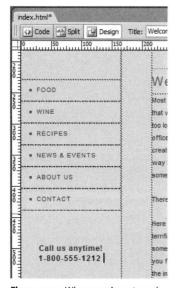

Figure 13.27 When you insert a snippet into a document, the text or other element the snippet contains appears on your page.

To use a snippet:

1. Position the insertion point in the document.

2. Highlight the snippet in the Snippets panel and do one of the following:

   Click the Insert button at the lower left of the Snippets panel.

   or

   Double-click the snippet name.

   or

   Drag the snippet from the Snippets panel onto the document.

3. The snippet appears in the document. Replace any dummy text with correct content (**Figure 13.27**).

✔ Tips

- The snippet preview pane won't display the snippet with any CSS shown. The snippet must be on a page before CSS rules take effect.

- Delete or modify snippets by highlighting them and using the Edit Snippet or Remove buttons at the lower right of the Snippets panel.

- Organize your snippets by dragging them into preexisting folders or creating new folders of your own naming.

- Don't use any special characters such as ampersans (&) or angle brackets (< and >) in snippet names.

WORKING WITH OTHER APPLICATIONS

When building a Web site, no single application can stand alone; in order to get the best results, you must orchestrate elements from a variety of programs. For example, you might get your text from Microsoft Word, data for a table from Microsoft Excel, and the site's images from Adobe Photoshop, Macromedia Fireworks, or any other image editing program.

Dreamweaver can help you expertly tie together these disparate elements into a unified Web site. It has special features that allow it to work with other programs, making it easy to incorporate files from those other programs in your pages.

In this chapter, you'll learn how you can use other programs to edit elements on a page you're working on in Dreamweaver; how you can use Dreamweaver's integration with Fireworks to edit and optimize images; and how you can import and modify Microsoft Office documents. You'll also learn how Dreamweaver and Macromedia Contribute work together to make editing your Web site easy, even for people who aren't Web savvy.

Assigning External Editing Programs

When you are working on your Web pages, you can launch another program to edit files that Dreamweaver can't edit itself, such as graphics and media files. For example, if you want to edit a JPEG file, you can have Dreamweaver use Fireworks or Photoshop or even something like Windows Paint. You specify an external editor for a particular file type.

Dreamweaver can use any programs that you have on your machine to edit files, but you'll need to tell Dreamweaver about these programs first. You do that in Dreamweaver's preferences.

To assign an external editor:

1. Choose Edit > Preferences (Dreamweaver > Preferences) or press Ctrl-U (Cmd-U).

   The Preferences dialog appears.

2. Click the File Types/Editors category.

   The File Types/Editors pane appears (**Figure 14.1**).

3. The field at the top of the pane, Open in Code view, has extensions of all kinds of files that Dreamweaver will automatically open in Code view. If you will be working on files of a type not listed, enter one or more extensions in the field, separated by a single space.

4. If you want to assign an external code editing program, such as Macromedia HomeSite, available for Windows only, click the Browse button, navigate to the program you want, and click OK (Choose).

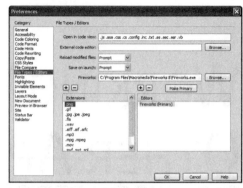

Figure 14.1 Use the File Types/Editors category of the Preferences to set which programs you want to use to edit particular kinds of files.

Figure 14.2 When you add a new file extension, you enter it at the bottom of the Extensions column.

If you assign an external code editor, Dreamweaver changes the Edit > Edit with External Editor menu choice to Edit > Edit with *[program name]*.

5. From the Reload modified files pop-up menu, choose what you want Dreamweaver to do when it detects that changes have been made in another program to a file that is open in Dreamweaver. Your choices are Prompt (Dreamweaver will ask you whether it should reload the page), Always, or Never.

6. From the Save on launch pop-up menu, choose whether Dreamweaver should always save the current document before starting the external editor, never save the document, or ask you if it should save the document.

7. If you have Macromedia Fireworks on your system, tell Dreamweaver its location: click the Browse button, navigate to Fireworks in the resulting Select External Editor dialog, and click OK (Choose). Dreamweaver uses Fireworks by default to edit most graphic files, and Fireworks has special features that allow it to update images directly on Dreamweaver pages.

8. The Extensions column has a list of graphic and media types. Click to select the media type for which you want to assign an external editor.

If the media type has a dialog appears already assigned, that editor appears in the Editors column.

or

To add a media type, click the plus (+) button above the Extensions column. A new entry appears at the bottom of the Extensions column. Type a new extension for the new media type (**Figure 14.2**).

Continues on next page

9. To add an editor, click the plus (+) button above the Editors column.

The Select External Editor dialog appears. Navigate to the program you want to use and click OK (Choose).

10. Repeat steps 8 and 9 for the rest of the media types in the Extensions column.

11. Click OK to dismiss the Preferences dialog.

✔ Tips

■ If you prefer to use Adobe Photoshop as your image editor, set it to be the external image editor for JPEG, GIF, and PNG files.

■ Dreamweaver can make some edits to graphic files itself, including resizing the image, adjusting its brightness and contrast, cropping it, and more. See Chapter 8 for more information.

■ On the Mac, Dreamweaver can use Bare Bones Software's BBEdit, a popular text editor, as its external code editor. In the File Types/Editors pane of Preferences, there is a check box labeled Enable BBEdit Integration (**Figure 14.3**). Select this check box to make BBEdit the external code editor. This also changes the Edit > Edit with External Editor menu choice to Edit > Edit with BBEdit. For more information about using BBEdit to edit your code, see Chapter 15.

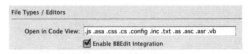

Figure 14.3 On the Mac, a single check box enables integration with BBEdit.

Edit in   *Optimize in*
Fireworks   *Fireworks*

Figure 14.4 Use the Edit button in the Property Inspector to begin modifying an image with Fireworks.

Editing Images with Fireworks

You can use Macromedia Fireworks to edit images on your Dreamweaver pages, and the two programs work together to make it easier. When you start editing an image in Dreamweaver, Dreamweaver hands the image off to Fireworks. It's in Fireworks that you'll make the changes you want. Then you tell Fireworks that you're done editing the image and you want to go back to Dreamweaver. Fireworks saves the image and sends it back to Dreamweaver, which then updates the Web page with the modified image.

You can also have Fireworks objects on your Web pages, and Dreamweaver opens Fireworks when you need to make any changes to those objects. For example, in Fireworks you can create navigation bars, complete with links and rollover effects. Fireworks saves these navigation bars as HTML tables, with associated images. Fireworks makes it easy to export its navigation bars to Dreamweaver, and Dreamweaver recognizes that the navigation bar was created in Fireworks, so that when you attempt to edit the navigation bar in Dreamweaver, Fireworks automatically launches.

In this chapter, we only have room to barely touch on the cool things you can do with Fireworks. For lots more information, we recommend *Macromedia Fireworks MX 2004 for Windows & Macintosh: Visual QuickStart Guide*, by Sandee Cohen.

To edit images with Fireworks:

1. Select the image on the Dreamweaver page.

2. Click the Edit button in the Property Inspector (**Figure 14.4**).

Continues on next page

Fireworks launches and displays the Find Source dialog. This gives you the choice to edit a PNG file that could be the original Fireworks file (**Figure 14.5**). That's because PNG is Fireworks' native format, and files that you create in Fireworks are saved as PNGs, then, if necessary exported to JPEG or GIF for use on your Web site. Fireworks provides more editing options for PNG files than it does for other formats. So if you create images in Fireworks, you can often have two copies of the image: the PNG source and the exported JPEG or GIF.

3. If you originally created the image in Fireworks and want to edit the PNG, click Use a PNG.

   The Open dialog appears. Navigate to the PNG file, select it, and click OK (Choose).

   or

   If you want to edit the file itself, click Use This File.

   The image opens in Fireworks (**Figure 14.6**).

   Note that a status bar appears in the Fireworks document window and includes a Done button and the notation "Editing from Dreamweaver."

4. Make your changes in Fireworks.

5. Click Done in the Fireworks window.

   Fireworks saves and closes the image. Behind the scenes, it has told Dreamweaver to update the image on the Dreamweaver document page.

6. Switch back to Dreamweaver to continue your work.

   The updated image will be on the page.

✔ Tip

- If the image you updated appears on more than one page on your site, it will be updated on all of those pages, not just the one you are working on.

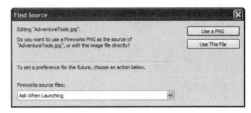

Figure 14.5 Fireworks gives you the choice to edit the file in the Dreamweaver page, or edit a Fireworks PNG source file.

Figure 14.6 When you are editing an image from Dreamweaver, Fireworks lets you know in a status bar at the top of the Fireworks document window and includes a Done button.

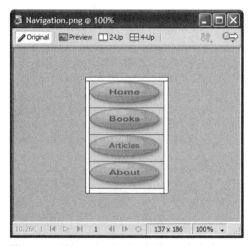

Figure 14.7 This navigation bar in Fireworks is destined for Dreamweaver.

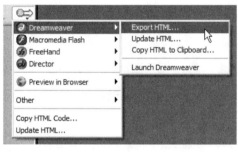

Figure 14.8 Use the Quick Export pop-up menu to begin sending the navigation bar to Dreamweaver.

Figure 14.9 Select your local site folder as the destination for the navigation bar.

To export Fireworks HTML to Dreamweaver:

1. In Fireworks, prepare and save the document (such as a navigation bar) that you want to export to Dreamweaver (**Figure 14.7**).

2. From the Fireworks Quick Export pop-up menu at the upper right of the document window, choose Dreamweaver > Export HTML (**Figure 14.8**).

   The Export dialog appears (**Figure 14.9**).

3. Navigate to the place in your local site folder where you want to save the Fireworks HTML file.

4. (Optional, but recommended) Click Put images in subfolder, then click Browse and select the images directory, so the different images that make up the Fireworks table don't clutter up the root directory of your site.

5. Click Export.

   Fireworks saves the HTML and associated images in your site folder.

To edit a Fireworks image or table:

1. In Dreamweaver, select the image or table that was originally created in Fireworks.

   Dreamweaver shows you in the Property Inspector that the object came from Fireworks, and shows you in the Src field the name of the original Fireworks PNG file (**Figure 14.10**).

2. Click the Edit button in the Property Inspector.

   or

   Right-click and choose Edit in Fireworks from the resulting shortcut menu.

   Fireworks launches and displays the PNG file for the object for editing (**Figure 14.11**). A status bar appears in the Fireworks document window, with a Done button and the notation "Editing from Dreamweaver."

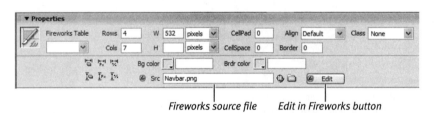

Fireworks source file   Edit in Fireworks button

Figure 14.10 The Dreamweaver Property Inspector recognizes objects from Fireworks, and shows you the name of the original Fireworks source file in the Src field.

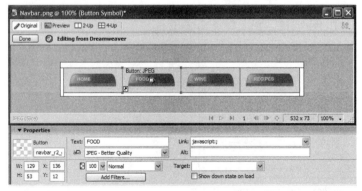

Figure 14.11 When you click the Edit in Fireworks button, the original PNG file opens for editing in Fireworks.

EDITING IMAGES WITH FIREWORKS

Figure 14.12 We've selected the borderless table that contains the navigation bar's components to show the slices that Fireworks creates.

3. Make the changes you want in Fireworks.

   In this case, I changed the name of the second button in the navigation bar by typing it into the Text field in the Fireworks Property Inspector.

4. Click Done in the Fireworks window.

   Fireworks saves and closes the object or table. Behind the scenes, it has told Dreamweaver to update the object on the Dreamweaver document page.

5. Switch back to Dreamweaver to continue your work.

   The updated object will be on the page.

✔ Tips

- When Fireworks creates a navigation bar (or any complex image that uses scripts), it slices the PNG file into many different pieces, some of which are buttons and some are spacers. Some of these pieces also have JavaScript associated with them, for functionality such as rollovers. When Fireworks exports the navigation bar to Dreamweaver, Fireworks converts the format of the slices to many different JPEG files and creates a borderless table to contain all the slices (**Figure 14.12**).

- Fireworks exports its images to JPEG or GIF formats, which are less flexible to edit than PNG files. For example, once you have exported an image from Fireworks' native PNG format, you can't easily go back and edit text, effects settings, or paths in the artwork. That is why it's important to keep the original PNG files, so that you can easily go back and edit your work. We recommend that you save your original Fireworks PNG files in the same folder with the exported files, which usually means your site's images folder.

Optimizing Images with Fireworks

You can *optimize* images that are in a Dreamweaver document using Fireworks. Optimization means that you can change the image from one format to another (for example, from PNG to JPEG); change the JPEG quality setting; crop the image; and more.

To optimize an image with Fireworks:

1. Select the image you want to optimize.

2. In the Property Inspector, click the Optimize in Fireworks button (Figure 14.4).

   or

   Choose Modify > Image > Optimize Image in Fireworks.

   Fireworks launches and displays the Find Source dialog. Choose whether to edit the file in Dreamweaver or as a Fireworks PNG source file. In this case, you're optimizing the file from Dreamweaver.

3. Click Use This File.

   The Optimize Images dialog appears, with your image displayed (**Figure 14.13**).

4. Make your adjustments to the image in the Optimize Images dialog.

5. Click Update.

   The image is saved and updated in the Dreamweaver document.

6. Switch back to Dreamweaver to continue your work.

Figure 14.13 You can make a variety of changes in Fireworks' Optimize Images dialog, including changing the graphics format.

Cleaning Up Word HTML

Back in Chapter 4, we learned how you can bring content from Microsoft Word into Dreamweaver with the Paste Special command, which allows you to preserve varying amounts of the formatting from the Word document. By using the Paste Special command, you will get very good results.

There's another way to get content from Word into Dreamweaver, though we don't recommend it (but you might have to deal with it anyway). Word can export its files as HTML documents, which can then be opened in Dreamweaver. The problem is that when Word (and other Microsoft Office applications) saves a document as a Web page, the HTML code created includes lots of excess or Microsoft-specific code that is designed to enable these Web pages to be brought back into Word or Excel more easily, but that most browsers don't need. This excess code can easily bloat the size of a Web page to two or three times the size of a Web page created entirely in Dreamweaver.

Happily, Dreamweaver has the ability to import a Word HTML document and clean up its code. It does this by eliminating Word-specific styles, removing nonstandard CSS, getting rid of empty paragraphs, deleting Microsoft-specific XML tags, and more. In short, if you have been given Word documents that were exported to HTML, Dreamweaver has the means to clean them up.

To clean up a Word HTML document:

1. Open the Word HTML document.

   The document appears on the screen.

2. Choose Commands > Clean Up Word HTML.

   Continues on next page

The Clean Up Word HTML dialog appears (**Figure 14.14**). Dreamweaver automatically detects whether the HTML was produced by Word 97/98 or Word 2000 or later.

3. Choose to turn on or off any of the options on the Basic or Detailed tabs of the dialog.

   By default, all of the options are turned on. We recommend that you leave things this way, unless you know that there are specific options you don't need.

4. Click OK.

   Dreamweaver processes the Word HTML document, then displays a dialog summarizing the results of the process (**Figure 14.15**).

5. Click OK.

   The converted document appears in the Dreamweaver document window.

✔ Tips

■ The Paste Special command does a better job of preserving the original formatting and styling of the Word document than the Clean Up Word HTML command.

■ Long Word documents may take more than a minute to complete processing, depending on the size of the document and the speed of your computer.

■ There is a third way to bring Word or Excel documents into Dreamweaver for Windows, but again, we don't recommend it. You can choose File > Import > Word Document or File > Import > Excel Document. After choosing the document you want from an Open dialog, Dreamweaver converts the document and inserts its contents into the current page. Unfortunately, you get approximately the same quality results as you would get if you exported the Word or Excel document to HTML, imported it into Dreamweaver, then used the Clean Up Word HTML command, which is to say, not as good as if you used Paste Special.

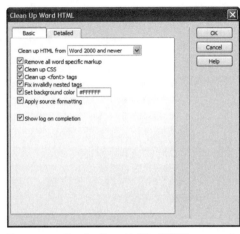

Figure 14.14 Use the Clean Up Word HTML command to optimize the HTML from Word documents that were exported as Web pages.

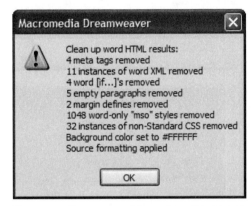

Figure 14.15 Dreamweaver lets you know the changes it made in the Word document.

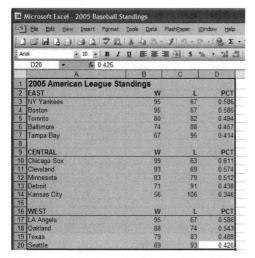

Figure 14.16 Began importing Excel worksheet data into Dreamweaver by selecting and copying the information in Excel.

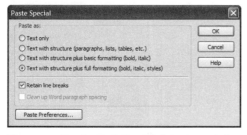

Figure 14.17 Use the Paste Special dialog to control how much formatting you want to maintain from the Excel worksheet.

Using Content from Excel

There are two kinds of information that you might want to use from Microsoft Excel on your Web pages. First, you may want the information in the worksheet—the data and calculations that make up all or part of the worksheet. Second, you may wish to place a graph taken from an Excel worksheet on a Web page.

In both cases, you'll copy and paste the information from Excel into your Dreamweaver document. Unfortunately, it's a bit harder to transfer a chart, so there are some extra steps, and there are different methods to get the job done on Windows and Mac.

To import Excel worksheet data:

1. In the Excel worksheet, select the information you want to bring into Dreamweaver (**Figure 14.16**).

2. Choose Edit > Copy, or press Ctrl-C (Cmd-C).

3. Switch to Dreamweaver.

4. Click in the document at the insertion point where you want the Excel information to appear.

5. Choose Edit > Paste Special.

   The Paste Special dialog appears (**Figure 14.17**). This dialog has four choices. The first choice, "Text only," pastes all the information from the worksheet into a single line. This jumbles all the information together, so don't use it. The next three choices paste the worksheet information as a table, retaining increasing amounts of formatting information from the original worksheet. In most cases, you'll find that the best choice is "Text with structure plus full formatting."

Continues on next page

6. Choose the formatting option you want.
7. Click OK.

   Dreamweaver pastes the Excel information into the document as a table (**Figure 14.18**).

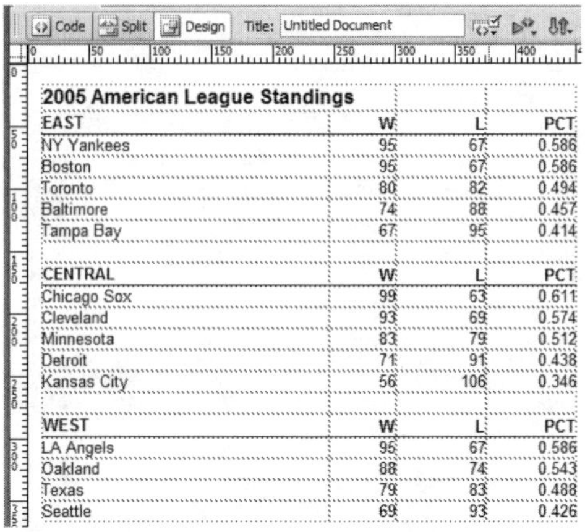

2005 American League Standings			
EAST	W	L	PCT
NY Yankees	95	67	0.586
Boston	95	67	0.586
Toronto	80	82	0.494
Baltimore	74	88	0.457
Tampa Bay	67	95	0.414
CENTRAL	W	L	PCT
Chicago Sox	99	63	0.611
Cleveland	93	69	0.574
Minnesota	83	79	0.512
Detroit	71	91	0.438
Kansas City	56	106	0.346
WEST	W	L	PCT
LA Angels	95	67	0.586
Oakland	88	74	0.543
Texas	79	83	0.488
Seattle	69	93	0.426

Figure 14.18 The Excel worksheet data appears in Dreamweaver as a table.

✔ Tips

- If you want to style the worksheet in Dreamweaver after import, you should use the "Text with structure plus basic formatting" choice in the Paste Special dialog. The reason is that the "Text with structure plus full formatting" choice creates CSS styles in your Dreamweaver document that make it difficult to restyle the table.
- If you want to use the Commands > Format Table command (see Chapter 9 for more information) to restyle a table after import from Excel, you may get an error message that tells you the command can't work on the table. That's because Dreamweaver inserts some code in the table that interferes with the Format Table command. To remove this code, switch to Code view, then look for one or more lines at the top of the table that begin with the `<col>` tag. Select those lines, then press Backspace (Delete) to get rid of them. Then switch back to Design view. You will now be able to use the Format Table command.

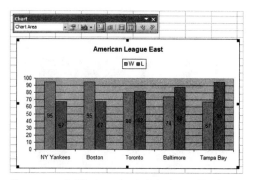

Figure 14.19 In Windows, begin bringing an Excel chart into Dreamweaver by selecting and copying the chart in Excel.

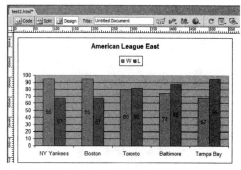

Figure 14.20 The Excel chart ends up on the Dreamweaver page as a graphic.

To import an Excel chart on Windows:

1. In the Excel worksheet, select the chart you want to bring into Dreamweaver (**Figure 14.19**).

   Dreamweaver can't accept a pasted graphic directly from Excel, but it *can* accept a pasted graphic from Word, so we'll use Word as an intermediary.

2. Launch Microsoft Word.

   A blank Word document appears.

   Both Excel and Word must be running before you start copying and pasting the Excel chart.

3. Back in Excel, make sure the chart is still selected, then choose Edit > Copy, or press Ctrl-C.

4. Switch to Word.

5. Choose Edit > Paste, or press Ctrl-V.

   The chart appears in the Word document.

6. In Word, select and copy the chart again by choosing Edit > Copy, or pressing Ctrl-C.

7. Switch to Dreamweaver.

8. Click in the Dreamweaver document to set the insertion point where you want the Excel chart to appear.

9. Choose Edit > Paste, or press Ctrl-V.

   The chart appears in the Dreamweaver document (**Figure 14.20**).

To import an Excel chart on the Mac:

1. In the Excel worksheet, select the chart you want to bring into Dreamweaver (**Figure 14.21**).

   Dreamweaver on the Mac cannot accept pasted graphics from other programs, so you must use a graphic program to create a GIF, JPEG, or PNG file. I used Fireworks, but you can use Photoshop or any other image editor.

2. Launch your image editor.

3. Switch back to Excel, make sure the chart is still selected, then choose Edit > Copy, or press Cmd-C.

4. Switch back to your image editor.

5. Choose Edit > Paste, or press Cmd-V.

   or

   If your image editor has a New from Clipboard command, use it; you will get a new image perfectly sized to the chart that is on the Clipboard.

   The chart appears in the image editor's document window.

6. Make any adjustments to the image that may be necessary. For example, the chart appeared in Fireworks with a resolution of 300 dpi, which created a too-large image. I reduced the resolution to 72 dpi, which shrank the image to a reasonable size.

7. Save and name the image in GIF, PNG, or JPEG format.

   The first two formats will probably look best.

8. In Dreamweaver, insert the chart image as you would add any image. See Chapter 8 if you need more information.

   The chart appears on the page (**Figure 14.22**).

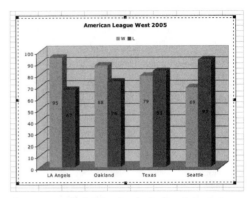

Figure 14.21 On the Mac, begin the Excel chart's journey by selecting and copying it in Excel.

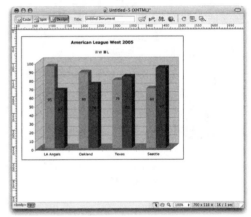

Figure 14.22 After you insert the saved chart image, it appears in Dreamweaver like any other image.

Working with Contribute

One of the difficulties faced by Web designers is the problem of maintaining a Web site in good order after you launch the site. Because Web sites need constant changing to remain vital, there is a need to update content throughout the site on a regular basis. But as a designer, you are probably reluctant to let everyday users make changes and updates to your Web sites for fear that minor mistakes will cause major problems.

That's where Macromedia Contribute comes in. With a combination of Dreamweaver templates and Contribute, you can allow virtually anyone who can use a word processor to make changes to your Web sites, without the possibility of accidentally breaking the site. Contribute users can only change page content within the template's editable areas, and the Contribute site administrator can restrict the Contribute user's editing abilities. Contribute allows designers to get back to the job of designing sites (rather than maintaining pages) and allows clients to maintain sites themselves (rather than trying to track down the designers to make small changes).

In Dreamweaver, besides designing your pages using Dreamweaver templates (see Chapter 13 for more information about templates), you need to set some Dreamweaver preferences so that your site is ready for the Contribute user. You can also launch Contribute to perform site administration from Dreamweaver.

✔ Tip

■ For lots more information about using Contribute, we recommend *Macromedia Contribute 3 for Windows and Macintosh: Visual QuickStart Guide*, by Tom Negrino.

To set your site to use Contribute:

1. Choose Site > Manage Sites.

   The Manage Sites dialog appears (**Figure 14.23**).

2. From the list of sites, select the site that you want to enable for Contribute.

3. Click Edit.

   The Site Definition dialog appears, set to the Advanced tab (**Figure 14.24**).

4. In the list on the left side of the dialog, click the Contribute category.

   The Contribute pane appears (**Figure 14.25**).

5. Select the Enable Contribute compatibility check box.

6. In the Site root URL text box, the URL of your site should appear. If it does not, enter it now.

7. Click the Test button.

   Dreamweaver connects to the Web site and confirms that the connection is working. Dreamweaver puts up an alert box letting you know the connection was successful.

8. Click OK to dismiss the confirmation alert.

9. Click OK to dismiss the Site Definition dialog.

Figure 14.23 In the Manage Sites dialog, choose the site for which you want to enable Contribute compatibility.

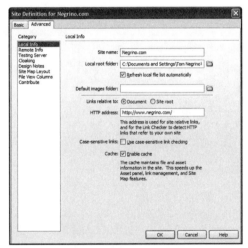

Figure 14.24 The Site Definition dialog allows you to make many settings that are associated with the particular site you chose in the Manage Sites dialog.

Figure 14.25 You enable Contribute compatibility in the Contribute pane of the Site Definition dialog.

Figure 14.26 Begin administering the Contribute site by entering your administrator password.

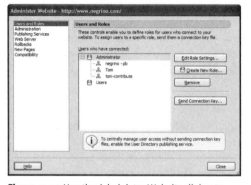

Figure 14.27 Use the Administer Website dialog to adjust user roles and permissions.

To administer a site in Contribute:

1. Choose Site > Manage Sites.

   The Manage Sites dialog appears.

2. From the list of sites, select the site that you want to enable for Contribute.

3. Click Edit.

   The Site Definition dialog appears.

4. In the list on the left side of the dialog, click the Contribute category.

   The Contribute pane appears (Figure 14.25).

5. Click Administer Site in Contribute.

   You must also have a copy of Contribute on your hard disk. The Administrator Password dialog appears (**Figure 14.26**).

6. Enter your Contribute administrator password, and click OK.

   The Contribute Administer Website dialog appears (**Figure 14.27**).

7. Make any administrative changes you desire, then click Close to dismiss the Administer Website dialog.

WORKING WITH CONTRIBUTE

Rollback and the Contribute Publishing Server

When you enable Contribute compatibility in Dreamweaver, you are setting up Dreamweaver to take advantage of two Contribute features. The first feature is *rollbacks*.

Contribute has the ability to rollback published pages—that is, revert to previously published versions of the pages. You can think of it as a sort of "Super Undo" for your Web page. The Contribute user can roll back to the last published version, or to any saved version, up to 99 previous versions. Enabling Contribute compatibility in Dreamweaver tracks page changes (using Dreamweaver's Design Notes feature) and marks pages as eligible for rollback, whether they are changed in Contribute or Dreamweaver.

The other feature is the Contribute Publishing Server (CPS), which is a Macromedia product designed for enterprises that have many Contribute users. CPS is a server application, created as a J2EE application, that provides central administration, tracks users and user access, and handles publishing activities for a Web site. The CPS can be installed on Windows, Linux, Mac OS X, or Solaris server machines.

The CPS server allows enterprise-sized organizations to deploy Contribute to dozens or hundreds of users. The CPS works with standard user directory systems, such as LDAP and Active Directory, to easily assign users to what Contribute refers to as *user roles*, which are the editing permissions granted to individual users. The CPS server also keeps track of page graphs and allows the Contribute site administrator to implement a publishing flow for pages. For example, administrators can force writers to submit pages to editors for review and approval before publishing the pages to the live Web site.

When you enable Contribute compatibility in Dreamweaver, Dreamweaver notifies the CPS every time you do a network operation such as checking in or checking out a file.

15

EDITING CODE

Dreamweaver is what's known as a *WYSIWYG* application; *WYSIWYG* is an acronym for "What You See Is What You Get." Given Dreamweaver's strengths as a design tool, why would anyone ever want to bother looking at code, much less editing it?

Believe it or not, there are people who purchase Dreamweaver who then spend most of their time in Code view. There are a number of reasons why; some of the more common we hear are:

- ◆ "It's perfect for control freaks like me who just want to change that one character or move things one pixel."

- ◆ "I learned tags before good WYSIWYG editors existed, so it's faster for me to make changes this way."

- ◆ "There are things I can do this way that can't be done any other way in Dreamweaver."

These are all perfectly valid reasons to want to use Code view (and there are plenty of other reasons). If you haven't before, check it out. You might find that Code view works best for you, or that it's useful when you simply want to tweak one small thing on your page.

Using the Coding Toolbar

Yes, it's another toolbar in Dreamweaver, but the Coding toolbar is a little different: it only shows up when you're in Code view, and it only acts on those things that you would deal with when you're in Code view.

To use the Coding toolbar:

1. If you're in Design view, click the Code button in the Document toolbar. This switches you into Code view, so you'll now see the tags (instead of the WYSIWYG appearance of your page) and the Coding toolbar. For instance, **Figure 15.1** shows a page in Design view, while **Figure 15.2** shows the same page in Code view.

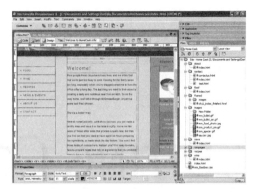

Figure 15.1 Here's the familiar Design view that you've grown to know and love.

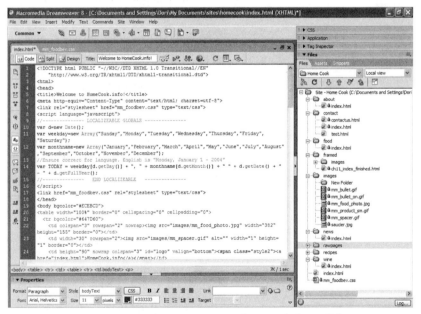

Figure 15.2 The Code view shows the exact same page but in a whole new light.

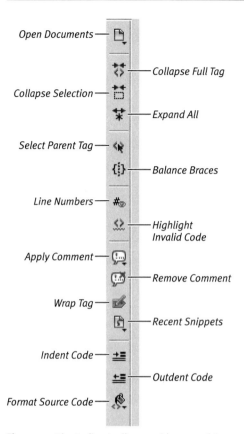

Open Documents —

—— Collapse Full Tag

Collapse Selection —

—— Expand All

Select Parent Tag —

—— Balance Braces

Line Numbers —

—— Highlight
Invalid Code

Apply Comment —

—— Remove Comment

Wrap Tag —

—— Recent Snippets

Indent Code —

—— Outdent Code

Format Source Code —

Figure 15.3 The Coding toolbar provides everything you need to manage text and tags.

2. On the left side of the document window, you'll see the Coding toolbar (**Figure 15.3**). Let's review its buttons, from top to bottom:

▲ **Open Documents:** The name of this button might make you think that it's a way to open documents, but that's incorrect; it actually offers a pop-up menu of all the items that are currently open.

▲ **Collapse Full Tag:** Collapsing code (and why you'd want to do it) is covered later in this chapter. For now, it's enough to know that this button will do it. Holding the Alt (or Option) key while clicking this button collapses everything outside the current tag.

▲ **Collapse Selection:** This button collapses the current selection of code, and holding down the Alt (or Option) key while clicking this button collapses everything outside the selection.

▲ **Expand All:** If any code on the page is collapsed, clicking this button expands it again.

▲ **Select Parent Tag:** This button causes the selection area to change to include the parent tag, based on the current cursor position.

▲ **Balance Braces:** If your current cursor position is inside a `<script>` or `<style>` tag, clicking this button causes the innermost set of braces ( ), { }, or [ ] to be selected. This also works inside external JavaScript and CSS files.

▲ **Line Numbers:** Toggles the display of line numbers in the current document. If they're currently displayed, they'll be hidden, and if they're currently hidden, they'll display.

Continues on next page

USING THE CODING TOOLBAR

▲ **Highlight Invalid Code:** If you enter tags that Dreamweaver doesn't like and you've chosen this option, your mistake will be highlighted in yellow. If you click in the highlighted area, the Property Inspector will tell you more about the error (**Figure 15.4**).

▲ **Apply Comment:** The pop-up menu on this button gives several choices, each of which wraps comments around the selected text:

Apply HTML Comment: Inserts <!-- and --!> before and after the selection (respectively).

Apply /* */ Comment: Wraps this type of comment around the selected CSS or JavaScript.

Apply // Comment: Inserts this type of comment at the beginning of each selected line of CSS and/or JavaScript.

Apply ' Comment: Inserts this type of comment at the beginning of each selected line of VBScript.

Apply Server Comment: If you're working on a server-side file such as PHP, JSP, or ColdFusion, Dreamweaver automatically detects the file type and inserts the correct type of comment.

▲ **Remove Comment:** Removes comment tags from the selected code.

Figure 15.4 It's always a good idea to tell Dreamweaver to highlight invalid code, so you can see problems at a glance.

Figure 15.5 The View Options button on the Document toolbar contains some very useful settings.

Figure 15.6 If you have too many buttons for your screen size, you'll find they're still accessible once you learn where they're hiding.

- If for some reason you don't like this toolbar and just want it to go away, you can do that just as you would with other Dreamweaver toolbars: choose View > Toolbars > Coding. And if you change your mind, that same command brings it back.

- Dreamweaver opens files in Design view by default. If you want all your HTML files to open in Code view instead, open the preferences and choose the File Types/Editors category. In the "Open in Code View" text box, add a space followed by .html. You can add any other file types where you want to use Code view by default by adding those file extensions, too.

▲ **Wrap Tag:** Opens the Quick Tag Editor (described later in this chapter) allowing you to wrap a tag around the selection.

▲ **Recent Snippets:** Allows you to insert a recently used snippet. Snippets are covered in Chapter 13: "Making Life Easier: Using Templates, Libraries, and Snippets."

▲ **Indent Code:** Takes the selection and moves it to the right, based on your chosen indentation preference in the Code Format settings (covered in "Text Editing Tips," later in this chapter).

▲ **Outdent Code:** Takes the selection and moves it to the left.

▲ **Format Source Code:** From this pop-up, you can choose whether to apply formatting to the file as a whole, or to just the current selection. Whichever you choose will be formatted as set in the Code Format settings, which can also be accessed via this pop-up.

✔ Tips

- Some of these options can also be set from the View Options button on the Document toolbar (**Figure 15.5**). There are a few extra ones there, also: Word Wrap, Hidden Characters, Syntax Coloring, and Auto Indent. Yes, this is different from the View Options button that you're used to in Design view; it changes its appearance based on whether you're in Design, Code, or Split view.

- If you appear to be missing a button or two, don't fret—your document window may just be smaller than the Coding toolbar. If that's the case, you'll see a couple of downward-facing arrows at the bottom of the toolbar. Click on those arrows and the missing buttons appear off to the side (**Figure 15.6**).

Layout for Coders (Windows only)

You may recall that way back in Chapter 1 we mentioned that you could choose between Designer layout and Coder layout. If you chose the latter, you might notice that your screen looks a little different than our screenshots. It's also possible that after using Code view for a bit, you decide that that's the way you want to work in the future, and so you decide to check out Coder layout. **Figure 15.7** shows you what Figure 15.2 looks like if you change the layout by choosing Window > Workspace Layout > Coder (**Figure 15.8**).

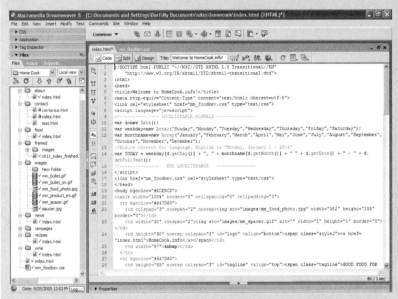

Figure 15.7 Coder layout is for those who want Dreamweaver to look as much as possible like HomeSite.

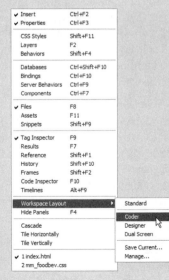

Figure 15.8 It's simple to switch from Designer to Coder layout, and back again.

If at some point you decide that not only do you just love Coder layout, but wish it had even more features for coders, check out the application HomeSite. Nope, we're not recommending that you buy something else, or even that you stop using Dreamweaver (far from it!). When you bought Dreamweaver 8 (or Studio 8), you also got a full-featured copy of HomeSite. **Figure 15.9** shows the same file again in HomeSite, and you'll notice that it looks awfully similar to Coder layout—that's because after Macromedia purchased HomeSite, they reworked their code tool based on HomeSite's functionality. Using HomeSite with Dreamweaver is covered later in this chapter (see "Using an External Editor").

Sorry, Mac users: there's no version of HomeSite for the Mac.

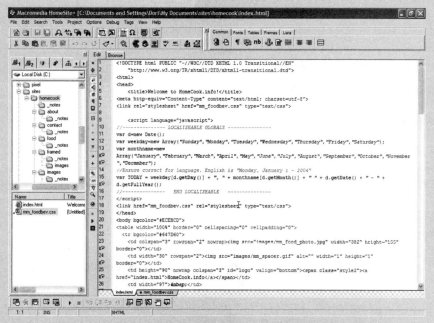

Figure 15.9 And here's that same page again, this time in Macromedia HomeSite.

Using Split View

Does losing your WYSIWYG view freak you out a little? Wish you had a way to see both Code and Design views at once? Well, that's exactly what the Split view is about. It splits the document window into two separate panes, so you can see both code and WYSIWYG at once.

To use Split view:

1. Whether you're in Design view or Code view, click the Split button in the Document toolbar. Your document window splits into two: one part for Design view, and one for Code view (**Figure 15.10**).

2. If you wish the two were reversed (you'd prefer Code on the top instead of Design or vice versa), use the View Options button on the Document toolbar (**Figure 15.11**). You've already seen how the button changes depending on which mode you're in (Code or Design). When you're in Split view, you get all the choices from the other two, plus a choice of whether or not Design view should go on top.

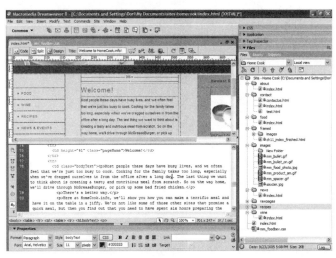

Figure 15.10 Split view is like training wheels for code—it lets you see how changing the design changes the code, and vice versa.

Figure 15.11 The View Options button has all of its choices visible when you're in Split view.

✔ Tips

■ If you update your page in Design view, Code view automatically updates in response. But if you update in Code view, the Property Inspector displays the message, "You have made changes to the code. To edit selection properties, click Refresh or press F5" (**Figure 15.12**).

■ When you're in Split view, the Coding toolbar only extends down the left side of the code pane, not down the full document window.

■ If you select anything in one view, the document automatically scrolls to show the same selection in the other view.

■ If you've never looked at HTML tags before, Split view can be a great way to familiarize yourself with which tags go with which elements of your design.

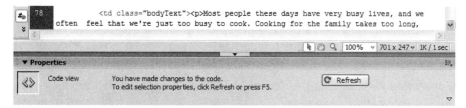

Figure 15.12 Changes to Design view automatically update Code view, but not vice versa—you'll need to refresh the Design view to see it updated.

Text Editing Tips

When you first start using Code view and see tags and markup for the first time, you'll find that there are a lot of things that Dreamweaver assumes you already know. In case you don't, here are a few handy tips:

◆ **Word Wrap:** You may want all of your paragraphs to be one long string of text, but if you have Word Wrap turned off, all your long lines will go off the right side of the document. Turn Word Wrap on using the View Options button on the Document toolbar (Figures 15.5, 15.11).

When you're entering code, be careful about putting in hard returns (where you press Enter/Return) versus the soft returns that Dreamweaver will display even though you didn't type anything in. If you want soft returns, just keep typing and Dreamweaver will handle it for you. If you want hard returns, you might as well turn Word Wrap off.

◆ **Syntax coloring:** At first, you might wonder why the text in the code editor is *so* many different colors. If all the colors confuse you and make you think about turning syntax coloring off, give it a try as-is. Syntax coloring is one of the best ways to learn what's what in code, as similar elements will have identical coloring.

Wish there were maybe fewer colors all at once? In the Code Coloring category in the Preferences, you can change any color to any other color. And if for some reason you want to make things even more tasteless, you can add unique background colors to each different foreground color. But you shouldn't.

◆ **Line numbers:** These are another matter of personal preference. Some people love them, while other people find them terribly annoying. What you'll want to note is how they work in conjunction with Word Wrap: soft-wrapped lines only get a single line number.

◆ **Indentation:** If you haven't worked with code before, you might not immediately get why indentation is so useful. But if you're trying to figure out where your divs begin and end, you'll get it and quickly when you can see them lined up with each other, with their contents indented.

There's no single "right" way to indent code. What we've found works best is to find one style that works for you, and then *stick to it*. It's the consistency that matters most, especially when you have multiple people working on a site.

If you want to manually indent/outdent your code, you can (with the Indent Code/Outdent Code buttons on the Coding toolbar; see Figure 15.3)—but we recommend instead turning on Auto Indent using the View Options button on the Document toolbar (Figures 15.5, 15.11).

◆ **Code formatting:** The last button on the Coding toolbar lets you format your source code (Figure 15.3). If your tags are all over the place because your code came from here and there (as happens to all of us), "Apply Source Formatting" can be found here. If you don't like the way that Dreamweaver formats your code by default, you can choose the Code Format Settings option, and you'll be presented with the Code Format category of the Preferences. Even if you don't know much about tags, it's easy to use this to put your text just where you want it (**Figure 15.13**).

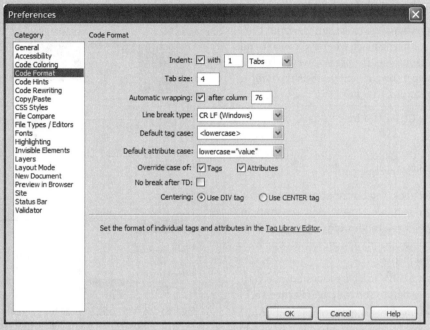

Figure 15.13 Dreamweaver lets you format your code precisely the way that you want it.

Using the Quick Tag Editor

If you prefer Design view (as do most people who've bought a WYSIWYG editor, after all) but wish you could type a little bit of HTML now and then without switching back-and-forth between modes, there's an answer: the Quick Tag Editor.

To use the Quick Tag Editor:

1. With your page in Design view, put the cursor in the place where you wish to add a tag, or select the tag you wish to change, or select the element you wish to wrap a tag around.

2. Press Ctrl-T (for Mac users, Cmd-T).

   or

   Click the Quick Tag Editor button 🖉 on the Property Inspector.

3. The Quick Tag Editor appears, in one of its three modes: Insert, Edit, or Wrap. In any of these modes, start typing, and the possible options appear in the code hints menu below.

   Insert HTML: This mode allows you to place a new tag on the page (**Figure 15.14**).

   Edit tag: This allows you to modify an existing tag, either to change it or to add attributes to it (**Figure 15.15**).

   Wrap tag: In this mode, you can wrap a new tag around an existing element (**Figure 15.16**).

4. To accept your changes and leave the Quick Tag Editor, press Enter. To leave the Quick Tag Editor without making any changes, press Escape.

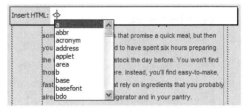

Figure 15.14 With the Quick Tag Editor, you can easily insert a new tag on the page.

Figure 15.15 The Quick Tag Editor also lets you edit existing tags.

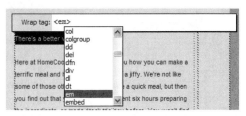

Figure 15.16 And lastly, you can tell the Quick Tag Editor that you want to wrap a tag around existing page elements.

USING THE QUICK TAG EDITOR

✔ Tips

- Dreamweaver tries to guess which Quick Tag mode you want to be in. If it guesses incorrectly, you can cycle through the three modes by pressing Ctrl-T (Cmd-T) again. Be careful about what's actually chosen when you do that, though—sometimes, the selected area can expand. For instance, if you've selected the text of a link with the goal of modifying that link, but you've also (accidentally) selected something outside the <a> (link) tag, you can find that you're modifying the <p> around the text instead of the link itself.

- If the Quick Tag Editor appears but it's covering an area you want to see, you can move it. Just click and drag in the area that displays the mode name to put it in the location you want.

Using the Tag Editor

You've seen the Quick Tag Editor; now here's the Tag Editor itself. It's not really slower than the Quick version, and it's handy for when you want more control than you can get in, say, the Property Inspector, but you don't want to deal with actual HTML tags.

To use the Tag Editor:

1. With your page in Design view, select an element where you wish to edit an existing tag. For instance, you can select an image, or the text of a link.

2. Right-click, and choose Edit Tag off the contextual menu.

   or

   Press Shift-F5.

   or

   From Dreamweaver's menu, choose Modify > Edit Tag.

3. The Tag Editor dialog for that particular tag appears. Every tag has a custom dialog of its own with a variety of categories in the left column. **Figure 15.17** shows the Tag Editor dialog for a `<img>` tag, while **Figure 15.18** shows the Tag Editor dialog for an `<a>` tag. Make any desired changes.

4. Click OK when complete.

✔ Tips

- Near the bottom right of the Tag Editor dialog is the Tag info disclosure arrow. Click it, and the dialog size increases to include a description of the tag you're modifying. For more information about this description, see "Using the Tag Chooser" and "Using the Code Reference," later in this chapter.

- You can also get into the Tag Editor from Code view by right-clicking on a tag (**Figure 15.19**).

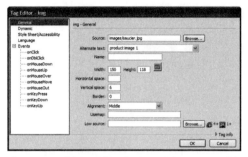

Figure 15.17 The Tag Editor for images lets you modify every possible attribute and event.

Figure 15.18 The Tag Editor for the *a* tag allows you to change attributes and events for links.

Figure 15.19 Right-click and this contextual pop-up appears with the available options.

Figure 15.20 The Tag Chooser lets you insert tags.

Using the Tag Chooser

If you're beginning to think that there are a lot of different ways to insert elements into a Dreamweaver page, you'd be right—except that you haven't even seen many of them yet. Here's a tool you might not have run across yet—Dreamweaver's Tag Chooser.

To use the Tag Chooser to insert tags:

1. With your page in Code view, put the cursor into the section of the document that you want to add to or edit.

2. Right-click, and a pop-up menu of the available options appears. Choose Insert Tag (Figure 15.19). The Tag Chooser dialog appears (**Figure 15.20**).

3. Click any of the icons or tag categories on the left side, and the matching tags will appear on the right.

4. Select one of the tags on the right, and click Insert. If the tag you chose contains angle brackets (< or >), it will be inserted into the page. Otherwise, a Tag Editor dialog appears, allowing you to enter the required information. For more about the Tag Editor dialog, see "Using the Tag Editor" earlier in this chapter.

5. When you are done with the Tag Chooser dialog, click Close.

To use the Tag Chooser to get tag information:

1. With the Tag Chooser open (Figure 15.20), select a tag on the right side.

2. Click the Tag Info button that's just above the Help button on the bottom left. The Tag Info reference area appears, along with useful information about the tag you selected (**Figure 15.21**).

   or

   Click the <?> button directly to the right of the Tag Info button. The same information appears, but in the Code Reference panel. For more information about the Code Reference panel, see "Using the Code Reference" later in this chapter.

✔ Tips

- If you're wondering where this option came from, it's one of the many options that was brought over from Macromedia HomeSite.

- You can also open the Tag Chooser by clicking on the right-most icon on the Insert Bar when you're in the Common category. If you do this when you're in Design view, Dreamweaver automatically switches you to Split view.

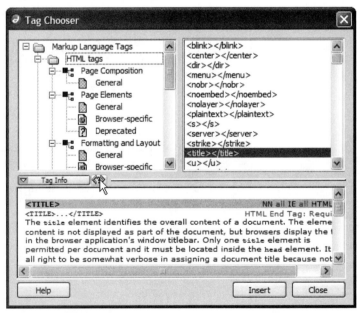

Figure 15.21 Select a tag, click the Tag Info button, and Dreamweaver displays a reference guide to that tag.

Collapsing Code

If you've spent much time working with tags and code, you'll often find yourself in a situation where you wish you could hide just some of it. Thankfully, that's now an option with Dreamweaver 8.

To collapse code:

1. In Code view, select the code that you want to collapse (**Figure 15.22**). The simplest way to do this is to click somewhere inside the area, and then click the Select Parent Tag button on the Coding toolbar (Figure 15.3).

Continues on next page

Figure 15.22 Select the code to collapse and then look for the vertical line on the left (on Windows, top; on Mac, bottom).

2. Just to the left of the code, you'll see a vertical line that goes from the beginning of the selected area to the end. Windows users will see a white box with a minus sign on each end and Mac users will see two gray triangles, the top one facing down and the bottom one facing up. Click one of these endpoints, and the selected code collapses (**Figure 15.23**). You'll now see the first part of the first line inside a highlighted box, plus a white box with a plus sign (Windows) or a right-facing gray arrow (Mac).

or

Click anywhere inside the tag you want to collapse, and click the Collapse Full Tag button on the Coding toolbar.

or

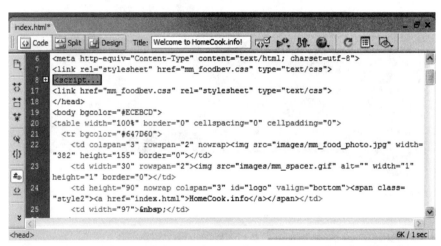

Figure 15.23 Click one of the icons on the endpoints of the line, and the selected text collapses to a single line.

Figure 15.24 You can also collapse code by right-clicking on the selection and choosing one of the collapse options.

Select the code you want to collapse, and click the Collapse Selection button on the Coding toolbar.

or

Click in a particular location on the page, and press the Alt (Option) key while clicking the Collapse Full Tag button on the Coding toolbar. This collapses everything *but* the full tag around your particular cursor position.

or

Select a segment of code, and press the Alt (Option) key while clicking the Collapse Selection button on the Coding toolbar. This collapses everything *but* the current selection.

or

Right-click inside a tag on the page, and choose Selection from the pop-up menu (**Figure 15.24**). From there, you can choose to Collapse Selection, Collapse Outside Selection, Collapse Full Tag, or Collapse Outside Full Tag.

To work with collapsed code:

◆ Put your cursor over the highlighted box, and a tip appears displaying all of the collapsed code (**Figure 15.25**).

◆ Collapse a section of code if you need to move it from one area of the page to another. You'll know that you're moving exactly what you want to move and no more.

◆ If you collapse a section of code and then save and close the page, the next time you open the page that section will still show as collapsed.

To expand code:

◆ Click the collapsed code symbol (the white box with a plus sign (Windows) or the right-facing gray arrow (Mac) to the left of the code you wish to expand.

or

Double-click the highlighted box.

or

Click the Expand All button on the Coding toolbar, which expands *all* the collapsed code on the page.

or

Right-click on the page, and choose Selection from the pop-up menu (Figure 15.24). From there, you can choose to Expand Selection or Expand All.

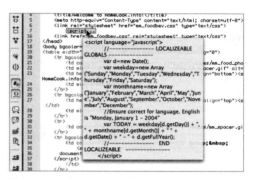

Figure 15.25 If you want to know what's collapsed, this tool tip gives you the info without actually expanding the code.

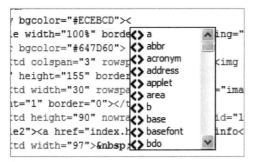

Figure 15.26 Start typing and the code hints pop-up menu appears.

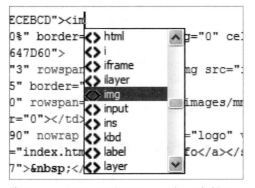

Figure 15.27 As you continue to type, the code hints narrow down your choices.

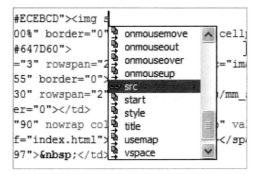

Figure 15.28 Code hints work for attributes as well as tags.

Using Code Hints

When it comes to working with HTML, not all text editors are created equally—and Dreamweaver's code hints are one reason why text editor fans will use its Code view rather than someone else's garden variety notepad-like application.

To use code hints:

1. Click anywhere on the page that you want to add a tag. Start a new tag by typing <, and the code hints appear in a pop-up menu (**Figure 15.26**).

2. Type in the first character or two of the tag, and the code hints menu should change to reflect your typing (**Figure 15.27**). When the hinted value is the tag you want, press Tab.

3. To add an attribute to your new tag, press the spacebar and continue to type. The code hints pop-up menu will appear again, this time displaying just the valid attributes for that tag (**Figure 15.28**). Again, choose the one you want and press Tab to get the full attribute added to your tag.

Continues on next page

USING CODE HINTS

4. If you select an attribute that needs to link to a file, the code hint changes to a Browse button (**Figure 15.29**). Click the button to browse to the file on your disk.

5. If you want to add an attribute to an existing tag, click immediately after the tag name (for instance, right after the g in <img), press the spacebar, and the attributes available will display (**Figure 15.30**).

6. To end a tag, type </, and the most recently opened tag will automatically be closed.

✔ Tips

■ If the code hints pop-up menu doesn't appear, press Ctrl-spacebar (Cmd-spacebar for Mac) to make it display.

■ You can use the arrows to move up and down through code hints to choose the tag or attribute you want.

■ If you're using XHTML and you end a tag with > rather than />, code hints will automatically change it to the proper format.

■ You can't modify an attribute with code hints; instead, delete the attribute and re-create it.

■ If you want a special character but can't remember the exact name of it (such as   for non-breaking space), just type in the first ampersand & and you'll get a code hint that lists all the possible characters you can enter.

■ If there's anything you don't like about how code hints work, you can change them to suit your taste by modifying the values in the Code Hints category of Dreamweaver's Preferences (**Figure 15.31**).

Figure 15.29 Code hints can tell you when the attribute needs a URL as its value.

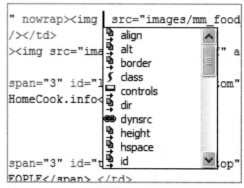

Figure 15.30 You can add an attribute to an existing tag—just click inside the tag and start typing.

Figure 15.31 Dreamweaver lets you make code hints work just the way you choose.

USING CODE HINTS

Figure 15.32 The Tag Inspector can be found in the Attributes tab of the Tag panel. Here's the Category view.

Figure 15.33 Or optionally, there's also the List view, which shows all that tag's attributes in alphabetical order.

Using the Tag Inspector

If you prefer to stay in Design view but every so often you just want to tweak something, the Tag Inspector is one of the simplest ways to do so. Along with the Tag Editor and Quick Tag Editor (covered earlier), it's a great way to modify existing tags, and it's a easy way to get used to what attributes exist for what tags.

To use the Tag Inspector:

1. If the Tag Inspector currently isn't displaying, choose Window > Tag Inspector from the menu.

2. If you're in Design view, click on an element on the page, or choose a tag from the tag selector. If you're in Code view, click anywhere inside a tag. The tag and its attributes appear in the Tag Inspector (**Figure 15.32**). Be sure the Attributes tab is selected.

3. There are two ways to view the attributes in the Tag Inspector: by category or as a list.

   ▲ To view by category, click the Show Category view button . Categories can be open or closed; to open a closed category, click the + button (Windows) or the right-facing triangle (Mac). To close an open category, click the - button (Windows) or the downward-facing triangle (Mac). When open, the list of attributes that fall into that category are displayed.

   ▲ To view as a list, click the Show List view button . This choice displays all the tag's attributes in an alphabetical list (**Figure 15.33**).

Continues on next page

USING THE TAG INSPECTOR

4. You can now modify, add, or delete attributes. There are different ways to edit different types of attributes:

▲ If you're adding or modifying an attribute with a value of a URL (**Figure 15.34**), you'll see the Point-To-File icon and a browse button to the right of the entry field. Alternatively, you can type into the entry box, which is also the case for most attributes.

▲ If your attribute has particular defined values, clicking in the value column displays a pop-up menu containing the valid values (**Figure 15.35**).

Figure 15.34 The standard Point-to-File and browse icons work the same way here as they do everywhere else in Dreamweaver.

Figure 15.35 For those attributes that can only have certain values, Dreamweaver lets you know what those possibilities are.

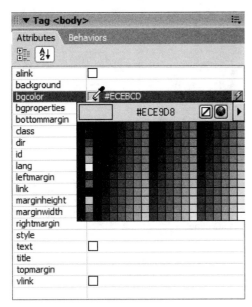

Figure 15.36 Instead of having to remember odd codes for colors, the color picker lets you choose the color you want.

▲ If the attribute contains a color, clicking on the small box in the value column brings up the standard color picker (**Figure 15.36**).

5. There's no OK or Accept changes button on the panel; simply clicking away from the attributes or off the panel implements your changes on your page.

✔ Tip

■ As you might remember from Chapter 1, it's also possible to change tag attributes in the Property Inspector. Because the Property Inspector only shows the most commonly used attributes, you'll want to use the Tag Inspector those times when you need to get at the others.

Using the Code Reference

It's often very handy to have a book close by when you're first starting to work with code (we recommend *HTML for the World Wide Web: Visual QuickStart Guide*, by Elizabeth Castro (Peachpit Press), by the way). If you don't happen to have a book nearby, don't fret—Dreamweaver's got several built-in.

To open the Code Reference tab:

◆ Right-click the element on the page that you have questions about, and select Reference from the pop-up menu (**Figure 15.37**). The Reference tab of the Results panel appears (**Figure 15.38**).

or

Follow the directions in "Using the Tag Chooser," above.

or

From Dreamweaver's menu, choose Window > Reference.

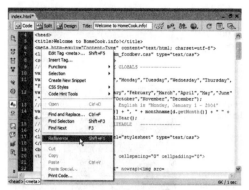

Figure 15.37 Picking Reference from this contextual pop-up menu displays the Reference tab of the Results panel.

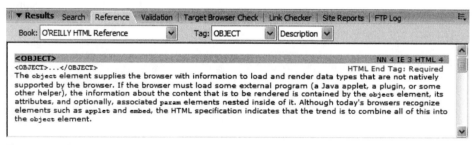

Figure 15.38 The Reference tab can display material about HTML, CSS, JavaScript, and more.

To insert code from the reference into your document:

1. In the Reference tab, find the code fragment you want, click it once, and the entire fragment will highlight (**Figure 15.39**).

2. Right-click the highlighted text and choose Copy from the pop-up menu.

3. Paste the copied code into your document wherever you want it.

✔ Tips

- If you don't like the size of the text in the code reference tab, you can change it. Right-click anywhere inside the panel and you'll have your choice of small, medium, or large text.

- The HTML, CSS, and JavaScript reference material included in Dreamweaver is all excerpted from Danny Goodman's book, *Dynamic HTML, The Definitive Reference* (O'Reilly Media). It's a darn good book, but for learning HTML, we still recommend the Visual QuickStart Guide.

- Besides that material, the code reference tab also includes information on ColdFusion, ASP, JSP, PHP, SQL, XML, and XSLT (and probably a few other three-letter acronyms, too). Lastly, there's also the *UsableNet Accessibility Reference*, a great resource for learning how to make your sites more accessible.

Figure 15.39 Click the code sample once, and it will highlight.

USING THE CODE REFERENCE

Validating Your Code

To *validate* your code is to make sure that it conforms to the W3C standards for whatever version of HTML or XHTML your page is in. There are a number of reasons for validating, but the most important is that if your page is valid, it's more likely to render better in more browsers—an amazing number of the page display errors we've seen could have been solved by making the site validate before it was uploaded to a live server.

To validate your HTML page:

◆ From Dreamweaver's menu, select File > Check Page > Validate Markup (**Figure 15.40**).

or

Press Shift-F6.

or

Click the Validate Markup button on the Document toolbar. A pop-up menu appears; from it, choose Validate Current Document (**Figure 15.41**).

or

Figure 15.40 This menu lets you validate both HTML and XHTML pages.

Figure 15.41 This menu lets you validate both HTML pages and sites, but no XHTML.

Click the green arrow 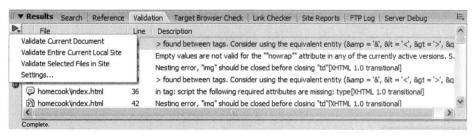 in the top-left corner of the Validation tab of the Results panel. A pop-up menu appears; from it, choose Validate Current Document (**Figure 15.42**).

The validation report appears in the Validation tab of the Results panel.

To validate your XHTML page:

◆ From Dreamweaver's menu, select File > Check Page > Validate as XML (Figure 15.40). The validation report appears in the Validation tab of the Results panel.

To use the validation report:

1. After you validate your page (by one of the above methods), the validation report appears in the Validation tab of the Results panel, displaying all of the errors and warning messages your page has generated (**Figure 15.43**).

Continues on next page

Figure 15.42 The Validate button on the Validation tab can also check your HTML.

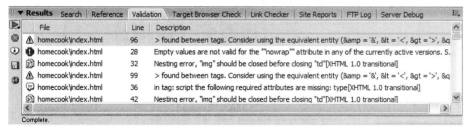

Figure 15.43 Validating this page resulted in a variety of different errors, messages, and warnings.

VALIDATING YOUR CODE

There are four types of messages:

Errors ❶: These are things that you *have* to fix in order for your page to be valid.

Warnings ⚠: These are things you should look at, but they aren't mandatory.

Nesting errors ▣: This is still an error that has to be fixed, but it's a specific type of error: it's displayed when there's a problem with nested tags. If an end tag wasn't found to close an opened tag, or if an `<img>` tag didn't end with a `/>` in an XHTML file, a nesting error would be shown.

Messages ▢: These are less serious than warnings, but things that Dreamweaver still thinks you should know about. If your HTML page is error-free, you'll get a message saying so (if your XHTML page is error-free, you'll get nothing at all).

2. To go to the problem line, double-click the error, and focus will shift to that line in the document. If you were in Design view when you did this, you'll be placed in Split view.

3. To get more information about an error, or just to see it in a reasonably sized font, select the error in the Validation tab and then click the More Info button ⊙ on the left toolbar of the panel. A Description dialog appears (**Figure 15.44**). Click OK to close the dialog.

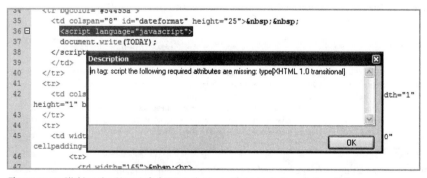

Figure 15.44 Clicking the More Info button gives you the error's Description dialog.

4. If you want to view the full report, click the Browse Report button ❂ on the left toolbar. A browser window opens displaying each error, along with its category, description, line number, and file location (**Figure 15.45**).

5. If you want to save the report for later, click the Save Report button ❒ on the left toolbar. You'll then see the standard Save As dialog, prompting you to save a new XML file.

✔ Tips

- As shown in Figures 15.41 and 15.42, you can also choose to validate the entire current local site or selected files in site. If you start this process and then decide to cancel it, click the Stop button ❂ on the left toolbar.

- If your site contains any XHTML pages, validating the entire site will cause many false errors to appear. Sadly, there doesn't appear to be a way to do sitewide validation if the site contains any XHTML files.

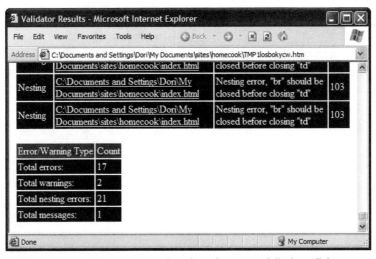

Figure 15.45 Viewing the error report launches a browser and displays all the errors, warnings, and messages.

Using an External Editor

No matter how much you love Dreamweaver, there may be times when you want to use a different text editor. There are many possible editors you might use, but the two most common are Macromedia HomeSite (on Windows) and BBEdit from Bare Bones (on the Mac).

To use an external editor:

1. In Dreamweaver's preferences, go to the File Types / Editors category. You'll see a dialog that looks like either **Figure 15.46** (Windows) or **Figure 15.47** (Mac).

2. If you're on a Mac and you want to use BBEdit as your external editor, click the Enable BBEdit Integration button, and you're done. Otherwise (on either platform), click the Browse button next to the External Code Editor text field, navigate to your application of choice, and click Open. Next, decide when you want to reload modified files, and when you want to save on launch. The choices for both are Always, Never, or Prompt.

3. Click OK to accept your changes.

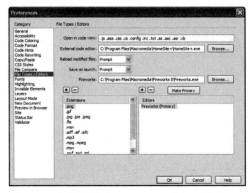

Figure 15.46 With Windows, you can pick any text editor by browsing to it and selecting it.

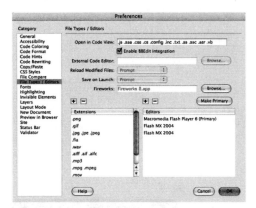

Figure 15.47 You can do the same on the Mac, but it's easier to just choose BBEdit.

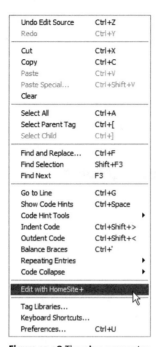

Undo Edit Source	Ctrl+Z
Redo	Ctrl+Y
Cut	Ctrl+X
Copy	Ctrl+C
Paste	Ctrl+V
Paste Special...	Ctrl+Shift+V
Clear	
Select All	Ctrl+A
Select Parent Tag	Ctrl+[
Select Child	Ctrl+]
Find and Replace...	Ctrl+F
Find Selection	Shift+F3
Find Next	F3
Go to Line	Ctrl+G
Show Code Hints	Ctrl+Space
Code Hint Tools	▶
Indent Code	Ctrl+Shift+>
Outdent Code	Ctrl+Shift+<
Balance Braces	Ctrl+'
Repeating Entries	▶
Code Collapse	▶
Edit with HomeSite+	
Tag Libraries...	
Keyboard Shortcuts...	
Preferences...	Ctrl+U

Figure 15.48 There's a new entry on this menu that lets you edit with your text editor of choice.

Figure 15.49 And the Mac menu shows BBEdit now, too.

4. To switch to your chosen editor, select Edit > Edit with HomeSite+ from Dreamweaver's menu (Windows) (**Figure 15.48**) or Edit > Edit with BBEdit (Mac) (**Figure 15.49**).

Continues on next page

If the application was closed, it will now launch, and the current page will open in the text editor and come to the front (**Figures 15.50** and **15.51**).

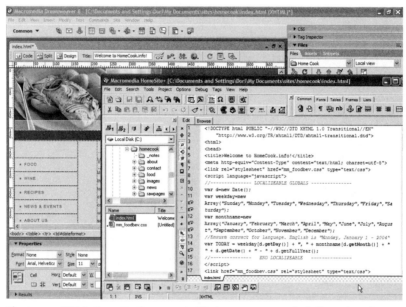

Figure 15.50 With both applications open in Windows, you can see both the code and the design.

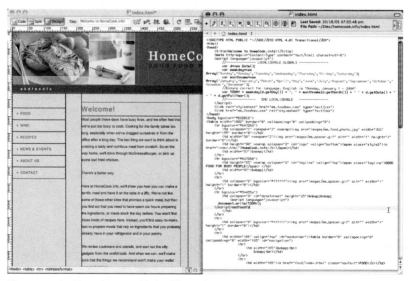

Figure 15.51 And here they are side by side on the Mac.

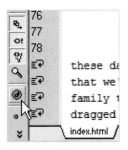

Figure 15.52 You can go in the reverse direction by choosing HomeSite's Dreamweaver button.

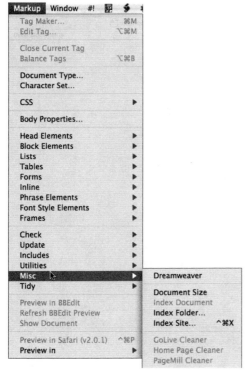

Figure 15.53 BBEdit has Dreamweaver integration under its Markup menu.

5. If you're in your chosen editor, and you want to switch back to Dreamweaver:

- ▲ In HomeSite: Click the Dreamweaver icon in the Editing toolbar (**Figure 15.52**).
- ▲ In BBEdit: Choose Markup > Misc > Dreamweaver (**Figure 15.53**).

✔ Tip

- The best part of using an external editor is being able to open your Dreamweaver window in Design view while you've got the text visible in the external editor. You can then change the file in either application, and the other changes to match. In some ways, this is more powerful than Dreamweaver's Split view, where any time you make a change to the code, you have to manually refresh Design view. Yes, this does mean that you'll need either a very large monitor or multiple monitors, but take our word for it—there's no such thing as too much screen real estate.

About Roundtrip HTML and Automatic Code Correction

Dreamweaver features what they refer to as *Roundtrip HTML*, meaning that you can modify your file in Dreamweaver, then in BBEdit, and then in Dreamweaver again without Dreamweaver changing what you've done in BBEdit. Except when it does change what you've done—but you can control this.

The Code Rewriting category of the Preferences (**Figure 15.54**) allows you to set what you do and do not want fixed. For instance, it can be handy to have Dreamweaver fix any badly nested or unclosed tags. Or maybe you want it to fix some types of files but not others (depending on their extension). That's all customizable here. We recommend turning on "Warn when fixing or removing tags" so that you're told what's being changed and when.

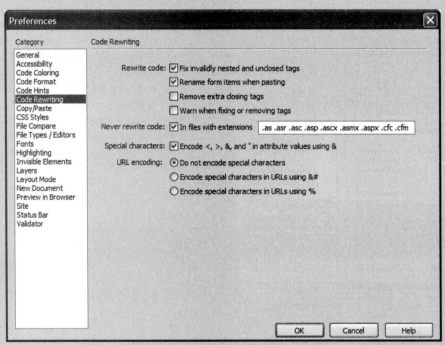

Figure 15.54 Use the Code Rewriting preference to tell Dreamweaver exactly what it can and cannot change.

MANAGING YOUR SITE

As you've seen the in the rest of this book, building a site means creating dozens, hundreds, or even thousands of files that must work together in order to present a dynamic, exciting Web site. Keeping track of and managing all these files, a process called site management, may not be an exciting job, but it is essential.

The problem of site management gets even more complex when, as is extremely common these days, you are just one member of a team that is responsible for building and maintaining the Web site. Imagine, for example, that you have two or three people who could be responsible for making changes to page content. It would be easy for one person to overwrite the changes already made by a coworker on the same page. That's where Dreamweaver's collaboration features come in. With Check In/Check Out, members of the team are notified when another person is already working on a particular file on the site.

In this chapter, you will learn how to manage the files and folders that make up your site; work with Dreamweaver's collaborative tools; and learn different ways of looking at and working with your site.

Planning for Site Expansion

When you're designing a site, you take the time to think about the site navigation so that your site visitors will have an easy time finding the information they need. But what about *your* needs? While you're building and maintaining a site, it's just as important for you to plan the folder structure so that you can easily and quickly find items you need to work on. Web sites have a disturbing tendency to grow, so when you set up your site, lay out your folder structure logically, and leave room for expansion in your site structure (**Figure 16.1**).

For example, if you have different sections of a site (as represented in the site's navigation), it's a good idea to create a folder for each section (which will contain all of the pages for the section). Then consider creating an images folder inside each section folder. After all, you will probably have images for each section that are used only in that section of the site. A separate images folder in the root of your site can handle images that are used globally throughout the site.

As your site grows, you can add additional folders for new sections from the site root, or you can add folders inside the existing section folders for new subsections.

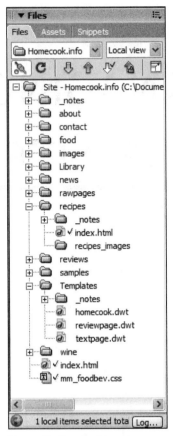

Figure 16.1 You should create your site structure with logical sections (shown here as folders), and plan for growth.

✔ Tips

- Make sure that you name your files and folders understandably. While you are creating a site, you may remember what the `med_sec_hed.html` file is used for, but when you come back to the site four months later, you might not have a clue, at least without opening the file and looking at it. Instead, name the file something like `media_home.html`, and it will make it easier for you to pick up where you left off. This also helps make your site easier for other people to maintain.

- Don't forget that there are some characters that you can't use in file and folder names, including space, #, &, @, /, and most other punctuation. Use a hyphen or underscore as substitutes for a space.

- If you create images folders inside section folders, give those images folders descriptive names, too. We like to use the name of the section, followed by an underscore, then images, like so: `recipes_images`.

Viewing the Site Map

When you need the bird's eye view of your Web site, Dreamweaver has a visual tool, the *Site Map*, which can help you see the links and relationships between the files on your site. The Site Map is a different view in the Files panel, and it allows you to see the links between the different files in the site in a tree display, descending from the site's index page (**Figure 16.2**). You can switch the Site Map between a purely graphic view of the tree structure, or a view of both the tree and the Files list simultaneously. You can also choose to view a file's name, or its page title (the title that appears in a Web browser).

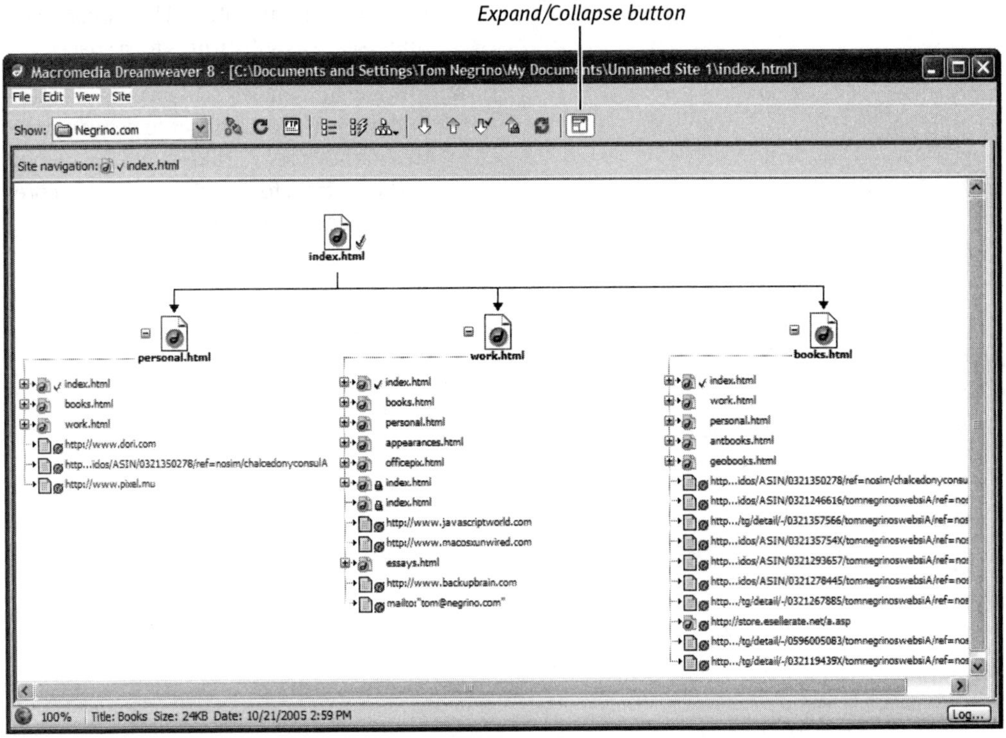

Expand/Collapse button

Figure 16.2 The Site Map shows you the structure of your site in a tree form, with lines and arrows showing links to files, and links from the files listed below each file.

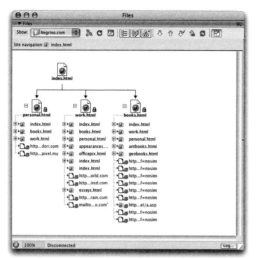

Figure 16.3 On the Mac, the Files panel expands into its own window when you display the Site Map.

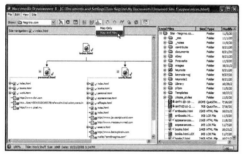

Figure 16.4 If you prefer, you can show the Files list next to the Site Map.

To show and hide the Site Map:

1. At the top of the Files panel, click the Expand/Collapse button.

   On Windows, the Dreamweaver window will be replaced by the Site Map (Figure 16.2).

   On the Mac, the Files panel will appear in a new window, displaying the Site Map (**Figure 16.3**).

2. (Optional) To view the Files list along with the Site Map, choose Map and Files from the Site Map pop-up menu in the toolbar at the top of the window.

   The Files list appears next to the Site Map (**Figure 16.4**).

3. When you're done with the Site Map, click the Expand/Collapse button again to toggle the window back to the normal Files panel.

✔ Tips

■ You must define the home page for a site before you can view the Site Map.

■ For the purposes of the Site Map, the home page, which is the starting point for the tree structure, does not have to be the index page of your site. So, for instance, if you have an initial splash page with an animation as the first page of the site that then automatically changes to the main page with content, you can make that main page the starting page for the Site Map. Just select the page you want in the Files panel, right-click, and choose Set as Home Page from the resulting shortcut menu.

To switch between file names and titles:

1. Display the Site Map.

2. On Windows, choose View > Site Map Options > Show Page Titles, or press Ctrl-Shift-T.

   or

   On Mac, from the Options menu at the upper-right corner of the Files window, choose View > Site Map Options > Show Page Titles, or press Cmd-Shift-T (**Figure 16.5**).

   The file names toggle to titles, or vice versa.

To set Site Map preferences:

1. To set what displays in the Site Map, choose Site > Manage Sites.

   The Manage Sites dialog appears.

2. Click Edit.

   The Site Definition dialog appears for the current site.

3. Click the Site Map Layout category from the Category list on the left side of the window.

   The Site Map Layout category appears (**Figure 16.6**).

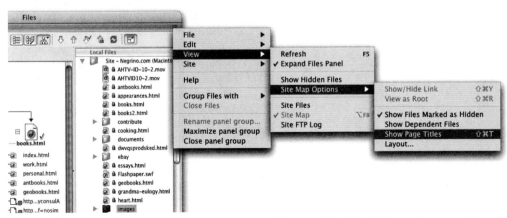

Figure 16.5 On the Mac, use the Options menu at the upper-right corner of the Files window to show page titles.

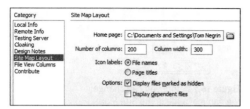

Figure 16.6 The Site Map Layout pane of the Site Definition dialog allows you to define the look of the Site Map.

4. Make one or more choices in this dialog:

▲ **Home page** allows you to set the home page for the Site Map, though it is easier to select the file you want to use as the home page in the Files panel, as explained in the previous tip.

▲ **Number of columns** sets the number of your site's pages that will display per row in the Site Map.

▲ **Column width** specifies how much space, in pixels, will be taken up by each column in the Site Map.

▲ **Icon labels** allows you to display either the file names or the page titles for the icons in the Site Map.

▲ **Options** allows you to display files that you've marked as hidden, or display dependent files, that is, files that a page needs to work properly, such as images and external style sheets.

5. When you're done, click OK at the bottom of the Site Definition dialog.

The Manage Sites dialog reappears.

6. Click Done.

Working with the Site Map

Besides viewing files and their relationships within your site, you can also use the Site Map to rename files, view and change links between files on your site, or create and link to new files.

To rename files in the Site Map:

1. Display the Site Map.

2. Click on an icon to select it.

   The icon highlights.

3. Depending on what is showing, below the icon, click the name of the file or the page title.

   The name or title highlights (**Figure 16.7**).

4. Type the new name, then press Enter (Return).

To create or change links in the Site Map:

1. Display the Site Map.

   The Site Map shows the links between files as lines.

2. Click on an icon to select it.

   The circular Point-to-File icon appears next to the file icon (**Figure 16.8**).

3. Click the Point-to-File icon, and drag to point to another file icon in the Site Map or Files list (**Figure 16.9**).

4. Release the mouse button.

   Dreamweaver creates the link between the two files.

Figure 16.7 Before you can change the name of a file in the Site Map, you must highlight it.

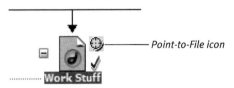

Point-to-File icon

Figure 16.8 Use the Point-to-File icon to create or change links.

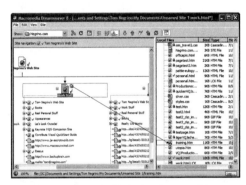

Figure 16.9 Point to the file in the Files panel that you want to link to.

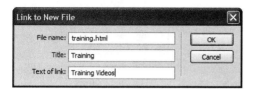

Figure 16.10 You can use the Link to New File dialog to create a new file and link to it in one step.

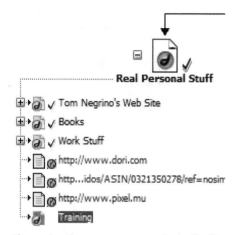

Figure 16.11 The new page appears in the Site Map, under the page that you linked to.

To create a new file and link it to an existing page:

1. Display the Site Map.

2. Click on a page's icon to select it.

3. Right-click the icon, then choose Link to New File from the resulting shortcut menu.

   The Link to New File dialog appears (**Figure 16.10**).

4. Fill out the File name, Title, and Text of link fields.

5. Click OK.

   The new page appears in the Site Map, linked to the existing page (**Figure 16.11**).

Setting Up Check In and Check Out

In Chapter 2, you saw how to copy selected files or folders between the local and remote sites in the Files panel using the Get file or Put file buttons. Get and Put works fine when you are the only person working on a site, but you don't want to use them when you are working on a site with other members of a team. In that case, you would like to prevent one person from accidentally undoing or overwriting changes made by another member of the team when the page is transferred back to the remote site.

When you are working with other people on a Web site, you will come to rely on Dreamweaver's ability to keep track of and manage who is working on a file. Known as Check In/Check Out, this feature prevents more than one team member from working on a particular file at a time. The feature also lets all members of the team know who is currently working on what file. Check In/Check Out replaces the use of Get and Put for sites that have Check In/Check Out enabled. When you want to work on a file, you check it out, and when you are done working on the file and want to send it back to the remote server, you check it in.

Dreamweaver shows the status of files in the Files panel. Files that are checked out to you appear with a green checkmark next to them, and files that are checked out by others appear with a red checkmark next to them. Files that are read-only (because they are files that Dreamweaver can't edit, or because the last time Dreamweaver connected to the remote server and checked their status they were checked out) appear with a padlock icon (**Figure 16.12**).

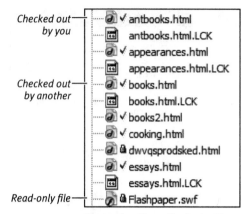

Figure 16.12 These files in the Files panel show their checked out status (though you can't tell the difference between the red and green checkmarks in this figure).

In order to get the Check In/Check Out system to work properly, there are two cardinal rules all members of the Web team must follow:

◆ All members of the team must enable Check In/Check Out and Design Notes in their site definitions.

◆ All members of the team must *always* use Dreamweaver or Contribute (and no other tools, such as an FTP program) to transfer files to and from the remote Web server.

✔ Tips

■ If Check In/Check Out is enabled for your site and you use the Get file or Put file button in the Files panel, rather than the Check In or Check Out button, Dreamweaver will transfer read-only versions of the file to and from the remote server.

■ When any team member checks out a file, Dreamweaver places a small text file on the remote site with the name of the checked out file plus the extension .LCK. You can see some of these files in Figure 16.12. Dreamweaver uses this file to store the Check Out name and e-mail address of the person who is using the file. When the file is checked back in, Dreamweaver automatically deletes the .LCK file.

SETTING UP CHECK IN AND CHECK OUT

To enable Check In/Check Out for your site:

1. Choose Site > Manage Sites.

   The Manage Sites dialog appears (**Figure 16.13**).

2. In the list of sites, click to select the site for which you want to enable Check In/Check Out and click Edit.

   The Site Definition dialog appears, set to the Advanced tab.

3. In the Category list on the left side of the dialog, click the Remote Info category.

   The dialog changes to show the Remote Info pane (**Figure 16.14**).

4. Select the check box next to "Enable file check in and check out."

5. Select the check box next to "Check out files when opening."

6. Enter a check out name.

   Because you may be working on a page using different programs or different systems, it's a good idea to use a name that describes the program and/or system you're working on. For example, in Figure 16.14, the check out name indicates "Tom, using Dreamweaver, on Windows." The check out name `tom-ct-mac` would indicate "Tom, using Contribute on Macintosh."

7. (Optional but recommended) Enter your email address in the Email address text box.

   This allows coworkers to easily send you email if they need to communicate with you about the status of a file.

8. Click OK.

   The Manage Sites dialog reappears.

9. Click Done.

Figure 16.13 Begin enabling Check In/Check Out in the Manage Sites dialog.

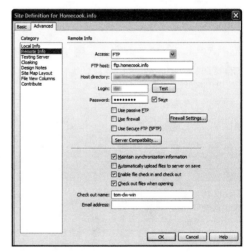

Figure 16.14 You enable Check In/Check Out in the Remote Info pane of the Site Definition dialog.

Figure 16.15 If someone else has already checked out a file, Dreamweaver lets you know and asks what you want to do.

Site pop-up menu

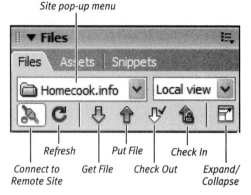

Figure 16.16 You'll check files in and out with the toolbar in the Files panel.

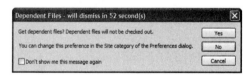

Figure 16.17 You can choose whether or not to download dependent files. If they haven't changed, don't bother.

✔ Tip

- If you make a mistake and check out the wrong file, you can revert to the version of the file on the remote server, even if you have modified and saved the checked out version on your machine. Just right-click on the checked out file in the Files panel, then choose Undo Check Out from the resulting shortcut menu. Dreamweaver removes your check out lock from the remote server, and the local copy of the file becomes read-only.

Checking Files In and Out

When Check In/Check Out is enabled for your site and you use the Check Out button at the top of the Files panel, Dreamweaver checks to see if anyone else is currently working on the file. If someone else has the file checked out, Dreamweaver displays a dialog asking if you want to override that check out (**Figure 16.15**). In general, it's a bad idea to do so, because it could lead to exactly the problems with multiple people working on the file that you want to avoid.

To check out a file for editing:

1. In the Files panel, from the Site pop-up menu, choose the site that contains the file you want to check out (**Figure 16.16**). The site must have Check In/Check Out enabled.

2. Click the Connect to Remote Site button. Dreamweaver connects to the remote site.

3. Choose the file (or files) you want to check out from the Files panel.

4. Click the Check Out button in the Files panel toolbar.
   The Dependent Files dialog appears (**Figure 16.17**).

5. If you need to also edit the dependent files, such as images or external style sheets, click Yes. In most cases, however, you will click No.
   Dreamweaver transfers the selected files, and puts green checkmarks next to the files in both the Local Files and the Remote Site views in the Files panel.

6. Make the changes you want to the checked out files.

To check in a file to the remote server:

1. In the Files panel, select the checked out file or files.

2. Click the Check In button in the Files panel toolbar.

   If the files you're checking in have not been saved, Dreamweaver prompts you to save them. After you save the files, Dreamweaver removes the green checkmarks from the files in the Files panel.

✔ Tips

■ You can have Dreamweaver automatically save unsaved files before checking them in by enabling the "Save files before putting" option in the Site category in Dreamweaver's Preferences.

■ If you save and close a file without checking it in, the copy of the file on the remote site will not be updated. You should always check a file in when you are done working with it.

Figure 16.18 Design Notes are XML files that Dreamweaver knows how to read.

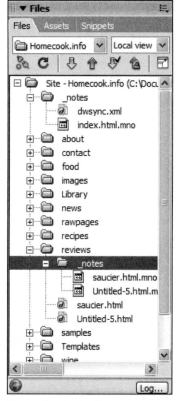

Figure 16.19 Design Notes appear in the special _notes folders Dreamweaver creates in your site.

Using Design Notes

Dreamweaver's Design Notes are XML files that Dreamweaver places on the site that can be used by Web team members to annotate changes or note when a file was modified and by whom. A Design Note is associated with a file on your site, but it is a separate XML file with different fields that can be read by the Macromedia programs (**Figure 16.18**). Design Note files aren't visible to your site's visitors.

You can create a Design Note yourself, and Dreamweaver and other programs in Macromedia Studio 8 can also make automated Design Note entries. For example, when you create an image in Fireworks, then export it to Dreamweaver, Fireworks creates (and places in the Dreamweaver site) a Design Note entry for the exported file, which could be in GIF or JPEG format. The entry records the name of the Fireworks source file (remember, the Fireworks file format is PNG) associated with the exported image in your site. That's how Dreamweaver and Fireworks know how to integrate the Fireworks source PNG with the exported site image when you go to edit it (refer to Chapter 8 for more information about editing Dreamweaver images with Fireworks).

Dreamweaver stores Design Notes in folders called _notes in each of the site folders that have files with associated notes (**Figure 16.19**). These notes folders contain one Design Note file for each site file that has a note.

To add a Design Note:

1. Open the file to which you want to add a Design Note, then choose File > Design Notes.

   or

   In the Files panel, select the file to which you want to add a Design Note, then right-click and choose Design Notes from the resulting shortcut menu.

   The Design Notes dialog appears, set to the Basic info tab (**Figure 16.20**). This tab shows you the file name and the location of the file at the top of the dialog.

2. (Optional) From the Status pop-up menu, choose the status you want to set for the Design Note.

   The preset statuses are draft, revision1, revision2, revision3, alpha, beta, final, and needs attention.

3. (Optional) if you want to date stamp your note, click the calendar icon in the dialog.

   The current date appears in the Notes field.

4. Type your note about the file.

5. Click OK.

   Dreamweaver saves the Design Note, and the Design Notes dialog disappears.

✔ Tips

- Macromedia Contribute also uses Design Notes to make note of when a Contribute user has updated a page. But Contribute doesn't have an interface to make specific notes; it just creates automated notes with the contributor's username and the page's modification date. Contribute Design Notes also keep track of rollbacks, which allow Contribute users to revert to previously published versions of pages.

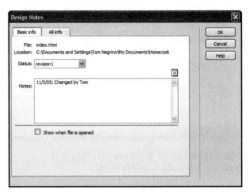

Figure 16.20 Use the Design Notes dialog to enter your notes.

- You must check out the file associated with a Design Note before you can add or modify the Design Note.

To modify a Design Note:

1. Open the file to which you want to add a Design Note, then choose File > Design Notes.

or

In the Files panel, select the file to which you want to add a Design Note, then right-click and choose Design Notes from the resulting shortcut menu.

The Design Notes dialog appears.

2. Make changes to the Status pop-up menu, or enter a new note in the Notes field.

If you click the calendar icon to add a new date stamp, the new note appears at the top of the dialog, and older notes appear below the newest entry, in reverse chronological order.

3. Click OK.

Generating Site Reports

A large part of site management, especially if you are managing a team working on the site, is keeping up with all of the things that are happening to the site. For example, let's say that you want to know which pages each of your team members is working on at the moment. Dreamweaver allows you to get a report of the checked out pages, and who has checked them out. Similarly, you can get reports on many other aspects of your site, listed in **Table 16.1**. Dreamweaver splits reports into two categories: Workflow, with reports detailing who has worked on the site and when; and HTML Reports, which search through files on your site looking for HTML errors.

Some reports allow you to enter parameters for the report that allow you to widen or narrow the criteria used for the report. All the reports, however, allow you to report on just the current document; the entire current local site; just selected files in the site; or files within a selected folder in the site.

Table 16.1

Dreamweaver Reports	
REPORT NAME	**DESCRIPTION**
Workflow Category	
Checked Out By	Reports file name and the name of the team member who has checked it out.
Design Notes	Shows the contents of the Design Note for files that have them.
Recently Modified	Shows the last modified date for the selected files, based on search criteria you specify.
HTML Reports Category	
Combinable Nested Font Tags	Finds markup with unnecessarily nested <font> tags.
Accessibility	Checks the selected pages for adherence to accessibility guidelines.
Missing ALT Text	Flags missing alternate text attributes for images on your pages.
Redundant Nested Tags	Reports unnecessarily repeated nested tags, i.e., <b><b> → example text</b></b>.
Removable Empty Tags	Shows any empty tags that can be safely removed.
Untitled Documents	Reveals documents where you have forgotten to enter a title.

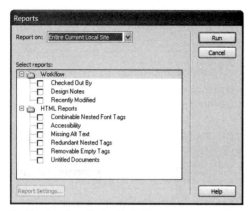

Figure 16.21 Specify the kind of site report you want in the Reports dialog.

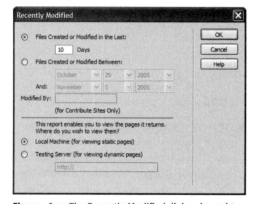

Figure 16.22 The Recently Modified dialog, brought up by the Report Settings button, allows you to specify the scope of the report. Other reports will have different Report Settings dialogs.

To get site reports:

1. Choose Site > Reports.

    The Reports dialog appears (**Figure 16.21**).

2. From the Report on pop-up menu, choose the scope of the report.

    Your choices are Current Document, Entire Current Local Site, Selected Files in Site, or Folder.

3. In the Select reports list, check the report or reports that you want to run.

    If the report you have selected allows you to choose report criteria, the Report Settings button becomes active.

4. (Optional) For reports that allow additional settings, click Report Settings, then complete the resulting settings dialog.

    Each report that allows additional settings has a different criteria dialog. **Figure 16.22** shows, for example, the criteria dialog for the Recently Modified report.

    After you click OK in the settings dialog, you return to the Reports dialog.

5. Click Run.

    Dreamweaver runs the report and shows the report output in the Site Reports tab of the Results panel below the Property Inspector (**Figure 16.23**).

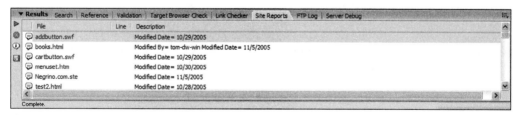

Figure 16.23 The report appears in the Results panel.

Checking for Broken Links

One of the more vexing problems with Web sites are broken links, that is, links that no longer point to valid destinations within your site. Dreamweaver usually does a pretty good job of updating links when you move or rename a page, but you can still end up with broken links if you cut or copy page content from one page to another on your site. Dreamweaver allows you to check all of the links on your site to make sure they are still valid and reports any broken links it finds. You can then easily open the file that contains the broken link to fix it.

To check for and fix broken links throughout your site:

1. Choose Site > Check Links Sitewide, or press Ctrl-F8 (Cmd-F8).

   Dreamweaver checks all the pages on your site and shows you files with broken links in the Link Checker tab of the Results panel (**Figure 16.24**).

2. Double-click on one of the results.

   The file with the broken link opens, with the broken link highlighted (**Figure 16.25**).

3. Using the Property Inspector, fix the broken link.

   For more information about using the Property Inspector to work with links, see Chapter 7.

4. Repeat steps 2 and 3 until you have eliminated all of the broken links.

Figure 16.24 Files with broken links appear in the Results panel.

Figure 16.25 To fix the broken link, double-click on one of the report results; the file with the broken link opens with the broken link highlighted.

✔ Tips

■ Dreamweaver only checks for the validity of links to documents within your site. If you have external links on your site (links that point to other sites on the Internet), Dreamweaver does not follow those links and make sure that those sites still exist and are reachable. If you need to validate external links, you will need to follow those links manually, in a Web browser.

■ You can also check for broken links on just the page you are editing. Choose File > Check Page > Check Links, or press Shift-F8.

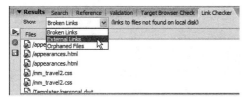

Figure 16.26 Choose either External Links or Orphaned Files to obtain a report on those items.

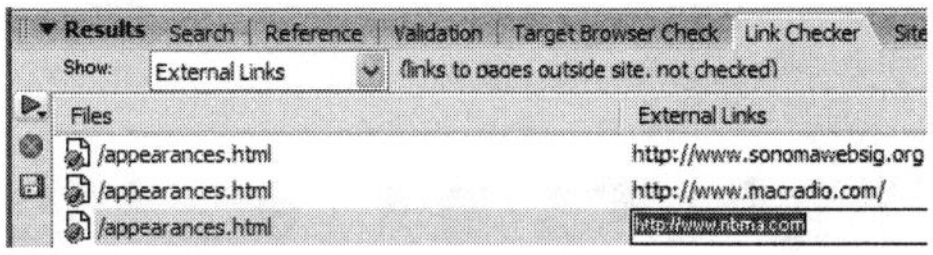

Figure 16.27 You can change external links right in the Results panel.

Finding External Links and Orphaned Files

You can get two other types of reports from Dreamweaver. The first is a list of links from your site to other sites, called *external links*, and the other is a report of *orphaned files*, which are files that have no links pointing to them. In the first case, after Dreamweaver finds the external links, you can (if needed) easily change them. In the case of orphaned files, you should create links to the files from your other Dreamweaver pages.

To find external links and orphaned files:

1. Choose Site > Check Links Sitewide, or press Ctrl-F8 (Cmd-F8).

   Dreamweaver checks all the pages on your site and shows you files with broken links in the Link Checker tab of the Results panel.

2. From the Show pop-up menu in the Results panel, choose External Links (**Figure 16.26**).

   or

   From the Show pop-up menu in the Results panel, choose Orphaned Files.

   Depending on your choice, the results appear in the Results panel.

3. (Optional) If you chose External Links in step 2, the Results panel shows a list of files and the external links that appear on them. Click on one of the links to highlight it and make it editable. You can then enter a new destination for the link (**Figure 16.27**).

   or

   (Optional) If you chose Orphaned Files in step 2, the Results panel shows a list of files with no links pointing to them. Double-click on a file name to open that file, or open other files in the Files panel to create links to the orphaned file.

Checking Browser Support

In terms of the HTML document type, Dreamweaver 8 creates XHTML 1.0 Transitional files by default, as discussed in Chapter 3. These files are readable and valid for all commonly used modern Web browsers. So you could consider Dreamweaver's ability to check files for browser support to be somewhat vestigial. But you may find you need to work on older pages that haven't been retrofitted for current browsers. Dreamweaver allows you to check your pages for errors with targeted browsers. It does this by keeping a database of browser profiles, which details how different browsers render pages. You can check individual pages, or check your whole site. Errors appear in the Results panel.

To define browsers for checking:

1. Open any file in your site.

2. From the Browser Check pop-up menu at the top of the document window, choose Settings (**Figure 16.28**).

   The Target Browsers dialog appears (**Figure 16.29**).

3. To enable a particular browser, select the check box next to its name. Choose from the pop-up menu next to the name to select the minimum version of that browser you want to check against.

4. Click OK to dismiss the Target Browsers dialog.

Figure 16.28 Use the Browser Check pop-up menu to make sure your pages will appear correctly in different browsers.

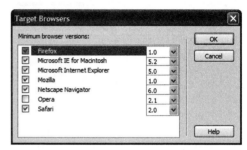

Figure 16.29 Choose the target browsers for your validation check.

To check the current document for browser support:

1. From the Browser Check pop-up menu at the top of the document window, choose Check Browser Support.

   If there are no errors found, a tooltip appears over the Browser Check pop-up menu stating "No browser check errors." Pop a cold one and relax.

2. If errors are found, a tooltip appears over the Browser Check pop-up menu stating the number of errors found. Choose Window > Results to see the errors.

   The Results panel opens with the errors displayed (**Figure 16.30**).

   There are three kinds of possible errors reported in the Results panel: *errors*, *warnings*, and *informational messages*. An error indicates a problem in the code that can cause serious visual problems with the page. A warning indicates that the page won't be displayed exactly correctly in the targeted browser, but the problem isn't serious. An informational message is used for code that isn't supported in a particular browser, but has no visual effect.

3. Double-click on an error in the Results panel to change the document window to Split view, highlighting the error in the Code and Design views.

4. Fix the error in Code view.

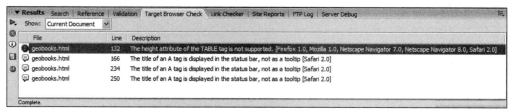

Figure 16.30 Errors in your document appear in the Results panel, along with names of the browsers affected by the errors.

To run a browser check on the entire current site:

1. In the Target Browser Check tab of the Results panel, click the Check Target Browsers pop-up menu (**Figure 16.31**).

2. Choose Check Target Browsers for Entire Current Local Site.

   Dreamweaver performs the browser check and places results in the Results panel.

3. Double-click on an error in the Results panel to change the document window to Split view, highlighting the error in the Code and Design views.

4. Fix the error in Code view.

Figure 16.31 Use the Check Target Browsers pop-up menu to run a browser check on your entire site.

Figure 16.32 Begin deleting a site in the Manage Sites dialog.

Figure 16.33 When you try to delete a site, Dreamweaver needs you to confirm your action.

Deleting Sites

When you will no longer be working with a site (perhaps because the project has been taken over by another developer), you can delete its site definition. This removes the site from the Manage Sites dialog, and from the Site pop-up menu in the Files panel. Of course, all the settings for the site are also deleted. You should be careful when you delete site definitions, because there's no way to undo the action.

To delete a site from Dreamweaver:

1. Choose Site > Manage Sites.

   The Manage Sites dialog appears (**Figure 16.32**).

2. From the list of sites, click on the site that you want to delete.

3. Click Remove.

   Dreamweaver alerts you that you cannot undo this operation (**Figure 16.33**).

4. Click Yes.

   Dreamweaver deletes the selected site.

✔ Tip

- While Dreamweaver is asking if you want to delete the site, the site itself (that is, the files in the local site folder on your hard drive) aren't touched. The only thing that's deleted are the site definitions: what Dreamweaver itself knows about your site. And of course, nothing is changed on the remote site.

DELETING SITES

467

Exporting and Importing Site Definitions

When you create a local site on your machine, Dreamweaver creates a local site definitions file with all the information about the site's settings, including information about the server connection, your server password, and any per-site preferences you may have set in the Site Definition dialog. If you need to move the site from one machine to another, or if you want to add members of your Web team and have them share the same site preferences, you must export the site definition. When you do that, Dreamweaver saves the site definition information as an XML file, with the .ste file extension.

Dreamweaver allows you to export the site definition in one of two ways. You can export it with your server username and password information (this facilitates you moving the site to a different machine), or you can export the site with the site preferences, but without your server logon information (this is good for adding coworkers to the site).

You can, of course, also import a site definition file that you had previously exported or one you receive from a colleague.

To export a site definition:

1. Choose Site > Manage Sites.

   The Manage Sites dialog appears (**Figure 16.34**).

2. From the list of sites, click on the site you want to export.

3. Click Export.

   The Exporting site dialog appears (**Figure 16.35**).

Figure 16.34 You begin exporting a site definition in the Manage Sites dialog.

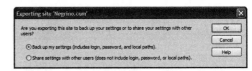

Figure 16.35 Choose whether or not you want to include your login information in the exported site definition file.

4. Click "Back up my settings (includes login, password, and local paths)" if you plan to move the site to another machine.

or

Click "Share with other users (does not include login, password, or local paths)" if you want to create a site definition file that does not include your server login information.

5. Click OK.

The Export Site dialog appears.

6. Navigate to where you want to save the site definition file, make sure that the name Dreamweaver has given the file is okay (by default it gives the file the name of your site and appends the `.ste` file extension), then click Save.

Dreamweaver saves the site definition file onto your hard disk.

You'll return to the Manage Sites dialog.

7. Click Done.

To import a site definition:

1. Choose Site > Manage Sites.

The Manage Sites dialog appears.

2. Click Import.

The Import Site dialog appears.

3. Navigate to and select the site definition file you want to import.

4. Click Open.

Dreamweaver imports the site definition and adds it to the list of sites in the Manage Sites dialog.

5. Click Done to dismiss the Manage Sites dialog.

✔ Tips

■ You can use the ability to export the site definition file as a way to back up your site's settings, but this is no substitute for a regular and comprehensive backup strategy covering all of the important documents on your hard drive.

■ If you happen to work on multiple computers and multiple sites, and each of the computers has a copy of Dreamweaver, you can export your site definitions for all of your sites, then copy them to a USB flash drive. You could then plug in the flash drive on whichever computer you happen to be working on, and you will have your site settings, including your server passwords. Of course, you would need to resynchronize the remote site with a newly created copy that would then become the local site folder on the machine you are working on. See Chapter 2 for more information about synchronizing sites.

EXPORTING AND IMPORTING SITE DEFINITIONS

WHERE TO LEARN MORE

Once you've worked through this book, you should be well on your way to creating great Web pages with Dreamweaver. But Dreamweaver is such a broad and deep program that there is plenty more to learn about it and about building Web sites in general.

In this appendix, we'll point to several of the most helpful Dreamweaver-oriented Web sites, other sites where you can learn more about building standards-compliant Web sites, and even mention a few other books that will help you deepen your knowledge of Dreamweaver.

As usual with products that can be found on the Internet, Web sites come, go, and change addresses with alarming regularity. The sites listed here were in existence when this book went to press (November 2005) and may be available when you check them out, or they may not. We are just reporting the URLs; we have no control over them. If you find a link that has become stale, we would appreciate it if you would drop a note to dw8@dreamweaverbook.com so that we can update the next edition of the book.

Find It Online!

You'll find an updated list of the sites and books in this appendix at this book's companion Web site, located at www.dreamweaverbook.com. We'll keep the Web site current with a list of Dreamweaver-oriented sites, and if eagle-eyed readers spot any errors in the book, we'll note them on the site, too.

Web Sites

Almost as soon as Dreamweaver came upon the scene, people began gathering online to discuss the program and to help each other use it. There are several Dreamweaver community sites, informational sites, places where you can purchase premade Dreamweaver templates, and sites from developers who have created new Dreamweaver extensions. This list is not by any means comprehensive, but they are sites that we have found to be helpful.

Of course, Macromedia has a variety of online support options as well. At press time, Macromedia was in the process of being acquired by Adobe, so chances are good that the URLs for the Macromedia sites we list below will change. We hope that the URLs will automatically redirect to the new addresses; otherwise, you may have to search for the resources. We'll also try to keep the list of links updated at this book's companion Web site, at www.dreamweaverbook.com.

Dreamweaver Documentation

http://www.macromedia.com/support/
→ documentation/en/dreamweaver

This should be your first stop when looking for answers to a Dreamweaver question (after this book, of course!). This site allows you to search Dreamweaver's LiveDocs (online manual) and the Product Support Knowledge Base (**Figure A.1**).

Dreamweaver Exchange

http://www.macromedia.com/exchange

This is the place to go when you're looking for Dreamweaver add-ons and extensions. At press time, there were more than a thousand items for download (**Figure A.2**).

Figure A.1 You can find the latest version of the Dreamweaver manuals, and search the Knowledge Base, at the Macromedia Dreamweaver Documentation site.

Figure A.2 Dreamweaver Exchange should be your first stop when you are looking for a Dreamweaver extension.

Figure A.3 Macromedia's weblog aggregator brings together interesting blog posts about Dreamweaver from all over the Web in one place.

Figure A.4 Project Seven makes a variety of great Dreamweaver extensions, such as the pop-up menu generator whose results are shown here.

Dreamweaver Weblogs

`http://weblogs.macromedia.com`

Once you go to the URL above, click the link for the Dreamweaver category. This site is an aggregator site that lists posts from many people's Dreamweaver-related weblogs (**Figure A.3**). It's a great way to keep up with the Dreamweaver community.

Dreamweaver Developer Center

`http://www.macromedia.com/devnet/`
`→ dreamweaver`

This site has tutorials and sample files focused on the new features of Dreamweaver 8, and articles that will help you better use Dreamweaver to build your sites.

Project Seven

`http://www.projectseven.com`

Project Seven is one of the premier developers of Dreamweaver extensions and page templates (**Figure A.4**). Their Pop Menu Magic extension helps you build extensive pop-up navigation menus for your site with almost no effort. And their PagePacks are collections of great-looking page layouts with an interface that lets you easily add those pages to your site.

Besides the paid products, the Project Seven site also contains many tutorials covering CSS, images, navigation, and more.

Dreamweaver Resources

`http://www.dreamweaverresources.com`

This site offers lots of page templates and other design elements (such as buttons and navigation bars) for sale, plus tutorials, FAQ lists, and other useful resources for Web site builders.

Dreamweaver FAQ

`http://www.dwfaq.com`

Here you'll find lots of FAQ (Frequently Asked Questions) lists covering all sorts of Dreamweaver topics. You'll also find pointers to Web building resources of all varieties, plus a search engine for the Macromedia Dreamweaver Newsgroup.

Community MX

`http://www.communitymx.com`

Tons of constantly updated content, page templates, tutorials, and extensions, are available on a subscription basis at Community MX (**Figure A.5**). Subscribers get the content at no extra charge; non-subscribers can purchase items à la carte; everyone can sign up for a free trial. The site also has support forums for subscribers, where the site partners guarantee a timely, useful response.

Figure A.5 Community MX provides a great deal of articles and tutorials for its subscribers.

Figure A.6 If you're serious about staying on the bleeding edge of Web development and running a Web-based business, you should be reading the Web magazine A List Apart.

Figure A.7 You can find many excellent CSS-based layouts at Position Is Everything.

A List Apart

`http://alistapart.com`

A List Apart is not Dreamweaver-specific, but it's essential reading nonetheless. This Web magazine has been around since 1998, and is still an invaluable resource for people who make Web sites (**Figure A.6**). You'll find great, well-written articles on virtually all aspects of building sites. Now, go check it out.

Position Is Everything

`http://www.positioniseverything.net`

At Position Is Everything, you'll find articles, example code, and explanations for laying out pages using CSS instead of old-style, table-based layout (**Figure A.7**). What could be better? Okay, you'll also find links to the sites of some of the best CSS gunslingers on the planet. Still not satisfied? How about demos of bugs found in specific browsers (thereby helping convince you that it's not your fault when your site looks weird in Internet Explorer).

WEB SITES

Other Online Resources

You can find interesting and useful help with Dreamweaver and Web sites in general if you go beyond just Web sites.

Dreamweaver Newsgroup

news://forums.macromedia.com/
→ macromedia.dreamweaver

Macromedia has a lively newsgroup for Dreamweaver users that gets many messages every day. You'll need a Usenet newsreader program to access this forum. Good ones are Microsoft Outlook or Outlook Express on Windows, or Microsoft Entourage or Panic Software's Unison on the Mac. Or, just send your browser to http://groups.google.com/group/macromedia.dreamweaver.

Wise-Women Mailing List

http://www.wise-women.org

Wise-Women is an online community, with a Web site and an email discussion list (**Figure A.8**). The purpose of the list is to provide women on the Web with a supportive atmosphere to deal with issues of Web development, design and consulting. Wise-Women was founded in 1999 by one of the authors of this book (Dori), and is going strong today. You'll find lots of useful information on the mailing list about using Dreamweaver, among many other subjects. And in case you're wondering, the community is not just for women only.

Figure A.8 The WiseWomen online community offers support and help for women and men alike.

Figure A.9 The Lynda.com Online Training Library offers 12 hours of video training on Dreamweaver 8.

Lynda.com Online Training Library

`http://www.lynda.com`

If you're more of a visual learner, Lynda.com offers an excellent series of video training programs that cover Dreamweaver and the rest of the Macromedia product line, as well as many other software packages (**Figure A.9**). You can purchase these training programs as CD-ROMs that you can view on your computer, or you can access the videos over the Internet through their Online Training Library, for which you'll need to purchase a subscription. One of us (Tom) produced *Contribute 3 Essential Training* for Lynda.com.

OTHER ONLINE RESOURCES

Other Books

Though the authors would naturally like to think that the book you've got in your hands is all you'll ever need to become a Dreamweaver expert, we recognize that you might just want a bit more information after you've completely devoured this book. There are approximately a million different Dreamweaver books on the market; here are some of the books we think are the best.

Macromedia Dreamweaver 8 Advanced for Windows and Macintosh: Visual QuickPro Guide

Written by Lucinda Dykes and also published by Peachpit Press, this book covers many of the aspects of Dreamweaver that aren't covered in the book you have in your hands. You'll find information on working with servers, setting up database connections, using SQL, and building database-backed Web sites with dynamic pages. You'll also find information on Dreamweaver 8's new XML and XSLT features.

Dreamweaver MX 2004 Killer Tips

Written by Joseph Lowery and Angela C. Buraglia for New Riders, this book delivers on the promise in its name, with hundreds of really great tips and tricks. Heck, you can call them killer tips! This book is not being updated for Dreamweaver 8 (because the authors didn't believe that there were enough great new hidden features in Dreamweaver 8 to warrant a new edition), but the existing edition is almost entirely still applicable to Dreamweaver 8, and is definitely worth your hard-earned dollars. Or lira. Or whatever.

Dreamweaver 8 Bible

Joseph Lowery is well known in the Dreamweaver community, and this massive Dreamweaver reference, published by Wiley, shows why. At a whopping 1,300 pages, we think this is perhaps the best comprehensive Dreamweaver reference book available.

Build Your Own Standards Compliant Website Using Dreamweaver 8

As we have mentioned again and again in the preceding pages, compliance with Web standards is important, and this book by Rachel Andrew, published by SitePoint, drills you in creating flexible, easy-to-maintain Web sites using strict XHTML and CSS with Dreamweaver 8. The author is the director of a Web solutions company in the U.K., and she is a member of the Web Standards Project, spearheading that organization's Dreamweaver Task Force (`http://www.webstandards.org/act/campaign/dwtf/`), which worked with Macromedia to improve Dreamweaver's standards compliance.

OTHER BOOKS

Customizing and Extending Dreamweaver

One of the best things about Dreamweaver is that it is both customizable and incredibly extendable. What's the difference? *Customizable* means that you can change the keyboard shortcuts to suit your style of working, and of course you can customize using Dreamweaver's Preferences. That's fine, but *extensibility,* the ability to add new features to the program, is where the real action is.

As you've seen in the rest of this book, Dreamweaver can do an awful lot. But just because Dreamweaver is amazingly capable doesn't mean that it does absolutely everything that people want it to do. Macromedia allows software developers to write add-ons, called extensions, which add new features to Dreamweaver. These new features can range from the mundane (add new Flash button styles) to the amazing (full pop-up menu generators with associated page templates).

In this appendix, we'll show you how to customize Dreamweaver's keyboard shortcuts, and how to find, acquire, and install Dreamweaver extensions.

Customizing Keyboard Shortcuts

Sometimes the keyboard shortcuts that come with Dreamweaver aren't quite what you want. For example, some shortcut keys used for editing code with BBEdit (on Mac) or HomeSite (on Windows) aren't the same as the shortcuts used for the equivalent commands in Dreamweaver 8. No problem; you can change Dreamweaver shortcuts to match those in your favorite code editor. In fact, Dreamweaver 8 comes with shortcut key sets for those two code editors, which makes it a snap to change shortcut keys and increase your productivity.

Of course, you can also change any keyboard shortcut, add ones to menu items that may not already have them, or delete shortcut keys you don't like. You can also print out a cheat sheet of keyboard commands, to help you learn them.

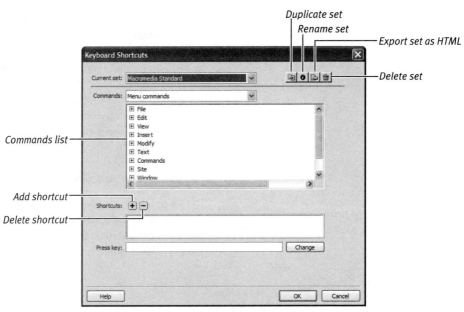

Figure B.1 Begin customizing your Dreamweaver experience in the Keyboard Shortcuts dialog.

Figure B.2 Enter the name of your new keyboard shortcuts set.

To change between shortcut key sets:

1. Choose Edit > Keyboard Shortcuts (Dreamweaver > Keyboard Shortcuts).

    The Keyboard Shortcuts dialog appears (**Figure B.1**).

2. Choose the keyboard shortcuts that you want from the Current set pop-up menu.

    Your choices are: Macromedia Standard, which includes the standard shortcut keys for Studio 8; Dreamweaver MX 2004, a slightly different set found in the previous edition of Dreamweaver; BBEdit, which modifies the code editing keyboard shortcuts to match those used by the popular Macintosh code editor; and HomeSite, which modifies the code editing keyboard shortcuts to match the popular Windows code editor.

3. Click OK.

    Dreamweaver changes its keyboard shortcuts to match the set that you chose.

To create a personalized set of keyboard shortcuts:

1. Choose Edit > Keyboard Shortcuts (Dreamweaver > Keyboard Shortcuts).

    The Keyboard Shortcuts dialog appears (Figure B.1).

2. From the Current set pop-up menu, choose the keyboard shortcuts set that you want to use as the basis for your personalized set.

3. Click the Duplicate set button.

    The Duplicate Set dialog appears (**Figure B.2**).

4. Type the name for your duplicate set.

5. Click OK.

    Dreamweaver creates the duplicate set and makes it the active set. You can then personalize it, as shown next.

To add or change a keyboard shortcut:

1. In the Keyboard Shortcuts dialog, choose the kind of command you want to modify from the Commands pop-up menu (**Figure B.3**).

   This pop-up menu differs on Windows and Mac, with more choices (and more functionality) on Windows. Besides Menu commands, Code editing, Document editing, and Snippets keyboard shortcuts, Dreamweaver for Windows also allows you to set keyboard shortcuts for the Site panel and the Site window.

   Depending on what you chose, the Commands list changes.

2. In the Commands list, navigate to the command that you want to change. Click the + icon next to the name of the menu to expand the choices for that menu.

   The menu choices will be shown with any existing shortcut keys (**Figure B.4**).

3. Click on the command that you want to change.

   The shortcuts assigned to the command appear in the Shortcuts text box (**Figure B.5**).

4. To add a shortcut, click the Add shortcut button.

   A new blank line appears in the Shortcuts text box.

   or

   To change an existing shortcut, select it in the Shortcuts text box.

5. Click in the Press key text box.

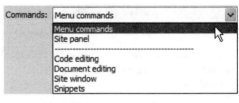
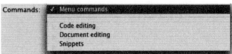

Figure B.3 You can customize keyboard shortcuts for more items on Windows (top) than on Mac (bottom).

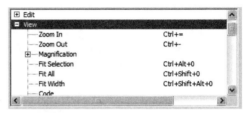

Figure B.4 Click the + buttons to display menu choices in an indented tree form.

Figure B.5 Select the shortcut key that you want to change.

Figure B.6 You can print your keyboard command cheat sheet from a Web browser.

6. Press the key combination you want to use for the shortcut key.

If the key combination is already in use, Dreamweaver lets you know with a message at the bottom of the Keyboard Shortcuts dialog.

7. Click Change.

The new shortcut appears in the Shortcuts text box.

8. Click OK to save your changes and dismiss the Keyboard Shortcuts dialog.

To export a keyboard command cheat sheet:

1. Choose Edit > Keyboard Shortcuts (Dreamweaver > Keyboard Shortcuts).

The Keyboard Shortcuts dialog appears (Figure B.1).

2. Click the Export set as HTML button.

The Save as HTML file dialog appears.

3. In the Save as text box, give the exported file a name, then navigate to where you want to save the HTML file.

4. Click Save.

Dreamweaver saves the list of keyboard commands to your hard disk as an HTML file. You can then open it in Dreamweaver or any Web browser (**Figure B.6**).

Finding and Installing Extensions

You add extensions to Dreamweaver using Macromedia Extension Manager, a program that was installed when you installed Dreamweaver on your system. After you install an extension, it appears as part of Dreamweaver. Where it appears within the program depends on what kind of extension it is. For example, if you have installed an extension that provides additional Flash buttons, those buttons will appear in the Insert Flash Button dialog. An extension that provides new ways to add pop-up menus may appear in the Commands menu. And extensions that add new scripting behaviors will appear in the Behaviors panel. Because Dreamweaver is almost infinitely extensible, the extensions you add can appear almost anywhere within the program.

You can find extensions in a variety of ways. Some extensions are free for downloading, and others are paid products. Many extension developers have Web sites where they host (and sometimes sell) their extensions. A Google search for "Dreamweaver extensions" will result in a large number of useful results.

But the most common way to find Dreamweaver extensions (and also extensions for other Macromedia products, such as Fireworks, Flash, etc.) is to use the Macromedia Exchange site, at www.macromedia.com/exchange/. The Dreamweaver Exchange portion of the site has lists and short descriptions of more than a thousand extensions.

Figure B.7 The Dreamweaver Exchange site lists more than a thousand extensions.

In Dreamweaver, it's easy to go to the Dreamweaver Exchange site. Just choose Help > Dreamweaver Exchange, and your default Web browser will open to the site (**Figure B.7**). From the Exchange site, or from an extension developer's site, download the extension file to your hard disk. Then you're ready to use Macromedia Extension Manager to install the extension.

To install an extension:

1. If it's running, quit Dreamweaver by choosing File > Quit (Dreamweaver > Quit).

2. Launch Macromedia Extension Manager by double-clicking its icon.

   On Windows, you'll find it in C:\Program Files\Macromedia\Extension Manager. On Mac, you'll find it in /Applications/ Macromedia Extension Manager/.

   The Macromedia Extension Manager window appears (**Figure B.8**).

Continues on next page

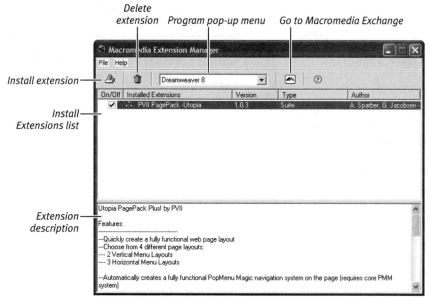

Delete extension   Program pop-up menu   Go to Macromedia Exchange

Install extension

Install Extensions list

Extension description

Figure B.8 Use the Macromedia Extension Manager program to install or remove extensions.

3. From the Program pop-up menu at the top of the Extension Manager window, choose Dreamweaver 8.

Any extensions you have installed for Dreamweaver 8 appear in the Installed Extensions list.

4. Click the Install extension button.

The Select Extension to Install dialog appears (**Figure B.9**).

5. Navigate to and select the extension file you wish to install.

6. Click Install.

A license dialog appears.

7. Click Accept.

The Extension Manager installs the extension and reports success with an alert dialog.

8. Click OK to dismiss the alert dialog.

The new extension appears in the Installed Extensions list.

9. Choose File > Exit (Extension Manager > Quit Extension Manager).

10. Launch Dreamweaver to use the new extension (**Figure B.10**).

✔ Tips

■ If you have more than one version of Dreamweaver installed (perhaps you didn't want to remove an older copy immediately when you upgraded to Dreamweaver 8), you can have different sets of extensions installed for each version.

■ Because each extension works differently, you will need to refer to the instructions that came with the extension to discover how to access the extension from within Dreamweaver.

Figure B.9 Find and select the extension file that you want to install.

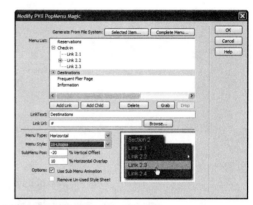

Figure B.10 Extensions can provide a complete user interface, as in this example, PopMenu Magic, which helps you easily create a wide variety of pop-up navigation menus.

CASCADING STYLE SHEETS REFERENCE

This appendix lists the CSS2 properties as defined by the W3C at `http://www.w3.org/TR/REC-CSS2`. Although the specification was standardized in May 1998, as of this writing, many of these properties are as yet unimplemented in any browser. The next version, CSS 2.1, was still at the Working Draft stage at the time this was written. The goal of the CSS 2.1 specification is to clarify CSS2 so that it is closer to what browser makers have actually implemented. However, Dreamweaver 8 properties mostly match those in CSS2; those properties not in Dreamweaver are shown below in italics.

This list is complete except for the aural properties (those used for speech synthesis for the visually disabled). Dreamweaver does not support aural style sheets.

If you want to learn more, we recommend *Cascading Style Sheets: The Definitive Guide, 2nd Edition*, by Eric A. Meyer. The book lives up to its name, including exhaustive descriptions of CSS through versions 2.1.

Table C.1

Basic Concepts

PROPERTY NAME	VALUE
In HTML	link
	<style>...</style>
	<x style="declaration;">
Grouping	x, y, z {declaration;}
Contextual selectors	x y z {declaration;}
Class selector	.class
ID selector	#ID
At-rules	@import
	@font-face
	@media
	@page
Important	!important

Table C.2

Pseudo-Elements and Pseudo-Classes

PROPERTY NAME	VALUE
after	:after
anchor	a:active
	a:focus
	a:hover
	a:link
	a:visited
before	:before
first	:first
first-child	:first-child
left	:left
paragraph	p:first-letter
	p:first-line
right	:right

Table C.3

Color and Background Properties

PROPERTY NAME	VALUE
background	<background-color>
	<background-image>
	<background-repeat>
	-<background-attachment>
	<background-position>
background-attachment	scroll
	fixed
background-color	<color>
	transparent
background-image	<url>
	none
background-position	<percentage>
	<length>
	top
	center
	bottom
	left
	right
background-repeat	repeat
	repeat-x
	repeat-y
	no-repeat
color	<color>

Table C.4

Font Properties

PROPERTY NAME	VALUE
font	<font-style>
	<font-variant>
	<font-weight>
	<font-size> / <line-height>
	<font-family>
	caption
	icon
	menu
	message-box
	small-caption
	status-bar
font-family	<family-name>
	cursive
	fantasy
	monospace
	sans-serif
	serif
font-size	<absolute-size> (xx-small - xx-large)
	<relative-size> (smaller - larger)
	<length>
	<percentage>
font-size-adjust	<number>
	none

Table C.4 *(continued)*

Font Properties

PROPERTY NAME	VALUE
font-stretch	normal
	wider
	narrower
	ultra-condensed
	extra-condensed
	condensed
	semi-condensed
	semi-expanded
	expanded
	extra-expanded
	ultra-expanded
font-style	normal
	italic
	oblique
font-variant	normal
	small-caps
font-weight	normal
	bold
	bolder
	lighter
	100 – 900

Table C.5

Text Properties	
PROPERTY NAME	**VALUE**
content	<string>
	<url>
	<counter>
	open-quote
	close-quote
	no-open-quote
	no-close-quote
counter-increment	<identifier>
	<integer>
	none
counter-reset	<identifier>
	<integer>
	none
direction	ltr
	rtl
letter-spacing	normal
	<length>
line-height	normal
	<number>
	<length>
	<percentage>
quotes	<string>
	none
text-align	left
	right
	center
	justify
text-decoration	none
	underline
	overline
	line-through
	blink

Table C.5 *(continued)*

Text Properties	
PROPERTY NAME	**VALUE**
text-indent	<length>
	<percentage>
text-shadow	none
	<color>
	<length>
text-transform	capitalize
	uppercase
	lowercase
	none
unicode-bidi	normal
	embed
	bidi-override
vertical-align	baseline
	sub
	super
	top
	text-top
	middle
	bottom
	text-bottom
	<percentage>
	<length>
white-space	normal
	pre
	nowrap
word-spacing	normal
	<length>

Table C.6

Box Properties

PROPERTY NAME	VALUE
border	<border-width>
	<border-style>
	<color>
border-bottom	<border-width>
	<border-style>
	<color>
border-bottom-color	<color>
border-bottom-style	<border-style>
border-bottom-width	<border-width>
border-collapse	collapse
	separate
border-color	<color>
	transparent
border-left	<border-top-width>
	<border-style>
	<color>
border-left-color	<color>
border-left-style	<border-style>
border-left-width	<border-width>
border-right	<border-top-width>
	<border-style>
	<color>
border-right-color	<color>
border-right-style	<border-style>
border-right-width	<border-width>
border-spacing	<length>
border-style	none
	dotted
	dashed
	solid
	double
	groove
	ridge
	inset
	outset
border-top	<border-top-width>
	<border-style>
	<color>
border-top-color	<color>
border-top-style	<border-style>
border-top-width	<border-width>

Table C.6 *(continued)*

Box Properties

PROPERTY NAME	VALUE
border-width	thin
	medium
	thick
	<length>
bottom	<length>
	<percentage>
clear	none
	left
	right
	both
float	left
	right
	none
height	<length>
	<percentage>
	auto
margin	<margin-width>
margin-bottom	<margin-width>
margin-left	<margin-width>
margin-right	<margin-width>
margin-top	<margin-width>
marker-offset	<length>
	auto
max-height	<length>
	<percentage>
	none
max-width	<length>
	<percentage>
	none
min-height	<length>
	<percentage>
min-width	<length>
	<percentage>
padding	<padding-width>
padding-bottom	<padding-width>
padding-left	<padding-width>
padding-right	<padding-width>
padding-top	<padding-width>
width	<length>
	<percentage>
	auto

CASCADING STYLE SHEETS REFERENCE

Table C.7

List Properties

PROPERTY NAME	VALUE
list-style	<list-style-type>
	<list-style-position>
	<list-style-image>
list-style-image	<url>
	none
list-style-position	inside
	outside
list-style-type	disc
	circle
	square
	decimal
	decimal-leading-zero
	lower-roman
	upper-roman
	lower-greek
	lower-alpha
	lower-latin
	upper-alpha
	upper-latin
	hebrew
	armenian
	georgian
	cjk-ideographic
	hiragana
	katakana
	hiragana-iroha
	katakana-iroha
	none

Table C.8

Positioning Properties

PROPERTY NAME	VALUE
caption-side	top
	bottom
	left
	right
clip	auto
	<shape>
display	block
	inline
	list-item

Table C.8

Positioning Properties *(continued)*

PROPERTY NAME	VALUE
display *(continued)*	run-in
	compact
	marker
	table
	inline-table
	table-row-group
	table-header-group
	table-footer-group
	table-row
	table-column-group
	table-column
	table-cell
	table-caption
	none
empty-cells	show
	hide
left	<length>
	<percentage>
	auto
overflow	visible
	hidden
	scroll
	auto
position	static
	absolute
	relative
	fixed
right	<length>
	<percentage>
	auto
table-layout	auto
	fixed
top	auto
	<length>
	<percentage>
visibility	collapse
	visible
	hidden
z-index	auto
	<integer>

Table C.9

Page Properties

Property Name	Value
marks	crop
	cross
	none
orphans	<integer>
page	<identifier>
	auto
page-break-after	auto
	always
	avoid
	left
	right
page-break-before	auto
	always
	avoid
	left
	right
page-break-inside	avoid
	auto
size	<length>
	auto
	portrait
	landscape
widows	<integer>

Table C.10

User Interface Properties

Property Name	Value
cursor	<url>
	auto
	crosshair
	default
	pointer
	move
	e-resize
	ne-resize
	nw-resize
	n-resize
	se-resize
	sw-resize
	s-resize
	w-resize
	text
	wait
	help
outline	<outline-color>
	<outline-style>
	<outline-width>
outline-color	<color>
	invert
outline-style	<border-style>
outline-width	<border-width>

Table C.11

Units	
PROPERTY NAME	VALUE
Length Units	em
	ex
	px
	in
	cm
	mm
	pt
	pc
Color Units	#000
	#000000
	(RRR,GGG,BBB)
	(R%,G%,B%)
	<keyword>
URLs	<url>

INDEX

A

A List Apart Web site, 475
About pane button (CSS Styles panel), 135
absolute links, 208
absolute positions, boxes, 172
Access key option, 297
Accessibility category (Preferences dialog), 221
Action field, 293
Action menu commands, 123
Add Browser dialog, 75
Add rule button (CSS Styles panel), 135
Add shortcut button, 484
address bars, adding favicon, 239–240
administration, site, 405
Advanced mode (Site Definition dialog), 32
advanced selectors, CSS (Cascading Style Sheets), 143–145
Align command (Text menu), 104
alignment
    images, 227
    text, 104
All mode button (CSS Styles panel), 135, 145–147
All Rules pane (CSS Styles panel), 135
Alt property, images, 228
anchors, links, 215–216
Andrew, Rachel, Build Your Own Standards Compliant Website Using Dreamweaver 8, 479
animation, 241
    inserting, 242–243
    placeholders, 242
Appearance category (Page Properties dialog), 77–78, 155
application category (Insert Bar), 9

Apply // Comment button (Coding toolbar), 410
Apply /**/ Comment button (Coding toolbar), 410
Apply ' Comment button (Coding toolbar), 410
Apply Comment button (Coding toolbar), 410
Apply HTML Comment button (Coding toolbar), 410
Apply Server Comment button (Coding toolbar), 410
Arrange Panels command (Window menu), 18
Assets command (Window menu), 224
Assets panel, inserting images, 224
assigning, editing programs, 388–390
Attach External Style Sheet dialog, 164
Attach stylesheet button (CSS Styles panel), 135
attributes, advanced text searches, 120
Authorized Training section (Start Page), 4
automatic corrections, code, 442

B

<b> tag, 99
Background category (CSS Rule definition dialog), 138
backgrounds
    CSS properties, 490
    images added to page, 235–236
    tables, 262
Balance Braces button (Coding toolbar), 409
Basic mode (Site Definition dialog), 32
behaviors, 333, 334
    adding, 335–336
    deleting, 337
    editing, 336
    grayed-out, 335
    order, 337
    Swap Image Restore, 341

INDEX

INDEX

INDEX